CROCHET

Novelties
from Turn-of-the-Century Sources

edited by Jules & Kaethe Kliot

The latter half or the nineteenth century reflected great achievements in lace making, with the true hand made laces of bobbin lace and needle lace giving way to the much easier-to-execute techniques of crochet, and tape lace. These "simpler" laces which initially tried to mimic the true laces, eventually came into their own, developing designs unique to the technique. The success of this development is evidenced by the many crochet pattern books printed for the mass market from the 1880's to 1918 recording the rich designs of a previous era, most manuals displaying the talents of the popular contemporary artists. These works essentially disappeared by the mid teems not to resurface till the mid 30's and then with the mush simpler anonymous designs of a new era.

The work of this book is taken from several manuals of crochet designs from the early 20th century and should serve as a valuable resource for the crocheter as well as historian and collector.

CONTENTS

Note: Numbers in [ ] refer to page numbers of this book. Other page references are from original publications.

SUPPLIES: Fine crochet hooks, to size 16, Novelty Braid and fine crochet threads available from:
LACIS, 2982 Adeline Street, Berkeley, CA 94703

LACIS
PUBLICATIONS
3163 Adeline Street, Berkeley, CA 94703

© 1996, LACIS
ISBN 0-916896-82-X

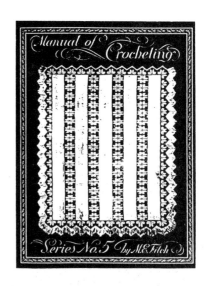

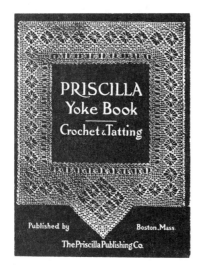

"The time is never lost, that is devoted to work."—Emerson.

INTRODUCTION

T HE production of a book for Art Needlework involves the duty of rendering to the needleworker all possible assistance for her task. With this aim in view, the Publisher now points with satisfaction to his conception of "duty fulfilled":

(1) A short explanation of stitches and terms used, is printed in the beginning of the book, to avoid errors.

(2) Complete and concise directions are given for **each and every** illustration shown.

(3) Where at all possible, some threads were left unfinished, in order to enable the crocheter to distinguish the size of thread used.

The same attitude of "helpfulness to the needleworker first" was carried out in her previous publications, and thus the Publisher hopes the needleworker will agree with her regarding the "VIRGINIA SNOW" publications, that they are the needleworker's true helpmates, that they are instruction books in the fullest sense of the word.

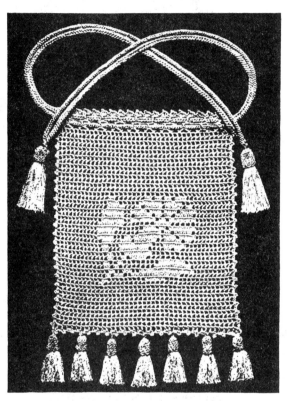

Fig. 1—Filet Crochet Bag.

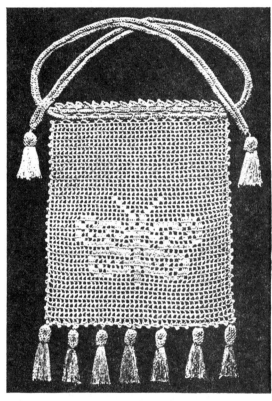

Fig. 2.—Filet Crochet Bag.

General Directions for Filet Crochet.

A few explanatory remarks about the principal features of Filet Crochet are made here, in order to facilitate the understanding of the directions.

Two kinds of square meshes are used, namely: the **open** and the **solid** mesh.

In order to make a number of **open** meshes, say, ten open meshes, make a ch. of 3 times the number of meshes, namely: a ch. of 30 — add 1 ch. — then 5 more ch. — and turn — skip 8 ch. st. — 1 d. c. in the 9th st., counting back from hook (thus completing the first open mesh) — *ch. 2 — skip 2 ch. st. — 1 d. c. in the 3d ch. st. (thus completing

the next open mesh) — repeat from*, until there are 10 open meshes. For second row of open meshes, turn the work — make a ch. of 5 — 1 d. c. in the 2d d. c. of preceding row —*ch. 2 — skip 2 st. — 1 d. c. in the next d. c. — repeat from*.

For a **solid** mesh, you would continue after 1 d. c. with — 2 d. c. over ch. of 2 — 1 d. c. over next d. c., thus showing 4 d. c. for 1 separate solid mesh; to 2 solid meshes there are 7 d. c.; to 3 solid meshes there are 10 d. c., and so on. For second row of solid meshes, turn the work — make a ch. of 3 — 1 d. c. in the 2d d. c. of preceding row — 2 d. c. over the next 2 d. c. (thus completing 1 solid mesh).

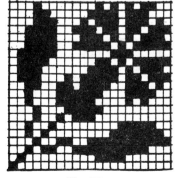

Fig. 29A.

These two designs can be used for front and back of the same bag — or the two sides may be made alike.

For the 41 meshes, make ch. 129.

FIRST ROW: 1 d. c. in 9th st. counting back from hook — make 40 more open meshes.

For the balance of the design, follow the illustration (Fig. 29a and b) and general directions for Filet Crochet above — and bear in mind to always make a ch. of 5 for turning at the end of each row. There are 47 rows of Filet Crochet in all.

Fig. 29B.

Abbreviation of Terms.

ch. = Chain Stitch.   d. c. = Double Crochet.
sl. st. = Slip Stitch.   t. c. = Treble Crochet.
s. c. = Single Crochet.   p. = Picot.

Repetition Mark means:
To repeat directions printed between these two stars as many times as stated in each case.

Explanation of Stitches.

Fig. 3.

Fig. 3. Chain Stitch (ch. st.). To start, tie a slip-knot over hook — *thread over hook — and draw through a loop* — continue this until the required length is reached.

Fig. 4.

Fig. 4. Slip Stitch (sl. st.). On a chain — put hook through the work — thread over hook — and draw through both, stitch and loop on hook at the same time.

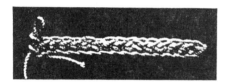

Fig. 5.

Fig. 5. Single Crochet (s. c.). On a chain — put hook through the work — thread over hook — draw through work — thread over hook — and draw through both loops.

Fig. 6.

Fig. 6. Double Crochet (d. c.). On a chain — thread over hook — put hook through the work — thread over hook — draw through work, showing 3 stitches on hook — thread over hook — draw through 2 loops — thread over hook — draw through 2 loops.

Fig. 7.

Fig. 7. Treble Crochet (t. c.). On a chain — thread over hook twice — put hook through the work — thread

over hook — draw through work, showing 4 stitches on hook — thread over hook — draw through 2 loops — thread over hook — draw through 2 loops - - thread over hook — draw through last 2 loops.

Fig. 8.

Fig. 8. Picot (p.). On a chain — join the last 4 ch. sts. by putting hook through the 4th stitch, counting back from hook, with 1 s. c. — then continue work.

Crocheted Cords.

Fig. 9.

Fig. 9. Take double thread and make two chains to the desired length.

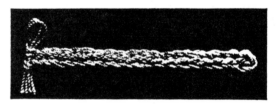

Fig. 10.

Fig. 10. For the two lengths, take double thread and make chains of 1½ yds. each — turn — 1 sl. st. in each chain stitch, picking up the two top strands.

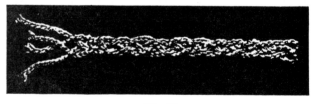

Fig. 11.

Fig. 11. Make four separate chains of 1½ yds. each, and braid same.

Fig. 12.

Fig. 12. Ch. 2 — 1 s. c. in 1st ch. — *1 s. c. in left outside loop of preceding s. c. — repeat from* until the desired length is reached.

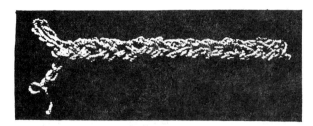

Fig. 13.

Fig. 13. Make a chain of about 5 yds. — take very coarse bone crochet hook — and crochet a chain again with these 5 yds. of chain.

Fig. 14.

Fig. 14. Ch. 3 — *thread over hook — put hook through 1st ch. made — thread over hook — draw through work — repeat from*, until there are 9 loops on hook — then thread over hook — and draw through all 9 loops — ch. 1, showing a large loop — thread over hook — hook through the large loop — thread over hook — and so on, as before. This cord can also be used as trimming, see Fig. 31.

Fig. 15.

Fig. 15. Ch. 4 — skip 1 ch. st. — 1 s. c. each in next 3 sts. — *ch. 1 — turn — 3 s. c. in 3 s. c. — repeat from* to desired length.

Fig. 16.

Fig. 16. FIRST ROW: Ch. 4 — and join with a sl. st.

SECOND ROW: 5 s. c. in this ring.

THIRD ROW: 1 s. c. in each s. c. of preceding row, picking up the inside thread.

FOURTH ROW: 1 s. c. in each s. c., picking up from the outside of work the thread below the top row of s. c. (which is the **top mesh of Second Row**). It will be easier to find the location of the correct stitch to be picked up, by counting back from the hook to the fifth last stitch.

By working in the way described, the top meshes will turn inside and make the padding of cord; continue same as Fourth Row, until there are two lengths of 24″ each — and join by sewing together.

Fig. 17.

Fig. 17. FIRST ROW: Ch. 4 — and join with a sl. st.

SECOND ROW: 5 s. c. in this ring.

THIRD ROW: 1 s. c. in each s. c. of preceding row, picking up the inside thread.

FOURTH ROW: At outside of work — 1 s. c. in each s. c., picking up from **back** the thread, going straight up below the top meshes of s. c. of preceding row. It will be easier to find the location of the correct stitch to be picked up, by counting back from the hook to the fifth last stitch.

By working in the way described, the top meshes will turn inside and make the padding of cord; continue same as Fourth Row, until there are two lengths of 24″ each — and join by sewing together.

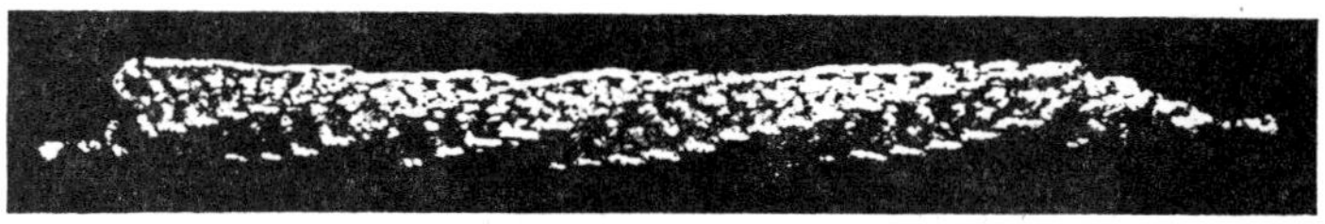

Fig. 18.

Fig. 18. FIRST ROW: Ch. 4 — and join with a sl. st.

SECOND ROW: 5 s. c. in this ring.

THIRD ROW: 1 s. c. in each s. c. of preceding row, picking up the inside thread.

FOURTH ROW: At outside of work — 1 s. c. in each s. c., picking up from **front** the thread, going straight up below the top meshes of s. c. of preceding row, and without turning the work. It will be easier to find the location of the correct stitch to be picked up, by counting back from the hook to the fifth last stitch.

By working in the way described, the top meshes will turn inside and make the padding of cord; continue same as Fourth Row, until there are two lengths of 24″ each — and join by sewing together.

Fig. 19.

Tassels and Ball.

Fig. 19. Cut 14 to 18 lengths of thread (3″ each) — fold them once — take new thread and make slip-knot — wind thread over center of tassel 4 times — ch. 4.

FIRST ROW of top of Tassel: Ch. 4 — join with a sl. st.

SECOND ROW: 10 s.c. over ring.

THIRD ROW: 1 s.c. over each s.c. of preceding row.

Make six more rows, same as Third Row. Draw chain of tassel through the crocheted top.

Fig. 20. A popcorn st. consists of 6 d.c., all in the same place — take out hook — put hook through top st. of 1st d.c. — draw last loop through, to form a pocket.

FIRST ROW: Ch. 5 — and join with a sl. st.

SECOND ROW: Ch. 3 — 5 d.c. over ring — close for a ppc. st. through ch. of 3 and 5 d.c. — ch. 2 — *1 ppc. st. over ring — ch. 2 — repeat from*, until there are 4 ppc. — and join to the ch. of 3.

THIRD ROW: Ch. 3 — 5 d.c. over ch. of 2 of preceding row — close for a ppc. st. — ch. 2 — *1 ppc. over next ch. of 2 — ch. 2 — repeat from* all around — and join to ch. of 3.

FOURTH ROW: Ch. 1 — 1 s.c. over ch. of 2 of preceding row — *1 s.c. over next ch. of 2 — repeat from* all around — join to 1st s.c. with a sl. st.

FIFTH ROW: Ch. 10 for string of tassel.

Fig. 21. Make a chain 6″ long — break thread — fold chain once — make with this double chain 3 knots, very loosely — put ends of chain inside of the knots — sew around this tightly and from each side with invisible stitches — crochet with same thread ch. 8.

Fig. 22. FIRST ROW: Ch. 3 — and join with a sl. st.

SECOND ROW: 8 s.c. in ch. of 3 — and join with a sl. st.

THIRD ROW: Ch. 1 — *1 s.c. in 1st s.c., always picking up the outside thread of loop — 2 s.c. over next s.c. — repeat from*, until the end of the row.

THE NEXT THREE ROWS: Ch. 1 — 1 s.c. over each s.c. of preceding row. If a larger ball is to be made, add as many more such rows as required.

LAST ROW: Stuff ball with cotton and decrease. Ch. 1 — *1 s.c. over 1st s.c. — 1 s.c. over next s.c. — skip 3d s.c. — repeat from*, until the end of the row. Break off thread, leaving ½ yd.; put this ½ yd. through sewing needle and draw the last loops together — take crochet hook, pick up a loop of last row — and make ch. 10 — knot ch. of 10 once — and sew ball to bag.

Fig. 23. Over cardboard, 4″ wide — wind thread about 100 times — cut threads at one end and wind a thread over what is now the center, tightly 3 times, leaving thread sufficiently long to pass through a needle, and sew to bag afterwards.

About ½″ below this thread, wind over tassel another thread 10 times, tightly and evenly, which completes the top of the tassel; fasten this thread by passing it up and down in center of parts just wound.

Make chain about ¾ yd. long — make simple knots in chain, about 2″ apart — sew to bottom of wound part, making loops to the length of the tassel — this will give 4 loops of the chain.

Fig. 20.

Fig. 22.

Fig. 23.

Fig. 24. Over cardboard, 3″ wide — wind thread about 60 times — cut threads at one end and wind a thread over what is now the center, tightly 3 times — leave thread sufficiently long to make ch. 4 afterwards and to sew to bag.

About ½″ below this thread, wind over tassel another thread several times, which makes the neck of tassel — fasten this thread at inside of neck. For cord over neck of tassel, make Fig. 12 about 1″ long, and sew tightly around tassel.

Fig. 25. Purse with Rose.

FIRST ROW: Ch. 6 — and join with a sl. st.

SECOND ROW: *1 s.c. over ring — ch. 2 — 3 d.c. — ch. 2 — 1 s.c. — repeat from*, until there are 5 petals to the rose.

THIRD ROW: Ch. 4 — at the back of the first petal of preceding row, 1 sl. st. through the 2d s.c. (which is the last st. forming the petal) — *ch. 4 — at the back of the next petal, 1 sl. st. through the 2d s.c. — repeat from*, until there are 5 ch. of 4.

FOURTH ROW: Over each ch. of 4 of preceding row — *1 s.c. — ch. 2 — 5 d.c. — ch. 2 — 1 s.c., all over same ch. — repeat over next ch. of 4 from*, until there are 5 petals.

FIFTH ROW: Same as Third Row.

SIXTH ROW: Same as Fourth Row. Break off thread and fasten.

SEVENTH ROW: 1 sl. st. over 1st ch. of 2 of preceding row — ch. 4 — *skip 1 d.c. — 1 d.c. in next d.c. — ch. 2 — repeat from* — 1 d.c. over ch. of 2 — ch. 2 — 1 d.c. over ch. of 2 of next petal — ch. 2 — and continue all around — and join with a sl. st.

Fig. 24.

EIGHTH ROW: Ch. 2 — 2 d.c. over ch. of 2 of preceding row — ch. 2 — *3 d.c. over next ch. of 2 — ch. 2 — repeat from* all around — and join with a sl. st.

NINTH ROW: Ch. 5 — 3 d.c. over ch. of 2 of preceding row — ch. 2 — *3 d.c. over next ch. of 2 — ch. 2 — repeat from* all around — and join the last d.c. with a sl. st. into 3d st. of ch. of 5.

TENTH ROW: Ch. 3 — 3 d.c. over ch. of 5 of preceding row — *ch. 2 — 4 d.c. over ch. of 2 — repeat from* all around and join with a sl. st.

ELEVENTH ROW: Ch. 5 — *4 d.c. over ch. of 2 of preceding row — ch. 2 — repeat from* all around. Break off thread and fasten.

For other side of bag, duplicate the directions of the above eleven rows, then lay one on top of the other (roses outside) — and work:

Border, always over both (front and back together):

1 sl. st. over the last d.c. of any group of 4 d.c. of the outside rows — ch. 3 — *1 sl. st. over 1st d.c. of next group — ch. 5 — 1 sl. st. over last d.c. of same group — ch. 3 — repeat from* — and continue, until there are 5 groups of 4 d.c. left. Break off thread and fasten.

For Beading and Edging, at the top of bag:

FIRST ROW: 1 s.c. over 1st d.c. of group of 4 d.c. — ch. 5 — *1 d.c. between 1st and 2d d.c. — ch. 2 — 1 d.c. between 3d and 4th d.c. — ch. 2 — 1 d.c. over ch. of 2 — ch. 2 — repeat from*, until the end of the row.

SECOND ROW: Ch. 4 — turn — 4 d.c. over ch. of 2 of preceding row — *ch. 2 — skip 1 ch. of 2 — 1 s.c. over next ch. of 2 — 4 d.c. over same ch. — repeat from*, until the end of the row — ch. 4 and fasten in preceding row.

For the other side of bag, repeat Edging as above.

For Cord, see Fig. 9.

Fig. 25. Purse with Rose.

Fig. 26. Purse with Flap.

Fig. 26. Purse with Flap.

FIRST ROW: Ch. 4 — join with a sl. st.

SECOND ROW: Ch. 3 — 7 d.c. over ring.

THIRD ROW: Ch. 3 — turn — 2 d.c. in each d.c. of preceding row. (Total, 14 d.c.)

FOURTH ROW: Ch. 3 — turn — increase by 1 d.c. in 1st, 7th, 14th st. (Total, 17 d.c.)

FIFTH ROW: Ch. 3 — turn — increase 1 d.c. in 1st, 9th, 17th st. (Total, 20 d.c.)

SIXTH ROW: Ch. 3 — turn — increase 1 d.c. in 1st, 10th, 20th st. (Total, 23 d.c.)

SEVENTH ROW: Ch. 3 — turn — increase 1 d.c. in 1st, 8th, 16th, 23d st. (Total, 27 d.c.)

EIGHTH ROW: Ch. 3 — turn — increase 1 d.c. in 1st, 9th, 18th, 27th st. (Total 31 d.c.)

NINTH ROW: Ch. 4 — turn — 6 t.c. — 3 d.c. — 3 half d.c. (for one-half d.c., start like the d.c. — and draw thread through the 3 loops on hook) — 7 s.c. — 3 half d.c. — 3 d.c. — 6 t.c.

TENTH ROW: Ch. 3 — turn — 1 d.c. in each st. of preceding row. (Total, 31 d.c.)

Make 26 more rows, same as Tenth Row. Fold back to Eleventh Row — and starting at lower right-hand corner, join front and back of bag by 2 s.c. over each d.c. When reaching the flap — 1 s.c. over d.c. as before — *ch. 3 — 1 d.c. in s.c. just made, between the two upright threads — 1 d.c. in same place — 1 s.c. over next d.c. — repeat from* all around the flap — continue on left side of bag with 2 s.c. over each d.c. Finish with snap fastener.

Fig. 27.
Purse with Popcorn Stitch.

Fig. 27. Purse with Popcorn Stitch.

Material—Use Collingbourne's American Maid or Japsilk Cordoney.

FIRST ROW: Ch. 158 — add another ch of 5 for turning.

SECOND ROW: 1 d.c. in 6th ch. st., counting back from hook — *ch. 1 — skip 1 ch. — 1 d.c. in next st. — repeat from*, until the end of the row; ch. 105 — turn.

THIRD ROW: 1 sl. st. in last d.c. of preceding row — ch. 3 — 1 ppc. in next d.c. (for 1 popcorn st. — see Fig. 20) — *ch. 2 — skip 1 d.c. — 1 ppc. in next d.c. — repeat from*, until the end of the row.

FOURTH ROW: Ch. 3 — *1 d.c. in 1st d.c. of ppc. — ch. 1 — 1 d.c. in last d.c. of next ppc. — ch. 1 — repeat from*, until the end of the row; ch. 105 — turn.

FIFTH ROW: 1 sl. st. in last d.c. of preceding row — ch. 3 — *skip ch. of 1 — 1 d.c. over next d.c. — ch. 1 — repeat from* until the end of the row.

Make 8 more rows, ppc. stitches on every 3d row; a ch. of 105 after each 2d row. Fold into the desired shape and slip-stitch along the edge over front and back; draw the 6 ch. of 105 through top of flap.

For **Ring**, fill a ⅝″ brass ring closely with s.c. — pull the 6 ch. of 105 through the ring, about half way down the chains — and slip the loop, thus formed, over the ring.

Fig. 28. Filet Crochet Purse.

FIRST ROW: Ch. 132.

SECOND ROW: Skip 4 ch. st. — 1 d.c. in the 5th st., counting back from hook — 1 d.c. in each ch. until the end of the row — ch. 105 — turn.

THIRD ROW: 1 d.c. over 1st d.c. of preceding row — 28 more d.c. over as many d.c. of preceding row — 1 open mesh (for 1 open mesh, ch. 2 — skip 2 st. — 1 d.c. over 3d st.) — 69 more d.c. over as many d.c. of preceding row — here the work has to be folded into a bag shape in order to allow one side of ch. of 105 to be laid over the d.c. just finished — 1 open mesh — and the ch. of 105 now appears surrounded by the open mesh, so the bag can be pulled open — 8 more open meshes — 1 additional d.c. — ch. 3 — turn.

FOURTH ROW: 1 d.c. over 2d d.c. of preceding row — 2 d.c. over ch. of 2 — 1 d.c. over 1 d.c. — 7 open meshes — here bring other side of ch. of 105 over the d.c. just finished — 2 d.c. over ch. of 2 — 66 more d.c. over d.c. of preceding row — 3 open meshes — 26 d.c. — ch. 105 — turn.

FIFTH ROW: 1 d.c. over 1st d.c. of preceding row — 22 more d.c. — 5 open meshes — 65 more d.c. over d.c. of preceding row — lay one side of ch. of 105 over d.c just finished — 1 d.c. over next d.c. — 2 d. c. over ch. of 2 — 1 d.c. over d.c. — 5 open meshes — 2 d.c. over ch. of 2 — 5 more d.c. — ch. 3 — turn.

For the balance of this design, follow the illustration. A ch. of 105 is to be made at the end of each alternate row; care should be taken that the ch. of 105 always is laid between the corresponding d.c.'s of each row. After 14 rows are completed, sew up the sides of purse.

For **Border around Flap,** make:

1 sl. st. between 2 d.c. over side of flap — *ch. 5 — skip 2 d.c. — 1 sl. st. in 3d d.c. — repeat from* around the edge of flap.

The **Ring** is a ⅝″ brass ring (inside measurement), filled closely with s.c. — pull the 6 ch. of 105 through the ring, about half-way down the chains — and slip the loop, thus formed, over the ring.

Fig. 30.   For Beading and Edging.

FIRST ROW: 1 s.c. over ch. of 2 of last mesh — *ch. 5 — skip 1 ch. of 2 — 1 s.c. over next ch. of 2 — repeat from*, until the end of the row.

SECOND ROW: Ch. 6 — turn — 1 t.c. over ch. of 5 of preceding row — *ch. 5 — 1 t.c. over next ch. of 5 — repeat from*, until the end of the row.

THIRD ROW: Same as Second Row.

FOURTH ROW: Ch. 3 — turn — *2 d.c. over ch. of 5 of preceding row — 1 p. — 2 d.c. over same ch. — 1 sl. st. over next ch. of 5, producing the slanting effect — repeat from*, until the end of the row.

After front and back of the Bag is finished, lay one on top of the other and work.

Picot Border, over front and back together:

1 sl. st. over ch. of 5 of Beading — 1 p. — ch. 3 — 1 sl. st. over next ch. of 5 — 1 p. — ch. 3 — 1 sl. st. over ch. of 2 — *1 p. — ch. 3 — skip 1 ch. of 2 — 1 sl. st. over next ch. of 2 — repeat from*.

For Cord, see Fig. 10; for Tassel, see Fig. 19.

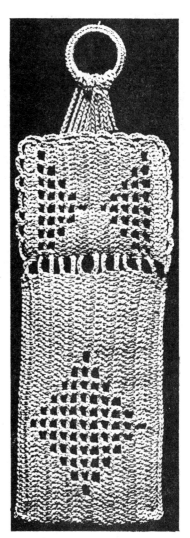

No. 28.   Filet Crochet Purse.

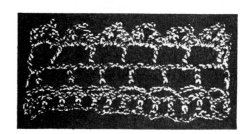

Fig. 30.

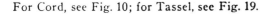

Fig. 31. Bag with Inserted Medallions.

No. 31. Bag with Inserted Medallions.

Fig. 32.

FIFTH ROW: 2 sl. st. over ch. of 5 of preceding row — ch. 4 — 1 t.c. over same ch. — ch. 4 — *2 contracted t.c. over next ch. of 5 — (for 2 contracted t.c., start 'ike the t.c., until you have drawn twice through two loops, leaving 2 st. on hook — then start next t.c., until you have drawn twice through two loops — then thread over hook — draw through all three loops) — ch. 4 — repeat from* all around — and join in top of ch. of 4 with a sl. st.

SIXTH ROW: *3 p. — 5 s.c. over ch. of 4 of preceding row — repeat from* all around. Break off thread and fasten.

SEVENTH ROW: *1 s.c. in center of 2d p. of preceding row — ch. 5 — repeat from* all around.

Make four medallions to a bag, buttonhole to the cloth of bag over Seventh Row.

For the **Beading** (Fig. 33):

FIRST ROW: *2 s.c. in cloth of bag — 1 p. — 2 s.c. in cloth of bag — ch. 15 — repeat from* all around and join. Break off thread and fasten.

SECOND ROW: *3 s.c. over center of ch. of 15 of preceding row — ch. 2 — 1 p. — ch. 2 — repeat from* all around.

For **Edging** at bottom of bag (Fig. 34):

FIRST ROW: Fasten thread in cloth — ch. 5 — *1 d.c. in cloth — ch. 2 — repeat from*, until the end of the bag is reached.

SECOND ROW: Ch. 1 — turn — *2 s.c. over ch. of 2 of preceding row — 3 p. — 2 s.c. over same ch. — repeat from*, until the end of the row.

For Cord, see Fig. 12; for Trimming, see Fig. 14.

FIRST ROW: For the Medallion (Fig. 32) — ch. 9 — and join with a sl. st.

SECOND ROW: Ch. 1 — 16 s.c. over ring.

THIRD ROW: Ch. 4 — *1 d.c. in s.c. of preceding row — ch. 1 — repeat from* all around — and join to ch. of 4 in the 3d st.

FOURTH ROW: Ch. 1 — 1 s.c. over ch. of 1 of preceding row — *ch. 5 — 1 s.c. over next ch. of 1 — repeat from* all around and join in 1st s.c.

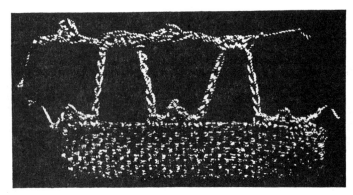

Fig. 33.

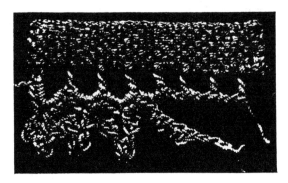

Fig. 34.

[10]

Fig. 35. Bag with Filet Crochet Medallions.

FIRST ROW: Ch. 124.

SECOND ROW: Skip 4 st. — 1 d. c. in 5th st., counting back from hook — 1 d. c. in each st., until the end of the row.

THIRD ROW: Ch. 3 — turn — 2 d. c. over 2 d. c. — 19 open meshes — 2 more d. c. over 2 d. c. — 19 open meshes — 2 more d. c. over last 2 d. c.

For the balance of the design, follow the illustrations (Fig. 36 and 37) and general directions for Filet Crochet, given on page 3 — and bear in mind to always make a ch. of 3 when turning.

For **Top of Bag**, over the square medallions (Fig. 38), work a row of open meshes over last row of solid meshes.

FIRST ROW: *Ch. 5 — skip 2 d. c. — 3 d. c. in 3d d. c. — ch. 2 — 2 d. c. in same st. — ch. 2 — 1 d. c. in same st. — repeat from*, until the end of the row.

SECOND ROW: Ch. 5 — turn — *3 d. c. over ch. of 2 between 2 and 1 d. c. of preceding row — ch. 2 — 2 d. c. over same st. — ch. 2 — 1 d. c. over same ch. — ch. 5 — repeat from*, until the end of the row.

Continue more rows, same as Second Row, until the desired length is reached.

Fig. 38. For **Beading**, continue:

FIRST ROW: With ch. 5 — turn — *skip 2 st. — 1 d. c. in 3d st. — ch. 2 — repeat from*, until the end of the row.

SECOND ROW: Ch. 6 — turn skip 1 ch. of 2 — *1 t. c. over next ch. of 2 — ch. 5 — skip 2 ch. of 2 — repeat from*, until the end of the row.

THIRD ROW: Ch. 6 — turn — 1 t. c. over centre of ch. of 5 — *ch. 5 — 1 t. c. over next ch. of 5 — repeat from*, until the end of the row.

FOURTH ROW: Ch. 5 — turn — *skip 2 st. — 1 d. c. in 3d st. — ch. 2 — 1 d. c. in d. c. — ch. 2 — repeat from*.

FIFTH, SIXTH and SEVENTH ROWS: Same as First and Second Rows for top of Bag. When two sides of bag are finished, fasten them together by one row of edging, as described in Fig. 38.

For Cord, see Fig. 11; for Ball, see Fig. 22.

Use Collingbourne's American Maid Cordonnet, size 20.

Fig. 35. Bag with Filet Crochet Medallions.

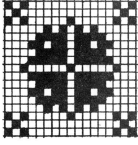

Fig. 36.

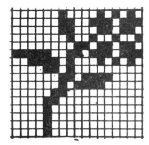

Fig. 37.

Fig. 38.

Fig. 39. Bag with Knot-Stitch and Long Tassel.

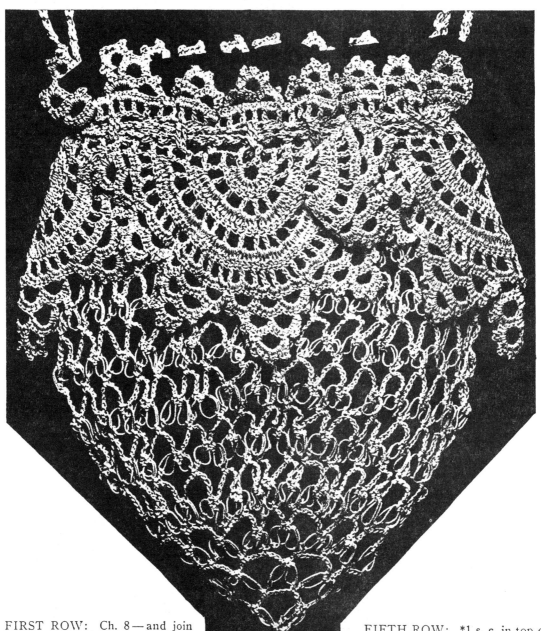

Fig. 40. FIRST ROW: Ch. 8 — and join with a sl. st.

SECOND ROW: *Ch. 1 very tight — draw the loop about ⅝″ long — thread over hook — draw through long loop, keeping the long loop in position with thumb and forefinger — 1 s. c. very tight over thread just drawn through, picking it up to the left of long loop — ch. 1 very tight — this completes 1 kn. st. — repeat from* — then 1 s. c. over ring of ch. of 8 — and repeat from Second Row 3 more times. Then 1 more kn. st. — fasten with 1 s. c. in top of 1st kn. st. made.

THIRD ROW: *1 sl. st. in top of next kn. st. — ch. 10 — 1 s. c. in top of next kn. st. — repeat from* all around — then 1 more s. c. in same kn. st.

FOURTH ROW: 2 kn. st. — 1 s. c. over ch. of 10 of preceding row — 2 kn. st. — 1 s. c. over same ch. of 10 — *2 kn. st. — 1 s. c. over next ch. of 10 — 2 kn. st. — 1 s. c. over same ch. of 10 — repeat from* all around — 1 more kn. st. (Total, 17 kn. st.) — 1 s. c. in top of 1st kn. st.

FIFTH ROW: *1 s. c. in top of next kn. st. — ch. 10 — 1 s. c. in top of next kn. st. — repeat from* all around (Total, 8 ch. of 10) — 1 s. c. in each of next 2 s. c. — 1 sl. st. each in next 2 ch. st.

SIXTH ROW: Same as Fourth Row. (Total, 33 kn. st.)

SEVENTH ROW: Same as Fifth Row. (Total, 16 ch. of 10.)

EIGHTH ROW: Same as Fourth Row. (Total, 65 kn. st.)

NINTH ROW: Same as Fifth Row. (Total, 32 ch. of 10.) This ends the increasing.

TENTH ROW: 3 more sl. st. over ch. of 10 — *2 kn. st. — 1 s. c. over next ch. of 10 — repeat from* all around — 1 more kn. st. — 1 s. c. in top of 1st kn. st.

ELEVENTH ROW: Same as Ninth Row; continue alternately, same as Tenth and Eleventh Rows.

[12]

TWENTY-SECOND ROW: Same as Tenth Row.

TWENTY-THIRD ROW: After 1 s. c. in top of 1st kn. st. — *1 s. c. in top of next kn. st. — ch. 4 — 1 s. c. in top of next kn. st. — repeat from* twice — 1 s. c. in top of next kn. st. — ch. 3 — 1 s. c. in top of next kn. st. — and repeat from Twenty-third Row all around — and join to 1st s. c.

Fig. 41. TWENTY-FOURTH ROW: Ch. 6 — skip 2 st. of preceding row — 1 d. c. in 3d st. — *ch. 2 — skip 2 st. — 1 d. c. in 3d st. — repeat from*, until there are 7 d. c. — ch. 5 — turn — 1 s. c. in 1 d. c., forming a semicircle — ch. 3 — 1 sl. st. in next d. c. — turn — 11 d. c. over ch. of 5 — skip 2 ch. st. of preceding row — 1 d. c. in next st. — ch. 2 — skip 2 st. — 1 d. c. in next st. — ch. 2 — turn — skip 1 d. c. of 11 d. c. — 1 d. c. in next d. c. — ch. 2 — skip 1 d. c. — 1 d. c. in next d. c. — *ch. 2 — 1 d. c. in next d. c. (without skipping a stitch) — repeat from*, until there are 7 d. c. in all — ch. 2 — skip 1 d. c. — 1 d. c. in next d. c. — ch. 2 — 1 sl. st. in d. c. of foundation, to form semicircle — ch. 3 — 1 sl. st. in next d. c. of foundation — turn — 3 d. c. over ch. of 2 — *4 d. c. over next ch. of 2 — repeat from*, until the end of semicircle — skip 2 ch. st. of preceding row — 1 d. c. in next st. — ch. 2 — skip 2 st. — 1 d. c. in next st. — ch. 2 — turn — *skip 1 d. c. — 1 d. c. in next d. c. — ch. 2 — repeat from* all around — and join last ch. of 2 to d. c. of foundation with a sl. st. — ch. 3 — 1 sl. st. in next d. c. of foundation — turn — 3 d. c. over ch. of 2 — *4 d. c. over next ch. of 2 — repeat from*, until the end of semicircle — skip 2 ch. st. of preceding row — 1 d. c. in next st. — ch. 2 — skip 2 st. — 1 d. c. in next st. — ch. 2 — turn — *skip 1 d. c. — 1 d. c. in next d. c. — ch. 2 — repeat from* all around — and join last ch. of 2 to ch. of 6 of foundation with a sl. st. — ch. 1 — turn continue for

Small Scallop: *With 3 s. c. each over the 1st 4 ch. of 2 — ch. 5 — turn — 1 s. c. in 6th s. c. — ch. 5 — 1 s. c. in 1st s. c. made — ch. 1 — turn — 2 s. c. over ch. of 5 — 1 p. — 4 s. c. over same ch. — 2 s. c. over next ch. of 5 — ch. 5 — turn 1 s. c. in centre of 4 s. c. — ch. 1 — turn — 2 s. c. over ch. of 5 — 1 p. — 1 s. c. — 1 p. — 1 s. c. — 1 p. — 2 s. c. over same ch. — 2 s. c. over remaining st. of next ch. of 5 — 1 p. 2 s. c over same ch. — and repeat from* — then 3 s. c. over next ch. of 2 and start for

Large Scallop: *By making 3 s. c. each over the next 6 ch. of 2 — ch. 5 — turn — 1 s. c. in the 12th s. c. — ch. 5 — 1 s. c. in 6th s. c. — ch. 5 — 1 s. c. in 1st s. c. — ch. 1 — turn — 2 s. c. over ch. of 5 — 1 p. — 4 s. c. over same ch. — 6 s. c. over next ch. of 5 — 2 s. c. over next ch. of 5 — ch. 5 — turn — 1 s. c. in centre of 6 s. c. — ch. 5 — 1 s. c. in centre of 4 s. c. — ch. 1 — turn — 2 s. c. over ch. of 5 — 1 p. — 4 s. c. over same ch. — 2 s. c. over next ch. of 5 — ch. 5 — turn — 1 s. c. in centre of 4 s. c. — ch. 1 — turn — 2 s. c. over ch. of 5 — 1 p. — 1 s. c. — 1 p. — 1 s. c. — 1 p. — 2 s. c. over same ch. — 2 s. c. over next ch. — 1 p. — 2 s. c. over same ch. — 2 s. c. over next ch. — 1 p. — 2 s. c. over same ch. — and repeat from* twice; then 3 s. c. over next ch. of 2 — and 2 more small scallops as described above; join by 1 sl. st. to 1 d. c.

Ch. 2 — skip 2 ch. st. of preceding row — 1 d. c. in next st. — repeat from — then repeat from Twenty-fourth Row three times (making, however, only ch. 2 instead of ch. of 6 at the outset). Finish the row with a sl. st. in the 3d st. of ch. of 6.

Turn the four semicircles over outside of bag, so the Twenty-third Row (of chain stitches) appears as the top of the bag.

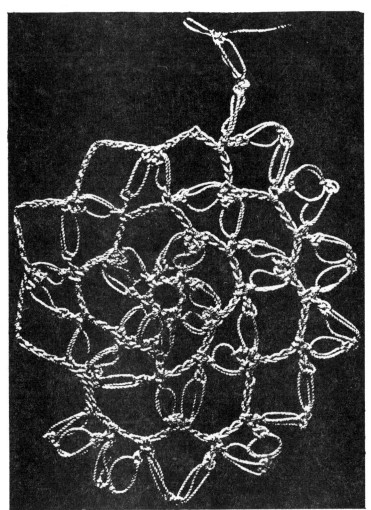

Fig. 40.

Fig. 41.

For Beading:

FIRST ROW: Over Twenty-third Row — ch. 4 — 1 t. c. over next ch. st. — *ch. 4 — skip 1 ch. of 2 — 2 t. c. over next ch. of 2 — repeat from* all around — and join to last st. of ch. of 4.

SECOND ROW: Ch. 4 — *skip 1 st. — 1 d. c. over next st. — ch. 1 — repeat from* all around — and join to 3d st. of ch. of 4.

THIRD ROW: See directions for Small Scallop of Twenty-fourth Row — all around.

For Cord, see Fig. 13; for Tassel, see Fig. 23.

[13]

Fig. 42. Knot-Stitch Bag with Border of Woven Flowers.

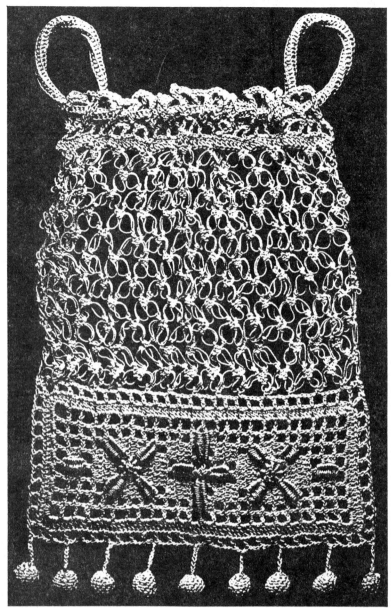

Fig. 42. Knot-Stitch Bag with Border of Woven Flowers.

To start border, make ch. 30 for 8 open meshes.

FIRST ROW: Skip 8 ch. st. — 1 d.c. in the 9th st., counting back from hook — 7 more open meshes.

For the balance of the design, follow the illustration (Fig. 43) and general directions for Filet Crochet, given on page 3 — and bear in mind to always make a ch. of 5 for turning. When the design is finished,

Ch. 3 — work around the entire outside — 3 d.c. over each ch. of 2 and 8 d.c. in the corners — and join last d.c. with sl. st. to ch. of 3.

For next row, ch. 5 — 1 d.c. between 3 and 3 d.c. of preceding row — *ch. 2 — 1 d.c. between the next 3 and 3 d.c. — repeat from* all around. For turning the corners, make 1 d.c. in center of 8 d.c. — ch. 5 — 1 d.c. in same st. — and continue as before.

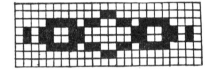

Fig. 43

To make center of **Flower** (Fig. 44), use sewing needle and fasten thread to the center point of four squares — then* carry thread to a corner of four squares — and in going back to center point, wind it twice around 1st thread — repeat from* for each corner, making a spider effect. Make a back stitch over 1 d.c. of spider — slip needle under next bar of spider — back stitch over the bar — continue back stitches, 3 times all around.

For petals, start from a corner of spider — *carry thread across the solid mesh and slip under corner of solid mesh — bring back to starting point, slipping it under bar of spider — repeat from* twice. Then insert needle in the middle — carry thread under three threads of foundation to right — insert in middle — carry under 3 threads to left — and so on, until petal is filled. Make 4 petals to each flower, and fill in balance of design as per illustration.

Work another border piece like this — join the two by sewing bottom and two sides together.

The **Knot-Stitch** (kn. st.) — Fig. 45 — is worked all around.

FIRST ROW: 1 s.c. over 1st ch. of 2 of border — *ch. 1 very tight — draw the loop about 5⁄8″ long — thread over hook — draw through long loop, keeping the long loop in position with thumb and forefinger — 1 s.c. very tight over thread just drawn through, picking it up to the left of long loop — ch. 1 very tight — this completes 1 kn. st. — repeat from* — skip 1 ch. of 2 — 1 s.c. over next ch. of 2 — then repeat again from "*ch. 1 very tight" — all around — do not close this row, but fasten last kn. st. with 1 s.c. in top of 1st kn. st. made, and over 1 s.c. together — 1 s.c. in top of next kn. st. — then continue.

SECOND ROW: Ch. 1 very tight — long loop and so on, as before. Make 12 rows in all.

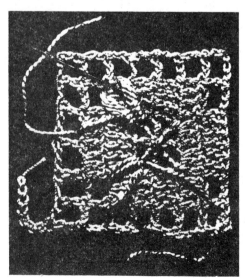

Fig. 44.

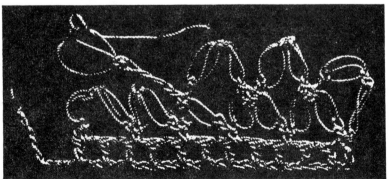

Fig. 45.

[14]

For Beading (Fig. 46):

FIRST ROW: *1 s. c. in top of kn. st. — 1 s. c. in top of next kn. st. — ch. 5 — repeat from* all around — and join to 1st s. c. with a sl. st.

SECOND ROW: Ch. 3 — d. c. in each st. of preceding row, all around — and join to 3d ch. st.

THIRD ROW: Ch. 5 — *skip 2 d. c. — 1 d. c. in 3d d. c. of preceding row — ch. 2 — repeat from* all around and join to 3d st. of ch. of 5.

FOURTH ROW: Ch. 15 — 1 s. c. over 2d ch. of 2 — *ch. 15 — 1 s. c. over next ch. of 2 — repeat from* all around. Break off thread and fasten.

FIFTH ROW: 4 s. c. over centre of ch. of 15 of preceding row, all around — and join to 1st s. c. with a sl. st.

For Cord, see Fig. 18; for Ball, see Fig. 22.

Fig. 47. Venetian Crochet Bag

FIRST ROW: Commence in the centre of middle star with ch. 4 — and join with a sl. st.

SECOND ROW: Ch. 6 — 1 d. c. over ring — *ch. 3 — 1 d. c. — repeat from* 5 times — ch. 3 — join with a sl. st.

THIRD ROW: 3 s. c. over each ch. of 3 of preceding row.

FOURTH ROW: Ch. 8 — 1 d. c. in 1st space between 3 and 3 s. c. of preceding row — *ch. 5 — 1 d. c. between next 3 and 3 s. c. — repeat from* all around — ch. 5 — join with a sl. st.

FIFTH ROW: *8 s. c. over ch. of 5 of preceding row — ch. 1 — turn — make 7 rows of s. c. for the petal, going forward and backward, and catching the loop always over the back thread, decreasing each row one st. at the end — (ch. 1 at end of each row of s. c. and turn). When petal is finished, go down on left side of petal with a sl. st. in each row of s. c. — repeat from*, until there are 8 petals in all — break off thread and fasten.

SIXTH ROW: *1 s. c. in the top st. of petal — ch. 5 — 1 t. c. between 8 and 8 s. c. of preceding row (the bottom of petal) — ch. 5 — repeat from* all around.

SEVENTH ROW: 9 s. c. over each ch. of preceding row.

EIGHTH ROW: 1 s. c. in each s. c. of preceding row, giving the scalloped effect.

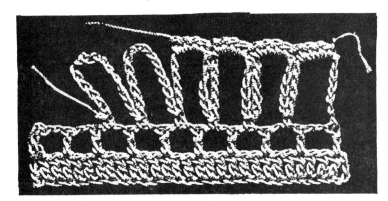

Fig. 46.

Fig. 47. Venetian Crochet Bag.

Fig. 48.

NINTH ROW: (Fig. 48.) *Ch. 9 — 1 s.c. in the 9th s.c. of scallop of preceding row — ch. 1 — turn — 8 s.c. over next 4 ch. st. of ch. of 9 — ch. 1 — turn — 5 more rows of 8 s.c., going forward and back and catching the loop always over the back thread — (ch. 1 at end of each row of s.c. and turn) — ch. 4 — 1 s.c. in the 9th s.c. of next scallop — repeat from*, until there are 8 squares.

TENTH ROW: 3 sl. st. over 1st 3 ch. st. of ch. of 9 of preceding row — *3 s.c. over remaining st. of ch. of 9 — 1 s.c. in each row of s.c. going up the right side of square — 3 s.c. in top of square, all in same st. — 7 s.c. along the following side of square — 5 s.c. over ch. of 4 of preceding row — 3 s.c. over 1st 4 st. of next ch. of 9 — ch. 5 — turn — 1 s.c. in center of 5 s.c. just made — ch. 1 — turn and going back, work over ch. of 5 — 3 s.c. — ch. 3 for picot effect — and 3 s.c. — then repeat from* all around. Break off thread and fasten.

ELEVENTH ROW: *1 s. c. in top of square — ch. 12 — 1 s. c. in picot of ch. of 3 — ch. 12 — repeat from* all around — and join in 1st s.c. with a sl. st.

Fig. 49.

TWELFTH ROW· Fill each ch. of 12 of preceding row with s.c. Break off thread and fasten.

Work the **Corner Medallions** separately (Fig. 49):

FIRST ROW: Ch. 4 — and join into a ring with a sl. st.

SECOND ROW: Ch. 3 — 17 d.c. over ring.

THIRD ROW: Ch. 1 — *1 s.c. in 1st d.c. of preceding row — 2 s.c. in next d.c. — repeat from* all around.

FOURTH ROW: Ch. 4 — 1 d.c. in s.c. of preceding row — ch. 1 — *1 d.c. in next s.c. — ch. 1 — repeat from* all around — join with a sl. st.

Fig. 50.

FIFTH ROW: Ch. 2 — *1 p. — 1 s.c. over ch. of 1 of preceding row — repeat from* until there are 22 p. — to join to outside row of big center star — ch. 2 — take out hook — put through 1 s.c. of outside row — (at about center of loop of s.c.) — pull loop through — ch. 2 — and finish p. by 1 s.c. as usual — 3 more p. as before — join next and last p. as described, in about the center st. of next loop of s.c.

Make 3 more Medallions for the remaining corners of bag.

For **Filling Effects** on the sides of bag, fasten thread in the 3d p. of corner medallion (Fig. 50):

Fig. 51.

FIRST ROW: Ch. 12 — 1 s.c. in about 3d s.c. from joining point of corner medallion — *ch. 1 — turn — 3 s.c. over ch. of 12 — 1 p. — 3 s.c., completing one stem — ch. 9 — turn — 1 s.c. in loop of s.c. at about even distance from previous stem — repeat from*, until there are 5 or 6 stems — then about ch. 5 — fasten in 3d p. of next corner medallion — ch. 1 — turn.

SECOND ROW: 1 s.c. over each ch. just made — *1 s.c. in top st. of stem — 5 s.c. over next ch. — 1 s.c. in top st. of stem — (see Fig. 51) — 2 s.c. over next ch. — ch. 5 — turn — 1 s.c. in center of 5 s.c. (between two stems) — ch. 5 — 1 s.c. in 2d s.c. of next 5 s.c. — ch. 1 — turn — 2 s.c. over ch. of 5 — 1 p. — 4 s.c. over same ch. — 2 s.c. over next ch. of 5 — ch. 5 — turn — 1 s.c. in centre of 4 s.c. — ch. 1 — turn — 2 s.c. over ch. of 5 — 1 p. — 1 s.c. — 1 p.

— 1 s.c. — 1 p. — 2 s.c. over same ch. — 2 s.c. over remaining st. of next ch. of 5 — 1 p. — 2 s.c. — 5 s.c. over next ch. — repeat from*, until the end of the row.

For two more sides of bag, repeat from "For Filling Effects."

The **Top** of the bag is made by making the First and Second Row of "For Filling Effects" as far as "See Fig. 51," until six stems are completed — then two more rows of twelve stems each — and finish with Edging, Fig. 51.

Both sides are to be worked alike, but only one side with the Edging, Fig. 51. Sew the two sides together with invisible stitches on three sides of bag, just behind the Edging and around the Corner Medallions.

For Cord, see Fig. 16.

Fig. 52.   Filet Crochet Band for Bag.

Fig. 52.   Filet Crochet Band for Bag.

This Bag can be worked, one side only, or two sides alike.

For the 18 open meshes, make ch. 60.

FIRST ROW: 1 d. c. in the 9th st., counting back from hook — make 17 more open meshes.

SECOND ROW: Ch. 3 — turn — 1 d. c. in each st. of preceding row.

THIRD, FOURTH and FIFTH ROWS: Ch. 5 — turn — skip 2 st. — 1 d. c. in 3d st. of preceding row — 17 more open meshes.

For the balance of the design, follow the illustration (Fig. 53) and general directions for Filet Crochet, given on page 3 — and bear in mind to always make a ch. of 5 for turning.

For the small **Picot Border,** along the upper edge of the band:

FIRST ROW: 3 d. c. over each space.

SECOND ROW: Ch. 3 — *1 p. — skip 2 d. c. — 1 d. c. over 3d d. c. of preceding row — repeat from* all around.

For **Beading** and **Edging** (Fig. 54):

FIRST ROW: Ch. 16 — 1 d. c. in 4th st., counting back from hook — *ch. 4 — 1 s. c. in 5th ch. st. from d. c. — ch. 4 — 1 d. c. in 6th st. from s. c. — 1 d. c. in next st.

SECOND ROW: Ch. 3 — turn — 1 d. c. in d. c. of preceding row — ch. 5 — 1 s. c. in s. c. of preceding row — ch. 5 — 2 d. c. over 2 d. c.

THIRD ROW: Ch. 3 — turn — 1 d. c. — ch. 10 — 2 d. c. over 2 d. c.

FOURTH ROW: Ch. 3 — turn — 1 d. c. — repeat from*, until the desired length is reached.

FIFTH ROW: On outside of Beading, over the row of d. c. — ch. 5 — *1 d. c. over next d. c. — ch. 2 — repeat from*, until the end of the row.

SIXTH ROW: On opposite side of Beading — same as Fifth Row.

SEVENTH ROW: Ch. 5 — turn — then open meshes, until the end of the row.

EIGHTH ROW: Ch. 3 — turn — *1 p. — 1 d. c. over d. c. — repeat from*, until the end of the row.

For Cord, see Fig. 13; for Ball, see Fig. 22.

Fig. 53.

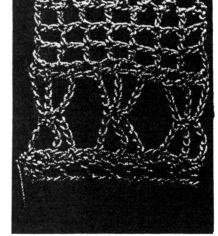

Fig. 54.

Fig. 55. Irish Crochet Band for Bag.

(To be used like in Fig. 52.)

Fig. 55. Irish Crochet Band for Bag.

FIRST ROW: For the raised flower (see Fig. 56), ch. 7 — and join with a sl. st.

SECOND ROW: Fill the ring closely with s. c.

THIRD ROW: Ch. 6 — *skip 1 s. c. — 1 d. c. in next s. c. — ch. 3 — repeat from* all around — and join to 4th st. of ch. of 6 with a sl. st.; this completes a 2d ring.

FOURTH ROW: Ch. 5 — 1 s. c. over d. c. inside of 2d ring — *ch. 5 — 1 s. c. over next d. c. — repeat from* all around.

THE NEXT SIX ROWS: Same as Fourth Row.

ELEVENTH ROW: *Ch. 5 — 1 s. c between 2 d. c. over ch. of 3 (of Third Row) — repeat from* all around.

TWELFTH ROW: The filling. *ch. 2 — 1 p. — ch. 2 — 1 s. c. over ch. of 5 of preceding row — repeat from* all around.

THIRTEENTH ROW: *Ch. 2 — 1 p. — ch. 2 — 1 p. — ch. 2 — 1 s. c. over ch. of 2 of preceding row (after the 1 p.) — repeat from* all around.

FOURTEENTH ROW: Same as Thirteenth Row, but 1 s. c. always between the 2 p.

Make three of these raised flowers.

For the **Star**: FIRST ROW: Ch. 5 — and join with a sl. st.

SECOND ROW: Ch. 3 — 18 d. c. over ring.

THIRD ROW: *Ch. 5 — skip 1 d. c. — 1 s. c. in next d. c. — repeat from* all around.

Make four more rows like Third Row, increasing on each new row the chains by 1 ch. st. Break off thread and fasten. Make three of these stars.

For the small **Squares** (see Fig. 57), start with ch. 12 — turn — 1 d. c. in 9th st., counting back from hook — ch. 2 — 1 d. c. in the 1st ch. made — ch. 5 — turn — 1 d. c. in centre d. c. of row below — ch. 2 — 1 d. c. in 3d ch. st., counting back from centre d. c. — turn — fill with s. c. all around the square. Break off thread and fasten. Make twelve of these squares.

When the raised flowers. stars and squares are finished, join them with s. c. and picots, and add more filling where required. To prepare for border, straighten both edges by means of a row of chain stitches, and catch with s. c., d. c. or t. c. over different fillings.

For **Outside Border**, over row of chain stitches:

FIRST ROW: Ch. 5 — skip 2 ch. st. — 1 d. c. over 3d ch. st. — *ch. 2 — skip 2 ch. st. — 1 d. c. over 3d ch. st. — repeat from*, until end of row — and join with a sl. st into 3d ch. st.

SECOND ROW: Ch. 3 — 2 d. c. over ch. of 2 of preceding row — *3 d. c. over next ch. of 2 — repeat from*, until end of row — and join with a sl. st.

THIRD ROW: Ch. 5 — *1 d. c. between 3 and 3 d. c. of preceding row — ch. 2 — repeat from*, until end of row.

For **Inside Border**: FIRST, SECOND and THIRD ROWS: Same as corresponding rows of Outside Border.

FOURTH ROW (see Fig. 56): 15 s. c. (3 over each ch. of 2) — turn — *ch. 5 — 1 s. c. in the 5th s. c. — repeat from* twice — ch. 1 — turn — 8 s. c. over ch. of 5 — 8 s. c. over next ch. of 5 — 4 s. c. over next ch. of 5 — turn — *ch. 5 — 1 s. c. in centre of 8 s. c. — repeat from* — ch. 1 — turn — 8 s. c. over ch. of 5 — 4 s. c. over next ch. of 5 — turn — ch. 5 — 1 s. c. in centre of 8 s. c. — ch. 1 — turn — 8 s. c. over ch. of 5 — *4 s. c. over remaining ch. st. of ch. of 5 — repeat from* — 3 s. c. over next ch. of 2 — and repeat from Fourth Row.

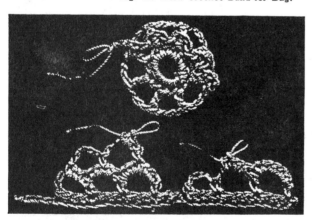

Fig. 56.

Fig. 57.

Fig. 58. Venetian Crochet Band for Bag.

(To be used like in Fig. 52.)

FIRST ROW: For star with picot corners, ch. 7 — and join with a sl. st.

SECOND ROW: 24 s. c. over ring.

THIRD ROW: 1 s. c. in each s. c. of preceding row.

FOURTH ROW: *Ch. 5 — skip 3 s. c. — 1 s. c. each in next 3 s. c. — repeat from* all around.

FIFTH ROW: *12 s. c. over ch. of 5 of preceding row — 1 s. c. each in next 3 s. c. — repeat from* all around.

SIXTH ROW: 1 s. c. in each s. c of preceding row.

SEVENTH ROW: Same as Sixth Row.

EIGHTH ROW: *1 s. c. each in the next 10 s. c. of preceding row — ch. 6 — skip 5 s. c. — repeat from* all around.

NINTH ROW: *1 s. c. each in the next 10 s. c. of preceding row — 8 s. c. over ch. of 6 — repeat from* all around.

TENTH ROW: *1 s. c. each in first 10 s. c. of preceding row — ch. 5 — turn — skip 4 s. c. — 1 s. c. in the 5th s. c. — ch. 5 — skip 4 s. c. — 1 s. c. in 5th s. c. — ch. 1 — turn — 3 s. c. over ch. of 5 — 1 p. — 3 s. c. over same ch. — 2 s. c. over next ch. of 5 — ch. 5 — turn — 1 s. c. in 2d s. c. after picot — ch. 1 — turn — 2 s. c. over ch. of 5 — 1 p. — 2 s. c. — 1 p. — 2 s. c. — 1 p. — 2 s. c. — 1 s. c. over remaining ch. st. of next ch. of 5 — 1 p. — 3 s. c. over same ch. — 1 s. c. each over the next 8 s. c. of preceding row — repeat from* all around. Break off thread and fasten.

When making the four-pointed star, join the picot star through the picots, as you go along; make four picot stars.

For the Four-Pointed Star:

FIRST ROW: Ch. 12 — 1 d. c. in the 9th st., counting back from hook — ch. 2 — 1 d. c. in the 1st ch. st. made — ch. 5 — turn — 1 d. c. in centre d. c. of row below — ch. 2 — 1 d. c. in the 3d ch. st., counting back from centre d. c. This completes a square with four openings.

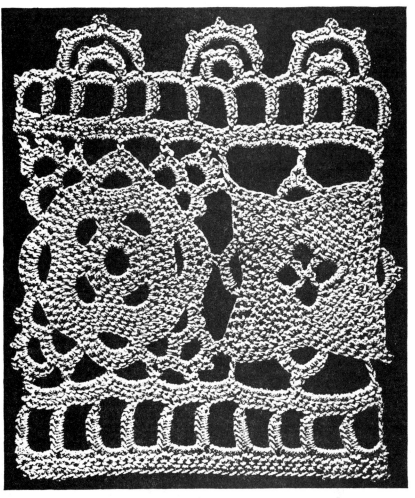

Fig. 58. Venetian Crochet Bag for Band.

SECOND ROW: 5 s. c. over last d. c. of preceding row — 10 s. c. over outside of each opening, all around.

THIRD ROW: For each corner, *make 9 rows of s. c., building over 1st 10 s. c. of preceding row, going forward and back, decreasing each row by 1 st. at the end (ch. 1 at end of each row of s. c., and turn). Go down on left side of corner, with a sl. st. in each row of s. c. — repeat from*, until there are four corners. Break off thread and fasten.

FOURTH ROW: 1 sl. st. in top st. of 1st corner — *1 p. — 1 s. c. each over the next 12 st. (down the first corner and up the next) — ch. 5 — turn — 1 sl. st. in centre of 12 s. c. — ch. 1 — turn — 3 s. c. over ch. of 5 — 1 p. — 3 s. c. over same ch. — continue the s. c. until top of the second corner is reached — repeat from* all around. Break off thread and fasten.

Make two Four-Pointed Stars. It has been said occasionally that Venetian Crochet looks more attractive on the wrong side; as this is a matter of taste, it is merely sugggested to give this matter some thought before starting with the

Inside Border:

FIRST ROW: 1 s. c. in 1st p. of Four-Pointed Star — ch. 10 — 1 d. c. in next p. — ch. 10 — 1 d. c. in p. of same star — ch. 2 — 1 s. c. in last p. of 1st loop of picot star — ch. 4 — 1 s. c. in next p. — ch. 4 — 1 s. c. in centre of next loop — ch. 4 — 1 s. c. in next p., and so on, all around.

SECOND ROW: Fill chains of First Row closely with s. c.

THIRD ROW: 1 s. c. over each s. c. of preceding row.

FOURTH ROW (Fig. 59): Ch. 12 — *1 s. c. in the 4th s. c. of preceding row — ch. 1 — turn — 6 s. c. over 4 ch. st. of ch. of 12 — ch. 8 — skip 3 s. c. — repeat from*, until the end of the row.

FIFTH ROW: 10 s. c. over ch. of 12 of preceding row

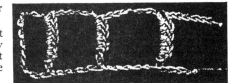

Fig. 59.

Fig. 60.

— (Fig. 60) — *4 s. c. over next ch. — ch. 5 — turn — fasten in top st. of stem — ch. 1 — turn — 2 s. c. over ch. of 5 — 1 p. — 2 s. c. — 1 p. — 2 s. c. — 2 s. c. over next ch. — ch. 10 — turn — 1 s. c. in 2d s. c. from stem — ch. 1 — turn — 4 s. c. over ch. of 10 — 1 p. — 4 s. c. — 1 p. — 1 p. — 4 s. c. over same ch. — 4 s. c. over remaining ch. st. of next ch. — 6 s. c. over next ch. — repeat from*, until the end of the row.

For Outside Border:

FIRST, SECOND, THIRD and FOURTH ROWS: Same as corresponding rows of Inside Border.

FIFTH ROW: 10 s. c. over ch. of 12 of preceding row —*6 s. c. over next ch. — repeat from*, until end of row.

SIXTH ROW: 1 s. c. in each s. c. of preceding row.

For **Edging,** at top of bag (Fig. 61):

FIRST ROW: Make chain of required length — join with sl. st.

SECOND ROW: Ch. 1 — 1 s. c. in each ch.

THIRD ROW: Ch. 1 — 1 s. c. in 1st s. c. of preceding row — ch. 12 — *skip 5 s. c. — 1 s. c. in 6th s. c. — ch. 1 — turn — 7 s. c. over ch. of 12 — ch. 9 — turn — repeat from* all around.

FOURTH ROW: 7 s. c. over each remaining st. of ch. of 9.

FIFTH ROW: Ch. 1 — 1 s. c. over each s. c.

Fig. 61.

Fig. 62. Coronation Braid Band for Bag.

(To be used like in Fig. 52.)

FIRST ROW (Fig. 63): Ch. 5 — and join with a sl. st.

SECOND ROW: Ch. 6 — *1 d. c. over ring — ch. 3 — repeat from*, until there are 5 d. c. — join to 3d st. of ch. of 6 with a sl. st.

THIRD ROW: Ch. 3 — 5 d. c. over 1st ch. of 3 of preceding row — and close for 1 popcorn stitch (see Fig. 20) — ch. 4 — *1 ppc. st. over next ch. of 3 — ch. 4 — repeat from* all around and join to 3d st. of ch. of 3.

FOURTH ROW: Ch. 3 — 5 d. c. over ch. of 4 of preceding row and close for 1 ppc. st. — ch. 8 — *1 ppc. st. — ch. 8 — repeat from* all around — and join to 3d st. of ch. of 3 — break off thread and fasten. Sew centre of flower closely together in back to produce clustered effect. Make six flowers.

FIFTH ROW (Fig. 64): 1 sl. st. in centre of ch. of 8 of preceding row — 1 s. c. over same place — 2 s. c. over fine part of Coronation Braid and over same ch. of 8 together — 4 more s. c. over same ch. — *4 s. c. over next ch. of 8 — form a loop of 2 knots of braid — 2 s. c. after 2d knot and over same ch. of 8 together — 4 more s. c. over same ch. — repeat from* — 4 s. c. over next ch. of 8 — form a loop of 2 knots of braid — 2 s. c. after 2d knot and over same ch. of 8 together — ch. 8 — 1 s. c. over next fine part of braid — ch. 8 — join to next flower with a sl. st. in centre of ch. of 8 — and repeat from Fifth Row, until all six flowers are joined — and join last ch. of 8 to the sl. st. of first flower. Turn the work — and continue on opposite side of flower, same as Fifth Row — and catch the 1 s. c. over fine part of braid (between 2 ch. of 8) in the 1 s. c. of other side. When all around, break off thread and fasten.

SIXTH ROW: 1 sl. st. in centre of 1st ch. of 8 of preceding row — *1 t. c. in centre of next ch. of 8 — ch. 4 — 3 contracted t. c. in the 2 s. c. over braid (for 3 contr. t. c., start like the t. c., until you have drawn twice through 2 loops, leaving 2 st. on hook — then start next t. c., until you have drawn twice through the 2 loops — leaving 3 st. on hook — then start 3d t. c., until you have drawn twice through 2 loops — then thread over hook — draw through all 4 loops) — ch. 5 — 1 s. c. in 1st loop of braid — ch. 5 — 3 contr. t. c. in 2 s. c. over braid — ch. 5 — 1 s. c. in next loop of braid — ch. 5 — 3 contr. t. c. — ch. 5 — 1 s. c. in next loop of braid — ch. 5 — 1 sl. st. in centre of ch. of 8 — repeat from* all around. Break off thread and fasten.

Fig. 62. Coronation Braid Band for Bag.

Fig. 63.

[20]

SEVENTH ROW: *Over ch. of 5 of preceding row, just before 1 s. c. over centre loop of braid—3 s. c.—3 s c. over next ch. of 5—ch. 3—3 contr. t. c. in 1 s. c. over next loop of braid—ch. 2—3 contr. t. c. in same s. c.—ch. 2—3 contr. t. c. in same s. c.—3 contr. t. c. in s. c. over 1st loop of braid of next star—ch. 2—3 contr. t. c. in same s. c. —ch. 2—3 contr. t. c. in same s. c.—ch. 3— repeat from* all around—and join to 1st s. c.

EIGHTH ROW: Ch. 6—1 d. c. between 3 and 3 s. c.—*ch. 3—skip 3 st.—1 d. c. in 4th st.—repeat from* all around—ch. 3— join to 3d st. of ch. of 6.

NINTH ROW: Ch. 4—*skip 1 st.—1 d. c. in 2d st. of preceding row—ch. 1—repeat from* all around—and join to 3d st. of ch. of 4.

TENTH ROW: Ch. 1—*1 s. c. over ch. of 1 and fine part of braid together—1 s. c. over ch. of 1—2 s. c. over next ch. of 1—2 s. c. over next ch. of 1—form a loop of 2 knots of braid—repeat from* all around— and join with sl. st. Break off thread and braid and fasten.

ELEVENTH ROW: *2 s. c. over fine part of braid at the top of loop—ch. 5—repeat from* all around— and join to 1st s. c.

TWELFTH ROW: Ch. 1—1 s. c. in 2d s. c. of preceding row—**5 s. c. over ch. of 5—2 s. c. over 2 s. c. —ch. 1—turn—1 d. c. in centre of 5 s. c.—*ch. 1—1 d. c. in same s. c.—repeat from*, until there are 5 d. c.— ch. 1—1 s. c. in 1st s. c. made—ch. 3—turn—1 s. c. over ch. of 1—*ch. 3—1 s. c. over ch. of 1 between 2 d. c.— repeat from* 3 times—ch. 3—5 s. c. over ch. of 5 of preceding row—2 s. c. over 2 s. c.—repeat from** all around.

On opposite side of work:

THIRTEENTH ROW: Same as Sixth Row.

FOURTEENTH ROW: *Over ch. of 5 of preceding row, just before 1 s. c. over centre loop of braid—3 s. c. —3 s. c. over next ch. of 5—ch. 4—3 contr. t. c. in top of 3 contr. t. c. of preceding row—ch. 3—3 contr. t. c. in top of same 3 contr. t. c.—ch. 4—1 s. c. over ch. of 4 of preceding row—ch 4—3 contr. t. c. in top of 3 contr. t. c.—ch. 3—turn—1 s. c. in top of last 3 contr. t. c. of precious star—ch. 1—turn—1 s. c. over last ch. of 3—1 p.—1 s. c. over same ch.—ch. 3—3 contr. t. c. in top of 3 contr. t. c.—ch. 4—repeat from* all around— and join to 1st s. c.

FIFTEENTH ROW: Same as Eighth Row.

SIXTEENTH ROW: Same as Ninth Row.

SEVENTEENTH ROW: Ch. 1—*2 s. c. over ch. of 1—repeat from* all around—and join with a sl. st.

Fig. 65. Irish Crochet Bag.

For the rose (Fig. 66 and 67):

FIRST ROW: Ch. 6—and join with a sl. st.

SECOND ROW: Ch. 6—1 d. c. over ring—*ch. 3 —1 d. c. over ring—repeat from* twice—ch. 3—join with a sl. st. to 3d st. of ch. of 6.

THIRD ROW: Ch. 1—1 s. c. over ch. of 3 of preceding row—*5 d. c. over same ch.—1 s. c. over same ch. —1 s. c. over next ch. of 3—repeat from* all around— then ch. 1—turn the petal over towards you—1 s. c. **over** (not in) 3d st. of ch. of 6, at back of petal.

FOURTH ROW: *Ch. 5—1 s. c. **over** 1 d. c. of Second Row—repeat from* all around—join last ch. of 5 to 1st s. c. with a sl. st.

FIFTH ROW: *1 s. c. over next ch. of 5 of preceding row—7 d. c.—1 s. c. over same ch.—repeat from* all around—then ch. 1—turn the petal over towards you —1 s. c. over 1 s. c. of Fourth Row, at back of petal.

SIXTH ROW: *Ch. 7—1 s. c. over 1 s. c. of next petal—repeat from* all around—join last ch. of 7 to 1st s. c. with a sl. st.

SEVENTH ROW: *1 s. c. over next ch. of 7 of preceding row—9 d. c.—1 s. c. over same ch.—repeat from* all around.

EIGHTH ROW: Ch. 1—1 p.—ch. 1—1 p.—ch.

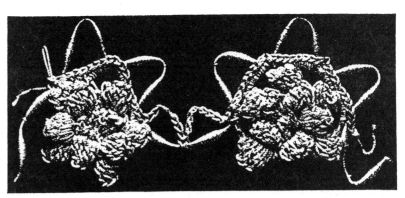

Fig. 64.

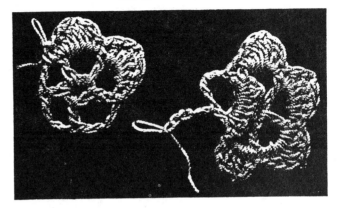

Fig. 66.

Fig. 67.

1 (these 5 st. will be called "1 picot bow")—*1 s. c. in 1st d. c. of 9 d. c. of preceding row—1 p. bow—1 s. c. in 6th d. c. of 9 d. c.—1 p. bow.—repeat from* all around —and join last p. bow with 1 s. c. over 1st p. bow made, between the 2 p.

NINTH ROW: *1 p. bow—1 s.c. over next p. bow, between 2 p.—repeat from* all around, until you reach the last p. bow of preceding row, to which join a p. bow with a sl. st. between 2 p. Break off thread and fasten.

Make **Second Rose,** the first eight rows as described above.

NINTH ROW: 1 p. bow—1 s. c. over next p. bow, between 2 p.—*then ch. 1—1 p.—ch. 5—take out hook —slip work over Ninth Row of previous rose, between 2 p.—now close for 1 p. as usual, but around the Ninth Row of previous rose—ch. 1—1 s. c. over next p. bow —repeat from*—then complete Ninth Row as usual.

Make **Third Rose,** the first eight rows as described above.

[21]

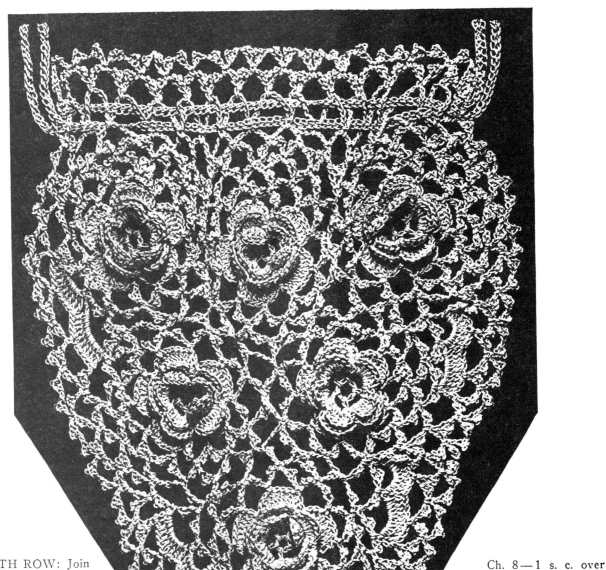

NINTH ROW: Join 1st p. bow to Second Rose, as before, over the 5th p. bow of Ninth Row — join 2d p. bow to same rose, over the 4th p. bow of Ninth Row — join 3d p. bow over p. bow of First Rose — then complete Ninth Row as usual.

The **Fourth Rose**, the upper one to the right is joined to the First Rose in the 4th and 5th p. bow from the joining point of the First and Second Rose — then complete Ninth Row as usual.

The **Fifth Rose**, the centre of three roses, is joined to Third Rose over its 4th p. bow of Ninth Row — join to First Rose over its next 2 p. bows — join to Fourth Rose over 2 p. bows — then complete Ninth Row as usual.

The **Sixth Rose** is joined to Third Rose over the 2 top p. bows and joined to Fifth Rose over 2 p. bows — then complete Ninth Row as usual. Break off thread and fasten.

For **Edging** around the bag:

FIRST ROW: 1 s. c. in corner p. bow of Sixth Rose — 1 p. bow each over the next 6 p. bows, always fastening with 1 s. c. between 2 p. — *then ch. 6 — turn — skip 1 p. bow — 1 s. c. over next p. bow — ch. 6 — 1 s. c. over next p. bow — ch. 3 — turn — 9 d. c. over ch. of 6 — 10 d. c. over next ch. of 6 — 6 p. bows — repeat from* — make 2 more p. bows — repeat from* to* twice — then along the top of bag:

Ch. 8 — 1 s. c. over next p. bow — ch. 6 — 1 s. c. over next p. bow — *ch. 6 — 1 d. c. over next p. bow — repeat from* twice — ch. 6 — 1 s. c. — ch. 6 — 1 s. c. — and so on, catching with s. c. or d. c. as required — join last ch. of 6 to 1st p. bow of Edging.

SECOND ROW: P. bows all around, catching with a s. c. between 2 p. of preceding row and over the 2 figures of d. c., until top of bag is reached — join last p. bow to 3d st. of ch. of 8 with 1 s. c. — ch. 12 — 1 s. c. over remaining st. of same ch. of 8 — ch. 12 — *1 s. c. over center of next ch. of 6 — ch. 12 — repeat from*, until the end of the row — join last ch. of 12 to 1st p. bow of this row.

THIRD ROW: 1 p. bow — turn — 1 s. c. over center of last ch. of 12 — *1 p. bow — 1 s. c. over center of next ch. of 12 — repeat from*, until the last ch. of 12 is reached.

FOURTH ROW: 1 p. bow — turn — 1 s. c. over last p. bow of preceding row — *1 p. bow — 1 s. c. over next p. bow — repeat from*, until the end of the row. Break off thread and fasten.

Make another piece like this for back of bag — and join the two by making a row of p. bows over the last row of both.

For Cord, see Fig. 12; for Tassel, see **Fig. 23**.

Fig. 65. Irish Crochet Bag.

Fig. 56.   Fig. 57.   Fig. 58.   Fig. 59.

LINGERIE CORDS.

Lingerie Cords.

Material: Collingbourne's American Maid, Size 5.

Fig. 56. Ch. 4 — turn — 1 s.c each in first 2 st. made — *ch. 1 — turn — 1 s.c. in each s.c. — repeat from* until the desired length is reached. For the small tassel — ch. 50 — break off thread, leaving it ½ yard long — put this ½ yard in embroidery needle — fold the chain once — leaving the threaded end one inch shorter and knot the folded chain twice — then sew to cord by the shorter end — put other end of chain through the loop and inside of knots — with sewing thread sew up from all sides.

Fig. 57. Ch. 3 — *thread over hook — put hook through first ch. made — thread over hook — draw through work — repeat from*, until there are 7 loops on hook — then thread over hook — and draw through all 7 loops — ch. 1, showing a large loop — thread over hook — hook through the large loop — thread over hook — and so on, until the desired length is reached. Break off thread and fasten.

For the STAR:

FIRST ROW: Ch. 6 — and join with a sl. st.

SECOND ROW: Ch. 4 — 1 d.c. over ring — *ch. 1 — 1 d.c. — repeat from* 7 more times — ch. 1 — 1 sl. st. in third st. of ch. of 4.

THIRD ROW: Ch. 3 — 1 s.c. over ch. of 1 of preceding row — *ch. 3 — 1 s.c. over next ch. of 1 — repeat from* all around and join to first ch. of 3. Leave enough thread to sew to cord.

Fig. 58. FIRST ROW: Make ch. 1½ yards long.

SECOND ROW: 1 sl. st. in each ch. st., picking up one thread only — break off thread and fasten.

For the TASSEL:

FIRST ROW: Ch. 6 — and join with a sl. st.

SECOND ROW: *Ch. 3 — 1 s.c. over ring — repeat from 3 more times — ch. 3 — 1 sl. st. in first st. of ch. of 3.

THIRD ROW: *Ch. 3 — 1 s.c. in ch. of 3 of preceding row — repeat from* all around — ch. 3 — 1 sl. st. in first st. of ch. of 3.

FOURTH ROW: 1 s.c. over first ch. of 3 — 1 s.c. over each following ch. of 3 — 1 sl. st. in first s.c. made — ch. 3 — leave enough thread to sew to cord.

Fig. 59. FIRST ROW: Make ch. 1½ yards long.

SECOND ROW: *Skip 1 st. — 1 s.c. in next st., picking up one thread only — ch. 1 — repeat from* until the end of the ch. — break off thread and fasten.

FOR THE SHAMROCK:

FIRST ROW: Ch. 6 — and join with a sl. st.

SECOND ROW: Ch. 1 — turn — *3 s.c. over ring — ch. 3 — turn — 1 s.c. in first s.c. made — turn — 1 s.c. over ch. of 3 — 5 d. c. — 1 s.c. over same ch. — repeat from* twice and finish with 1 sl. st. over ring — leave enough thread to sew to cord.

Fig. 32. Motif.

Fig. 33. Rings and Edging.

Fig. 31. Bag.

This bag is very handsome and yet quite simple to make; it should be lined with Messaline Silk in the color desired.

Fig. 32, 33, 34, 35 are used in the illustration of this bag — and C.B. used is Size 3.

Fig. 32. Form loops of braid as per illustration.

FIRST ROW: 2 s.c. over fine part of braid — *ch. 5 — 2 s.c. — ch. 5 — 2 s.c. — ch. 15 — 2 s.c. — repeat from*.

SECOND ROW: *5 s.c. over ch. of 5 of preceding row — 5 s.c. over next ch. — turn — ch. 15 — fasten with 1 s.c. in the 10th st., counting back from last s.c. — turn — 20 s.c. over ch. of 15 — 20 s.c. over next ch. — repeat from*.

THIRD ROW: Turn — 1 s.c. in each s.c. of preceding row, excepting the first and last s.c. of each scallop — repeat around.

FOURTH ROW: Turn — *skip the first and last stitch of each scallop — 2 s.c. — 1 p. — 3 s.c. — 1 p. — 3 s.c. — 1 p. — repeat until you have 5 p. on each scallop — 2 s.c. — repeat from*.

Make 16 motifs — join together in the center picot.

To make the large **ring**, shown in the background:

FIRST ROW: Ch. 11 — and join — have 17 s.c. over ch. and join with a sl. st.

SECOND ROW: Turn — ch. 1 — 1 s. c. in each s. c. of preceding row — join.

THIRD ROW: Turn — ch. 2 — 2 s. c. — 1 p. — *1 s. c. in last s. c. — 1 s. c. in next st. of preceding row — ch. 5 — insert hook through center of p. of last motif and draw loop through — ch. 5 — 1 s. c. in last s. c. — 1 s. c. — 1 p. — repeat from*.

For small figure, insert hook through center of p. of first motif — ch. 6 — slip loop through second p. of next motif — ch. 6 — 1 s. c. in the p. of the first motif — ch. 6 — slip loop through second p. of third motif — ch. 6 — fasten with 1 s. c. in the p. of first motif.

Fig. 33. FIRST ROW: Ch. 20 — and join.

SECOND ROW: Make 40 s. c. over ring — join with a sl. st.

THIRD ROW: Turn — ch. 2 — 1 s. c. in each s. c. of preceding row.

FOURTH ROW: Turn — ch. 2 — 3 s. c. — 1 p. — 3 s. c. — 1 p. — repeat until you have 14 p.

To join rings together, make a ch. of 4 — slip loop through p. of next ring — ch. 4 — 3 s. c. — ch. 4 —

Have 12 rings in all and join every other one to motifs of bag by two loops of a ch. of 8.

At last make scallop on the rings.

FIRST ROW: Insert hook through p. — ch. 12 — fasten with a s. c. in second p. — ch. 12 — 1 s. c. — ch. 10 — 1 s. c. — ch. 12 —

SECOND ROW: *15 s. c. over ch. of 12 of preceding row — 5 s. c. over next ch. of 12 — turn — ch. 12 — fasten with a sl. st. in eleventh st., counting back from last s. c. — turn — have 15 s. c. over ch. — 10 s. c. on next ch. — 8 s. c. on ch. of 10 — repeat from*.

THIRD ROW: Turn — 1 s. c. in each s. c. of preceding row, excepting the first and last st. of each scallop.

FOURTH ROW: Turn — *4 s. c., leaving out the first and last st. of each scallop — 1 p. — 4 s. c. — 1 p. — 4 s. c. — 1 p. — 4 s. c. — 1 p. — 4 s. c. — 1 p. — 4 s. c. — repeat from*.

Fig. 34. Make two tassels of seven large loops of C. B., having four knots of braid to each one — seven small loops around, having two knots of braid in each one — two tassels, having only four large loops and five small loops — leave two ends of braid on each tassel, as shown in the illustration.

Make two crochet balls for each tassel:

FIRST ROW: Ch. 15 — join — have 20 s. c. over ch. — make 5 rows of s. c., crocheting around — then slip the two ends of braid through the ball and gather stitches together at top — the two balls are made exactly alike, the effect of the smaller one at the bottom is produced by pressing it down after it is put on the tassel.

Fig. 35. Fold C. B. as per illustration.

FIRST ROW: 3 s. c. around fine part of braids — ch. 8 — 3 s. c. — ch. 8 — 3 s. c. —

SECOND ROW: Turn — 3 s. c., picking up the 3 s. c. of preceding row — ch. 8 — 3 s. c. —

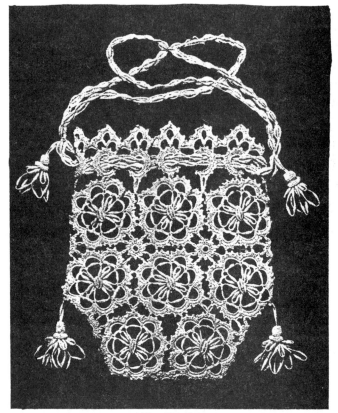

Fig. 31. Bag.

Fig. 34. Tassel

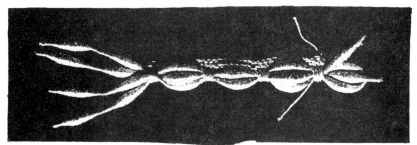

Fig. 35. Cord.

Fig. 61. Pin Cushion.

Fig. 62, 63 and 64 are used in the illustration of this Pin Cushion—C. B. used is Size 1.

Fig. 61. Pin Cushion.

Fig. 62. Figure of C. B. as per illustration.

FIRST ROW: 2 s. c. over fine part of braid — *ch. 4 — 2 s. c. in next loop — ch. 6 — 2 s. c. — ch. 6 — 2 s. c. — repeat from*. — Finish row with 1 s. c. in the first s. c.

1 s. c. over same ch. — ch. 1 — 1 p. — ch. 1 — 1 p. — ch. 1 — 1 s. c. over next ch. of 6 — ch. 1 — 1 p. — ch. 1 — 1 p. — ch. 1 — 1 s. c. over same ch. — ch. 1 — 1 p. — ch. 1 — 1 p. — ch. 1 — 1 s. c. over ch. of 4 — repeat from*.

Fig. 62. Motif.

SECOND ROW: Ch. 1 — 1 p. — ch. 1 — 1 p. — ch. 1 — 1 s. c. over ch. of 4 — *ch. 1 — 1 p. — ch. 1 — 1 p. — ch. 1 — 1 s. c. over ch. of 6 — ch. 1 — 1 p. — ch. 1 — 1 p. — ch. 1 —

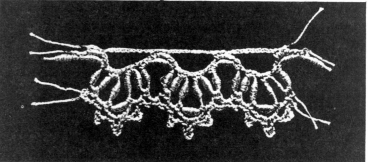

Fig. 64. Edging.

Join three motifs, as shown in Fig. 61 — around these motifs crochet a chain of 5 — fastened with 1 s.c. over each ch. of 1 between the picots — excepting between the motifs a chain of 13 should be made — when turning the corners, a ch. of 7 should be made.

Fig. 63. FIRST ROW: 2 s.c. over fine part of braid — *form a loop of two knots of braid — 2 s.c. — ch. 5 — 2 s.c., leaving a knot of braid between — repeat from*.

SECOND ROW: On opposite side of braid — 2 s.c. over fine part of loop — *ch. 7 — 2 s.c. over next loop — repeat from*.

THIRD ROW: Over Second Row — 1 s.c. in the first s.c. — ch. 4 — 1 d.c. in the next s.c. — ch. 3 — *2 d.c. over ch. of 7 — ch. 3 — 2 d.c. in the 2 s.c. — ch. 3 — repeat from*.

FOURTH ROW: On the opposite side of braid — 1 s.c. in the second s.c. — ch. 4 — 1 d.c. in the next s.c. — ch. 3 — *2 d.c. over ch. of 5 — ch. 3 — 2 d.c. in the 2 center s.c. — ch. 3 — repeat from*.

Fig. 64. FIRST ROW: 2 s.c. over fine part of braid — ch. 5 — 2 s.c., leaving one knot of braid between — *ch. 1 — form a loop of two knots of braid — 2 s.c. — ch. 1 —

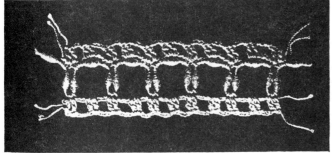

Fig. 63. Beading.

form a loop of 3 knots of braid — 2 s.c. — ch. 1 — form a loop of two knots — 2 s.c. — ch. 5 — 2 s.c., leaving one knot of braid between — repeat from*.

SECOND ROW: On opposite side of braid — *2 s.c. in first loop — ch. 2 — 1 s.c. in next loop — ch. 6 — 1 s.c., leaving one knot of braid between — ch. 2 — 2 s.c. in next loop — ch. 3 — repeat from*.

THIRD ROW: Over second row — 1 s.c. in the first s.c. — ch. 2 — 2 s.c. over ch. of 2 — *ch. 1 — 1 p. — ch. 1 — 2 s.c. over ch. of 6 — ch. 1 — 1 p. — ch. 1 — 2 s.c. over same ch. — ch. 1 — 1 p. — ch. 1 — 2 s.c. over ch. of 2 — ch. 2 — 2 s.c. over ch. of 3 — ch. 2 — 2 s.c. over ch. of 2 — repeat from*.

FOURTH ROW: On opposite side of braid — 3 s.c. over ch. of 5 — *ch. 8 — 3 s.c. over next ch. of 5 — repeat from*.

Appliqué the motifs and beading on the linen by buttonholing.

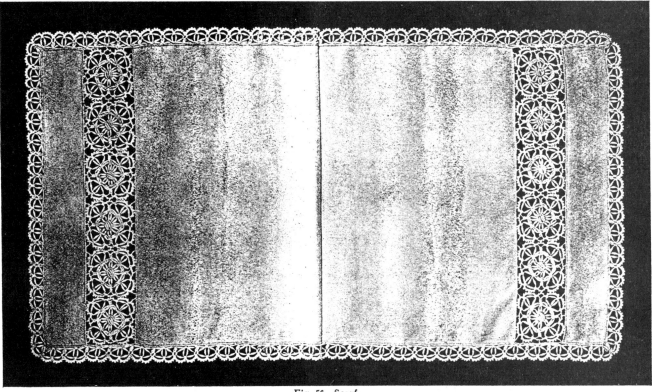

Fig. 56. Scarf.

Fig. 56. Scarf

Figs. 57 and 58 are used in the illustration of this scarf — C.B. used is Size 5.

Fig. 57. Figure of C.B. as per illustration — make two separate figures — to crochet, start at the inside of the outside figure.

FIRST ROW: *2 s.c. over fine part of braid — 1 s.c. in center loop — 2 s.c. — ch. 8 — 3 s.c. — ch. 8 — repeat from*.

SECOND ROW: *1 s.c. in the center of the 5 s.c. of preceding row — ch. 4 — slip chain through loop of braid of inside figure — 1 s.c. in the last s.c. — ch. 7 — 1 s.c. in the center of the 3 s.c. of preceding row — ch. 4 — slip chain through next loop of braid — 1 s.c. in the last s.c. — ch. 7 — repeat from*.

THIRD ROW: Start at the outside of the outside figure — *3 s.c., catching inside loop at the same time — ch. 12 — 3 s.c. over fine part of braid, leaving one knot between — ch. 6 — 3 t.c. over fine part of braid and in center of 3 s.c. of the First Row — ch. 6 — 3 s.c. — ch. 12 — repeat from*.

FOURTH ROW: *3 s.c. over ch. of 12 of preceding row — 1 p. — 3 s.c. — 1 p. — 3 s.c. — 1 p. — 3 s.c. — 1 p. — 3 s.c. — 1 p. — 3 s.c. over next ch. of 6 — make 3 p. — 3 s.c. over next ch. of 12 — 1 p. — 3 s.c. — 1 p. — repeat same until you have 5 p. — repeat from*.

After crocheting the second motif, join them together in the third p. of the 5 p. — and in the second p. of the 3 p.

At last, crochet a ch. on both sides of border — *1 s.c. in the fourth p. — ch. 9 — 1 d.c. in center of 3 p. — ch. 9 — 1 s.c. in the second p. — ch. 9 — 1 l.t.c. in the fifth p. — ch. 4 — 1 l.t.c. in the first p. of the 5 p. — ch. 9 — repeat from*.

Fig. 58. FIRST ROW: For inside of edging — 3 s.c. over fine part of braid — *ch. 8 — form the loops of braid as per illustration — 3 s.c. around both loops — ch. 8 — 3 s.c. — repeat from*.

SECOND ROW: For outside edging — work on opposite side of braid figure — *3 s.c. in loop of braid — ch. 12 — 3 s.c., catching both loops together — ch. 12 — 3 s.c. — ch. 1 — 1 l.t.c. in the center of the 3 s.c. of First Row — ch. 1 — repeat from*.

THIRD ROW: *3 s.c. over ch. of 12 of preceding row — 1 p. — 3 s.c. — 1 p. — 3 s.c. — 1 p. — 3 s.c. — 1 p. — 3 s.c. — repeat from*.

After placing the motifs and edging on the linen, appliqué on by buttonholing.

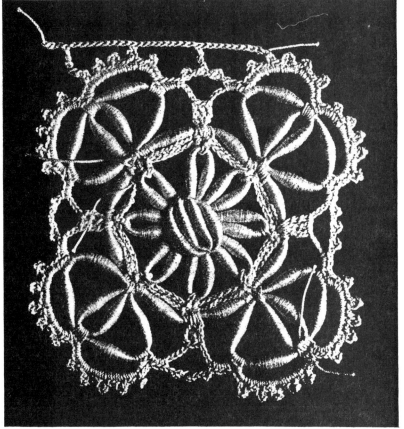

Fig. 57. Motif.

Fig. 58. Edging.

Fig. 59. Pillow.

Fig. 60 is used in illustration of this pillow — C.B. used is Size 4.

Fig. 60. Join 8 small loops of C.B. together — then make 4 large loops of four knots of braid each — have 2 small loops inside of each large loop.

FIRST ROW: *3 s.c. over fine part of both, the small loop and the outside loop — ch. 10 — 3 s.c. over outside loop, leaving one knot of braid between — ch. 10 — 3 s.c. over both loops as before — ch. 3 — repeat from* — finish row with 1 s.c. in the first s.c.

SECOND ROW: Ch. 2 — *1 s.c. over ch. of 10 of preceding row — ch. 1 — 1 p. — ch. 1 — 1 p. — ch. 1 — 1 s.c. over same ch. of 10 — ch. 1 — 1 p. — ch. 1 — 1 s.c. over same ch. of 10 — ch. 1 — 1 p. — ch. 1 — 1 p. — ch. 1 — 1 s.c. over next ch. of 10 — ch. 1 — 1 p. — ch. 1 — 1 p. — ch. 1 — 1 s.c. over same ch. of 10 — ch. 1 — 1 p. — ch. 1 — 1 p. — ch. 1 — 1 s.c. over same ch. of 10 — ch. 1 — 1 p. — ch. 1 — 1 p. — ch. 1 — repeat from* — finish row with 1 s.c. in ch. of 2.

THIRD ROW: Ch. 2 — 1 s.c. over ch. of 1 between the first 2 p. of preceding row — ch. 2 — 1 p. — ch. 1 — 1 p. — ch. 2 — 1 s.c. over ch. of 1 between the next 2 p. — ch. 2 — 1 p. — ch. 1 — 1 p. — ch. 2 — 1 s.c. over ch. of 1 between the next 2 p. — ch. 2 — 1 p. — ch. 1 — 1 p. — ch. 2 — 1 s.c. over ch. of 1 between the next 2 p. — ch. 2 — 1 p. — ch. 1 — 1 p. — ch. 2 — 1 s.c. over ch. of 1 between the next 2 p. — ch. 1 — 1 p. — ch. 1 — 1 p. — ch. 1 — 1 s.c. over ch. of 1 between the 2 p., leaving 4 p.

Fill in the center of the motif with French knots.

For the center of the pillow, arrange nine motifs for a square effect, as per Fig. 59 — and join these nine motifs together by crocheting around this square a chain of 3 — fastened with 1 s.c. in each p. — excepting between the motifs, a chain of 12 should be made — when turning the four corners of the square, make a ch. of 6, thus maintaining a perfectly square effect.

For the corners of the pillow, arrange three motifs each, as per Fig. 59 — and join them together. Around the joined motifs, crochet a chain of 3 — fastened with 1 s.c. in each p. — when turning corners, however, a ch. of 6 should be made.

Appliqué on by buttonholing.

The **tassel,** which is shown in illustration of Fig. 59, is made by folding a piece of C.B. into forty to fifty loops, each loop containing from 17 to 20 knots of braid.

When making the first loop, allow for a loose end of 14 to 16 inches of braid — each loop is joined together with a threaded needle — after the necessary number of loops has been made, fold the loose end three times and fasten securely to the tassel; the purpose of this folded end is to allow the tassel to hang loose from the pillow, when sewed on.

The rings over the tassel are made with another piece of braid, in carrying the braid around and over the tassel, until sufficiently heavy.

Fig 60. Motif.

Fig. 23. Jabot.

Fig. 23. Jabot.

Fig. 24, 25, 26 are used in the illustration of this Jabot — and C.B. used is Size 1.

Fig. 24. Figure of C.B. as per illustration.

FIRST ROW: 1 s.c. over fine part of braid — *ch. 5 — 1 s.c. in next loop — ch. 6 — 1 s.c., leaving a knot between — repeat from*.

SECOND ROW: *1 s.c. over preceding row — 6 d.c. — 1 s.c. — repeat from*.

THIRD ROW: *Ch. 6 — 1 s.c. in the first row, taken between the petals in back of work — repeat from*.

FOURTH ROW: *1 s.c. over loop of preceding row — 8 d.c. — 1 s.c. — repeat from*.

FIFTH ROW: Ch. 2 — slip through center of scallop from back of work — ch. 7 — *1 d. c. in the next st. — ch. 3 — 1 d.c. in preceding row, leaving 2 sts. between — 1 d.c. in second st. of next scallop — ch. 3 — 1 d.c., leaving two sts. between — ch. 3 — repeat from*.

SIXTH ROW: After finishing fifth row with 1 s.c. over ch. of 7 — ch. 6 — *1 d.c. in same place — ch. 3 — 1 d.c in same place — ch. 3 — 1 d.c. in same place, making 3 loops in each scallop — ch. 2 — 1 d.c. between the two d.c. of preceding row — ch. 2 — 1 d.c. in next loop — ch. 3 — repeat from*.

SEVENTH ROW: 2 s.c. over ch. of 6 — 1 p. — *2 s.c. — 2 s.c. over next ch. — 1 p. — 2 s.c — 2 s.c. over next ch. — 1 p. — 2 s.c. — 2 s.c. over ch. of 2 — 2 s.c. in next ch. — 2 s.c. — 1 p. — repeat from*.

EIGHTH ROW: Ch. 2 — slip through center of first picot — ch. 6 — 1 d.c. in center of next p. — *ch. 3 — 1 d.c. in same place — ch. 2 — 1 d.c. in next p. — repeat from* until you have crocheted on three scallops.

NINTH ROW: Turn — ch. 6 — *1 d.c. over ch. of 3 of preceding row — ch. 3 — 1 d.c. in same place — ch. 2 — repeat from*.

TENTH ROW: Turn — make 1 s.c. over each ch. of 3.

When the two motifs are finished, sew them together.

Fig. 24. Motif.

Fig. 25. Each loop of C.B. to have four knots — join 6 such loops of braid together, leaving two even ends of the length desired.

For the crochet ball, make a ch. of 12 — and join — 13 s.c. over ch. of 12 — make 4 more rows of 13 s.c. — slip the two ends of braid through and fasten the ball at the top, joining the last row of s.c. together.

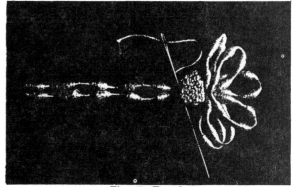

Fig. 25. Tassel.

Fig. 26. Fold C.B. as per illustration.

FIRST ROW: 2 s.c. — ch. 6 — 2 s.c. — ch. 6.

SECOND ROW: Insert hook on opposite side of braid — then same as First Row.

THIRD ROW: Make 9 s.c. over every ch. of 6.

FOURTH ROW: On opposite side of braid — same as Third Row.

Fig. 26.

LUXURA TAFFE BAG

Use *Collingbourne's* Luxura Artificial Silk Crochet

2 black, 1 delft, 1 yellow, 1 green, 1 red, 1 grey.

First Row.—Color black, ch. 6, join, 12 s. c. in ring, join.

Second Row.—In this and all following rows take up back rib. ch. 3, 1 s. c. in 1 st., ch. 3, 1 s. c. in next ch. 3 and repeat around, join with sl. st.

Third Row.—1 s. c. in 1st ch., 5 s. c. in next, 1 s. c. in 3rd ch., skip the s. c. and repeat the same in the following ch. 3, continue around, join.

Fourth Row.—Turn, 2 s. c. in 1st 2 sts., 3 s. c. in center st., 2 s. c. in next 2 sts., sk. 2 sts., repeat around, join.

Fifth Row.—Turn, sk. 1st st., 2 s. c., 5 s. c. in center, 2 s. c., sk. 2, repeat around, join.

Sixth Row.—Color yellow. Turn, sk. 1st st., 3 s. c., 3 s. c. in center, 3 s. c., sk. 2, repeat around, join.

Seventh Row.—Turn, sk. 1st st., 3 s. c., 5 s. c. in center st., 3 s. c., sk. 2, repeat around, join.

Eighth Row.—Color black, turn, sk. 1st st., 4 s. c., 3 s. c. in center, 4 s. c., sk. 2, repeat around, join.

Ninth Row.—Turn, sk. 1, 4 s. c., 5 s. c. in center, 4 s. c., sk. 2, repeat, join.

Tenth Row.—Turn, sk. 1, 5 s. c., 3 s. c. in center, 5 s. c., sk. 2, repeat, join.

Eleventh Row.—Turn, sk. 1, 5 s. c., 5 s. c. in center, 5 s. c., sk. 2, repeat, join.

Twelfth Row.—Turn, sk. 1, 6 s. c., 3 s. c. in center, 6 s. c., sk. 2, repeat, join.

Thirteenth Row.—Turn, sk. 1, 6 s. c., 5 s. c. in center, 6 s. c., sk. 2, repeat, join.

Fourteenth Row.—Turn, sk. 1, 7 s. c., 3 s. c. in center, 7 s. c., sk. 2, repeat, join.

Fifteenth Row.—Turn, sk. 1, 7 s. c., 5 s. c. in center, 7 s. c., sk. 2, repeat, join.

Sixteenth Row.—Turn, sk. 1, 8 s. c., 3 s. c. in center, 8 s. c., sk. 2, repeat, join.

Seventeenth Row.—Turn, sk. 1, 8 s. c., 5 s. c. in center, 8 s. c., sk. 2, repeat, join.

Eighteenth Row.—Turn, sk. 1, 9 s. c., 3 s. c. in center, 9 s. c., sk. 2, repeat, join.

Nineteenth Row.—Turn, sk. 1, 9 s. c., 5 s. c. in center, 9 s. c., sk. 2, repeat, join.

Twentieth Row.—Turn, sk. 1, 10 s. c., 3 s. c. in center, 10 s. c., sk. 2, repeat, join.

Twenty-first Row.—Turn, sk. 1, 10 s. c., 5 s. c. in center, 10 s. c., sk. 2, repeat, join.

Twenty-second Row.—Turn, sk. 1, 11 s. c., 3 s. c. in center, 11 s. c., sk. 2, repeat, join.

Twenty-third Row.—Turn, sk. 1, 11 s. c., 5 s. c. in center, 11 s. c., sk. 2, repeat, join.

Twenty-fourth Row.—Color red, turn, sk. 1, 12 s. c., 3 s. c. in center, 12 s. c., sk. 2, repeat, join.

Twenty-fifth Row.—Turn, sk. 1, 12 s. c., 3 s. c. in center, 12 s. c., sk. 2, repeat, join.

Twenty-sixth and **Twenty-seventh Rows.**—Color black. Same as twenty-fifth row.

Continue same as last row, making:

4 rows of delft.
2 rows of black.
6 rows of green.
2 rows of black.
4 rows of yellow.
2 rows of white.
2 rows of red.
14 rows of grey.
2 rows of yellow.
2 rows of delft.

Finish Off.—Begin with black on top of point * in center and next st. of point, 1 s. c. in each. In the following sts. 2 h. d. c., 2 d. c., 2 tr. c., 2 d. tr. c., 2 d. tr. tr. c. Now wind silk 5 times around needle, insert in next st., sk. sts., silk once over needle, insert in next, pull through 4 ls., then work off 2 at a time. In following sts., 2 d. tr. tr. c., 2 d. tr. c., 2 tr. c., 2 d. c., 2 h. d. c., 1 s. c., repeat from * around, join, 1 row of 1 s. c. in each 2 sl. sts. at beginning of next row, ch. 3, 9 d. c., ch. 3, sk. 3, 9 d. c., repeat around, 1 row of 1 s. c. in each st.

With red Luxura, 11 s. c., * ch. 4 from p., ch. 4. p., ch. 4, p., 1 s. c., in beginning of 1st p., sk. 1, 11 s. c., repeat from * around and finish off.

Strings for Bag.—With black, ch. 2, 1 s. c. in 1st ch., turn, ch. 1, 1 s. c. in st., s. c. 1 of previous row, turn. Repeat the desired length and make 2 strings.

Tassel for Bottom of Bag.—Wind all the colors together around a cardboard 6 inches long as many times as you want the tassel. Fasten in center and cut in half. Crocheted top for the tassel ch. 23, join, ch. 1, 1 s. c. in each ch., taking up back rib; continue without joining for 4 rows, decrease by skipping 1 s. c. and 2 s. c. in next 2 sts. until closed, ch. 14, 1 s. c. in top of bell shape, 20 s. c. in one. On the bottom of the bell make 1 row of 2 s. c., 1 p., 2 s. c., pull tassel up through center of bell and fasten all to bag.

HAND BAG.

Materials: 2 ounces BELDING's black "Pure Thread" Crochet Silk, 1 large bunch of black jet cut beads, and a No. 2 steel hook.

String the beads on the silk before you begin to crochet, and always push the bead on the silk before you take the stitch.

Chain 150 stitches, join in a ring, use the short crochet stitch and crochet 2 plain rows; when you work the 2nd row, take up both stitches in the top of the 1st row.

3rd and 4th rows plain with beads.

Start the squares by crocheting * 5 short crochet and 5 stitches with beads; continue this for 5 rows, when you will have a complete row of squares.

Start the next row with 5 stitches with beads, then 5 short crochet, and continue for 5 rows.

You will find you have a plain square over a beaded one; repeat from * until you have 18 rows of squares, which you may finish with 2 plain rows of beads and 20 rows of plain crochet for the top. This will make a bag 9½ by 7 inches.

In all bead-work the beads will be on the wrong side of the work, and the article being made must be turned after it is finished.

For a finish across the bottom, fill brass rings with crochet, and tie in heavy silk tassel made of strands of crochet silk. Finish top with a strip of silk 7 inches deep. Turn it down at the top. If preferred, make a fringe of beads for bottom. Make a casing with frill. Use ribbon to draw the bag together.

FANCY BAG.

Materials: 1½ ounces BELDING's "Pure Thread" Crochet Silk, 1 yard silk, satin or plush, and 4½ yards of ribbon 1¼ inches wide.

To make the large rosettes.—Make 13 ch. Join.

1st round.—3 ch., 1 tr. in first st., 4 ch., 2 tr. till there are seven points to the star. Join.

2nd round.—2 ch. and a row of str. around the star by making 4 str. in each loop, and 2 str. on the upper edge of the points of the star. Join.

3rd round.—3 ch., 1 tr. in first st., 2 tr., 3 ch. and 2 tr. in every fourth st. to end of round. Join.

4th round.—2 ch., 4 str. in each loop, and 4 str. on the upper edge of the tr. to end of row. Join.

5th round.—3 ch., 1 tr. in first st., 4 ch., 2 tr. in the third and fourth sts. to the end of round. Join.

6th round.—2 ch., 4 str. in loop, and 2 str. in upper edge of tr. to end of round. Join.

7th round.—3 ch., 1 tr. in first st., 6 ch., 2 tr. in fifth and 6th sts. to end of round. Join.

8th round.—1 str. between the tr. in the foundation, 8 tr. in each loop to end of round.

To make the small rosettes.—Make 13 ch. Join.

1st round.—2 ch., 1 tr. in every first st., 4 ch. and 2 tr. till there are seven points in the star. Join.

2nd round.—3 ch., 1 str. in every first st., 4 str. in loop, 2 str. on the upper edge of tr. to end of round. Join.

3rd round.—6 ch. in every third st. to end of round.

These rosettes are arranged upon the bag as illustrated, and after making a row of ch. stitches and a row of tr. with 3 ch. between them, on the lower edge of the second row of rosettes, a less number of rosettes is placed below on the gathered end of the bag, as shown in the cut. The rosettes should not be crocheted too loosely. The width of the satin or plush forms the length of the bag and the hem above the gathers on the upper end, may be lined with satin of a contrasting color matching the rosettes. Fawn-color or light brown on blue, or cardinal and old gold on brown velvet are very elegant combinations.

TOBACCO BAG No. 1.

This bag is made of Belding's cardinal red and gold-colored "Pure Thread" Crochet Silk, about an ounce of each. Use a medium size steel hook.

Commence at the center of bottom of bag with red silk, work 8 ch., and join in a ring.

1st round.—24 tr. under the ch., join to the 1st tr. with a sc. To commence the next round, work 3 ch. to take the place of a tr. ; this applies to each round, so that we shall not repeat the directions.

2nd round.—1 tr. into 1 st., 2 tr. into the next ; repeat all around.

3rd to 6th rounds.—With gold silk work 1 tr. into each of 2 st., 2 tr. into next ; repeat.

7th round.—With red silk, 1 tr. into each of 2 st., 2 tr. into the next ; then with gold silk make 1 tr. into each of 6 st. ; repeat from beginning of round. In order to make the number of stitches right, so

62

that the Vandyke pattern come evenly, you must either pass over a st. or work twice into a st. at the end of round if necessary.

8th round.—With red silk make 1 tr. in each of the 4 red st., 2 red into the 1st gold, 1 gold into each of four next gold, 2 red into next gold, then repeat from beginning of round.

9th round.—1 red into each st. of red, 1 red into next gold; 1 gold into each of 2 next gold, 1 red into next gold; repeat from beginning of round.

10th and 11th rounds.—Work entirely with red silk, 1 tr. in each st.

The 11th round should have 154 sts.

12th round.—The Greek key pattern is commenced in this round. With red, make 2 tr. into a st., 1 tr. into each of 2 next st., 2 into the next; with gold 1 tr. into each of 10 st. Repeat from the beginning of the round.

13th round.—1 tr. with red into each red st. of last round, 1 gold into each of 2 next gold, 1 red into each of 6 next gold, 1 gold into each of 2 next gold. Repeat from beginning of round.

14th round.—1 red into each of 5 red, 2 into the next, 1 gold into each of 2 gold, 1 red into each of 4 next st., 1 gold into each of 7 next st. Repeat from beginning.

15th round.—With red, 1 tr. into each of 7 st., 1 gold into each of 2 st., 1 red into each of 4 next st., 1 gold into each of 2 next st., 1 red into each of 5 next st. Repeat from the beginning of round.

16th round.—1 gold into each of 7 red tr., 1 into each of 2 gold, 1 red into each of the next red st., 1 gold into each of 7 next st. Repeat from beginning of round.

Now work about 2 inches in red with 1 tr. into each st. without increase or decrease. Then work another Greek key pattern, as described in 12th to 16th rounds, omitting the increase. Work two rounds plain in red.

For the frill at the top:

1st round.—With red, 1 tr. into a st., 2 ch., miss 2 st., 1 tr. in next; repeat all around.

2nd round.—1 dc. in each st. of last round.

3rd round.—1 tr. in each of 2 st., 2 ch., miss 2, and repeat.

4th round.—Like 2nd. The 3rd and 4th rounds are repeated twice more.

Now, with red silk, finish the diamond at the bottom of the bag by

[32]

working lines of chain stitches from the depth between the points to the center of 1st row, either with a needle or crochet hook.

Make a crochet ch. and run it through the 1st row of holes, and finish the ends with small silk pompons. Line the bag with chamois skin.

TOBACCO BAG No. 2.

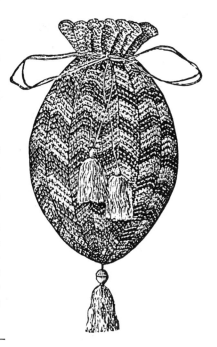

Use BELDING's "Pure Thread" Crochet Silk, two shades, and a steel hook.

Ch. 5 with darkest shade, and work upon it dc., gradually increasing the number of st. until there are 30. Then begin the points by working 2 dc., divided by 1 ch. in each 3rd st. In the next row the increase will be in each 5th st., and so on until there are 15 st. between each point. Then begin to miss the middle st. between the points, and continue working thus until the bag is the size required. The change from one color to the other should always be in the middle between 2 points, and 3 rows are worked with each color. The pouch is finished with silk cord and tassels. A brass ring tassel is made for the bottom.

BON-BON BAG.

A bon-bon bag in the shape of a lily is shown in many of the art stores. The petals are of cardboard about six inches in length, covered with white and lined with yellow satin. These are sewed together for a length of four inches, leaving the tops of the petals to curl over. Make a pretty crocheted bag of BELDING's "Pure Thread" Crochet Silk and put into the top of the blossom. Have a row of holes round top to put in ribbon for drawing-strings. A short stem and two leaves of green satin finish the bottom.

To crochet the bag part, make a chain, fasten it round, then 1 tr. in every other st. with a ch. of 1 between the next and all following rows, 1 tr. in every space with 1 ch. between. Finish the top with a row of shells. Run in narrow ribbon drawing strings, or the bag may be in shell stitch, 2 double in 1st stitch, 1 ch., 2 double in same stitch, the 2nd shell in 5th stitch from the last. These bags find a ready sale at fairs.

SUSPENDERS.

These are crocheted over a cord foundation. The tabs are worked separately, lengthwise.

Begin at the back end with a foundation of 22 sts. and crochet in rounds, going back and forth, as follows :

1st round.—Pass over the next st., 10 sc. on the following 10 sts., 3 sc. on the next st., 10 sc. on the following 10 sts.

2nd round (on a cord foundation, fastened to the next edge st. with several sts.) One ch., pass over the next st. in the preceding round, 10 sc. on the upper veins of the next 10 sts., 3 sc. on the following st., 10 sc. on the next 10 sts. Repeat always the second round until the requisite length is obtained, passing the foundation cord loosely from one round to another, so that it forms a small loop.

The row of points on the outer edge of the suspenders is worked as follows : Beginning at the corner on one side, work * 1 sc. on the next cord loop, at the same time catching the single ch. there, one point consisting of 3 ch. and 3 dc. on the first of these, and repeat from *. On the ends of the suspenders pass over 2 sts. with each point and work the sc. on the upper veins of the respective stitches. Work each of the back tabs on a foundation of 38 sts., the last 23 of which are closed in a ring for a buttonhole ; to do this, work going back 15 sc. the last 15 st., then turn the work and crochet the first round as follows : One ch., 15 sc. on the upper veins of the next 15 sc., 23 sc. on the following 23 foundation sts., 15 sc. on the free veins of the next 15 foundation sts.

2nd round.—Turn the work, 1 ch., going back on the st. in the preceding round, work always 1 sc. on the upper veins of each st., but at the under edge of the tab widen several sts. so that the work may not draw.

3rd round (inserted round).—Carry the thread to the eleventh of the 11 sts. worked last, and crochet 11 sc. on the upper veins of the last 11 sts. in the preceding round. Repeat three times the 2nd and 3rd rounds but in the last two inserted rounds, instead of 11 sts. work 15 sts. on the last 15 sts. in the preceding round. Next follow two rounds like the 2nd round. The double tab on the front of the suspenders is worked in two parts, for each of which make a foundation of 60 ch., close the last 20 in a ring for a buttonhole, going back on the next 40 sts., and working first 5 sc. on the following 5 sts., and for two additional buttonholes work twice alternately 10 ch., pass over 10 sts., 5 sc. on the next 5 sts., and then 5 sc. on the last 5 sts. Next follow a round like the 1st round and 3 rounds like the 2nd round of the back tab, which completes this part. The second part is worked in the same manner, and both these parts are then placed side by side, and the 7 sts. nearest the top on the sides turned toward each other are overseamed together from the wrong side. The finished tabs are sewed to the wrong side of the suspenders.

GARTER.

Materials : ½ ounce BELDING's "Pure Thread" Crochet Silk. 1 yard white satin ribbon No. 5, ³₄ of a yard of white silk elastic, and a fine steel hook.

1st, 2nd and 3rd rows.—Crochet back and forth with short crochet stitch, taking always the back part of the stitch, and remembering to make 1 ch. when the work is turned at the end.

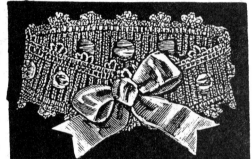

4th row.—5 sc., 8 ch. ; miss 8 stitches, 5 sc.

The next four rows are crocheted in sc. stitch. Repeat these last five rows until the strip is 1 inch longer than the required size.

The border consists of 1 row of tr. with 1 ch. between them, and a picot edge made as follows : 3 sc., 5 ch., and fasten back into the 1st ch. with a sc. stitch ; 5 ch., fasten to second stitch and to foundation with a tr. ; 5 ch., fasten to 2nd stitch and 5 sc. on foundation. Repeat this edge for the entire length. Lace the elastic through the openings and cover the fastening with a bow of ribbon.

PURSE.

A great many ladies prefer the kind of purses that were carried by our great grandmothers, and many beautiful designs have appeared from time to time. A very elegant one is worked with dark blue and red silk. The ends are worked in single crochet on a foundation of small brass rings, and the center is worked crosswise in an open-work design, on which lengthwise rows are crocheted.

Begin the purse at one end, both sides of which are worked lengthwise in connection, first working the middle row of crochet rings with BELDING's "Pure Thread" Crochet Silk, as follows : 13 times in succession work always 11 sc. on one-half of a brass ring three-eighths of an inch in diameter, then 22 sc. on the 14th brass ring, always going back on the 2nd half of the 1st 13 rings; work 13 times alternately 1 sc. on the vein between the next two rings, 11 sc. on the next ring, finally, 1 sl. on the 1st sc. in this round. On each side of these middle rounds work 3 similar rounds alternately with blue and red silk, but in working these rounds always fasten the middle st. of every 11 sc. worked on the 1st half of a ring to the middle st. on the corresponding ring in the preceding round. (To do this drop the st. from the needle, insert the latter in the upper veins of the corresponding st., and draw the dropped stitch through.) Lay the finished end of the purse double, and in connection with it work with blue silk the center of the purse, always goin forward, as follows:

1st round.—* 3 ch., three times alternately 5 sc. on the middle 5 sc. at the top of the next ring crocheted with blue silk, 9 ch., pass over the next (red) ring; then 5 sc. as before on the st. of the next ring, and repeat once, from *; finally, 2 sl. on the first 2 st. in this round.

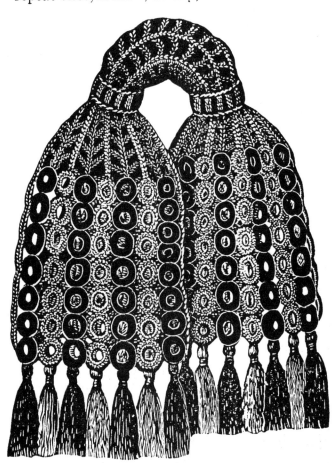

2nd round.—4 ch., the first 3 of which count as first dc., * three times alternately 3 dc. separated each by 1 ch. on the upper veins of the 1st, 3rd and 5th sc. in the preceding round, 9 ch.; then 3 dc. separated by 1 ch. on the 1st, 3rd and 5th of the next 5 sc., 1 ch., 1 dc. on the middle of the next 3 ch., 1 ch., and repeated once from *, but instead of the last dc. and single ch. work 1 sl. on the third of the 3 ch. counting as first dc. in this round.

3rd to 34th rounds.—Like the 2nd round, but working the dc. always on the corresponding dc. in the preceding round, and in the 11th to the 24th rounds forming the slit, for which crochet, going back and forth, and always turning the work so that the middle 9 ch. on the side above which the slit is worked are always drawn over to the next round in a loop.

In the last round of the center fasten each dc. to the sc. in the corresponding ring of the second end of the purse worked previously. Join the sides on both ends with red silk, beginning always at the under edge, as follows: Six times alternately with 1 sc. fasten together the middle st. of the next rings above one another, 6 ch.; then fasten together the next two rings with 1 sc., 3 ch., 1 sl. on the middle of the 3 ch. in the next round of the center; fasten the thread and cut it off. With similar silk work on both sides of the purse one round in sc. as follows: 6 times 9 sc. on the next ch., then 5 sc. on the following 3 ch., 34 times 4 sc. on the vertical veins of each single dc. on the side of the next 34 rounds of the center, then 5 sc. on the next 3 ch., six times 9 sc. on the next 6 ch. On the center crocheted crosswise, work six times two lengthwise rounds, going back and forth, as follows: Begin the round, going forward, with 1 sl. on the middle st. of the next at the top of one end, which was passed over, then always 3 ch., with 1 sc. catch the middle of the next 9 ch. of the center; finally, 3 ch., 1 sl. on the middle st. of the ring there. In the round going back work always 4 sc. on the next 3 ch., and finally 1 sl. on the same st. on which the first sl. in these two rounds was worked; fasten the thread and cut it off. Finish the slit with two rounds, which are worked in connection with the two lengthwise rounds of the center bordering the slit; for the round going forward work along the slit always alternately 3 ch., 5 sc. on the next loop, and then on the side nearest the slit work the 2nd round, crocheting always alternately 5 sc. on the next 3 ch., 3 ch. Then work the round going forward to the end, work the round going back to the slit, finish the 2nd round on the other side of the slit, and then also the round going back, with which the slit is bordered in connection. Furnish the purse with the steel rings overcast with buttonhole stitches, as shown, and trim the ends with silk tassels.

SIMPLE PURSE.

Materials: ½ ounce BELDING's "Pure Thread" Crochet Silk, a fine steel crochet hook, a pair of bars and chain, and one fancy steel tassel for bottom.

Ch. 6, join, and work in the circle, 12 sc.

2nd round—Widen in every other st. in this row, which will give you 18 dc.
3rd round.—Widen in every 3rd st.
4th round.—Widen in every 4th st.
5th round.—Widen in every 5th st.
6th round.—Widen in every 6th st.
7th round.—Widen in every 7th st.
8th round.—Widen in every 8th st.
9th round.—Widen in every 9th st.
10th round.—Widen in every 10th st.
11th round.—Widen in every 11th st.
12th round.—Widen in every 12th st.

Work 20 rounds without widening or narrowing.

After this, work half way around the purse with tr. crochet, then turn and work back. Repeat until you have done eight rows, and then fasten one of the bars by crocheting the sts. over it.

Work the other half in the same way.
Fasten silk securely, and finish point with an ornamental tassel.

MISER'S PURSE.

Materials: 1 ounce BELDING's "Pure Thread" Crochet Silk and a steel hook.

Ch. 212. Work on it a row of tr., each 2 separated by 1 ch., skipping

1 ch. of foundation. Make 46 tr., ch. 120, and cut off silk. Repeat, until 11 rows of tr., each ending with 120 ch., have been made. Fold the strip thus made together, letting the end with the chs. come 6 tr. from the other end, which is to make the flap. Crochet the long edges together with a row of sc., and work a row of trs. across the double end, and also across the end of the flap.

Pass the chs. through the back of the bag thus made, 1 ch. between every row of trs. except in the middle, where there will be 2 ch. Now make another bag like this, except that the chs. are omitted. Pass chs. from first bag through back of second bag, and sew them neatly to the front. Finish purse by fringes of beads and rings.

BUTTON COVERS.

Use Belding's "Pure Thread" Crochet Silk, a fine steel hook, and button molds of the size desired.

Make a chain of 3 stitches; join into this chainwork 6 short crochet stitches.

2nd row.—Short crochet stitch, widening every other stitch.

3rd and all following rows the same, widening three times each row until the cover is the size of the button for which it is desired. Now work one row of long crochet stitches, narrowing every other stitch; fasten and break silk, leaving a needleful to draw it with after the mold is put in. If the cover is wished for a large button, any small pattern may be used; but the simple short crochet stitch is most suitable.

TIDY.

The diamonds may be of one shade of silk, the wheels of another, or the tidy may be all one color. It will take about 2 ounces of Belding's "Pure Thread," Crochet Silk. Use a steel hook.

For One Diamond.—Chain 8 st. and join round.

1st round.—Into this work as follows: (2 tr., 5 ch.) 4 times, join last 5 ch. to 1st tr.

2nd round.—(3 tr., 3 ch., 3 tr.) into the 1st 5 ch. of the 1st round, 1 ch., (3 tr., 3 ch., 3 tr.) into the 2nd 5 ch. of 1st round, 1 ch., (3 tr., 3 ch., 3 tr.) into 3rd 5 ch. of 1st round, 1 ch. (3 tr. 2 ch., 3 tr.) into 4th 5 ch. of 1st round, 1 ch. joined to 1st tr. of this round.

3rd round.—4 ch., 1 sc. into 3 ch. of last round, * 7 ch., 1 sc. in same 3 ch., 7 ch., 1 sc. in same 3 ch., 7 ch., 1 sc. in same 3 ch., 4 ch., 1 sc. in the 1 ch. of last round. Repeat from * 3 times more.

4th round.—* 3 ch., 7 tr. into ch. of 7, 1 sc. in same 7 tr., 1 sc. in next ch. of 7, 1 sc., 7 tr. in next ch. of 7, 3 ch., 1 sc. in sc. of last round. Repeat from * 3 times more. Fasten on wrong side.

For One Rosette.—Ch. 10, join round. Into this work 16 dc.

2nd round.—* 7 ch., 1 sc. in 2d dc. of 1st round. Repeat from * 7 times more.

3rd round.—* 7 ch., 1 sc. in center of 7 ch. of 2nd round. Repeat from * 7 times more.

4th round.—* 1 slip stitch, 9 tr., 1 slip stitch into 1st ch. of 7 in 3rd round. Repeat from * 7 times more. Fasten at back. Make as many of each as you wish the tidy large, then sew together. Make the tassels all round of knitting silk. Five only are shown in cut.

BABY'S SOCK IN PANEL STITCH.

Materials : ½ ounce BELDING'S "Pure Thread" Blue Crochet Silk, a very little white knitting silk, and a medium-sized crochet hook.

This pretty stitch is worked in nearly the same manner as crazy-stitch, but being worked round and round instead of back and forth, the effect is entirely different. With the blue silk make a ch. of 31 stitches, *very* loose, as it will draw up in working and make a non-elastic edge if care is not taken in this respect. Join in a round.

1st round.—1 dc. in the 1st stitch of the chain, 2 ch., 3 tr in. the same stitch in which the dc. was placed, thus giving the effect of 4 tr. in one stitch of the foundation. Repeat, always missing 1 ch. of the foundation, and beginning with 1 dc.

2nd round.—1 dc. between the 2 ch., and the 1st tr. in the preceding round. 2 ch., 3 tr. in the same place. Repeat. Practically, the shells in the 1st round consist of 4 tr., and the dc. of the 2nd round between the 1st and 2nd tr. All succeeding rounds are like the 2nd. Work 14 rounds. Begin the 15th by making 36 ch., miss 4 shells and begin with the dc. in the 5th shell. Work around as before and when you reach the long ch., work on that as on the foundation. This begins the foot, leaving an opening on the top of the foot. Work 3 rounds plain. In the 4th round narrow (by missing one shell) at the

toe and at the heel. Work the 5th round plain, then narrow in every round until you have 9 rounds in all. Turn the foot on the wrong side, and beginning at the heel, crochet the foot together. This is better than sewing it, and is easily done by laying the shells exactly opposite each other, and fastening each pair together by a single crochet. About 4 ch. stitches will be needed between each sc. to keep the foot straight.

Now take the white silk, make a ch. of 31 rather tight stitches, turn, make 1 tr. in the 5th ch., 1 ch., 1 tr. in the 7th ch., etc. There must be 14 tr. in the row, including the one made in turning, by the ch. stitches. The tr. in the next row are placed in the spaces between the tr. of the 1st row. Repeat. Work 3 rows plain, then narrow at the beginning of every row (by missing one space) until there are but 3 stitches left. Work the 3 and fasten off. The piece thus made is for the top of the foot, and must be crocheted in with double crochet stitches, on the right side, using the blue silk. It will fit in smoothly at the ankle and the sides of the foot; but at the toe, the sock must be "gathered" to fit the piece, thus giving the requisite fullness over the toe. Work a row of tr. separated by 1 ch., around the top of the leg, making a place to run a cord, or narrow ribbon, and finish with any fancy edge.

A pretty one is as follows:
1st row.—1 dc. on the 1st tr., * 7 ch., 1 dc. on 3rd tr. Repeat from *.
2nd row.—4 tr. in the 4th of the 7th ch. Repeat.
3rd row.—1 dc. between the first 2 groups of tr., 6 ch. Repeat.

BABY'S HOOD.

Materials : 1½ ounces BELDING's "Pure Thread" Crochet Silk, and a steel crochet hook of moderate size.
Make 25 ch.
1st row.—*1 dc. into 1st ch., 2 ch.; 3 tr. into same ch., miss 2, 2 ch., 1 dc. into 3rd. *Repeat.
2nd row.—*3 ch., 3 tr. into first dc. of last row, 1 dc. into 2 ch. of last row. *Repeat, making 25 rows which form crown of cap. Break off and fasten on at the ch. stitches, which must form back of cap, and

make a mesh as follows : To begin, make 5 ch., take up one loop as for a tr., putting the needle in 3rd ch., then still holding the loop on needle, take another loop, putting the needle in 1st stitch, draw the thread through 2 loops at once until only 1 is left on the needle. 2nd mesh.—Make 1 tr. into every 3 ch., 2 ch. between each mesh making it wide enough to take satin ribbon No. 4; work mesh around the crown.

Top of Head.—Repeat 2nd row, working every mesh until 12 rows are done.

Repeat row for mesh.

Repeat 2nd row 3 times.

Make 1 row of dc. round neck of cap.

Cape.—* 1 tr. into 2nd hole, then 1 tr. back into 1st hole, forming cross stitch. Repeat, making 7 rows.

8th row.—Take up * 3 loops as for a tr., keep them on the needle and take up 3 more on the next stitch ; draw the silk through the 4 loops, draw through 3. Repeat.

9th row.—Repeat 7th row.

Round the front of cap make shells to meet those already made, making a double front.

Edge.—* Make 10 tr. for shell, turning over the needle twice into 3rd ch., 1 dc. into next 3rd ch. * Repeat round the cap and round cape, miss 2 cross-stitches into 3rd.

Last Row.—3 ch. and a dc., into every tr., missing the dc. between the shells.

Line with wadded silk.

LAMP SHADE.

Materials : 1 ounce BELDING's " Pure Thread " Crochet Silk, and a fine steel hook.

Make a ch. large enough to fit the neck of the lamp shade, and join in a ring.

1st round.—Ch. 9, pass by 4 stitches, 1 dc. in next. Repeat all round.

2nd round.—Ch. 9, 1 dc. in 5th stitch of 9 ch. of previous row ; 9 ch., 1 dc. in 5th stitch of next 9 ch., and repeat all the way round.

Repeat 2nd round till work is of required length. Tie in heavy fringe of the silk. If wished, lace may be basted under the fringe. Finish the top with a row of holes and shell edge. Make cord and tassels of the silk, run through holes, draw up shade.

FRINGE, No. 1.

This pattern is worked crosswise in rows, and is used in various kinds of ornamentation, such as tidies, lamp-shades, etc., when made from BELDING's " Pure Thread " Crochet Silk in colors, or for dress-trimming when made from black.

Make a chain of 35 stitches.

1st row.—3 dc. in 4th stitch, 3 ch., 3 dc. in same stitch; fasten to next 3rd stitch of chain, 6 ch., miss 6 ch., 3 dc. in 7th, 3 ch., 3 dc. in same ; fasten to next 3rd chain, 6 ch., miss 6, put 3 dc. in 7th, 3 ch., 3 dc. in same ; fasten to next 3rd stitch ; 6 ch., miss 6 ch., 3 dc. in 7th stitch of chain, 3 ch., 3 dc. in next chain stitch, 5 ch. stitches and turn.

2nd row.—3 dc. around next chain of 3, worked between the last 3 dc. in preceding row, 3 ch., 3 dc. around same; fasten around 1st stitch of next chain of 6, 6 ch., 3 dc. around next chain of 3, 3 ch., 3 dc. around same chain, fasten ; 6 ch., 3 dc. around next chain of 3, 3 ch., 3 dc. around same chain, fasten ; 6 ch., 3 dc. around next chain of 3, 3 ch., 3 dc. a.ound same, work 6 ch. Turn.

3rd row.—3 dc. around next chain of 3 of 2nd row, 3 ch., 3 dc., around same chain, fasten, 6 ch., 3 dc. around next chain of 3, 3 ch., 3 dc. around same chain, fasten, 6 ch., 3 dc. around next chain of 3, 3 ch., 3 dc. around same, fasten, 6 ch., 3 dc. around next chain of 3, 3 ch., 3 dc. around same, fasten in 1st stitch of chain of 5 of last row.

4th row.—5 ch., dc. around next chain of 3 of 3rd row, 3 ch., 3 dc. around same, fasten, 6 ch., 3 dc. around next chain of 3, 3 ch., 3 dc. around same, fasten, 6 ch., 3 dc. around next chain of 3, 3 ch., 3 dc. around same, fasten, 6 ch., 3 dc. around next chain of 3, 3 ch., 3 dc. around same ; work around next chain of 6, * 2 dc., 3 ch.*. Repeat 5 times, stopping before 3 ch. Fasten by 1 sc. in last 3rd dc. of 1st row.

5th row.—Turn, * 1 sc., 3 dc., 1 sc. around chain of three.* Repeat 4 times ; 3 ch., 3 dc. around next chain of 3 of last row, * 3 ch., 3 dc. around same, fasten, 6 ch., 3 dc. around next chain of 3 ; repeat to the end of the row. Finally, make 5 ch. instead of 3.

Begin again from 2nd row.

For the heading, fasten the silk to the end of the work, then crochet 1 sc. in every stitch of the edge.

The 2nd row of heading is worked as follows ;

Turn * 3 dc. in next sc. of last row, miss next sc., fasten in following sc., miss 1, * repeat to the end of the row.

FRINGE, No. 2.

Make any number of chain stitches divisible by 9, and half as long again as desired when finished. as it takes up in working.

1st row.—* 1 dc. in each of 1st 9 ch.; 9 ch., miss 8, 1 dc. in next 9 ch.*

Repeat to end of row, finishing with 9 dc.

Every row has to be worked on the right side of the work ; consequently the silk has to be broken at the end of every row.

2nd row.—* 9 dc., 9 ch.* Repeat to the end of the row, finishing with 9 dc.

3rd row.—*9 dc. 4 ch., 1 sc. through 5th chain stitch of 2nd and 3rd rows, drawing tightly together ; 4 ch.* Repeat.

4th row.—* 9 dc., 9 ch.* Repeat.

5th row.—* 9 dc., 9 ch.* Repeat.

6th row.—* 9 dc., 9 ch.* Repeat.

7th row.—* 9 dc., 4 ch., 1 sc. through the 5th stitch of chain of 5th and 6th rows ; 4 ch.* Repeat.

8th row.—Repeat 5th row.

9th row.—Dc. to end of row.

Heading.—* 6 dc. in 3rd dc., miss 2; fasten on 3rd by 1 sc.* Repeat.

To finish off the lower edge. work * 10 tr. in 5th dc.. 1 sc. in 9th dc., 4 ch., 1 sc. in 5th stitch of chain of the last row ; 4 ch., 1 sc. in 1st of the next 9 dc.* Repeat.

The fringe is put in every other loop of the edge of the last described row. This pattern is a very desirable one for an inexperienced worker, as it is composed almost entirely of two kinds of stitches—double crochet. separated by chain. The lower edge can be fringed as heavily as desired.

FRINGE, No. 3.

This, if made from BELDING's "Pure Thread" Crochet Silk, is an exceedingly handsome design. It is worked across the width, making a very pretty edging even if the fringe finishing the edge is omitted.

Make a ch. of 43 stitches.

1st row.—3 dc. in the 5th ch. stitch, 3 ch., 3 dc. in the same 5th ch. stitch, 9 ch., miss 12 ch.. 3 dc. in 13th, 3 dc. in same, 9 ch., miss 12 ch.. 3 dc. in 13th, 3 ch., 3 dc. in next stitch, 7 ch., miss 4 ch., fasten in 5th with a dc. Turn.

2nd row.—3 ch.. 12 dc. around last ch. of 7 stitches. * 3 dc., 3 ch., 3 dc. around next ch. of 3, 4 ch.. fasten in 5th ch. stitch of last row, 4 ch. * Repeat, then make 3 dc., 3 ch., 3 dc. around last ch. of 3. Turn.

3rd row.—2 ch., 3 dc., 3 ch.. 3 dc., around next ch. of 3, 9 ch., 3 dc., 3 ch., 3 dc. around next ch. of 3, 9 ch., 3 dc., 3 ch., 3 dc. around next ch. of 3, * 1 dc. in next dc.. 1 ch. * Repeat 10 times ; at the end fasten in 1st stitch of foundation ch. Turn.

4th row.—3 ch., * 1 dc., around chain of one of last row, 2 ch. * Repeat 9 times. Then 3 dc., 3 ch., 3 dc. around next ch. of three, etc. Work to the end as in 2nd row. Turn.

5th row.—2 ch., 3 dc., 3 ch., 3 dc., 9 ch., 3 dc., 3 ch., 3 dc., 9 ch., 3 dc., 3 ch., 3 dc. ; then 1 ch. * 1 dc. around next ch. of two, 3 ch. ; * repeat 9 times. Turn.

6th row.—* 5 ch., 1 sc. around next chain of 3 ; * repeat 8 times ;

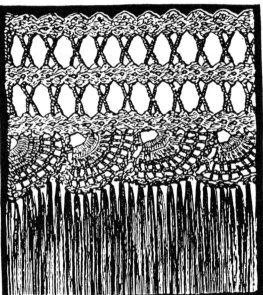

then 5 ch., 1 sc. around next ch. of 1, 3 dc., 3 ch., 3 dc. around next ch. of 3, 4 ch., etc., like 4th row. Turn.

7th row.—2 ch., 3 dc., 3 ch., 3 dc.. 9 ch., 3 dc , 3 ch., 3 dc., 9 ch., 3 dc., 3 ch. 3 dc., then 7 ch. ; fasten around 2nd ch. of 5 of 6th row. Turn.

8th row.—3 ch., 12 dc. around last ch. of 7 ; go on working like 2nd row. Turn.

9th row.—Work up to scallop like 3rd row ; then make * 1 dc. in next dc., 1 ch. ; * repeat 11 times, then fasten around 3rd ch. of 5 of 6th row. Turn.

10th row.—3 ch., * 1 dc. around next ch. of one of last row, 2 ch. ; * repeat 10 times ; work to the end of row, like 4th row.

11th row.—Work up to the scallop like 5th row, then 1 ch., * 1 dc. around next ch. of 2, 3 ch. ; * repeat 11 times, fasten in 4th ch. of 5 of 6th row. Turn.

12th row.—* 5 ch., 1 sc. around next ch. of 3 ; * repeat 10 times ; then continue to work 5 ch., 1 sc. around next ch. of 1, 3 dc., etc., like 6th row.

The following scallops are worked after directions in second scallop, as the foundation ch. makes a difference in the number of stitches in the first.

Fasten fringe in the chains of 5 on the edge of every scallop.

FIGURE 1

Bedroom Slipper. No. 1

Art. 1116, Pearl Cotton No. 3, Color Shades 200 and 203

Make a chain of 22 st; allow 1 st to turn.

1st row. 10 s, taking up back part of st, 3 s in next st, 10 s in next 10 st; turn.

2d row. Crochet across without widening; turn.

3d row. Crochet back, widening with 3 s in center st.

4th row. Crochet across plain.

5th row. Widen, continue until there are 20 ribs for the vamp.

Then crochet 22 st on one side of vamp. Work back and forth until where joined to other side of vamp the slipper will fit sole.

This is for size No. 5.

Make a beading around top of slipper by making d with 1 ch between, continuing around top.

White pearl cotton for the cuff of slipper.

Ch 18 st; allow one for turning. Crochet back and forth in 17 st, taking front part of st, until the strip is long enough to fit around top of slipper.

Decorate cuff with embroidery silk; green for the leaves, worked with the lazy-daisy stitch, and forget-me-nots in blue French knots with yellow centers.

FIGURE 2

Bedroom Slipper. No. 2

Art. 1116, Pearl Cotton No. 3, Color Shades 200 and 224

Work the same as No. 1.

Decorate cuffs with lazy-daisy stitch, using green embroidery silk for leaves. Small flowers are worked with pink silk and yellow for centers.

3

FIGURE 3. RUNNER FOR LIBRARY OR DINING ROOM

Runner for Library or Dining Room

Art. 131, N. E. T. (Crochet Twist), White or Ecru

CHAIN 365; allow 8 ch for 1st sp.

1st row. 119 sp, ch 5; turn.

2d row. 1 sp, 352 d, 1 sp, ch 5; turn.

3d row. 1 sp, 4 d, 115 sp, 4 d, 1 sp, ch 5; turn.

4th row. 1 sp, 4 d, 115 sp, 4 d, 1 sp, ch 5; turn.

5th row. 1 sp, 4 d, 115 sp, 4 d, 1 sp, ch 5; turn.

6th row. 1 sp, 4 d, 115 sp, 4 d, 1 sp, ch 5; turn.

7th row. 1 sp, 4 d, 115 sp, 4 d, 1 sp, ch 5; turn.

8th row. 1 sp, 4 d, 115 sp, 4 d, 1 sp, ch 5; turn.

9th row. 1 sp, 4 d, 115 sp, 4 d, ch 5; turn.

10th row. 1 sp, 4 d, 74 sp, 4 d, 40 sp, 4 d, 1 sp, ch 5; turn.

11th row. 1 sp, 4 d, 30 sp, 4 d, 9 sp, 7 d, 4 sp, 7 d, 28 sp, 7 d, 37 sp, 4 d, 1 sp, ch 5; turn.

12th row. 1 sp, 4 d, 8 sp, 7 d, 27 sp, 10 d, 1 sp, 10 d, 20 sp, 19 d, 2 sp, 10 d, 8 sp, 7 d, 5 sp, 13 d, 21 sp, 4 d, 1 sp, ch 5; turn.

13th row. 1 sp, 4 d, 20 sp, 16 d, 6 sp, 13 d, 7 sp, 34 d, 16 sp, 28 d, 2 sp, 7 d, 17 sp, 7 d, 3 sp, 13 d, 7 sp, 4 d, 1 sp, ch 5; turn.

14th row. 1 sp, 4 d, 3 sp, 25 d, 2 sp, 10 d, 17 sp, 10 d, 2 sp, 16 d, 2 sp, 7 d, 7 sp, 34 d, 3 sp, 10 d, 6 sp, 19 d, 7 sp, 19 d, 3 sp, 7 d, 9 sp, 13 d, 1 sp, 4 d, 1 sp, ch 5; turn.

15th row. 1 sp, 4 d, 1 sp, 19 d, 5 sp, 13 d, 3 sp, 16 d, 10 sp, 34 d, 2 sp, 16 d, 3 sp, 10 d, 3 sp, 10 d, 10 sp, 25 d, 12 sp, 4 d, 3 sp, 16 d, 1 sp, 19 d, 1 sp, 4 d, 3 sp, 4 d, 1 sp, ch 5; turn.

16th row. 1 sp, 4 d, 4 sp, 4 d, 2 sp, 28 d, 2 sp, 13 d, 11 sp, 22 d, 10 sp, 22 d, 3 sp, 7 d, 4 sp, 13 d, 1 sp, 22 d, 13 sp, 25 d, 1 sp, 10 d, 4 sp, 4 d, 2 sp, 10 d, 2 sp, 4 d, 1 sp, ch 5; turn.

17th row. 1 sp, 4 d, 1 sp, 4 d, 6 sp, 4 d, 3 sp, 10 d, 1 sp, 22 d, 13 sp, 16 d, 2 sp, 16 d, 3 sp, 7 d, 3 sp, 7 d, 6 sp, 13 d, 9 sp, 10 d, 13 sp, 16 d, 1 sp, 19 d, 3 sp, 10 d, 4 sp, 4 d, 1 sp, ch 5; turn.

18th row. 1 sp, 4 d, 4 sp, 19 d, 3 sp, 31 d, 8 sp, 7 d, 2 sp, 13 d, 5 sp, 10 d, 5 sp, 10 d, 4 sp, 7 d, 3 sp, 7 d, 3 sp, 13 d, 3 sp, 7 d, 9 sp, 10 d, 2 sp, 22 d, 1 sp, 16 d, 1 sp, 4 d, 8 sp, 4 d, 1 sp, ch 5; turn.

19th row. 1 sp, 4 d, 9 sp, 4 d, 1 sp, 16 d, 3 sp, 13 d, 2 sp, 13 d, 11 sp, 7 d, 1 sp, 7 d, 3 sp, 4 d, 3 sp, 7 d, 4 sp, 16 d, 7 sp, 10 d, 5 sp, 25 d, 6 sp, 25 d, 2 sp, 25 d, 5 sp, 4 d, 1 sp, ch 5; turn.

20th row. 1 sp, 4 d, 9 sp, 19 d, 1 sp, 16 d, 9 sp, 19 d, 5 sp, 4 d, 11 sp, 22 d, 2 sp, 7 d, 3 sp, 4 d, 2 sp, 4 d, 3 sp, 7 d, 9 sp, 16 d, 1 sp, 16 d, 2 sp, 19 d, 11 sp, 4 d, 1 sp, ch 5; turn.

21st row. 1 sp, 4 d, 8 sp, 10 d, 1 sp, 19 d, 1 sp, 19 d, 1 sp, 13 d, 7 sp, 7 d, 7 sp, 7 d, 3 sp, 4 d, 3 sp, 22 d, 1 sp, 7 d, 9 sp, 10 d, 3 sp, 13 d, 7 sp, 22 d, 1 sp, 25 d, 8 sp, 4 d, 1 sp, ch 5; turn.

22d row. 1 sp, 4 d, 6 sp, 34 d, 2 sp, 16 d, 9 sp, 7 d, 2 sp, 10 d, 9 sp, 34 d, 3 sp, 7 d, 4 sp, 4 d, 8 sp, 4 d, 5 sp, 16 d, 1 sp, 16 d, 1 sp, 40 d, 6 sp, 4 d, 1 sp, ch 5; turn.

23d row. 1 sp, 4 d, 5 sp, 46 d, 1 sp, 10 d, 1 sp, 19 d, 3 sp, 7 d, 8 sp, 4 d, 5 sp, 4 d, 5 sp, 13 d, 1 sp, 16 d, 11 sp, 7 d, 2 sp, 4 d, 9 sp, 10 d, 2 sp, 40 d, 6 sp, 4 d, 1 sp, ch 5; turn.

24th row. 1 sp, 4 d, 7 sp, 13 d, 4 sp, 16 d, 2 sp, 4 d, 9 sp, 7 d, 2 sp, 16 d, 8 sp, 19 d, 1 sp, 10 d, 6 sp, 4 d, 5 sp, 4 d, 8 sp, 4 d, 3 sp, 19 d, 1 sp, 10 d, 6 sp, 31 d, 5 sp, 4 d, 1 sp, ch 5; turn.

25th row. 1 sp, 4 d, 6 sp, 28 d, 2 sp, 4 d, 1 sp, 13 d, 1 sp, 19 d, 3 sp, 4 d, 8 sp, 4 d, 6 sp, 4 d, 5 sp, 10 d, 1 sp, 22 d, 8 sp, 7 d, 2 sp, 10 d, 1 sp, 4 d, 10 sp, 22 d, 1 sp, 4 d, 4 sp, 7 d, 7 sp, 4 d, 1 sp, ch 5; turn.

26th row. 1 sp, 4 d, 11 sp, 37 d, 8 sp, 13 d, 11 sp, 10 d, 2 sp, 16 d, 1 sp, 13 d, 3 sp, 4 d, 8 sp, 7 d, 6 sp, 4 d, 4 sp, 28 d, 1 sp, 4 d, 2 sp, 16 d, 1 sp, 13 d, 6 sp, 4 d, 1 sp, ch 5; turn.

27th row. 1 sp, 4 d, 7 sp, 7 d, 3 sp, 13 d, 1 sp, 4 d, 1 sp, 4 d, 1 sp, 22 d, 4 sp, 4 d, 7 sp, 4 d, 9 sp, 4 d, 3 sp, 25 d, 2 sp, 22 d, 11 sp, 10 d, 6 sp, 16 d, 2 sp, 19 d, 11 sp, 4 d, 1 sp, ch 5; turn.

28th row. 1 sp, 4 d, 12 sp, 13 d, 2 sp, 19 d, 6 sp, 4 d, 3 sp, 10 d, 1 sp, 7 d, 4 sp, 25 d, 1 sp, 25 d, 2 sp, 4 d, 11 sp, 4 d, 7 sp, 4 d, 5 sp, 10 d, 1 sp, 7 d, 1 sp, 4 d, 2 sp, 7 d, 3 sp, 16 d, 6 sp, 4 d, 1 sp, ch 5; turn.

29th row. 1 sp, 4 d, 5 sp, 31 d, 1 sp, 10 d, 1 sp, 4 d, 1 sp, 4 d, 8 sp, 4 d, 5 sp, 7 d, 6 sp, 16 d, 2 sp, 4 d, 2 sp, 19 d, 1 sp, 25 d, 4 sp, 37 d, 4 sp, 10 d, 2 sp, 7 d, 2 sp, 13 d, 12 sp, 4 d, 1 sp, ch 5; turn.

30th row. 1 sp, 4 d, 12 sp, 10 d, 5 sp, 7 d, 1 sp, 7 d, 3 sp, 10 d, 4 sp, 19 d, 5 sp, 25 d, 1 sp, 4 d, 2 sp, 7 d, 1 sp, 4 d, 1 sp, 25 d, 7 sp, 7 d, 4 sp, 4 d, 5 sp, 7 d, 1 sp, 52 d, 5 sp, 4 d, 1 sp, ch 5; turn.

31st row. 1 sp, 4 d, 4 sp, 43 d, 1 sp, 10 d, 3 sp, 10 d, 1 sp, 19 d, 9 sp, 28 d, 1 sp, 4 d, 3 sp, 4 d, 1 sp, 28 d, 4 sp, 19 d, 6 sp, 10 d, 4 sp, 13 d, 19 sp, 4 d, 1 sp, ch 5; turn.

32d row. 1 sp, 4 d, 18 sp, 19 d, 2 sp, 7 d, 8 sp, 4 d, 2 sp, 10 d, 2 sp, 31 d, 4 sp, 7 d, 1 sp, 31 d, 13 sp, 10 d, 5 sp, 16 d, 4 sp, 7 d, 1 sp, 22 d, 4 sp, 4 d, 1 sp, ch 5; turn.

33d row. 1 sp, 4 d, 5 sp, 22 d, 5 sp, 19 d, 6 sp, 4 d, 15 sp, 16 d, 2 sp, 4 d, 2 sp, 10 d, 1 sp, 4 d, 1 sp, 34 d, 1 sp, 4 d, 15 sp, 4 d, 3 sp, 16 d, 17 sp, 4 d, 1 sp, ch 5; turn.

34th row. 1 sp, 4 d, 15 sp, 25 d, 1 sp, 4 d, 18 sp, 19 d, 3 sp, 10 d, 3 sp, 4 d, 1 sp, 16 d, 1 sp, 10 d, 16 sp, 7 d, 5 sp, 22 d, 4 sp, 16 d, 7 sp, 4 d, 1 sp, ch 5; turn.

35th row. 1 sp, 4 d, 7 sp, 10 d, 4 sp, 28 d, 4 sp, 7 d, 16 sp, 13 d, 1 sp, 19 d, 3 sp, 19 d, 3 sp, 10 d, 14 sp, 13 d, 3 sp, 31 d, 13 sp, 4 d, 1 sp, ch 5; turn.

36th row. 1 sp, 4 d, 11 sp, 28 d, 4 sp, 16 d, 16 sp, 4 d, 3 sp, 19 d, 2 sp, 4 d, 1 sp, 22 d, 4 sp, 16 d, 14 sp, 7 d, 5 sp, 28 d, 7 sp, 10 d, 3 sp, 4 d, 1 sp, ch 5; turn.

37th row. 1 sp, 4 d, 3 sp, 10 d, 7 sp, 28 d, 4 sp, 4 d, 1 sp, 7 d, 1 sp, 4 d, 11 sp, 13 d, 1 sp, 25 d, 3 sp, 31 d, 2 sp, 4 d, 14 sp, 19 d, 9 sp, 16 d, 9 sp, 4 d, 1 sp, ch 5; turn.

38th row. 1 sp, 10 d, 3 sp, 37 d, 2 sp, 28 d, 2 sp, 13 d, 8 sp, 4 d, 1 sp, 34 d, 2 sp, 13 d, 2 sp, 31 d, 8 sp, 19 d, 1 sp, 4 d, 5 sp, 25 d, 6 sp, 13 d, 3 sp, 4 d, 1 sp, ch 5; turn.

39th row. 1 sp, 4 d, 3 sp, 13 d, 8 sp, 7 d, 1 sp, 10 d, 4 sp, 4 d, 2 sp, 16 d, 9 sp, 31 d, 2 sp, 19 d, 1 sp, 31 d, 2 sp, 4 d, 7 sp, 34 d, 4 sp, 55 d, 1 sp, 4 d, 1 sp, ch 5; turn.

40th row. 1 sp, 4 d, 9 sp, 31 d, 7 sp, 25 d, 6 sp, 4 d, 4 sp, 28 d, 1 sp, 19 d, 3 sp, 28 d, 4 sp, 10 d, 4 sp, 13 d, 2 sp, 4 d, 14 sp, 7 d, 1 sp, 10 d, 1 sp, 4 d, 2 sp, 4 d, 1 sp, ch 5; turn.

41st row. 1 sp, 4 d, 1 sp, 10 d, 2 sp, 7 d, 2 sp, 7 d, 11 sp, 4 d, 3 sp, 19 d, 1 sp, 13 d, 4 sp, 10 d, 1 sp, 16 d, 2 sp, 25 d, 1 sp, 28 d, 3 sp, 4 d, 8 sp, 16 d, 7 sp, 16 d, 3 sp, 10 d, 9 sp, 4 d, 1 sp, ch 5; turn.

42d row. 1 sp, 4 d, 10 sp, 10 d, 3 sp, 7 d, 10 sp, 19 d, 7 sp, 4 d, 2 sp, 10 d, 1 sp, 13 d, 2 sp, 25 d, 4 sp, 10 d, 8 sp, 19 d, 1 sp, 7 d, 6 sp, 4 d, 9 sp, 4 d, 5 sp, 19 d, 1 sp, 4 d, 1 sp, ch 5; turn.

43d row. 1 sp, 4 d, 1 sp, 25 d, 4 sp, 7 d, 5 sp, 7 d, 6 sp, 13 d, 1 sp, 10 d, 10 sp, 10 d, 3 sp, 28 d, 3 sp, 10 d, 5 sp, 4 d, 7 sp, 13 d, 1 sp, 10 d, 13 sp, 13 d, 10 sp, 4 d, 1 sp, ch 5; turn.

44th row. 1 sp, 4 d, 11 sp, 7 d, 14 sp, 7 d, 3 sp, 10 d, 8 sp, 4 d, 5 sp, 7 d, 3 sp, 7 d, 1 sp, 22 d, 11 sp, 19 d, 1 sp, 16 d, 8 sp, 16 d, 6 sp, 10 d, 1 sp, 10 d, 2 sp, 4 d, 1 sp, ch 5; turn.

45th row. 1 sp, 4 d, 2 sp, 22 d, 21 sp, 13 d, 1 sp, 16 d, 11 sp, 19 d, 6 sp, 7 d, 5 sp, 4 d, 10 sp, 4 d, 33 sp, 4 d, 1 sp, ch 5; turn.

46th row. 1 sp, 4 d, 33 sp, 4 d, 6 sp, 7 d, 2 sp, 4 d, 13 sp, 16 d, 13 sp, 10 d, 1 sp, 7 d, 1 sp, 7 d, 22 sp, 10 d, 5 sp, 4 d, 1 sp, ch 5; turn.

47th row. 1 sp, 4 d, 29 sp, 4 d, 4 sp, 4 d, 2 sp, 10 d, 14 sp, 10 d, 14 sp, 16 d, 5 sp, 7 d, 32 sp, 4 d, 1 sp, ch 5; turn.

48th row. 1 sp, 4 d, 31 sp, 7 d, 7 sp, 10 d, 30 sp, 10 d, 39 sp, 4 d, 1 sp, ch 5; turn.

49th row. 1 sp, 4 d, 73 sp, 7 d, 40 sp, 4 d, 1 sp, ch 5; turn.

50th row. 1 sp, 4 d, 115 sp, ch 5; turn.

51st row. 1 sp, 4 d, 115 sp, ch 5; turn.

52d row. 1 sp, 4 d, 115 sp, ch 5; turn.

53d row. 1 sp, 4 d, 115 sp, ch 5; turn.

54th row. 1 sp, 4 d, 115 sp, ch 5; turn.

55th row. 1 sp, 4 d, 115 sp, ch 5; turn.

56th row. 1 sp, 352 d, 1 sp, ch 5; turn.

57th row. 119 sp.

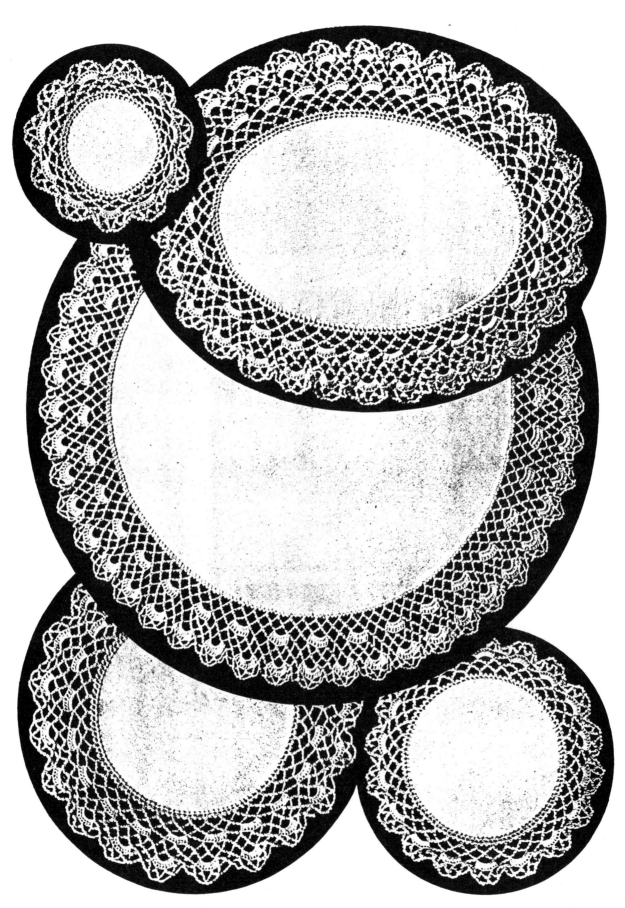

FIGURE 4.   LUNCHEON SET

ART. 1116, PEARL COTTON No. 5, WHITE

Luncheon Set.   Figure 4

After having made a narrow hem on the linen crochet over the hem.

1st row. * 1 picot (p), 1 d, repeat from * around d'oyley, allowing 6 p for each scallop.

2d row. * 4 ch, skip 2 p, 1 s in the next p of row before, repeat from *. After having joined rows make a ch of 2, fasten with 1 s in back of 2d p, ch 1, 1 s between the 4th p of 1st loop. When starting each row repeat same.

3d row. * 4 p with 1 s between each p, repeat from *.

4th row. * ch 9, 1 s between each of 4 p; turn, ch 3, 14 d over ch of 9; turn, ch 5, skip 2 d, 1 d in next st, * ch 1, skip 1 d, 1 d in next st, repeat from * until there are 7 d, 3 p, 1 s between the next 4 p, repeat from last *.

5th row. * 4 p, 1 s over ch of 1 after the 3d d, 4 p, 1 s in the last d, 4 p, 1 s in the ch of 5, repeat from *.

6th row. * 4 p, 1 s between the 4 p of row before, repeat from *.

7th row. Ch 10, 1 s between the 4 p of row before; turn, ch 3, 16 d over ch of 10; turn, ch 5, skip 2 d, * 1 d in next d, ch 1, skip 1 d, repeat from * until there are 8 d, 2 p, 1 s between the 4 p, 4 p, 1 s between next 4 p, repeat from beginning of row with a ch of 10.

8th row. 4 p, 1 s over ch of 1 after the 2d d, 4 p, leaving 3 d between, 4 p, 1 s in the last d, 4 p, 1 s between next 4 p, 2 p, 1 s over ch of 5, repeat from beginning of row.

9th row. * 4 p, 1 s between the 4 p, repeat from *, skip over the 2 p into next loop. For the two small d'oyleys make only the last 5 rows.

Corner of Edging for Crocheted Bedspread.   (Cover Design.)   Figure 5

Bedspread Crochet Cotton

CHAIN 38; turn, 1 d in 4th st, which counts for 1 d.

1st row. 7 d, 9 sp, ch 5; turn.

2d row. 10 sp, 4 d, ch 6; turn.

3d row. 1 d in 4th st, 1 d in 5th st, 4 d over next 4 d, 5 sp, 7 d, 3 sp, ch 5; turn.

4th row. 2 sp, 10 d, 6 sp, 4 d, ch 6; turn.

5th row. 1 d in 4th st, 1 d in 5th st, 4 d over next 4 d, 6 sp, 4 d, 1 sp, 4 d, 2 sp, ch 5; turn.

6th row. 2 sp, 10 d, 7 sp, ch 6; turn.

7th row. 7 d, 3 sp, 13 d, 1 sp, 7 d, 2 sp, ch 5; turn.

8th row. 2 sp, 4 d, 1 sp, 7 d, 1 sp, 7 d, 4 sp, 4 d, ch 6; turn.

9th row. 7 d, 5 sp, 16 d, 3 sp, ch 5; turn.

10th row. 1 sp, 4 d, 12 sp, 4 d, ch 3; turn.

11th row. 7 d, 5 sp, 16 d, 3 sp, ch 5; turn.

12th row. 2 sp, 4 d, 1 sp, 7 d, 1 sp, 7 d, 4 sp, 4 d, ch 3; turn.

13th row. 7 d, 3 sp, 13 d, 1 sp, 7 d, 2 sp, ch 5; turn.

14th row. 2 sp, 10 d, 7 sp, 4 d, ch 3; turn.

15th row. 7 d, 6 sp, 4 d, 1 sp, 4 d, 2 sp, ch 5; turn.

16th row. 2 sp, 10 d, 6 sp, 4 d, ch 3; turn.

17th row. 7 d, 5 sp, 7 d, 3 sp, ch 5; turn.

18th row. 10 sp, 4 d, ch 3; turn.

19th row. 7 d, 9 sp, ch 5; turn.

20th row. 10 sp, 4 d, ch 6; turn.

21st row. 7 d, 5 sp, 7 d, 3 sp, ch 5; turn.

22d row. 2 sp, 10 d, 6 sp, 4 d, ch 6; turn.

23d row. 7 d, 6 sp, 4 d, 1 sp, 4 d, 2 sp, ch 5; turn.

24th row. 2 sp, 10 d, 7 sp, 4 d, ch 6; turn.

25th row. 7 d, 3 sp, 13 d, 1 sp, 7 d, 2 sp, ch 5; turn.

26th row. 2 sp, 4 d, 1 sp, 7 d, 1 sp, 7 d, 4 sp, 4 d, ch 6; turn.

27th row. 7 d, 5 sp, 16 d, 2 sp; turn, sl st across one sp, ch 5.

28th row. 12 sp, 4 d, ch 3; turn.

29th row. 7 d, 5 sp, 16 d; turn, sl st across 1 gp of d, ch 3; turn.

30th row. 7 d, 1 sp, 7 d, 4 sp, 4 d, ch 3; turn.

31st row. 7 d, 3 sp, 13 d; turn, sl st across 1 gp of d, ch 5.

32d row. 6 sp, 4 d, ch 3; turn.

33d row. 7 d, 4 sp; turn, sl st across one sp, ch 5.

34th row. 3 sp, 4 d, ch 3; turn.

35th row. 7 d, 1 sp; turn, sl st across one sp, ch 3.

36th row. 4 d, ch 6; turn.

1st row of mitre. 1 d in 4th st of ch, 1 d in next, sl st to corner of gp, sl st across gp and up to corner of sp.

2d row. 1 sp, 4 d, ch 6; turn.

3d row. 7 d, 2 sp, sl st across sp and to corner of next sp; turn.

4th row. 4 sp, 4 d, ch 6; turn.

5th row. 7 d, 5 sp, sl st across sp and to corner of gp; turn.

6th row. 7 sp, 4 d, ch 6; turn.

7th row. 7 d, 3 sp, 13 d, 1 sp, sl st across gp and to corner of next gp; turn.

8th row. 1 sp, 7 d, 1 sp, 7 d, 4 sp, 4 d, ch 6; turn.

9th row. 7 d, 5 sp, 16 d, 1 sp, sl st across sp and to corner of next sp; turn.

10th row. 4 d, 12 sp, 4 d, ch 3; turn.

11th row. 7 d, 5 sp, 16 d, 1 sp, 4 d, 3 sp, ch 5; turn.

The design starts again with 12th row.

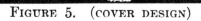

FIGURE 5. (COVER DESIGN)

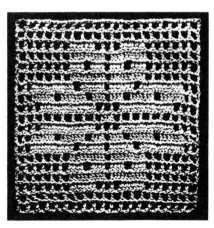

FIGURE 6. INSERTION FOR BEDSPREAD

FIGURE 7

Scarf in Cross-Stitch Embroidery
Art. 1116, Pearl Cotton No. 3, Color Nos. 203 and 214

The scarf as shown is worked with two shades of blue on material having a sq. weave; or cross-stitch canvas basted on plain material may be worked in the same way. See Fig. 9 for working model.

FIGURE 8. WORKING MODEL FOR FIGURE 7

Purse

Art. 131, N. E. T. (Crochet Twist), White or Ecru

Begin with 6 chain, join into ring by slip stitch.

1st round. 4 ch, for long treble (thread over needle twice). 3 ch, making 7 in all, 1 l t into the ring, 3 ch, 1 l t into the ring, * 3 ch, 1 l t into the ring, repeat from * until there are 8, 1 l t into the ring, after the last l t work 3 ch, sl st into the top of the 4 ch worked from the 1st l t.

2d round. 3 d, 5 ch, 3 d into the 1st sp of 3 ch of previous round, * 3 d, 5 ch, 3 d into the next sp, repeat from * into each of the 8 sp; there will be 6 d between each p of 5 ch.

3d round. * 9 ch, 1 l t into the d over the 1st l t between 2 p of the previous round, 9 ch, 1 d into the d over the next l t between 2 p, repeat from * into each of the l t, after the last 9 ch, sl st into the 1st 9 ch instead of the the d.

4th round. After the last sl st of the previous round work 12 ch from the medallion, sl st into the 10th loop from the needle, into this ring work 2 d, 5 ch, 2 d, 5 ch, 2 d, 5 ch, 2 d, 5 ch, 2 d, 5 ch, 2 d, 2 ch, 1 d into the same d in the circle as the 12 ch was begun from, and into the 1st sp of 9 ch work 4 d, draw the thread through the 1st p on the side of the ring just worked, 6 d into the same sp of 9 ch 1 d into the t of the previous round, * 12 ch, sl st into the 10th loop from the needle, into this ring work 2 d, 5 ch, 2 d, 5 ch, 2 d, 5 ch, 2 d, 5 ch, 2 d, 5 ch, 2 d, 2 ch, 1 d into the t of the previous round, into the next sp of 9 ch work 10 d, 1 d into the d of the previous round, 12 ch, sl st into the 10th loop from the needle, into this ring work 2 d, 3 ch, draw the thread through the 4th d from the needle of the 10 d of the previous sp, 2 ch, 2 d, 5 ch, 2 d, 5 ch, 2 d, 5 ch, 2 d, 5 ch, 2 d, 2 ch, 1 d into the same d as the 12 ch was begun from, 4 d into the next sp of 9 ch, draw the thread through the 1st p on the ring just worked, 6 d into the same sp, 1 d into the next t of the previous round, repeat from * around circle. When making the last 10 d on the last sp of 9 ch work first 6 d, then draw thread through the 1st p on the ring just worked, and then work 4 d into same sp, finish off firmly with a needle. Join one medallion to another by the last round on the pattern the following way: ** Begin with the small ring on the corner of the medallion and work 12 ch, sl st into the 10th loop from the needle, into this ring work 2 d, 3 ch, draw the thread through the 4th d from the needle of the 10 d of the previous sp, 3 ch, 2 d into the ring, 5 ch, 2 d, 3 ch, draw the thread through the 3d p on the corner ring of the previous pattern, 3 ch, 2 d into the ring, 5 ch, 2 d, 5 ch, 2 d, 2 ch, 1 d into the same d as the 12 ch was begun from, 4 d into the next sp of 9 ch, draw the thread through the 1st p on the side of ring just worked, 6 d, 1 d into the t of previous round, draw the thread through the 3d p on the next ring on the side of previous pattern, 10 d into the next sp of 9 ch, 1 d into the d of the previous round, 12 ch, sl st into the 10th loop from the needle, into this ring work 2 d, 3 ch, draw the thread through the 4th d from the needle of the 10 d of the previous sp, 2 ch, 2 d into the ring, 5 ch, 2 d, 3 ch, draw the thread through the 3d p on the next corner ring of the previous pattern, 3 ch, 2 d into the ring, 5 ch, 2 d, 5 ch, 2 d, 2 ch, 1 d into the d on which the 12 ch was begun from, repeat from ** for all the joinings. After 2 rows are joined together there should be 4 p of 5 ch joined to each other at the corners of each pattern. When joining down the sides and across the bottom there should be a pattern or small flower on each side joined by the p at the top. There are 18 medallions which form the bag. Around the top of the bag make 1 row of t (thread over needle twice), except when there is a p, when you make a single crochet. There are 3 medallions which make the flap. Join them together, following the directions for joining medallions of bag; when joining to the row of mesh around the top of bag make the connection directly over the medallion on bag. Fasten feather-bone across back in hem of lining.

For the Strings

Join the thread to the corner of bag, ch 65, draw the ch through 1st mesh between flap and bag and join with d to a large bone ring, ch 65 and draw thread through same mesh, join with d to the same place where 1st ch of 65 started, 3 d into next sp, 1 d into next sp, ch 64, skip one mesh and pass the chain through the next, 1 d to ring, ch 64, pass the ch through the same mesh and continue across bag, making each ch about 1 less as you go towards the center of bag and increase 1 st as you go towards the other end, being careful to have the chains the correct length, and finish with 65 ch.

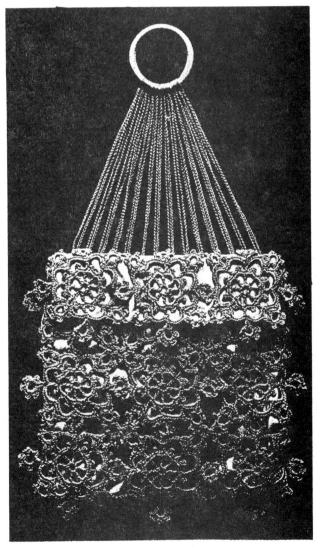

FIGURE 9

9

Knot-Stitch Bag

N. E. T. (Crochet Twist), White or Color

Cross-stitch embroidery is worked with 3 shades of pink and 1 of green. Have two bands 1½ inches wide, join. Work cross-stitch design on same as shown in illustration, or any other decoration may be used. The knot stitch is made by drawing up the stitch on the hook about ½ inch, pass the hook between the single thread and the loop and make 1 s. Draw up another ½-inch loop, fasten with 1 s as before, 1 s into the band, repeat around bag.

The second row of knot stitch is made by fastening the ½-inch loops with a s each side of s in row before.

There are 4 rows of knot stitch between bands.

Work 6 rows of knot stitch for the top, using the second and third rows for the cord to run through.

For the bottom make 3 rows, then divide the bag into 4 parts and each time reaching them draw 2 loops together at the same time to narrow, continue until the bag is narrowed to a point.

Make a tassel of material used.

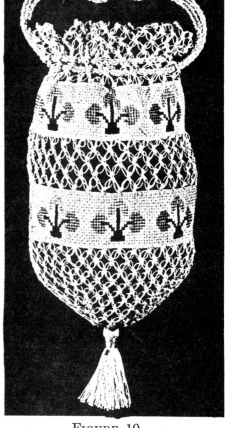

Cord

Ch 5, join, make 5 s around ring, picking up outside loop; continue picking up outside loop until the desired length is made.

Crochet Work Bag

CHAIN 12, join in ring.

1st row. Ch 4, 23 d in ring, join with sl st.

2d row. Ch 11, skip 1 d, 1 t (thread over hook twice), **draw thread through the first d of ring, thread over hook, draw through 2 loops, thread over hook once, skip one d on ring, put hook through the next st, thread over hook, draw through loop, thread over hook, draw through 2 loops, thread over hook, draw through 2 loops, thread over hook, draw through 2 loops, thread over hook, draw through 2 loops, ch 2, thread over hook, put hook through the middle st of the t, thread over hook, draw through, thread over hook, draw through 2 loops, thread over hook, draw through the last 2 loops, ch 4, thread over hook twice, put hook through the next st and draw loop through, repeat from *.** This is called a crossed treble crochet. Make 8 c t around ring after last c t, make ch of 6, 1 d in next d on ring sl st into 2d st of 1st 11 ch; turn, sl st back over 2 st of last 6 ch, ch 2; turn, sl st into 4 st of 1st 11 ch.

3d row. Ch 1, * 8 s over ch of 4, 4 s in the c t, repeat from *.

Work 4 more rows of s around.

8th row. Ch 3, 1 d in 1st s, ch 1, 1 d in next s, ch 1, 1 d in next s, repeat around.

9th row. Ch 11, * skip 2 d, 1 c t, leaving 2 d between c t, ch 4, repeat from *.

10th row. 4 s over ch of 4, 4 s in c t, repeat around.

Make 4 rows more of s.

15th row. Ch 7, * skip 1 s, 2 t in next s, ch 2, repeat from *.

16th row. Ch 3, 2 d over ch of previous row, ch 3, * skip 4 t, 1 s over ch of 2, ch 3, skip 4 t, 3 d over ch of 2, ch 4, 3 d in same place, ch 3, repeat from *, join row with sl st. Ch 2, draw loop through center of last ch so as to begin next row from center of loop.

17th row. Ch 3, 2 d over same loop, ch 3, * 3 d in ch of 4 between the 6 d, ch 4, 3 d in same place, ch 3, repeat from *, join row.

18th row. Ch 3, 2 d over 1st loop, ch 3, 1 s over ch of 3, ch 3, 3 d over ch of 4, ch 4, 3 d in same place, repeat same.

Repeat next row from 17th row. Make 22 rows in all like 17th and 18th rows.

Next row for scallop, * 8 d in ch of 4 with 1 ch between, 1 d in 1 s, repeat from *.

Last row. * 1 p, 1 d in 1 ch, 1 p, 1 d in 1 ch, repeat from *.

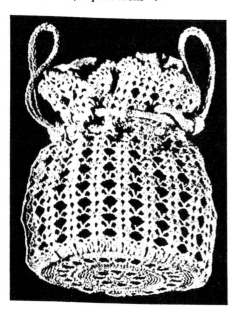

FIGURE 11

BOTTOM OF FIGURE 11

FIGURE 10

10

FIGURE 12

FIGURE 13.   SMALL NUT BASKET

Large Nut Basket

 Art. 1151, No. 30 Cordonnet

1st row. Ch 5, join to make ring, 8 s in ring, join with sl st.
2d tow. 2 s into each st, join.
3d row. 2 s into 1st st, 1 s into next, 2 s into 3d st, 1 s into next, continue around, join.
4th row. 2 s into 1st st, 1 s into each of 10 next st, 2 s into 4 st, 2 s into next 2 st, continue around, join.
5th row. 2 s into 1st st, 1 s into next 3 st. Continue widening, being careful to keep work flat until the 21st row is worked, when there should be 108 st. Work 3 rows with 108 st in each row.
25th row. Ch 3 for 1 d, 4 d, 1 sp, 4 d, 1 sp. 4 d, repeat around, join the last ch of 2 to 1st d.
26th row. Ch 5, 1 sp, 4 d, 1 sp, 4 d, continue and join, repeat until there are 6 rows of sp and d.
33d row. 1 s into each st, join.
34th row. Ch 3, * skip 1, 26 s, ch 2, repeat from * 3 times, join.
35th row. Ch 2, * 6 d with 1 ch between into sp, ch 2, skip 1, 24 s into next 24 st, ch 1, repeat from * 3 times, at end of row, after 24 s are made, join to 1st ch from beginning.
36th row. Ch 3, * 1 d into sp before 1st d, ch 2, 1 d into next sp, continue until 7 d with 2 ch between are made, ch 2, skip 2, 20 s into following st, ch 2, repeat from * 3 times, at end row, after last 20 s are made, join to 1st ch from beginning.
37th row. Ch 4, * 1 d into 1st sp before 1st d, ch 3, 1 d into next sp. ch 3, continue until 8 d with 3 ch between are made, ch 3, skip 2, 16 s, ch 3, repeat from *, after last 16 s are made join to 1st ch.
38th row. Ch 5, * 1 d in 1st sp before d, ch 4, 1 d in next sp, ch 4. continue until 9 d are made, ch 4, skip 1, 14 s, ch 4, repeat from * 3 times, after last 14 s join.
39th row. Ch 6, 1 d in 1st sp, ch 5, 1 d in next sp, continue until 10 d are made, ch 5, skip 2, 10 s, ch 5, repeat from * 3 times, join.
40th row. Ch 7, * 1 d in 1st sp, ch 6, 1 d in next sp, continue until 11 d are made, ch 6, skip 1, 8 s, ch 6, repeat from * 3 times, join.
41st row. Ch 8, * 1 d into 1st sp, ch 7, 1 d in next sp, continue until 12 d are made, ch 7, skip 2, 4 s, ch 7, repeat from * 3 times, join.
42d row. Ch 9, * 1 d into 1st sp, ch 8, 1 d into next sp, continue until 12 d are made, ch 7, skip 2, 4 s, ch 7, repeat from * 3 times. join.

Handle
Ch 5, join to make ring, 4 d, ch 2, 3 d into ring; turn, * ch 3, 4 d, ch 2, 3 d into sp of 2 ch; turn, repeat from * for 7½ inches. Sew to basket between two scallops on opposite sides.

Feet
Ch 9, skip 1, 2 s into each ch; turn, 1 s into each st; turn, make 10 more rows of 12 s. Fill with cotton and sew together along side. Sew to bottom of basket, having 4 feet in all.

Baby's Rattle
(To be Hung on Carriage)

 Art. 1116, Pearl Cotton No. 5, Pink and White

1st row. Pink rows. Ch 5, join in ring, ch 1 to turn.
2d row. 8 s in ring, ch 1.
3d row. 2 s in each of 8 s, ch 1.
4th row. 2 s in each of 16 st, ch 1.
5th row. 2 s in every other st of 4th row.
6th row. 1 s in every st.
7th row. Work with white pearl cotton. 1 s in every st.
8th row. Pink 3 rows. Increase to 64 st.
9th row. Increase to 68 st.
10th row. 1 s in each st of 9th row.
11th row. White. 1 s in each st.
12th, 13th, 14th rows. Pink. 1 s in each st.
  8 rows of white.
  Decrease in same count until a small place is left at top. Fill with cotton and trim as shown and close. The bells may be found at the Woolworth stores.

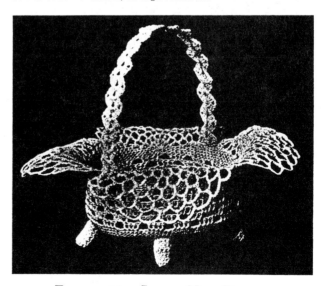

FIGURE 14.   LARGE NUT BASKET

11

FIGURE 15

Infants' Carriage Robe

Art. 131, N. E. T. (Crochet Twist)

CHAIN 71; turn, 1 d in 4th st, which counts for 1 d.

1st row.   4 d, 1 sp, 4 d, 3 sp, 28 d, 3 sp, 4 d, 1 sp, 4 d, ch 3; turn.

2d row.   13 d, 1 sp, 10 d, 5 sp, 10 d, 1 sp, 13 d, ch 3; turn.

3d row.   16 d, 9 sp, 16 d, ch 3; turn

4th row.   7 d, 1 sp, 10 d, 2 sp, 7 d, 1 sp, 7 d, 2 sp, 10 d, 1 sp, 7 d, ch 3; turn.

5th row.   4 d, 3 sp, 4 d, 2 sp, 10 d, 1 sp, 10 d, 2 sp, 4 d, 3 sp, 4 d, ch 3; turn.

6th row.   7 d, 1 sp, 7 d, 2 sp, 7 d, 3 sp, 7 d, 2 sp, 7 d, 1 sp, 7 d, ch 3; turn.

7th row.   16 d, 5 sp, 4 d, 5 sp, 16 d, ch 3; turn.

8th row.   16 d, 2 sp, 7 d, 3 sp, 7 d, 2 sp, 16 d, ch 3; turn.

9th row.   7 d, 5 sp, 10 d, 1 sp, 10 d, 5 sp, 7 d, ch 3; turn.

10th row.   4 d, 7 sp, 7 d, 1 sp, 7 d, 7 sp, 4 d, ch 3; turn.

12

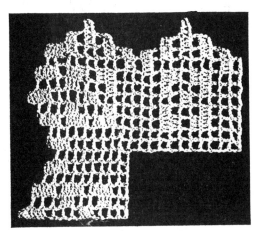

FIGURE 16
CORNER OF INFANTS' CARRIAGE ROBE

11th row. 4 d, 2 sp, 7 d, 1 sp, 7 d, 5 sp, 7 d, 1 sp, 7 d, 2 sp, 4 d, ch 3; turn.
12th row. 4 d, 1 sp, 10 d, 1 sp, 10 d, 3 sp, 10 d, 1 sp, 10 d, 1 sp, 4 d, ch 3; turn.
13th row. 4 d, 1 sp, 7 d, 3 sp, 7 d, 3 sp, 7 d, 3 sp, 7 d, 1 sp, 4 d, ch 3; turn.
14th row. 4 d, 4 sp, 4 d, 9 sp, 4 d, 4 sp, 4 d, ch 3; turn.
This completes one-half of design, work back 13th, 12th, 11th, etc., to complete.

Edging

CHAIN 32; turn, 1 d in 8th ch, which counts for 1 sp.
1st row. 8 sp, ch 6; turn.

2d row. 1 d in 4th ch, 1 d in next ch, 1 d over d, 2 d in sp, 1 d over d, 7 sp, ch 5; turn.
3d row. 9 sp, ch 6; turn.
4th row. 1 d in 4th ch, 1 d in next ch, 1 d over d, 2 d in sp, 1 d over d, 1 sp, 7 d, 1 sp, 7 d, 2 sp, ch 5; turn.
5th row. 2 sp, 4 d, 3 sp, 4 d, 3 sp, ch 6; turn.
6th row. 7 d, 4 sp, 4 d, 4 sp, ch 5; turn.
7th row. 2 sp, 4 d, 3 sp, 4 d, 3 sp, ch 3; turn.
8th row. 7 d, 1 sp, 7 d, 1 sp, 7 d, 2 sp, ch 5; turn.
9th row. 9 sp, ch 3; turn.
10th row. 7 d, 7 sp, ch 5; turn.
11th row. 8 sp, ch 6; turn.
12th row. 7 d, 6 sp; turn, sl st over sp, ch 5.
13th row. 7 sp, ch 6; turn.
14th row. 7 d, 1 sp, 7 d, 1 sp, 4 d; turn, sl st across gp, ch 5.
15th row. 2 sp, 4 d, 3 sp, ch 6; turn.
16th row. 7 d, 4 sp; turn, sl st across sp, ch 3.
17th row. 4 d, 3 sp, ch 3; turn.
18th row. 7 d, 1 sp; turn, sl st across sp, ch 3.
19th row. 4 d, ch 6; turn.

1st row of mitre. 4 d, join to corner of gp, sl st across gp and to corner of sp; turn.
2d row. 2 sp, ch 6; turn.
3d row. 7 d, 1 sp, 4 d, sl st across side of gp and to corner of sp above; turn.
4th row. 1 sp, 4 d, 3 sp, ch 6; turn.
5th row. 7 d, 4 sp, 4 d, sl st over sp and to corner of gp; turn.
6th row. 3 sp, 4 d, 3 sp, ch 3; turn.
7th row. 7 d, 1 sp, 7 d, 1 sp, 7 d, sl st to corner of sp above; turn.
8th row. 8 sp, ch 3; turn.
9th row. 7 d, 7 sp, ch 5; turn.
10th row. 8 sp, ch 6; turn.
11th row. 7 d, 7 sp, ch 5; turn.
12th row. 9 sp, ch 6; turn.
Work 4th row, 5th row, 6th row, etc.

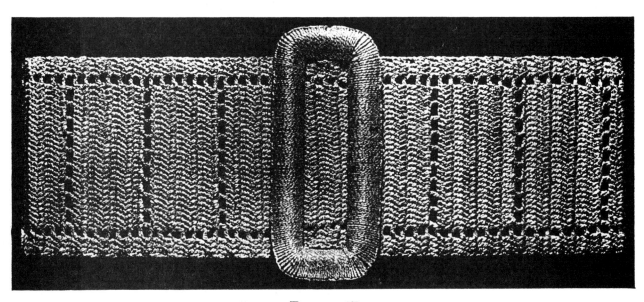

FIGURE 17

Tennis Girdle
Art. 1116, Pearl Cotton No. 3, White

CHAIN 43; turn.
1st row. 40 d, ch 3; turn.
2d row. 4 d, 11 sp, 4 d, ch 3; turn.
3d row. 4 d, 1 sp, 28 d, 1 sp, 4 d, ch 3; turn.
4th row. 5th, 6th, 7th, and 8th like 3d row.

9th row. Repeat 2d row.
10th row. Repeat 3d row.
Make girdle the desired length. The buckle forms may be found in department stores. Cover with crochet or buttonhole stitch. Fasten with hooks and eyes.

13

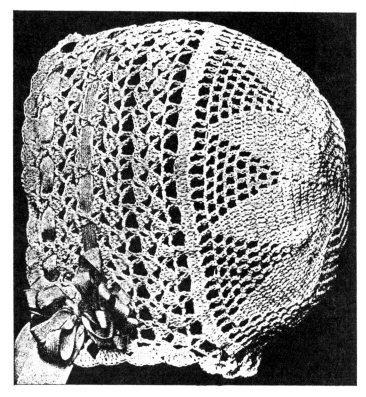

FIGURE 18

Baby's Cap

Pearl Cotton, No. 5

CHAIN 6, join in ring.

1st row. Ch 3, 26 d, in ring, join.

2d row. Ch 3, 2 d, ch 1, * 3 d, ch 1, repeat from *.

3d row. 5 d, ch 1 in each of 9 spokes of wheel.

4th row. 7 d, ch 1 in each of 9 spokes of wheel.

5th row. 9 d, ch 1 in each of 9 spokes of wheel.

6th row. 11 d, ch 1 in each of 9 spokes of wheel.

7th row. 13 d, ch 1 in each of 9 spokes of wheel.

8th row. 15 d, ch 1 in each of 9 spokes of wheel.

9th row. 17 d, ch 1 in each of 9 spokes of wheel.

10th row. * 15 d, ch 2, 1 d between spokes, ch 2, repeat from * in each spoke.

11th row. * 13 d, ch 2, 1 d, ch 2, 1 d, ch 2, repeat from *.

12th row. * 11 d, ch 2, 1 d, ch 2, 1 d, ch 2, 1 d, ch 2, repeat from *.

13th row. * 9 d, ch 2, 1 d, ch 2, 1 d, ch 2, 1 d, ch 2, 1 d, ch 2, repeat from *.

14th row. * 7 d, 6 sp, repeat from *.

15th row. * 5 d, 7 sp, repeat from *.

16th row. * 3d, 8 sp, repeat from *.

17th row. 1 d, ch 2, repeat.

18th row. * 1 d over d, 2 d in sp, 1 d over d, 2 d in sp, repeat from *.

19th row. * d, ch 2, d in same st, ch 2. skip 5, repeat from *.

20th row. * 3 d over 2 ch of last row, ch 2, 1 d, repeat from * in all except last 9 st, which are left for back of cap, turn.

21st row. * 3 d, ch 2, 1 d, repeat from *.

22d row. * d, ch 2, d, ch 2, repeat from * across row.

23d row. * 3 d, ch 2, 1 d, repeat from * across row in every 2d sp of 2 ch.

24th row. Same as 23d row, continue repeating 23d row until there are 28 rows. Make shell of 8 d in every 2d sp of 2 ch.

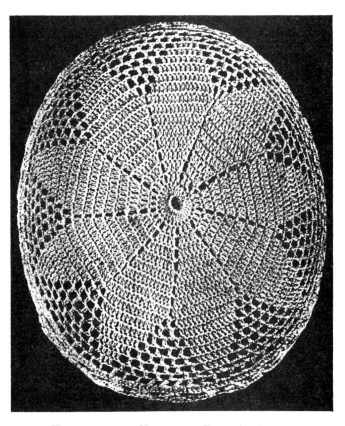

FIGURE 19. BACK OF BABY'S CAP

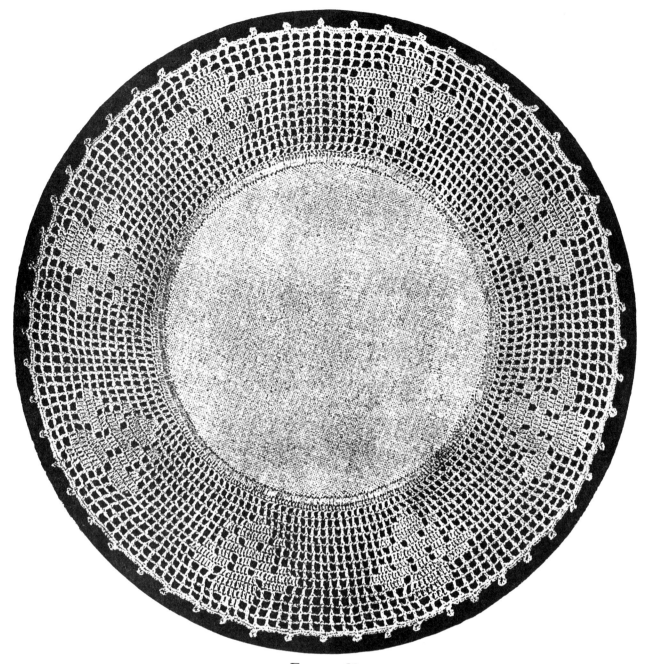

FIGURE 20

D'Oyley

◀W▶ N. E. T. (Crochet Twist), White or Ecru

Cut linen 7½ inches in diameter, hem.

1st row. 1 row of d around edge, ch 4.

2d row. Skip 1 d, 1 d in next d, ch 1, skip 1 d, 1 d in next d, continue around edge, making a number of sp divisible by 20, join last ch of 1 into 3d st of 1st 4 ch.

3d row. Ch 5, 1 row of sp having 2 ch between d around edge, joining the last 2 ch into 3d st of 1st 5 ch.

4th row. Ch 3, which counts for 1 d, 2 d in sp, 1 d over d, 19 sp, 4 d, 19 sp, 4 d, repeat around edge, joining last 2 ch into corner of 1st gp of 4.

5th row. Ch 3 for 1 d, 3 d over d, 2 d in sp, 1 d over d, 17 sp, 10 d, 17 sp, 10 d, repeat around edge. After the last 17 sp make 3 d, joining the last d into 1st d of gp, which completes the gp of 10.

6th row. Ch 3, 7 d, 1 sp, 4 d, 13 sp, 4 d, 1 sp, 10 d, 1 sp, 4 d, 13 sp, 4 d, 1 sp, 10 d, 1 sp, 4 d, 13 sp, repeat

around edge. After the last gr of 4 d make 1 sp, 3 d, joining the last d to 1 d of gp.

7th row. Ch 3, 4 d, 1 sp, 4 d, 15 sp, 4 d, 1 sp, 4 d, 1 sp, 4 d, 15 sp, repeat.

8th row. Ch 3, 10 d, 15 sp, 16 d, 15 sp, 16 d, repeat.

9th row. Ch 3, 4 d, 1 sp, 4 d, 1 sp, 4 d, 11 sp, 4 d, 1 sp, 4 d, 1 sp, 4 d, 1 sp, 4 d, 11 sp, repeat.

10th row. Ch 3, 4 d, 1 sp, 13 d, 9 sp, 13 d, 1 sp, 4 d, 1 sp, 13 d, 9 sp, repeat.

11th row. Ch 3, 7 d, 1 sp, 7 d, 11 sp, 7 d, 1 sp, 10 d, 1 sp, 7 d, 11 sp, repeat.

12th row. Ch 3, 7 d, 17 sp, 10 d, 17 sp, 10 d, repeat.

13th row. Repeat 12th row.

14th row. Ch 3, 4 d, 19 sp, 4 d, 19 sp, 4 d, repeat.

15th row. Ch 5, 1 d in middle of gp of 4, ch 2, 1 d in last d of gp, 19 sp, 2 sp over gp, 19 sp, repeat.

16th row. 3 s in sp, 1 s over d, 3 s in sp, 1 d over d, 3 s in sp, p over d, repeat around edge.

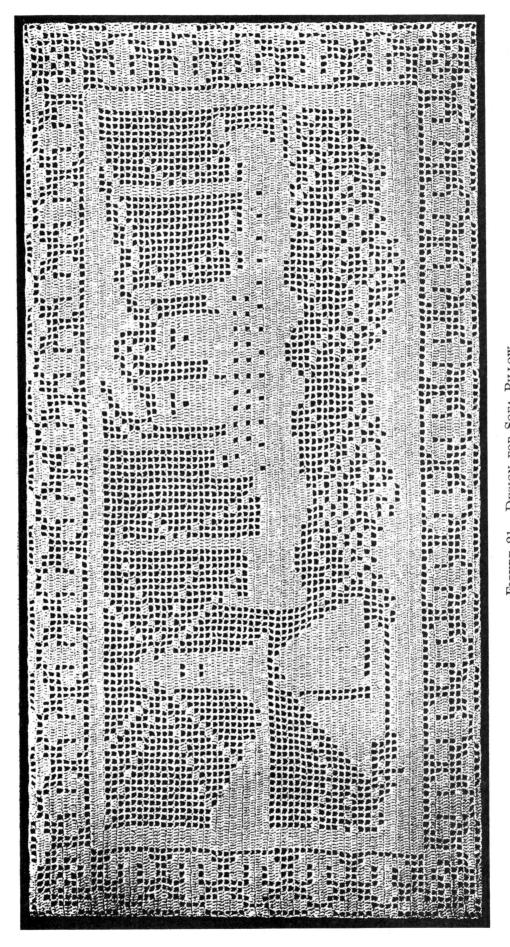

FIGURE 21. DESIGN FOR SOFA PILLOW

N. E. T. (CROCHET TWIST), WHITE OR COLOR

Marine Sofa Pillow

Art. 131, N. E. T. (Crochet Twist), White or Ecru

Make a chain of about 370 st; turn, 1 d in 8th ch, which counts for 1 sp.

1st row. 3 sp, 13 d, 6 sp, 13 d, 6 sp, 13 d, repeat until there are 23 gp of 13 d and 6 sp, 3 sp at end of row, ch 5; turn.

2d row. 1 sp, 7 d, 4 sp, 19 d, 4 sp, 19 d, 4 sp, repeat until there are 23 gp of 4 sp and 19 d, 7 d, 1 sp, at end of row, ch 5; turn.

3d row. 1 sp, 4 d, 7 sp, 7 d, 3 sp, 7 d, 3 sp, repeat until there are 41 gp of 7 d and 3 sp, 7 sp, 4 d, 1 sp at end of row, ch 3; turn.

4th row. 4 d, 2 sp, 4 d, 1 sp, 4 d, 7 sp, * 13 d, 6 sp, repeat from * until there are 19 gp of 6 sp and 13 d, 7 sp, 4 d, 1 sp, 4 d, 2 sp, 4 d at end of row, ch 3; turn.

5th row. 4 d, 3 sp, 4 d, 2 sp, 7 d, 5 sp, * 7 d, 8 sp, repeat from * until there are 19 gp of 7 d and 8 sp, 5 sp, 7 d, 2 sp, 4 d, 3 sp, 4 d at end of row, ch 3; turn.

6th row. 4 d, 2 sp, 4 d, 1 sp, 4 d, 2 sp, 4 d, 2 sp, * 7 d, 1 sp, 7 d, 1 sp, 7 d, 2 sp, repeat from * across, finish other end of row like first end. Finish design as shown in illustration.

Crown Edge for Marine Sofa Pillow

Crochet a row of d around pillow. Ch 5, skip 2 d, 1 d in next, * ch 2, skip 2, 1 d in next, repeat from * around pillow, joining last ch of 2 into 3d st of 1st 5 ch with a sl st, ch 1, 2 s in sp, 1 s in d, 2 s in sp, repeat until 6 sp have been filled with s, ch 7; turn, skip 5 s, 1 s in next s, ch 7; skip 5 s, 1 s in next s; turn, 2 s, p, 5 s in 1st sp, 5 s in next sp, ch 7; turn, 1 s in 3d st of 1st sp; turn, 2 s, p, 5 s, p, 2 s in sp, 2 s, p, 2 s in sp, where there are 5 s, repeat.

[59]

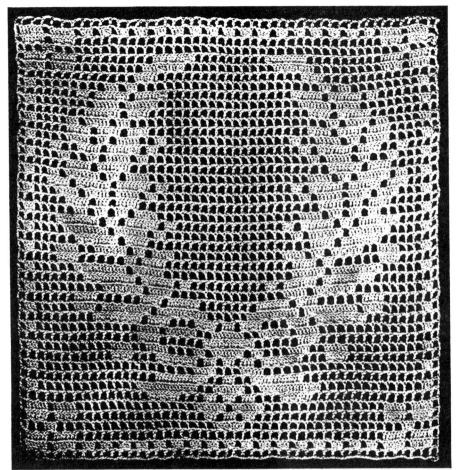

FIGURE 23

Medallion. 47 sp.

Art. 1116, No. 12, or Art. 1151, No. 40

CHAIN 149; turn, 1 d in 8th st, which counts for 1 sp.

1st row. 47 sp, ch 5; turn.

2d row. 1 sp, 7 d, 1 sp, 7 d, 1 sp,* 4 d, 1 sp, 4 d, 1 p, 4 d, 1 sp, repeat from * until there are 18 sp and 17 gr of d, 7 d, 1 sp, 7 d, 1 sp, ch 5; turn.

3d row. 1 sp, 7 d, 1 sp, 7 d, 35 sp, 7 d, 1 sp, 7 d, 1 sp, ch 5; turn.

4th row. 3 sp, 4 d, 18 sp, 10 d, 18 sp, 4 d, 3 sp, ch 5; turn.

5th row. 1 sp, 7 d, 1 sp, 7 d, 15 sp, 4 d, 1 sp, 4 d, 1 sp, 4 d, 15 sp, 7 d, 1 sp, 7 d, 1 sp, ch 5; turn.

6th row. 1 sp, 7 d, 1 sp, 7 d, 14 sp, 10 d, 1 sp, 10 d, 14 sp, 7 d, 1 sp, 7 d, 1 sp, ch 5; turn.

7th row. 15 sp, 10 d, 3 sp, 4 d, 1 sp, 4 d, 1 sp, 4 d, 3 sp, 10 d, 15 sp, ch 5; turn.

8th row. 1 sp, 4 d, 12 sp, 19 d, 2 sp, 10 d, 2 sp, 19 d, 12 sp, 4 d, 1 sp, ch 5; turn.

9th row. 16 sp, 16 d, 2 sp, 4 d, 2 sp, 16 d, 16 sp, ch 5; turn.

10th row. 1 sp, 4 d, 18 sp, 7 d, 3 sp, 7 d, 18 sp, 4 d, 1 sp, ch 5; turn.

11th row 11 sp, 7 d, 3 sp, 13 d, 1 sp, 4 d, 1 sp, 4 d, 1 sp, 4 d, 1 sp, 13 d, 3 sp, 7 d, 11 sp, ch 5; turn.

12th row. 1 sp, 4 d, 9 sp, 7 d, 2 sp, 7 d, 3 sp, 4 d, 1 sp, 10 d, 1 sp, 4 d, 3 sp, 7 d, 2 sp, 7 d, 9 sp, 4 d, 1 sp, ch 5; turn.

13th row. 14 sp, 7 d, 5 sp, 16 d, 5 sp, 7 d, 14 sp, ch 5; turn.

14th row. 1 sp, 4 d, 12 sp, 7 d, 1 sp, 10 d, 2 sp, 10 d, 2 sp, 10 d, 1 sp, 7 d, 12 sp, 4 d, 1 sp, ch 5; turn.

15th row. 9 sp, 16 d, 1 sp, 7 d, 3 sp, 7 d, 1 sp, 4 d, 1 sp, 7 d, 3 sp, 7 d, 1 sp, 16 d, 9 sp, ch 5; turn.

16th row. 1 sp, 4 d, 5 sp, 7 d, 1 sp, 16 d, 1 sp, 16 d, 5 sp, 16 d, 1 sp, 16 d, 1 sp, 7 d, 5 sp, 4 d, 1 sp, ch 5; turn.

17th row. 7 sp, 7 d, 5 sp, 7 d, 1 sp, 10 d, 7 sp, 10 d, 1 sp, 7 d, 5 sp, 7 d, 7 sp, ch 5; turn.

18th row. 1 sp, 4 d, 8 sp, 13 d, 1 sp, 7 d, 13 sp, 7 d, 1 sp, 13 d, 8 sp, 4 d, 1 sp, ch 5; turn.

19th row. 8 sp, 16 d, 1 sp, 10 d, 1 sp, 4 d, 9 sp, 4 d, 1 sp, 10 d, 1 sp, 16 d, 8 sp, ch 5; turn.

20th row. 1 sp, 4 d, 5 sp, 16 d, 1 sp, 10 d, 15 sp, 10 d, 1 sp, 16 d, 5 sp, 4 d, 1 sp, ch 5; turn.

21st row. 5 sp, 7 d, 5 sp, 4 d, 1 sp, 7 d, 15 sp, 7 d, 1 sp, 4 d, 5 sp, 7 d, 5 sp, ch 5; turn.

22d row. 1 sp, 4 d, 3 sp, 7 d, 2 sp, 10 d, 1 sp, 4 d, 1 sp, 7 d, 13 sp, 7 d, 1 sp, 4 d, 1 sp, 10 d, 2 sp, 7 d, 3 sp, 4 d, 1 sp, ch 5; turn.

23d row. 7 sp, 13 d, 1 sp, 7 d, 19 sp, 7 d, 1 sp, 13 d, 7 sp, ch 5; turn.

24th row. 1 sp, 4 d, 4 sp, 13 d, 1 sp, 10 d, 1 sp, 4 d, 15 sp, 4 d, 1 sp, 10 d, 1 sp, 13 d, 4 sp, 4 d, 1 sp, ch 5; turn.

25th row. 5 sp, 13 d, 1 sp, 4 d, 1 sp, 10 d, 1 sp, 4 d, 13 sp, 4 d, 1 sp, 10 d, 1 sp, 4 d, 1 sp, 13 d, 5 sp, ch 5; turn.

26th row. 1 sp, 4 d, 5 sp, 4 d, 1 sp, 4 d, 1 sp, 4 d, 1 sp, 7 d, 17 sp, 7 d, 1 sp, 4 d, 1 sp, 4 d, 1 sp, 4 d, 5 sp, 4 d, 1 sp, ch 5; turn.

27th row. 6 sp, 7 d, 1 sp, 4 d, 1 sp, 7 d, 21 sp, 7 d, 1 sp, 4 d, 1 sp, 7 d, 6 sp, ch 5; turn.

28th row. 1 sp, 4 d, 3 sp, 7 d, 1 sp, 7 d, 1 sp, 7 d, 1 sp, 4 d, 17 sp, 4 d, 1 sp, 7 d, 1 sp, 7 d, 1 sp, 7 d, 3 sp, 4 d, 1 sp, ch 5; turn.

29th row. 4 sp, 7 d, 1 sp, 10 d, 1 sp, 10 d, 1 sp, 4 d, 15 sp, 4 d, 1 sp, 10 d, 1 sp, 10 d, 1 sp, 7 d, 4 sp, ch 5; turn.

30th row. 1 sp, 4 d, 2 sp, 4 d, 1 sp, 10 d, 1 sp, 4 d, 1 sp, 7 d, 19 sp, 7 d, 1 sp, 4 d, 1 sp, 10 d, 1 sp, 4 d, 2 sp, 4 d, 1 sp, ch 5; turn.

31st row. 6 sp, 7 d, 1 sp, 10 d, 23 sp, 10 d, 1 sp, 7 d, 6 sp, ch 5; turn.

32d row. 1 sp, 4 d, 3 sp, 4 d, 2 sp, 4 d, 1 sp, 7 d, 1 sp, 4 d, 19 sp, 4 d, 1 sp, 7 d, 1 sp, 4 d, 2 sp, 4 d, 3 sp, 4 d, 1 sp, ch 5; turn.

33d row. 4 sp, 4 d, 2 sp, 7 d, 1 sp, 10 d, 1 sp, 4 d, 17 sp, 4 d, 1 sp, 10 d, 1 sp, 7 d, 2 sp, 4 d, 4 sp, ch 5; turn.

34th row. 1 sp, 4 d, 4 sp, 7 d, 1 sp, 4 d, 1 sp, 7 d, 2 sp, 4 d, 15 sp, 4 d, 2 sp, 7 d, 1 sp, 4 d, 1 sp, 7 d, 4 sp, 4 d, 1 sp, ch 5; turn.

35th row. 6 sp, 7 d, 1 sp, 7 d, 1 sp, 7 d, 19 sp, 7 d, 1 sp, 7 d, 1 sp, 7 d, 6 sp, ch 5; turn.

36th row. 1 sp, 4 d, 4 sp, 4 d, 1 sp, 7 d, 1 sp, 4 d, 23 sp, 4 d, 1 sp, 7 d, 1 sp, 4 d, 4 sp, 4 d, 1 sp, ch 5; turn.

37th row. 8 sp, 10 d, 1 sp, 7 d, 19 sp, 7 d, 1 sp, 10 d, 8 sp, ch 5; turn.

38th row. 1 sp, 4 d, 7 sp, 7 d, 1 sp, 10 d, 17 sp, 10 d, 1 sp, 7 d, 7 sp, 4 d, 1 sp, ch 5; turn.

39th row. 7 sp, 4 d, 1 sp, 10 d, 1 sp, 10 d, 15 sp, 10 d, 1 sp, 10 d, 1 sp, 4 d, 7 sp, ch 5; turn.

40th row. 1 sp, 4 d, 8 sp, 4 d, 1 sp, 4 d, 21 sp, 4 d, 1 sp, 4 d, 8 sp, 4 d, 1 sp, ch 5; turn.

41st row. 13 sp, 7 d, 17 sp, 7 d, 13 sp, ch 5; turn.

42d row. 1 sp, 7 d, 1 sp, 7 d, 8 sp, 13 d, 11 sp, 13 d, 8 sp, 7 d, 1 sp, 7 d, 1 sp, ch 5; turn.

43d row. 1 sp, 7 d, 1 sp, 7 d, 9 sp, 13 d, 9 sp, 13 d, 9 sp, 7 d, 1 sp, 7 d, 1 sp, ch 5; turn.

44th row. 3 sp, 4 d, 39 sp, 4 d, 3 sp, ch 5; turn.

45th row. 1 sp, 7 d, 1 sp, 7 d, 35 sp, 7 d, 1 sp, 7 d, 1 sp, ch 5; turn.

46th row. Repeat 2d row.

47th row. Repeat 1st row.

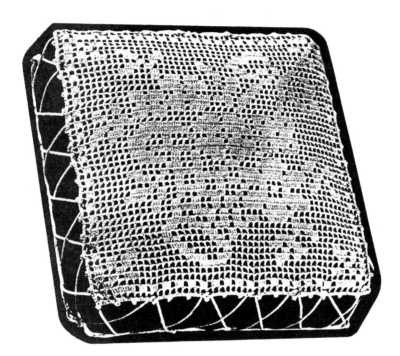

FIGURE 24

Medallion. 47 sp.

Art. 1116, No. 12, or Art. 1151, No. 50

CHAIN 149; turn, 1 d in 8th st, which counts for 1 sp.

1st row. 47 sp, ch 5; turn.

2d row. 1 sp, 4 d, 1 sp, 10 d, * 1 sp, 4 d, 1 sp, 4 d, 1 sp, 4 d, repeat from * until there are 18 sp, 17 gp of 4 d, 10 d, 1 sp, 4 d, 1 sp, ch 5; turn.

3d row. 2 sp, 4 d, 41 sp, 4 d, 2 sp, ch 5; turn.

4th row. 1 sp, 4 d, 1 sp, 4 d, 1 sp, 7 d, 33 sp, 7 d, 1 sp, 4 d, 1 sp, 4 d, 1 sp, ch 5; turn.

5th row. 1 sp, 4 d, 2 sp, 4 d, 11 sp, 4 d, 9 sp, 13 d, 12 sp, 4 d, 2 sp, 4 d, 1 sp, ch 5; turn.

6th row. 1 sp, 4 d, 1 sp, 4 d, 1 sp, 4 d, 9 sp, 10 d, 2 sp, 7 d, 8 sp, 7 d, 1 sp, 4 d, 7 sp, 4 d, 1 sp, 4 d, 1 sp, 4 d, 1 sp, ch 5; turn.

7th row. 3 sp, 4 d, 1 sp, 7 d, 5 sp, 7 d, 1 sp, 4 d, 9 sp, 4 d, 5 sp, 7 d, 7 sp, 7 d, 1 sp, 4 d, 3 sp, ch 5; turn.

8th row. 1 sp, 4 d, 4 sp, 4 d, 6 sp, 7 d, 5 sp, 7 d, 7 sp, 7 d, 1 sp, 7 d, 6 sp, 4 d, 4 sp, 4 d, 1 sp, ch 5; turn.

9th row. 10 sp, 4 d, 3 sp, 10 d, 7 sp, 4 d, 1 sp, 7 d, 5 sp, 7 d, 12 sp, ch 5; turn.

10th row. 1 sp, 4 d, 10 sp, 4 d, 5 sp, 7 d, 2 sp, 4 d, 10 sp, 4 d, 1 sp, 7 d, 8 sp, 4 d, 1 sp, ch 5; turn.

11th row. 11 sp, 10 d, 8 sp, 7 d, 1 sp, 7 d, 1 sp, 10 d, 2 sp, 7 d, 12 sp, ch 5; turn.

12th row. 1 sp, 4 d, 11 sp, 13 d, 2 sp, 4 d, 1 sp, 4 d, 1 sp, 4 d, 1 sp, 7 d, 2 sp, 10 d, 1 sp, 4 d, 11 sp, 4 d, 1 sp, ch 5; turn.

13th row. 14 sp, 16 d, 4 sp, 4 d, 1 sp, 4 d, 1 sp, 10 d, 2 sp, 4 d, 14 sp, ch 5; turn.

14th row. 1 sp, 4 d, 9 sp, 4 d, 2 sp, 13 d, 2 sp, 4 d, 1 sp, 4 d, 2 sp, 10 d, 1 sp, 10 d, 1 sp, 10 d, 9 sp, 4 d, 1 sp, ch 5; turn.

15th row. 11 sp, 34 d, 1 sp, 7 d, 1 sp, 4 d, 2 sp, 4 d, 2 sp, 4 d, 2 sp, 4 d, 11 sp, ch 5; turn.

16th row. 1 sp, 4 d, 5 sp, 10 d, 2 sp, 4 d, 2 sp, 4 d, 2 sp, 13 d, 2 sp, 4 d, 1 sp, 10 d, 3 sp, 10 d, 10 sp, 4 d, 1 sp, ch 5; turn.

17th row. 4 sp, 7 d, 3 sp, 4 d, 4 sp, 4 d, 1 sp, 4 d, 1 sp, 4 d, 2 sp, 4 d, 3 sp, 4 d, 2 sp, 13 d, 2 sp, 4 d, 1 sp, 10 d, 8 sp, ch 5; turn.

18th row. 1 sp, 4 d, 9 sp, 4 d, 3 sp, 4 d, 2 sp, 4 d, 2 sp, 4 d, 1 sp, 7 d, 1 sp, 10 d, 3 sp, 10 d, 2 sp, 7 d, 2 sp, 4 d, 3 sp, 4 d, 1 sp, ch 5; turn.

19th row. 6 sp, 4 d, 1 sp, 4 d, 2 sp, 34 d, 2 sp, 16 d, 2 sp, 4 d, 2 sp, 4 d, 1 sp, 7 d, 9 sp, ch 5; turn.

20th row. 1 sp, 4 d, 6 sp, 7 d, 3 sp, 4 d, 1 sp, 13 d, 3 sp, 4 d, 2 sp, 10 d, 1 sp, 10 d, 2 sp, 7 d, 5 sp, 4 d, 1 sp, ch 5; turn.

19

21st row. 4 sp, 10 d, 2 sp, 7 d, 3 sp, 16 d, 3 sp, 7 d, 4 sp, 4 d, 2 sp, 7 d, 14 sp, ch 5; turn.

22d row. 1 sp, 4 d, 8 sp, 13 d, 1 sp, 4 d, 2 sp, 4 d, 2 sp, 7 d, 2 sp, 4 d, 3 sp, 10 d, 5 sp, 7 d, 2 sp, 4 d, 3 sp, 4 d, 1 sp, ch 5; turn.

23d row. 7 sp, 7 d, 9 sp, 4 d, 1 sp, 10 d, 1 sp, 10 d, 1 sp, 4 d, 2 sp, 4 d, 3 sp, 10 d, 9 sp, ch 5; turn.

24th row. 1 sp, 4 d, 7 sp, 7 d, 1 sp, 19 d, 1 sp, 28 d, 1 sp, 10 d, 1 sp, 10 d, 9 sp, 4 d, 1 sp, ch 5; turn.

25th row. 11 sp, 4 d, 1 sp, 10 d, 1 sp, 4 d, 1 sp, 13 d, 1 sp, 13 d, 4 sp, 4 d, 3 sp, 7 d, 9 sp, ch 5; turn.

26th row. 1 sp, 4 d, 1 sp, 4 d, 2 sp, 4 d, 2 sp, 10 d, 2 sp, 4 d, 3 sp, 4 d, 2 sp, 4 d, 1 sp, 4 d, 1 sp, 4 d, 2 sp, 25 d, 9 sp, 4 d, 1 sp, ch 5; turn.

27th row. 12 sp, 7 d, 1 sp, 7 d, 2 sp, 13 d, 1 sp, 13 d, 1 sp, 25 d, 2 sp, 7 d, 1 sp, 7 d, 3 sp, ch 5; turn.

28th row. 1 sp, 4 d, 2 sp, 7 d, 1 sp, 4 d, 3 sp, 19 d, 2 sp, 25 d, 2 sp, 22 d, 9 sp, 4 d, 1 sp, ch 5; turn.

29th row. 11 sp, 4 d, 1 sp, 10 d, 1 sp, 4 d, 2 sp, 10 d, 1 sp, 10 d, 10 sp, 13 d, 6 sp, ch 5; turn.

30th row. 1 sp, 4 d, 2 sp, 7 d, 2 sp, 4 d, 1 sp, 7 d, 1 sp, 7 d, 6 sp, 7 d, 1 sp, 7 d, 3 sp, 10 d, 1 sp, 10 d, 9 sp, 4 d, 1 sp, ch 5; turn.

31st row. 13 sp, 4 d, 6 sp, 4 d, 5 sp, 7 d, 1 sp, 7 d, 1 sp, 16 d, 2 sp, 4 d, 2 sp, 4 d, 4 sp, ch 5; turn.

32d row. 1 sp, 4 d, 5 sp, 4 d, 3 sp. 4 d, 1 sp, 4 d, 1 sp, 10 d, 1 sp, 10 d, 3 sp, 4 d, 1 sp. 4 d, 6 sp, 4 d, 4 sp, 10 d, 3 sp, 4 d, 1 sp, ch 5; turn.

33d row. 4 sp, 7 d, 1 sp, 7 d, 3 sp, 4 d, 5 sp, 7 d, 1 sp, 10 d, 1 sp, 19 d, 1 sp, 16 d, 10 sp, ch 5; turn.

34th row. 1 sp, 4 d, 8 sp, 7 d, 1 sp, 7 d, 2 sp, 4 d, 1 sp, 4 d, 5 sp, 4 d, 2 sp, 7 d, 5 sp, 4 d, 1 sp, 7 d, 2 sp, 7 d, 2 sp, 4 d, 1 sp, ch 5; turn.

35th row. 5 sp, 7 d, 2 sp, 4 d, 1 sp, 4 d, 4 sp, 7 d, 2 sp, 7 d, 3 sp, 22 d, 15 sp, ch 5; turn.

36th row. 1 sp, 4 d, 13 sp, 10 d, 1 sp, 10 d, 2 sp, 4 d, 1 sp, 7 d, 2 sp, 7 d, 3 sp, 4 d, 1 sp, 4 d, 3 sp, 7 d, 2 sp, 4 d, 1 sp, ch 5; turn.

37th row. 4 sp, 7 d, 4 sp, 7 d, 1 sp, 7 d, 4 sp, 7 d, 1 sp, 4 d, 3 sp, 7 d, 1 sp, 7 d, 1 sp, 4 d, 14 sp, ch 5; turn.

38th row. 1 sp, 4 d, 7 sp, 7 d, 3 sp, 4 d, 8 sp, 7 d, 4 sp, 10 d. 2 sp, 4 d, 1 sp, 7 d, 2 sp, 7 d, 3 sp, 4 d, 1 sp, ch 5; turn.

39th row. 8 sp, 7 d, 1 sp, 4 d, 1 sp, 7 d, 2 sp, 7 d, 4 sp, 7 d, 8 sp, 4 d, 1 sp, 7 d, 10 sp, ch 5; turn.

40th row. 1 sp, 4 d, 10 sp, 4 d, 1 sp, 4 d, 7 sp, 4 d, 4 sp, 7 d, 6 sp, 4 d, 9 sp, 4 d, 1 sp, ch 5; turn.

41st row. 3 sp, 4 d, 1 sp, 7 d, 5 sp, 4 d, 3 sp, 10 d, 12 sp, 7 d, 2 sp, 7 d, 3 sp, 7 d, 1 sp, 4 d, 3 sp, ch 5; turn.

42d row. 1 sp, 4 d, 1 sp, 4 d, 1 sp, 4 d, 3 sp, 7 d, 4 sp, 4 d, 13 sp, 19 d, 6 sp, 4 d, 1 sp, 4 d, 1 sp, ch 5; turn.

43d row. 1 sp, 4 d, 2 sp, 4 d, 8 sp, 10 d, 26 sp, 4 d, 2 sp, 4 d, 1 sp, ch 5; turn.

44th row. Repeat 4th row.

45th row. Repeat 3d row.

46th row. Repeat 2d row.

47th row. Repeat 1st row.

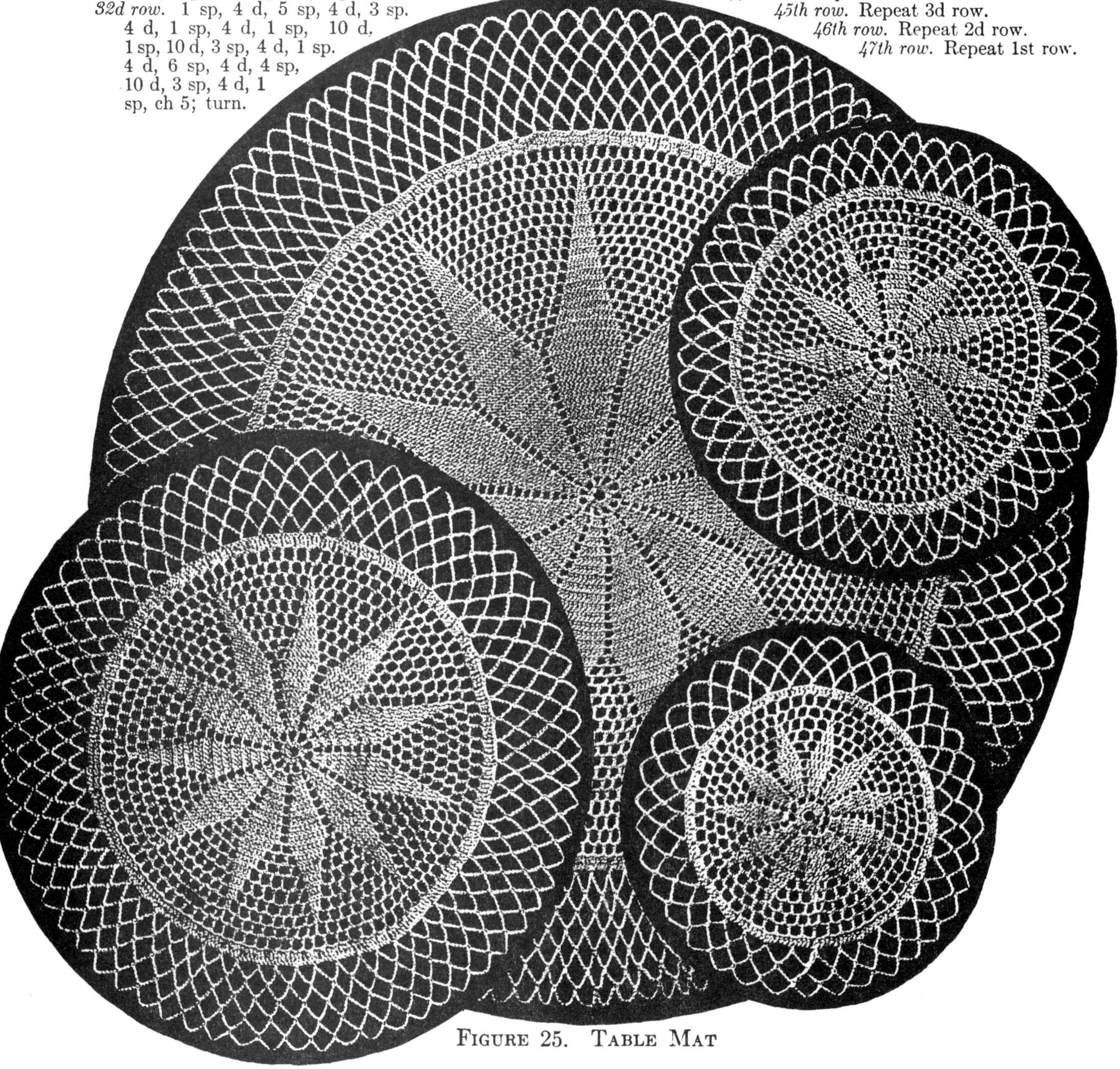

FIGURE 25. TABLE MAT

Table Mats. Figure 25. (Directions for Small Size)

N. E. T. (Crochet Twist)

CHAIN 9; join, 2 ch.

1st row. 22 s in ring. Fasten to 2 ch with sl st.

2d row. 5 ch, skip 1 s, 1 d in next, * 2 ch, skip 1 s, 1 d in next. Repeat from *9 times, 2 ch, 1 s in 3 d st of 5 ch.

3d row. 3 ch, 2 d in 1st sp, * 3 ch, 3 d in next sp. Repeat from * 9 times, 3 ch, fasten with sl st to 3 ch.

4th row. 3 ch, 1 d in d, 2 d in next d, * 3 ch, 2 d in next 2 d, 2 d in last d. Repeat from * 9 times, 3 ch, join with sl st to 2 ch.

5th row. 3 ch, 2 d in next 2 d, 2 d in last d, * 3 ch, 3 d in next 3 d, 2 d in last d. Repeat from * 9 times, 3 ch, sl st to 3 ch.

6th row. 3 ch, 3 d in 3 d, 2 d in last d, *3 ch, 4 d in next 4 d, 2 d in last d. Repeat from *9 times, 3 ch, sl st to 3 ch.

7th row. 3 ch, 4 d in 4 d, * 4 ch, 5 d in 5 d. Repeat from * 9 times, 4 ch, sl st to 3 ch.

8th row. 3 ch, 3 d in 3 d, * 4 ch, 1 d in sp, 4 ch, 4 d in next 4 d. Repeat from * 9 times, 4 ch, sl st to 3 ch.

9th row. 3 ch, 2 d in next 2 d, * 4 ch, 1 d in next sp, 4 ch, 1 d in next sp, 4 ch, 3 d in next 3 d. Repeat from * 9 times, 4 ch, 1 d in next sp, 4 ch, 1 d in next sp, 4 ch, 1 sl st in 3 ch.

10th row. 3 ch, 1 d in next d, * 4 ch, 1 d in next sp, 4 ch, 1 d in next sp, 4 ch, 1 d in next sp, 4 ch, 2 d in next 2 d. Repeat from *9 times, 4 ch, 1 d in next sp, 4 ch, 1 d in next sp, 4 ch, 1 d in next sp, 4 ch, 1 sl st in 3 ch.

11th row. 5 ch, 1 d in sp, 1 d with 3 ch between in each space and between 2 d around mat.

12th row. 5 ch, 1 d in sp, * 3 ch, 1 d in next sp. Repeat from * around.

13th row. 3 ch, 2 d in 1st sp, 1 d in d, 3 d in each of the remaining sp, 1 d in d, around mat.

14th row. 9 ch, 1 s in 5th d, 9 ch, 1 s in next 5th d. Repeat around, 1 s in st where ch started, sl st to 5th of 1st 9 ch.

15th row. Repeat 14th row.

16th row. Repeat 14th row.

FIGURE 26

Runner or Scarf

For Embroidery, Art. 1116, Pearl Cotton in Shades of Blue No. 5. For Crocheted Edge, No. 5, Shade No. 205 or 214

Crochet 1 row of sp around edge of runner, join. On sides of runner make 2 s in sp, 1 s over d, 2 s in next sp, 1 s over d, ch 7; turn, join with 1 s in 6th st; turn, 11 s in loop of 7 ch, * 2 s in next sp, 1 s over d, repeat 3 times from *, ch 7; turn, 1 s in 6th st; turn, 11 s in loop of 7 ch, repeat along side of runner. Across end make 2 s in 1st sp, 1 s over d, 2 s in next sp, 1 s over d, 2 s in next sp, 1 s over d, ch 7; turn, skip 4 s, 1 s in 5th st, ch 7, 1 s in 5th st; turn, 9 s in loop of 7 ch, 6 s in next loop, ch 7; turn, 1 s in middle st of 1st loop; turn, 11 s in loop of 7 ch, 4 s in next loop, * 2 s in sp, 1 s over d, repeat from * for 3 more sp, ch 7; turn, 1 s in 6th st; turn, 11 s in loop of 7 ch, repeat, having 2 sp between each scallop.

21

FIGURE 27

Nursery Laundry Bag

Art. 1116, Pearl Cotton, No. 8, White, or
Art. 1151, Cordonnet, No. 30

CHAIN about 128; turn, 1 d in 8th ch, which counts for 1 sp.

1st row. 40 sp, ch 5; turn.

2d row. 5 sp, 91 d, 5 sp, ch 5; turn.

3d row. 5 sp, 4 d, 28 sp, 4 d, 5 sp, ch 5; turn.

4th row. 3 sp, 10 d, 11 sp, 10 d, 14 sp, 10 d, 3 sp, ch 5; turn.

5th row. 3 sp, 4 d, 15 sp, 16 d, 12 sp, 4 d, 3 sp, ch 5; turn.

6th row. 1 sp. 10 d, 2 sp, 10 d, 7 sp, 7 d, 1 sp, 7 d, 10 sp, 10 d, 2 sp, 10 d, 1 sp, ch 5; turn.

7th row. 1 sp. 4 d, 2 sp, 4 d, 2 sp, 7 d, 11 sp, 16 d, 6 sp, 7 d, 2 sp, 4 d, 2 sp, 4 d, 1 sp, ch 5; turn.

8th row. 1 sp. 4 d, 3 sp, 4 d, 2 sp, 4 d, 5 sp, 19 d, 11 sp, 4 d, 2 sp, 4 d, 3 sp, 4 d, 1 sp, ch 5; turn.

9th row. 1 sp. 4 d, 1 sp, 4 d, 2 sp, 7 d, 13 sp, 7 d, 2 sp, 7 d, 5 sp, 7 d, 2 sp, 4 d, 1 sp, 4 d, 1 sp, ch 5; turn.

10th row. 1 sp, 4 d, 1 sp, 7 d, 1 sp, 7 d, 4 sp, 4 d, 3 sp, 7 d, 4 sp, 13 d, 6 sp, 7 d, 1 sp, 7 d, 1 sp, 4 d, 1 sp, ch 5; turn.

11th row. 1 sp. 4 d, 1 sp, 10 d, 2 sp, 4 d, 4 sp, 19 d, 3 sp, 7 d, 4 sp, 4 d, 2 sp, 4 d, 2 sp, 10 d, 1 sp, 4 d, 1 sp, ch 5; turn.

12th row. 1 sp. 4 d, 8 sp, 4 d, 5 sp, 7 d, 2 sp, 25 d, 10 sp, 4 d, 1 sp, ch 5; turn.

13th row. 1 sp. 4 d, 9 sp, 40 d, 5 sp, 4 d, 8 sp, 4 d, 1 sp, ch 5; turn.

14th row. 1 sp. 4 d, 8 sp, 4 d, 5 sp, 43 d, 8 sp, 4 d, 1 sp, ch 5; turn.

15th row. 1 sp. 4 d, 7 sp, 34 d, 1 sp, 10 d, 5 sp, 4 d, 8 sp, 4 d, 1 sp, ch 5; turn.

16th row. 1 sp. 4 d, 8 sp, 4 d, 6 sp, 10 d, 1 sp, 34 d, 6 sp, 4 d, 1 sp, ch 5; turn.

17th row. 1 sp. 4 d, 5 sp, 34 d, 1 sp, 13 d, 6 sp, 4 d, 8 sp, 4 d, 1 sp, ch 5; turn.

18th row. 1 sp. 4 d, 8 sp, 4 d, 7 sp, 13 d, 1 sp, 25 d, 1 sp, 7 d, 4 sp, 4 d, 1 sp, ch 5; turn.

19th row. 1 sp, 4 d, 4 sp, 7 d, 1 sp, 22 d, 1 sp, 16 d, 6 sp, 4 d, 1 sp, 4 d, 7 sp, 4 d, 1 sp, ch 5; turn.

20th row. 1 sp, 4 d, 6 sp, 4 d, 3 sp, 4 d, 6 sp, 16 d, 1 sp, 19 d, 1 sp, 4 d, 5 sp, 4 d, 1 sp, ch 5; turn.

21st row. 1 sp, 4 d, 5 sp, 7 d, 1 sp, 10 d, 2 sp, 16 d, 7 sp, 4 d, 3 sp, 4 d, 6 sp, 4 d, 1 sp, ch 5; turn.

22d row. 1 sp, 4 d, 5 sp. 4 d, 5 sp, 4 d, 7 sp, 16 d, 4 sp, 13 d, 4 sp, 4 d, 1 sp, ch 5; turn.

23d row. 1 sp, 4 d, 3 sp, 40 d, 2 sp, 4 d, 4 sp, 4 d, 7 sp, 4 d, 4 sp, 4 d, 1 sp, ch 5; turn.

24th row. 1 sp, 4 d, 3 sp, 4 d, 8 sp, 4 d, 1 sp, 13 d, 2 sp, 4 d, 2 sp, 25 d, 1 sp, 4 d, 3 sp, 4 d, 1 sp, ch 5; turn.

25th row. 1 sp, 4 d, 2 sp, 7 d, 3 sp, 16 d, 2 sp, 7 d, 2 sp, 16 d, 7 sp, 10 d, 3 sp, 4 d, 1 sp, ch 5; turn.

26th row. 1 sp, 4 d, 2 sp, 16 d, 5 sp, 13 d, 2 sp, 4 d, 2 sp, 4 d, 2 sp, 4 d, 2 sp, 22 d, 2 sp, 4 d, 1 sp, ch 5; turn.

27th row. 1 sp, 4 d, 2 sp, 10 d, 1 sp, 4 d, 3 sp, 7 d, 2 sp, 4 d, 2 sp, 28 d, 2 sp, 19 d, 2 sp, 4 d, 1 sp, ch 5; turn.

28th row. 1 sp, 4 d, 2 sp, 52 d, 2 sp, 4 d, 3 sp, 4 d, 5 sp, 10 d, 2 sp, 4 d, 1 sp, ch 5; turn.

29th row. 1 sp, 4 d, 3 sp, 4 d, 6 sp, 4 d, 3 sp, 4 d, 6 sp, 40 d, 2 sp, 4 d, 1 sp, ch 5; turn.

30th row. 1 sp, 4 d, 3 sp, 34 d, 7 sp, 4 d, 3 sp, 4 d, 10 sp, 4 d, 1 sp, ch 5; turn.

31st row. 1 sp, 4 d, 10 sp, 4 d, 3 sp, 4 d, 8 sp, 31 d, 3 sp, 4 d, 1 sp, ch 5; turn.

32d row. 1 sp, 4 d, 5 sp, 22 d, 9 sp, 4 d, 3 sp, 4 d, 10 sp, 4 d, 1 sp, ch 5; turn.

33d row. 1 sp, 4 d, 10 sp, 4 d, 3 sp, 4 d, 21 sp, 4 d, 1 sp, ch 5; turn.

34th row. 1 sp, 4 d, 21 sp, 4 d, 3 sp, 4 d, 10 sp, 4 d, 1 sp, ch 5; turn.

35th row. 1 sp, 4 d, 10 sp, 4 d, 3 sp, 4 d, 21 sp, 4 d, 1 sp, ch 5; turn.

36th row. 1 sp, 4 d, 1 sp, 10 d, 2 sp, 4 d, 14 sp, 4 d, 3 sp, 4 d, 3 sp, 4 d, 2 sp, 10 d, 1 sp, 4 d, 1 sp, ch 5; turn.

37th row. 1 sp, 4 d, 1 sp, 7 d, 1 sp, 7 d, 4 sp, 37 d, 8 sp, 7 d, 1 sp, 7 d, 1 sp, 4 d, 1 sp, ch 5; turn.

38th row. 1 sp, 4 d, 1 sp, 4 d, 2 sp, 7 d, 8 sp, 7 d, 2 sp, 13 d, 3 sp, 7 d, 3 sp, 7 d, 2 sp, 4 d, 1 sp, 4 d, 1 sp, ch 5; turn.

39th row. 1 sp, 4 d, 3 sp, 4 d, 2 sp, 4 d, 1 sp, 4 d, 1 sp, 4 d, 1 sp, 13 d, 3 sp, 10 d, 7 sp, 4 d, 2 sp, 4 d, 3 sp, 4 d, 1 sp, ch 5; turn.

40th row. 1 sp, 4 d, 2 sp, 4 d, 2 sp, 7 d, 7 sp, 13 d, 7 sp, 4 d, 3 sp, 7 d, 2 sp, 4 d, 2 sp, 4 d, 1 sp, ch 5; turn.

41st row. 1 sp, 10 d, 2 sp, 10 d, 3 sp, 13 d, 3 sp, 16 d, 7 sp, 10 d, 2 sp, 10 d, 1 sp, ch 5; turn.

42d row. 3 sp, 4 d, 12 sp, 19 d, 4 sp, 13 d, 6 sp, 4 d, 3 sp, ch 5; turn.

43d row. 3 sp, 10 d, 11 sp, 22 d, 10 sp, 10 d, 3 sp, ch 5; turn.

44th row. 5 sp, 4 d, 10 sp, 25 d, 10 sp, 4 d, 5 sp, ch 5; turn.

45th row. 5 sp, 91 d, 5 sp, ch 5; turn.

46th row. 40 sp.

For the Edge

Make long chain the length to be used; turn, 4 s, 1 p, 4 s, ch 9; turn, join with 1 s in 3d st beyond p; turn, 3 s, 1 p, 3 s, 1 p, 3 s, 1 p, 3 s in sp of 9 ch, 7 s, 1 p, 4 s, ch 9; turn, join with 1 s in 3d st beyond p; turn, 3 s, 1 p, 3 s, 1 p, 3 s, 1 p, 3 s in sp of 9 ch, repeat. Use two oval embroidery rings for top. One under flap and one outside.

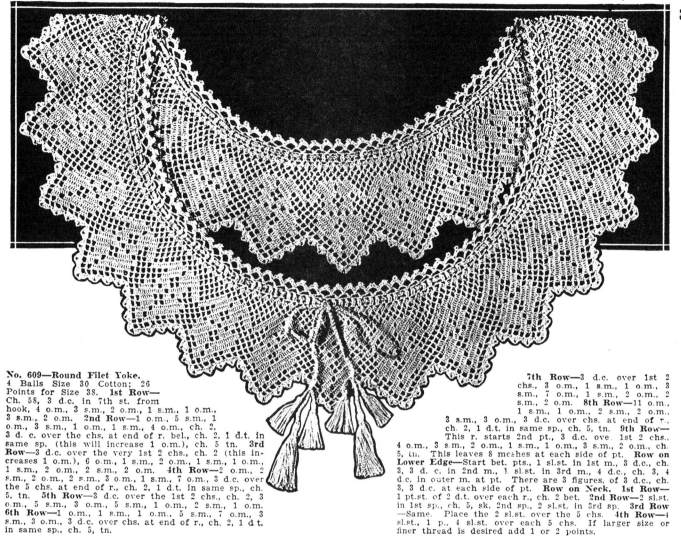

No. 609—Round Filet Yoke.
4 Balls Size 30 Cotton; 26
Points for Size 38. **1st Row**—
Ch. 58, 3 d.c. in 7th st. from
hook, 4 o.m., 3 s.m., 2 o.m., 1 s.m., 1 o.m.,
3 s.m., 2 o.m. **2nd Row**—1 o.m., 5 s.m., 1
o.m., 3 s.m., 1 o.m., 1 s.m., 4 o.m., ch. 2,
3 d.c. over the chs. at end of r. bel., ch. 2, 1 d.t. in
same sp. (this will increase 1 o.m.), ch. 5 tn. **3rd
Row**—3 d.c. over the very 1st 2 chs., ch. 2 (this in-
creases 1 o.m.), 6 o.m., 1 s.m., 2 o.m., 1 s.m., 1 o.m.,
1 s.m., 2 o.m., 2 s.m., 2 o.m. **4th Row**—2 o.m., 2
s.m., 2 o.m., 2 s.m., 3 o.m., 1 s.m., 7 o.m., 3 d.c. over
the 5 chs. at end of r., ch. 2, 1 d.t. in same sp., ch.
5, tn. **5th Row**—3 d.c. over the 1st 2 chs., ch. 2, 3
o.m., 5 s.m., 3 o.m., 5 s.m., 1 o.m., 2 s.m., 1 o.m.
6th Row—1 o.m., 1 s.m., 1 o.m., 5 s.m., 7 o.m., 3
s.m., 3 o.m., 3 d.c. over chs. at end of r., ch. 2, 1 d t.
in same sp., ch. 5, tn.

7th Row—3 d.c. over 1st 2
chs., 3 o.m., 1 s.m., 1 o.m., 3
s.m., 7 o.m., 1 s.m., 2 o.m., 2
s.m., 2 o.m. **8th Row**—11 o.m.,
1 s.m., 1 o.m., 2 s.m., 2 o.m.,
3 s.m., 3 o.m., 3 d.c. over chs. at end of r.,
ch. 2, 1 d.t. in same sp., ch. 5, tn. **9th Row**—
This r. starts 2nd pt., 3 d.c. ove 1st 2 chs.,
4 o.m., 3 s.m., 2 o.m., 1 s.m., 1 o.m., 3 s.m., 2 o.m., ch.
5, tn. This leaves 8 meshes at each side of pt. **Row on
Lower Edge**—Start bet. pts., 1 sl.st. in 1st m., 3 d.c., ch.
3, 3 d. c. in 2nd m., 1 sl.st. in 3rd m., 4 d.c., ch. 3, 4
d.c. in outer m. at pt. There are 3 figures, of 3 d.c., ch.
3, 3 d.c. at each side of pt. **Row on Neck. 1st Row**—
1 pt.st. of 2 d.t. over each r., ch. 2 bet. **2nd Row**—2 sl.st.
in 1st sp., ch. 5, sk. 2nd sp., 2 sl.st. in 3rd sp. **3rd Row**
—Same. Place the 2 sl.st. over the 5 chs. **4th Row**—4
sl.st., 1 p., 4 sl.st. over each 5 chs. If larger size or
finer thread is desired add 1 or 2 points.

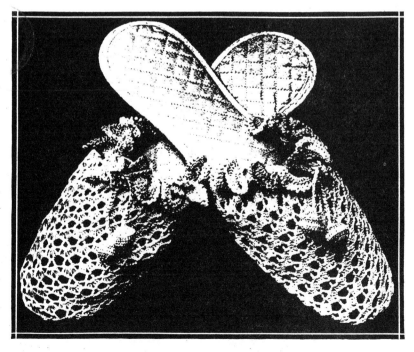

No 642—"Fluffy Mule"
Crochet Cotton, Size 25, 1 Ball—and 1 Spool Variegated Silkateen. Start
at right side of Slipper. **1st Row**—Ch. 14, 3 d.c. start in 4th st. from hook,
ch. 2, 3 d.c. in next 3 sts., ch. 1 sk. 1, 2 d.t. in next 2 sts., ch. 6, tn. **2nd
Row**—1 d.c., ch. 3, 1 d.c. over 1st d.c. bel., ch. 3, 1 d.c., ch. 3, 1 d.c. over 2
chs. bel., ch. 3, tn. **3rd Row**—3 d.c., ch. 2, 3 d.c. over 1st 3 chs. Same figure
over 2nd 3 chs., ch. 1, 2 d.t. over the 6 chs. Increase same way until there

No. 634—Napkin Ring
Cut goods the desired size and hem, sl.st. around.
2nd Row—(Start at pt.) ch. 5, 1 d.c. in next sl.st.,
ch. 2, 1 d.c. in next sl.st., ch. 2, 1 d.c. in next sl.st.,
ch. 2, 1 d.c. in 3rd sl.st., 3 at turn. **3rd Row**—10
sl.st. over the next 2 o.m., ch. 6, catch back into
5th sl.st., 10 sl.st. in loop of ch., 10 sl.st., ch. 6,
catch back into 5th sl.st., 10 sl.st. in loop of ch.

16 of these figures in one r. **Ruffle 1st Row**—4
sl.st. over each d.t., 4 sl.st. over the 6 chs. **2nd
Row**—2 d.c. in each st. **3rd Row**—1 d.c., ch. 1 over
each d. c. **4th Row**—Ch. 3 over each d.c. **Ornament 1st Row**—Ch. 4 form ring, 2 sl.st. in each st.
2nd Row—2 sl.st. in each of these 8 sts. **3rd Row**
—1 sl.st. in 1st sl.st., 2 sl.st. in 2nd sl.st., 1 sl.st. in
each one bel. for next 3 rows. Omit same way as
increasing is worked for last 3 rows. Fill out with
cotton before closing. Chain with 3 double threads
for cordeliere.

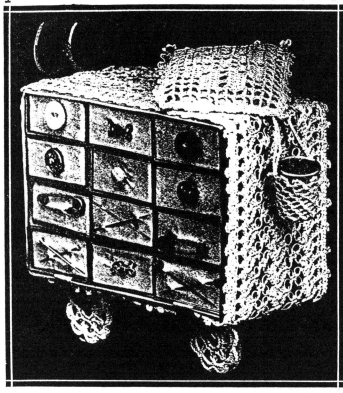

No. 620—Sewing Case

No. 30 Thread. **Insertion. 1st Row**—Ch. 40, 1 d.c. in 4th st. from hook, ch. 1, sk. 2, 3 d.c., ch. 2, 3 d.c., ch. 2, 3 d.c. in 4 sts., * 1 kn.st., sk. 5, 3 d.c., ch. 2, 3 d.c. in next 4 sts. * rep. once, ch. 1, sk. 1, 2 d.c., tn. **2nd Row**—Same as 1st r. **3rd Row**—1 d.c. over same, ch. 1, 3 d.c., ch. 2, 3 d.c. over 2 chs. in center, 1 sl.st. in 6th d.c., 1 kn.st., 1 sl.st. in 1st d.c. of next figure, 3 d.c., ch. 2, 3 d.c., 1 sl.st. in 6th d.c., 1 kn.st., rep. **Finishing Row at Side. 1st Row**—3 sl.st. over each r. **2nd Row**—4 sl.st. over same, 1 p., 4 sl.st. Insertion will be 15 1-2 in. long and is connected. **Thimble Holder. 1st Row**—Ch. 7, form ring, 22 d.c. in ring, close. **2nd Row**—Ch. 3, 1 sl.st., sk. 1, making 11 l.'s. Continue until there are 8 rows adding 1 ch.st. in each l. in 6th r. **9th Row**—Ch. 6 going back into 2nd st., ch. 2, 1 sl.st. in each l. A double ch. is used for holders. **Scissor Holder 1st Row**—Ch. 21, form ring, ch. 3, 1 d.c. in each st. **2nd Row**—Ch. 3, 1 sl.st., sk. 1, making 10 l.'s. Make 6 rows adding 1 ch.st. in each l. in last 2 rows. **9th Row**—2 sl.st., 1 p., 2 sl.st. in each l. A double ch. is used for holders. **Medallion on Wheel 1st Row**—Ch. 8, form r., 16 sl.st. in ring. **2nd Row**—Ch. 4, sk. 1, 1 d.c., * ch. 4, 1 d.c. in same st., sk. 1, 1 d.c., * 6 times. **3rd Row**—1 sl.st., 1 s.c., 5 d.c., 1 s.c., 1 sl.st. over each 4 chs. **Pin Cushion**—Ch. 44. **1st and 2nd Rows**—13 o.m. **3rd Row**—4 o.m., 2 s.m., 1 o.m., 2 s.m., 4 o.m. **4th Row** —Same as 3rd r. **5th Row**—2 o.m., 2 s.m., 1 o.m., 1 s.m., 1 o.m., 1 s.m., 1 o.m., 2 s.m., 2 o.m. **6th Row**—2 o.m., 3 s.m., 3 o.m., 3 s.m., 2 o.m. **7th Row**—6 o.m., 1 s.m., 6 o.m. Rep. in opp. direction. **Finishing Row. 1st Row**—3 sl.st. in each m., add 3 at cor. **2nd Row**—4 sl.st. over same, 1 p. Glue 12 small match boxes together, 3 rows of four each. Wind string around, let dry 24 hours. Requires 3 1-2 yds. ribbon as wide as height of box and 1-2 yd. the length of box. Sew narrow ribbon around each box. Sew on front of box whatever they will contain. Place lining, wide ribbon and insertion around whole case. Glue medallions in front of spools, which are used as wheels. These are tied with ribbon to the two lower boxes on each side. Fasten cushion on top and scissors and thimble holder at each side.

No. 617—Hot Roll Cover.

No. 50 Thread. **1st Row**—o. m. in linen, 3 o.m. over cor. **2nd Row**—3 d.c., 3 p., 3 d.c., ch. 1, sk. 1 o.m., sk. 2 over curve.

No. 633—"Heart Satchet."

1st Row—Ch. 53, 1 d. c. in 8th st. from hook, 23 o.m. in all, ch. 5, tn. **2nd Row**—Same. **3rd Row**—Begins design, follow pattern. **Edging**—3 sl.st. bet. each o.m. and 7 o.m., turn.

No. 621—Collar Bag

4 Balls, Size 10 Cotton. **Bottom. 1st Row**—Ch. 10, form ring, ch. 3, 28 d.c. in ring, j. **2nd Row**—Ch. 5, sk. 1, 3 d.c., * ch. 2, 3 d.c. * 5 times (there must be 3 d.c. 7 times). **3rd Row**—Ch. 5, sk. 2 chs., 5 d.c. over 3 d.c. (that is 2 d.c. in 1st and 2 d.c. in last d.c. bel.), ch. 2, rep. around. **4th Row**—Ch. 5, sk. 2 chs., 8 d.c. over 5 d.c. (that is 2 d.c. in 1st, 3rd and 5th d.c.), ch. 2, rep. **5th Row**—Ch. 5, sk. 2 chs., 10 d.c. over 8 d.c. (that is 2 d.c. in 1st and last d. c. bel.), ch. 2, rep. In this way 5th r is increased. Continue until 18 rows are worked. **19th Row**—14 o.m. over each one of the 7 parts. **20th Row** —3 sl.st. in each m. Fasten thread. **Filet and Upper Part. 1st Row** —Ch. 56, work 2 rows of 17 o.m. Then follow design. Work the 2 designs 5 times, then 1 r. of 17 o.m., j. **Lower Edge. 1st Row**—3 d.c. in each m. **2nd Row**—4 d.c. over same, sk. 5th d.c. Sew to bottom. **Upper Part 1st Row**—3 d.c. in each one of 4 o.m., 2 d.c. in 5th o.m. **2nd Row**—1 d.c. over same. **3rd Row**—2 d.c. in one st., ch. 4, sk. 4. **4th Row**—Same, placing the 2 d.c. over the 4 chs. Continue until there are 15 of these rows. **Edging. 1st Row**—4 d.c. over 4 chs., ch. 2 over 2 d.c. **2nd Row**—Ch. 7 going back into 2nd st., ch. 2, 1 sl.st. over 2 chs., sk. 4 d.c. **Cord**—Ch. with 3 double thread. **Ornaments. 1st Row**—Ch. 5, form ring, 2 sl.st. in each st. **2nd Row**—2 sl.st. in each st. Work 7 rows without increasing, fill with cotton, then 2 rows omitting same way as increasing is made.

No. 600—Filet "Butterfly" Towel

No. 30 Thread. **1st Row**—Ch. 38, 11 o.m.
2nd Row—11 o.m., ch. 10, tn. **3rd Row**—2
o.m. over the 10 chs., 3 o.m., 2 s.m., 6 o.m.
4th Row—5 o.m., 1 s.m., 2 o.m., 3 o.m.,
ch. 10, tn. **5th Row**—2 o.m. over the 10 chs.,
2 o.m., 1 s.m., 5 o.m., 1 s.m., 4 o.m. **6th Row**—
4 o.m., 1 s.m., 1 o.m., 1 s.m., 1 o.m., 1 s.m.,
1 o.m., 1 s.m., 4 o.m., ch. 10, tn. **7th Row**—
2 o.m. over the 10 chs., 1 o.m., 1 s.m., 1 o.m.,
1 s.m., 3 o.m., 1 s.m., 2 o.m., 1 s.m., 4 o.m.
8th Row—2 o.m., 1 s.m., 1 o.m., 1 s.m., 3 o.m.,
1 s.m., 1 o.m., 1 s.m., 1 o.m., 1 s.m., 1 o.m.,
1 s.m., 2 o.m. **9th Row**—2 o.m., 1 s.m., 6 o.m.,
1 s.m., 1 o.m., 1 s.m., 2 o.m., 1 s.m., 2 o.m.
10 Row—3 o.m., 2 s.m., 1 o.m., 1 s.m., 4 o.m.,
1 s.m., 2 o.m., 1 s.m., 2 o.m. **11th Row**—3 o.m.,
1 s.m., 3 o.m., 3 s.m., 1 o.m., 1 s.m., 5 o.m.
12th Row—6 o.m., 7 s.m., 4 o.m. Rep. in opp.
direction. **Finishing Row. 1st Row**—3 sl.st.
in each m. **2nd Row**—1 sl.st. over same, 1 p.
over each pt., 5 sl.st. bet. each of the 6 p.
over scallop.

No. 601—Shell Towel Edge.

No. 30 Thread. **1st Row**—Ch. 28, 1 sl.st. in
10th st. from hook, * ch. 7, sk. 6, 1 sl. st., *
rep. once, ch. 6, sk. 5, 1 sl.st., ch. 3, tn. **2nd
Row**—15 d.c. over 1st l., ch. 2, 1 sh. st. of 7
d.c. in center ch. st. of 2nd l., 1 loose ch.st.,
1 sh.st. in center ch.st. of 3rd l., ch. 4, 1 sl.st
in 5th ch.st. of last l., ch. 9, tn. **3rd Row**—
1 sl.st. over 1st d.c. of sh.st., ch. 4, 1 sh.st. in
the loose ch.st., ch. 4, 1 sl.st. in last d.c. of last
sh.st., ch. 2, 1 d.c. in 1st d.c. bel., ch. 1, 5 pt.st.
(of 3 d.c. each) over 15 d.c., ch. 4 bet. each,
ch. 6, tn. **4th Row**—Ch. 5 over each 4 ch., 1
sl.st., 1 d.c. over same bel., ch. 4, 1 sl.st. over
4 chs., ch. 7, 1 sl.st. over 2nd 4 chs. forming l.
over sh.st., ch. 7 to end of r., ch. 9, tn. **5th
Row**—* Ch. 7 (making 4th st. very loose), 1
sl.st. * rep. once, ch. 2, 1 d.c. over same, ch.
6, 1 sl.st. in 2nd l. bel. **Heading**—6 sl.st. in
each sp.

No 602—"Wave" Towel.

No. 30 Thread. **1st Row**—1 r. of o.m. in
linen. **2nd Row**—3 sl.st., ch. 1, 3 sl.st. over 1st
2 spaces, sk. 3rd and 4th sps., ch. 6. **3rd Row**
—14 d.c. over 6 chs., 1 sl.st. over the 1 ch.st.
4th Row—5 sl.st. over 5 d.c. in center of scallop, ch. 7, 1 tr.t. in last sl.st., 5 sl.st. over next
scallop. **5th Row**—16 d.c. over the 7 chs., 1
sl.st. over 3rd sl.st. bel. **6th Row**—Same as
4th R. 6 sl.st. instead of 5. **7th Row**—2 sl.st.
over 3rd and 4th sl.st. bel., 3 d.c., 4 p. with 3
d.c. bet. each over each 7 chs.

No 603—Insertion Towel.

No. 30 Thread. **1st Row**—Ch. 52, 1 d.c. in
4th st. from hook, ch. 2, sk. 2, 1 d.c., ch. 5,
sk. 5, 4 d.c. with 2 chs. bet. each in next st.,
ch. 5, sk. 5, 1 o.m., ch. 7 sk. 7. Rep. in opp.
direction. At end of r., 2 d.c., ch. 3, tn. **2nd
Row**—1 d.c. over same, 1 o.m., ch. 3, 1 sl.st.
over 5 chs., 4 d.c. in 1st sp., 3 d.c., ch. 1, 3
d.c. in 2nd sp., 4 d.c. in 3rd sp., 1 sl.st. over
next 5 chs., ch. 3, 1 o.m., 7 d.c. in (not over)
the 7 ch. sts., 1 o.m. Rep. in opp. direction.

NO. 605—MINT BASKET SHOWN ON FRONT COVER.

No. 30 Thread. **Upper Part. 1st Row**—Ch. 19, 15 d.c. start
in 4th st. from hook, ch. 3, tn. **2nd Row**—2 d.c., ch. 3, sk. 3,
3 d.c., ch. 3, sk. 3, 4 d.c., ch. 3, tn. **3rd Row**—15 d.c., that is
1 d.c. in each st. **4th Row**—Same as 2nd r. **5th Row**—Same
as 3rd r. **6th Row**—Same as 2nd r., then * ch. 3, 1 d.c. over
the 3 ch.sts. of r. bel. * twice, ch. 3, fasten on 3rd r., ch. 2,
fasten again, tn. **7th Row**—5 d.c. in 1st, 2nd and 3rd sp., 6
d.c. in 4th sp., 15 d.c., ch. 3, tn. **8th Row**—Same as 2nd r.,
then ch. 2, sk. 2 over scallop, * 1 d.t., ch. 3, 1 d.t. in next st.,
ch. 2, sk. 2, * sk. 3 after 2nd and 4th figure, making 6 figures
in all, ch. 2, fasten with 2 sl.st. on 1st r., tn. **9th Row**—3 d.c.,
ch. 3, 3 d.c. over each 3 chs., 1 sl.st. over each 2 chs., ch. 2,
15 d.c. Connect 1st and last little pt. Work 8 scallops for
basket. Join and sew to bottom. **Bottom 1st Row**—Ch. 55,
1 sl.st. in each st., 3 sl.st. in 1st and last ch.st.; going back on
other side by working same. **2nd Row**—Ch. 1, tn. (The turn-

ing after each r. gives rib effect), 2 sl.st. over same taking up
back thread, 3 sl.st. in 3rd sl.st., 1 sl.st. in each st., 3 sl.st. in
3rd last sl.st., 2 sl.st., over same, 3 sl.st. in last sl.st. Rep. same over
other side. **3rd Row**—Ch. 1, tn., 1 sl.st. over same taking up back
thread, 3 sl.st. in center sl.st. of every increasing. Continue
until there are 5 of these rows. Now increase in every other
r. only until there are 11 r. Fasten thread. **Handle. 1st Row**—
Ch. 11, 2 d.c. start in 4th st. from hook, ch. 2, sk. 2, 3 d.c., ch.
3, tn. **2nd Row**—7 d.c., ch. 3, tn. Continue to desired length
and sew to basket. **Wild Rose**—Pink, Green and Yellow Silkateen. **Petals of Pink. 1st Row**—Ch. 4, 6 d.c. in 1st ch.st. **2nd
Row**—Ch. 3, 10 d.c. over 6 d.c. **3rd Row**—Ch. 3, 6 d.c. over 1st
4 d.c., 2 s.c. over next 2 d.c., 6 d.c. over last 4 d.c., ch. 2, 1
sl.st. in r. bel. Fasten thread. Work 5 of these petals. **Calyx
of Green. 1st Row**—Ch. 4, form ring, 2 sl.st. in each ch.st.
2nd Row—2 sl.st. in each one bel. **3rd Row**—1 sl.st. over each
one bel. Work 3 more rows without increasing. **Center of
Yellow. 1st Row**—Ch. 4, form ring, 2 sl.st. in each ch.st. **2nd
Row**—2 sl.st. in each one bel. **3rd Row**—1 sl.st. in 1st sl.st., 2
sl.st. in 2nd sl.st. Wind green silkateen over wire for stems,
form hook of same, place in calyx, fill out with cotton, place
petals around and sew on.

No 612—Utility Bag

Five Spools White and 1 spool Colored Silkateen. 9-Inch Oval Hoop. **1st Row**—Ch. 10, form r., ch. 3, 23 d.c. in r., close. **2nd Row**—24 d.c., ch. 1 bet. each. **3rd Row**—48 d.c., ch. 1 bet. each. **4th Row**—1 d.c. in each st., making 96 d.c. **5th Row**—2 d.c., ch. 3, sk. 2, rep. 23 times. **6th Row**—Same as 5th r., increasing 2 d.c. and 3 chs., 3 times, making 2 d.c., 27 times. **7th Row**—2 d.c., ch. 3. Do not increase in this r. **8th Row**—Increase 2 d.c., 4 times, always increasing in center of increasing bel. (2 d.c., 31 times). **9th Row**—2 d.c., 35 times. **10th-11th Rows**—(Colored Thread). Same as 9th r. (Do not increase). **12-13-14-15-16th Rows**—(White Thread) worked the same but increasing in each r. and ending with the 16th r. of 2 d.c., 46 times. **17th Row**—(Colored Thread) 2 d.t., ch. 3, 2 d.t., ch. 8 over every other sp., making 23 of these figures. **18th Row**—2 d.t., ch. 3, 2 d.t., ch. 7. **19th Row**—2 d.t., ch. 3, 2 d.t., ch. 4 taking up the chs. of the 2 rs. bel. with 1 sl.st., ch. 4. Repeat these 3 rows twice in white; once in blue; then 3 times in white. **1st Upper Row**—1 sl.st. over 1st 3 chs., ch. 8 to next 3 chs. **2nd Row**—10 sl.st. over each 8 chs. **Upper Edge. 1st Row**—Ch. 15, 1 d.c. in 4th st. from hook, ch. 2, 1 d.c., ch. 5, tn. **2nd Row**—1 d.c. over same, ch. 2, 8 d.c. in 3rd sp. bel. ch. 2, 2 d.c. **Finishing Row.**—**1st Row**—1 sl.st. in 1st l. of 5 chs., ch. 2, 8 d.t. with 1 ch. bet. each in 2nd l., ch. 2. **2nd Row**—Ch. 3 over each d.t. On upper edge, ch. 1 p., 2 sl.st. Wind tape over hoop, sew bag to this. For strings ch. to desired length with double thread, fasten over hoop, then sew edging over it. **Tassel**—Wind thread over 3 fingers about 28 times, draw last thread thru all with hook, leaving loop on top. Wind thread tightly about 5 times,, 1-4 inch from top of tassel and cut.

No. 614—Pin Cushion Top.
1st Row—Ch. 6, form r., ch. 6, 15 d.t. with 2 ch. bet. each in r. Close. **2nd Row**—3 sl.st. in every sp. **3rd Row**—Ch. 5, 3 d.t. in 3 sts. (Keep last loop of thread on hook, pull thread thru all), ch. 6, 4 d.t. in next 4 sts., ch. 6, rep. 10 times. **4th Row**—9 sl.st. over each l. **5th Row**—Work thread up to center of 1st l., ch. 8, 1 sl.st. in center of next l., rep. 11 times. **6th Row**—Ch. 3, 12 d.c. in each l. **7th Row**—3 d.c., ch. 3, sk. 3, making 3 d.c. 24 times. **8th Row**—3 d.c. over 3 ch., ch. 4 over every 3 d.c. **9th Row**—3 d.c., ch. 3, 3 d.c. over every 4 chs. **10th Row**—3 d.c. over same, 3 d.c., ch. 3, 3 d.c. over 3 chs. in center, 3 d.c. over same (making 18 d.c. and 3 chs). **11th Row**—1 d.c. over each one bel., 3 d.c., ch. 3, 3 d.c. over 3 chs. in center (making 18 d.c. in this r.). **12th Row**—10 p. over 18 d.c. Connect 11th p. with 2nd one; this forms upper pt. with 8 p., 10 p. over next 18 d.c.; this forms lower pt. Connect 11th p with the 2nd last of upper pt.; this leaves 8 p. for lower pt.

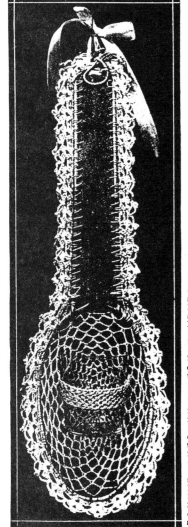

No. 636—Match Holder
Requires 1 Ball Size 30 Cotton and An Egg Beater. **Center of Spoon. 1st Row**—Tie thread close to handle, ch. 5, 1 sl.st. around wire, ch. 5, 1 sl.st. around wire, continue around. Make 6 rows same as 1st row, using a sl.st. in center of each ch. **8th Row**—Ch. 4, 1 sl.st. in center. **9th Row**—Same. **10th Row**—Ch. 3, 1 sl.st. in center. **11th Row**—Same. **12th Row**—Ch. 2, 1 sl.st. in center, ch. 1, sl.st. on both sides bringing both sides together. **Outside of Wire. 1st Row**—Tie thread at top, ch. 3, 1 sl.st. all around. **2nd Row**—Ch. 3, 1 d.c. in loop of ch., 2 d.c. in same loop, ch. 1, 1 d.c. in next loop, ch. 1, 2 d.c. in next loop, ch. 2, 2 d.c. in same loop, rep. around. **3rd Row**—Ch. 3, 2 d.c. in the center of the 2 ch., ch. 2, 3 d.c. in same place, ch. 1, 3 d.c. in the 2 chs. of next loop, ch. 2, 3 d.c. in same place, rep. around. **4th Row**—Ch. 5, 1 sl.st. under the 2 chs., ch. 5, 1 sl.st. in same place, ch. 5, 1 sl.st. bet. next shell, rep. around. **Band. 1st Row**—Ch. 3, 1 sl.st., ch. 3, 1 sl.st., ch. 5, tn. **2nd Row**—Ch. 3, 1 sl.st. in each loop, ch. 3, 1 sl.st., ch. 5, tn. Continue until length desired.

No 626—Wishbone Thimble Holder.
1 Spool Silkateen. **1st Row**—42 d.c. over each side of bone. **2nd Row**—2 d.c., ch. 2, sk. 2. Do not sk. any over pt. **3rd Row**—2 d.c. over same, 2 d.c. in sp., 3 d.c. in 3 sps. over pt. **4th Row**—1 d.c., ch. 3, 1 d.c. in same st., sk. 3. **5th Row**—Ch. 1, 1 sl.st. in 1st sp., 4 d.c. with 1 p. bet. each in 2nd sp. **Thimble Holder 1st Row**—Ch. 5, form ring, 2 sl.st. in each st. **2nd Row**—2 sl.st. in each st. **3rd Row**—1 sl.st. over 1st sl.st. 2 sl.st. in 2nd sl.st. **4th Row**—1 sl.st. in each st. **5th Row**—Same. **6th Row**—Increase 1 sl.st. in every 5th st. **7th Row**—1 sl.st. in each st. Continue working 7th row until there are 12 rows. **13th Row**—Ch 3, sk. 2, 1 sl.st. **14th Row**—Same, placing the sl.st. over the 3 chs. **15th Row**—Ch. 6, going back into 2nd st., ch. 2, 1 sl.st. in l. bel. Sew bet. wishbone. Chain with 3 double thread for cord.

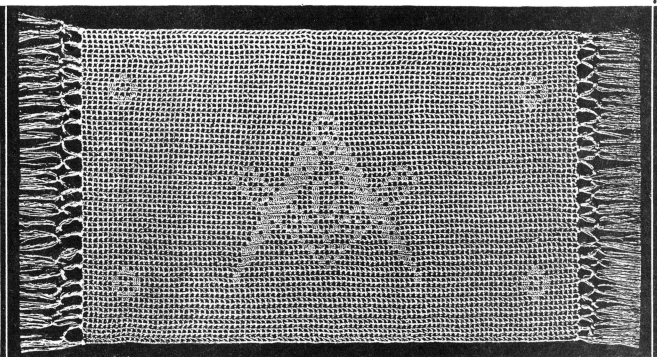

No. 643—Masonic Cushion
Crochet Cotton, Size 20, 5 Balls. Ch. 191—5 rows of 62 o.m. Follow design. **Fringe**—Cut cotton into strands 6 inches long, fold 10 strands in center and pull thru m. with hook from wrong side, make ch. and pull out. Knot fringe as shown in cut.

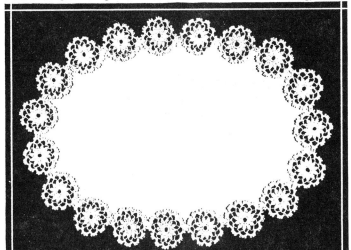

No. 646—Tray Cloth
Size 40 Cotton. **1st Row**—Ch. 10, form ring, 24 sl.st. in ring. **2nd Row**—Ch. 5, 1 pt.st. of 4 tr.t. in every 2 sts., ch. 7 bet. pt.st. **3rd Row**—Work thread to center of 1st l., * ch. 7, 2 sl.st. in next l. * 11 times. **4th Row**—4 sl.st., ch. 4, 2 sl.st., ch. 4, 2 sl.st., ch. 4, 4 sl.st over every l. of 7 chs. Connect medallions on 2 p. of 6th pt. leaving 3rd p. on outer edge unconnected.

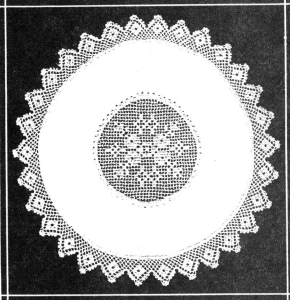

No. 651—Doilie With Filet Center—12 Inches Diameter.
Size 50 Cotton, 1 Ball. Filet center worked first. Ch. 26, 7 o.m., follow pattern. Increase 2 o.m. at each side for each one of the next 3 rows; increase 1 o.m. at each side in each r. from 4th to 8th r.; increase 1 o.m. in every other r. at each side until there are 14 rows. Then 7 rows of 35 m. Omit same way as increasing is made. **Picot Edge 1st Row**—3 sl.st. in each m. **2nd Row**—5 sl.st. over same, 1 p., 5 sl.st. Roll outer edge of linen bet. fingers and sl.st. over roll. **Edging. 1st—Row**—Ch. 21, 5 o.m. **2nd Row**—5 o.m. over same, ch. 2, 1 d.t. in st. of last d.c. **3rd Row**—Ch. 6, 1 d.c. over every 1st 2 chs., 2 o.m. over same, 3 s.m., 1 o.m. **4th Row**—1 o.m., 1 s.m., 1 o.m., 1 s.m., 3 o.m., ch. 2, 1 d.t., ch. 6, tn. **5th Row**—1 d.c. over the 1st 2 chs., 4 o.m., 3 s.m., 1 o.m. **6th Row**—9 o.m., ch. 2, 1 d.t. **Finishing Row**—2 sl.st. in 1st and 2nd m., 3 p. with 2 sl.st. bet. each over next 3 m., ch. 3, 4 d.c. with 1 p. bet. each in center m., ch. 3. Sew on sl.st. row.

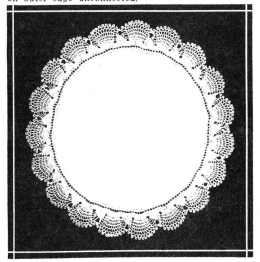

No. 650—Plate Doilie.
Crochet Cotton, Size 40, 1 Ball. Cut linen 8 1-2 inches in diameter. **1st Row**—1 d.c., ch. 2, 1 d.c. (189 meshes). **2nd Row**—3 d.t. in 1st m., 4 d.t. in 2nd m. **3rd Row**—Each design requires 35 d.t., making 19 designs. 11 sl.st. in 11 sts., ch. 5, sk. 5, 14 d.c. in 14 sts., ch. 5, sk. 5. **4th Row**—9 sl.st. over 11 sl.st., sk. 1st and last one, ch. 6, 13 d.c. over 14 d.c., start bet. 1st and 2nd d.c., ch. 1 bet. each ch. 6. **5th Row**—7 sl.st. over 9 sl.st., ch. 7, 12 d.c. over 13 d.c. (same way), ch. 1 bet. each ch. 7. **6th Row**—5 sl.st. over 7 sl.st., ch. 8, 11 d.c. over 12 d.c. (same way), ch. 2 bet. each, ch. 8. **7th Row**—3 sl.st. over 5 sl.st., ch. 8, 10 d.c. over 11 d.c., ch. 3 bet. each, ch. 8. **8th Row**—Work thread up on ch. with 4 sl.st., ch. 7 back to 2nd st., ch. 2, 1 sl.st. over every 3 chs., ch. 6 back to 2nd st., ch. 1 bet. pts.

8

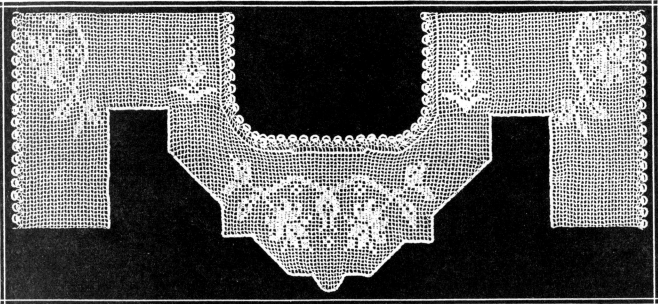

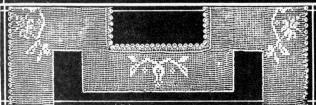

No. 635—Gladiola Gown Yoke.
Crichet Cotton, Size 30, 6 Balls. **1st Row**—Ch. 37, 1 d.c. in 8th st. from hook, ch. 2, 1 d.c. in 3rd ch., 11 o.m. in all, ch. 6, tn. **2nd Row**—1 d.c. in 1st d.c. of 1st r. continue to end making 12 o.m. in 2nd r., ch. 5, tn. **3rd Row**—Continue o.m. for 15 rows, increase 1 o.m. each r. Note.—At the end of r. always ch. 2, thread twice over hook and catch back in last

d.c. of last r., ch. 6. Always ch. 6 on increase side. On the decrease side work up to within the last o.m., t.c. in last d.c., ch. 3, tn., then 1 d.c. in next d. c. of last r. Follow pattern. Shoulder Strap, are 15 m. wide, continue for 48 rows, following pattern. Back of yoke is 21 m. wide, work same pattern as front and continue until you have 89 m. long. Join to back with sl.st. Sleeves—Tie thread where shoulder straps join front of yoke and make 48 o.m. for 1st row. **2nd Row**—Same, until you have 18 rows of o.m., then ch. 179, tn. **19th Row**—Make 108 o.m. Start design on 20th r., making 25 rows in wide part of sleeve. **Edging—1st Row**—Ch. 5, 1 d.c. in center of o.m., ch. 3, 1 sl.st. in top of 2nd d.c., ch. 3, 1 d.c. in center of 2nd o.m., sk. 3 o.m. bet. each loop. Making 36 loops on outside of sleeve. **2nd Row**—Ch. 3, 5 d.c. in loop (3 chs. make 6 in all), ch. 6, catch back in the 3 chs., then make 10 sl.st. in the ch., ch. 4, 1 sl.st. on top of sl.st., ch. 4, 6 d.c. in next loop and continue around. **Beading—1st Row**—1 sl.st. around inside of yoke, 3 sl.st. bet. each o.m. and 5 sl.st. at turn. **2nd Row**—Ch. 6, 1 t.c. in 3 sl.st., ch. 2, 1 t.c. in the next 3rd st., continue around. Edging, same as above.

No. 610—Tie Rack—Ecru.
Crochet Cotton, Size 10, 3 Balls. Ch. 44. 2 rows of 13 o.m., follow design, 2 rows of 13 o.m., ch. 29, make 8 o.m. over this ch., 13 o.m. over same, make a ch. of 27 of second ball of thread, connect on r. bel. and work 9 o.m. over this new ch. Work 30 o.m. over all and follow design which cover 45 rows. Fasten thread. Start over 10th o.m. with 13 o.m. and rep. small square. **1st Finishing Row**—3 d.c. in each m., 9 d.c. in cor. m., sk. 2 m. on concave corners. **2nd Row**—1 d.c. in each st., 4 d.c. in d.c. over cor., sk. 6 d.c. on concave corners. **Hanger—1st Row**—Ch. 180, 1 d.c. in each st., 3 d.c. in 60th st. and 3 d.c. in 120th st. **2nd Row**—1 d.c. in each st., 4 d.c. in cor. d.c.

No 618—Fancy Tea Apron.
Size 50 Cotton. **1st Row**—Ch. 9, form ring, ch. 4, * 3 d.t., ch. 3 in ring * twice, 3 d.t., ch. 1, 1 d.t., ch. 4, tn. **2nd Row**—3 d.t., ch. 3, 3 d.t. over 1st 3 chs., ch. 2, 3 d.t., ch. 4, 3 d.t. over 2nd 3 chs., ch. 2, 3 d.t., ch. 3, 3 d.t. over 3rd 3 chs., 1 d.t. in end of 1st r., ch. 4, tn. **3rd Row**—3 d.t., ch. 3, 3 d.t., ch. 3, 3 d.t. over 1st 3 chs., ch. 4, 1 sl.st. over 2 chs., 1 d.c., 11 d.t., 1 d.c. over 4 chs., 1 sl.st., rep. all but center figure in opp. direction, 1 d.t. in 2nd r., ch. 4, tn. **4th Row**—3 d.t., ch. 3, 3 d.t. over 1s* 3 chs., ch. 2, 3 d.t., ch. 4, 3 d.t. over 2nd

3 chs., ch. 1, 1 pt.st. of 2 d.t. over 4 chs., ch. 1, 3 d.t., ch. 4, 3 d.t. over center st. of scallop, rep. in opp. direction, 1 d.t. in r. bel., ch. 4, tn. **5th Row**—3 d.t., ch. 3, 3 d.t. over 1st 3 chs., ch. 4, 1 sl.st. over 2 chs., then same larger scallops over 4 chs., 3 sl.st. over next 3 sts., large scallop in center, rep. all in opp. direction, 1 d.t. in r. bel., ch. 5, tn. **6th Row**—2 sl.st. over 1st 3 chs., ch. 5, 2 sl.st. over 3 center sts. of large scallop, ch. 6, 1 pt.st. of 2 d.t. over center sl.st. in r. bel., ch. 6, 3 sl.st. over center scallop, rep. in opp. direction, ch. 3, tn. **7th Row**—6 d.c. in 1st sp., 7 d.c. in 2nd sp., 12 d.c. in each one of the next 6 sps., 7 d.c. in 2nd last and last sp., ch. 1, tn. **8th Row**—slst. over 1st 6 sts., ch. 8, sk. 9, 1 sl.st., ch. 8, sk. 9, 1 sl.st., tn., 4 sl.st., ch. 8, p. 8 sl.st. in 1st l., 6 sl.st. in 2nd l., ch. 8, fasten over 1st l., 4 sl.st., 1 p., 3 sl.st., 1 p., 3 sl.st., 1 p., 4 sl.st. in this l., 2 sl.st., 1 p., 4 sl.st. in remaining l., fasten with 1 tight sl.st. **9th Row**—Ch. 14, 1 sl.st., in center p., ch. 14, fasten on other side of scallop. **10th Row**—8 sl.st. (going up again), ch. 6 for leaf (making 2nd st. loosely), * 3 d.t. in the loose st., ch. 3, 1 sl.st. * (this forms 1 petal), twice, all in loose ch.st. 1 sl.st. over remaining ch. st. for stem, 8 sl.st. to top of scallop, work same leaf and rep. all over other side, 3 tight sl.st. over same, another leaf in last 2 sl.st. Work 5 sl.st over r. of d.c., 3 sl.st., 1 p., in every sp. over upper 2 sides of medallion, then 5 sl.st. and leaf at opp. end of leaf last made. Fasten thread. Start at left side, count 10 sts. from center st. of medallion, 1 sl.st., ch. 8 and work pt. in center same way as 1st st., ch. 8, 1 sl.st., tn. 6 sl.st., 1 p., 6 sl.st. for the 2 connecting l.'s bet. pts. **Edge—1st Row**—o.m. in linen (1 d.c., ch. 2, sk. 2, 1 d.c.). **2nd Row**—3 sl.st. in each m. **3rd Row**—1 sl.st., ch. 3, sk. 3, 1 d.c., ch. 3, 1 d.c. in next st., * ch. 6, sk. 7, 1 d.c., ch. 3, 1 d.c. in next st. * around. **4th Row**—1 sl.st. over the 6 chs. in center sl.st. of 2nd r., ch. 3, 1 sl.st., 1 s.c., 5 d.c., 1 s.c., 1 sl.st. in l. of 3 chs., ch. 2.

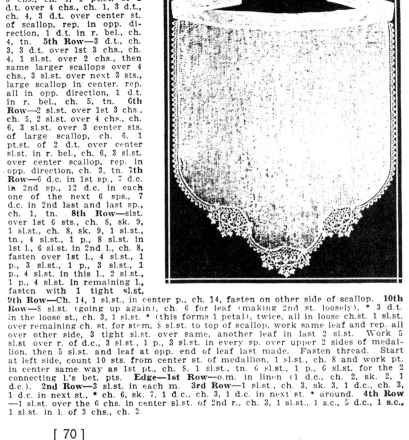

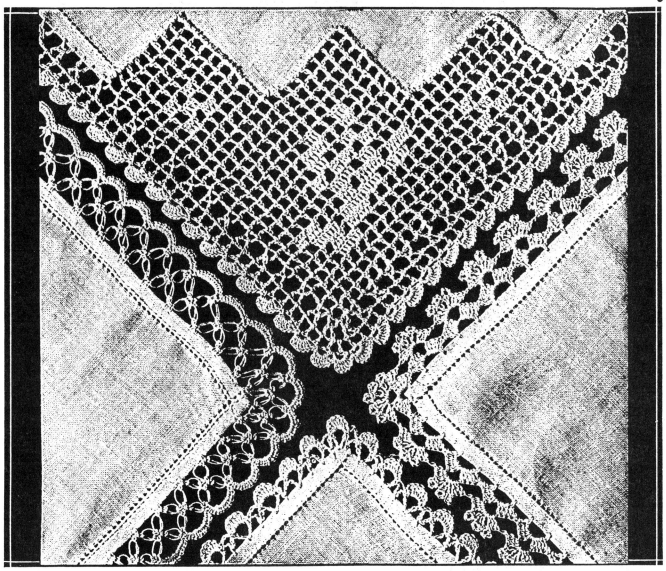

No. 622—Knot Stitch Kerchief Edge.
Size 70 Cotton Used on These Kerchiefs.
1st Row—2 sl.st., 1 kn.st. in linen, sk. 1-3 in. **2nd Row**—1 kn.st. over same. **3rd Row**—Ch. 7, 2 sl.st. over kn.st. **4th Row**—13 sl.st. over each 7 chs.

No 623—Shell Picot Kerchief Edge.
1st Row—1 sl.st. in linen, ch. 5, sk. 1-3 in. **2nd Row**—1 sl.st. in 1st l., 4 d.c., ch. 4, 4 d.c. in 2nd l. **3rd Row**—3 d.c., 1 p., 1 d.c., 1 p., 1 d.c., 1 p., 3 d.c. over 4 chs., ch. 1 to next pt.

No. 624—Filet Corner and Kerchief Edging.
1st Row—Ch. 80, 25 o.m. **2nd Row**—Same. Follow design for 8 rows of 25 meshes. **9th Row**—16 meshes. Work 8 rows of 16 meshes. **17th Row**—8 meshes. Work 9 rows of 8 meshes. Place over corner of handkerchief, sew on with buttonhole stiches. **Edging. 1st Row**—1 X.st., ch. 2, 2 X.sts. over cor. m. **2nd Row**—1 o.m. over X.st., add 1 o.m. at cor. **3rd Row**—1 sl.st. in 1st m., 1 d.c. in 2nd m., ch. 2, 6 d.c. over d.c. just made, fasten with 1 sl.st.

No. 625—Shell Kerchief Edge
1st Row—1 d.c., ch. 4, 1 d.c. in same st. in linen, sk. 1-5 in., ch. 3, 1 sl.st., ch. 3. **2nd Row**—1 sl.st., 1 s.c., 5 d.c., 1 s.c., 1 sl.st. in l. of 4 chs., ch. 3 to next l.

INSTRUCTIONS FOR NO. 604 AND 606 SHOWN ON FRONT COVER.

No 604—Bon Bon Basket.
No. 30 Thread. **1st Row**—Ch. 8, form ring, ch. 3, 23 d.c. in ring, j. **2nd Row**—Ch. 5, sk. 1, 11 d.c. with 2 chs. bet. each. **3rd Row**—Ch. 3, 5 d.c. in each sp. **4th Row**—Ch. 3, 1 d.c., ch. 2, 2 d.c. in one st. **5th Row**—Ch. 3, 5 d.c. in each sp. **6th Row**—Ch. 4, sk. 1, 1 d.c., ch. 1, sk. 2, 1 d.c., ch. 1, sk. 1, 1 d.c. Count 40 sps. **7th Row**—1 d.c. in 1st sp., sk. 2nd sp., 3 d.c., ch. 2, 3 d.c. in 3rd sp., sk. 4th sp. **8th Row**—1 d.c. over same, ch. 1, 3 d.c., ch. 2, 3 d.c. over same, ch. 1. **9th Row**—1 d.c. over same, ch. 1, 3 d.c., ch. 3, 3 d.c. over same, ch. 1. **10th Row**—1 d.c. over same, ch. 1, 3 d.c., ch. 5, 3 d.c. over same, ch. 1. **11th Row**—Turn working this row the other way. 1 sl.st. over 1 d.c., ch. 1, 4 d.c., 1 p., 3 d.c., 1 p., 4 d.c. over the 5 chs., ch. 1, 1 sl.st. over 1 d.c. **Handle 1st Row**—Ch. 80, 25 o.m. **2nd Row**—3 sl.st. in each m., 8 sl.st. in 1st and last m. **3rd Row**—4 d.c. over same, 1 p., sk. 1.

No. 606—Ball Holder
Size 40, 2 Balls. **1st Row**—Ch. 11, form ring, ch. 3, 30 d.c. in ring. **2nd Row**—Ch. 5, 14 d.c. with 2 chs. bet. each, sk. 1. **3rd Row**—Ch. 3, 63 d.c. in sps. **4th Row**—Ch. 6, sk. 1, 1 d.c., ch. 2, 4 d.c. over same, * 2, sk. 1, 1 d.c., ch. 1, 1 d.c., ch. 2, sk. 1, 4 d.c. * 5 times over 63 d.c. (this forms 7 parts of bottom). **5th Row**—1 sl.st., ch. 6, 1 d.c. in same sp., ch. 2, 8 d.c. over 4 d.c. (that is add 2 d.c. at each side), ch. 2, 1 d.c., ch.

2, 1 d.c. in center sp., ch. 2. **6th Row**—1 sl.st., ch. 6, 1 d.c. in same sp., 12 d.c. over 8 d.c. (that is add 2 d.c. at each side) ch. 2, 1 d.c., ch. 2. 1 d.c. in center sp., ch. 2. **7th Row**—1 sl.st., ch. 6, 1 d.c. in same sp., ch. 2, 14 d. c. over 12 d.c. (that is add 1 d.c. at each side), ch. 2, 1 d.c., ch. 2, 1 d.c. in center sp., ch. 2. **8th-9th-10th Rows**—Some way adding 1 d.c. at each side of each solid part. **11th Row**—12 o.m. over each solid part, ch. 2, 1 d.c., ch. 2, 1 d.c. in center sp., ch. 2. **12th Row**—3 d.c. in each m., sk. m. over center sp. **Filet Part 1st Row**—Work 83 o.m. over this solid r. **2nd Row**—82 o.m. over same, 1 s.m. (this starts flower design). **3rd Row**—Same. Placing the s.m., 1 m. to the left. **4th Row**—Again place the s.m., 1 m. to the left. **5th Row**—Follow pattern. Filet requires 20 r. in length, flower design 10 meshes, word design 33 m. There are 20 m. at each side bet. designs. **Upper Part. 1st Row**—3 d.c. in each m. **2nd Row**—2 d.c. over same, ch. 4, sk. 4. **3rd Row**—2 d.c. over 4 chs., ch. 4 over 2 d.c. Continue until there are 11 r. **12th Row**—1 pt.st. of 3 d.c. over 4 chs., ch. 5. **13th Row**—3 sl.st., 1 p., 3 sl.st. over every 5 chs., 1 tight sl.st. over pt.st. **Hanger. 1st Row**—Ch. 23, 6 o.m. **2nd Row**—6 o.m. **3rd Row**—2 o.m., 2 s.m., 2 o.m. **4th Row**—1 o.m., 1 s.m., 2 o.m., 1 s.m., 1 o.m. **5th Row**—2 o.m., 2 s.m., 2 o.m., then 2 rows of 6 o.m. Continue until desired length is reached. At ends omit 1 o.m. at each side for 3 rows. **Edge**—5 sl.st., 1 p. over every 2 m. all around hanger.

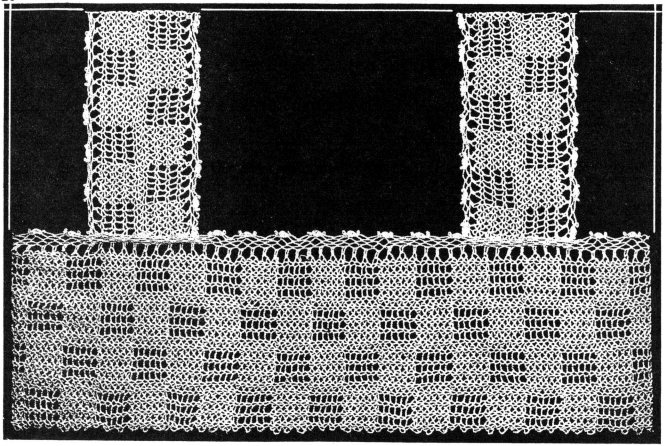

No. 632—Camisole.

Size 70 Cotton, 2 Balls. **1st Row**—Ch. 90, 1 d.c. in 8th st. from hook, ch. 2, 1 d.c. in same st., ch. 3, 1 d.c. in 5th ch., ch. 2, 1 d.c. in same st., rep. until there are 4 l.'s, * 1 d.c. in 5th st., ch. 2, 1 d.c. in same st., ch. 2, 1 d.c. in same st., ch. 2, 1 d.c. in same st., 1 d.c. in 5th ch., ch. 2, 1 d.c. in same st., ch. 2, 1 d.c. in same st., ch. 2, 1 d.c. in same st. * twice, ch. 5, tn. **2nd Row**—1 d.c. in middle l., ch. 2, 1 d.c. in same place, ch. 2, 1 d.c. in same place, ch. 2, 1 d.c. in same place. Follow pat-

tern. **Edging. 1st Row**—Tie thread in any l., ch. 3, 1 d.c. in same l., ch. 4 ,2 d.c. in next l., continue around. **2nd Row**—Ch. 6, 1 sl.st. from l. to l. **3rd Row**—Same. **4th Row**—Ch. 6, 1 sl.st. in next l., 1 p. (5 chs.), 6 d.c. in sl.st. bel., 1 sl.st. in 3rd l., 1 p., 1 sl.st., ch. 6 in next l., continue around. **Shoulder Strap. 1st Row**—J. on 1st r. of beading at front, ch. 5, 1 d.c. in same place, forming l., ch. 3, 1 d.c. in next l., ch. 2, 1 d.c. in same place, making 4 l.'s, * 1 d.c. in next l., ch. 2, 1 d.c. in same st., ch. 2, 1 d.c. in same st., ch. 2, 1 d.c. in same st. * 4 times. Makes the strap 2 blocks wide and finish with same edging.

No. 616—Mat, or Can Be Used As Bed Spread Square.

2 Balls No. 5 Cotton. **1st Row**—Ch. 9, form ring, ch. 4, 3 d.t., ch. 6 for cor., * 4 d.t., ch. 6 * twice, j., 1 sl.st. in each st., taking up front thread only, 7 sl.st. over 6 chs. at cor. Fasten thread. **2nd Row**—* 5 d.t. (that is 2 d.t. in 2nd st.), ch. 2, sk. 2 d.t. in center, 5 d.t. (that is 2 d.t. in 2nd last st.), taking up back thread only to obtain rib effect, ch. 6 * 3 times, 1 sl.st. in each st., taking up front thread, 7 sl.st. over 6 chs. at cor. **3rd Row**—9 d.t. (that is 2 d.t. in 2nd st.), ch. 2, sk. sp. bel., 9 d.t. (that is 2 d.t. in 2nd last st.), ch. 6 over cor., taking up back thread, 1 sl.st. in each st. Worked same way as above. **4th Row**—13 d.t. (that is 2 d.t. in 2nd st.), ch. 2, sk. sp. bel., 13 d.t. (that is 2 d.t. in 2nd last st.), ch. 6 over cor. taking up back thread, 1 sl.st. in each st. for rib. **5th Row**—17 d.t. worked same way as rows above. **6th Row**—21 d.t. **7th Row**—Start at cor. st., ch. 5, 1 X. st., that is ch. 1 and sk. 1 instead of 2, ch. 1, sk. 1, 1 d.t., ch. 5, sk. 4, 1 d.t., ch. 1, 1 X. st., ch. 1, sk. 1, 1 d.t., ch. 5, sk. 4. Work 5 of these figures over each side of square, ch. 7 over cor. **8th Row**—7 d.t. over 1st and last d.t. and 5 chs., ch. 5 over figure, 7 d.t., ch. 5, 7 d.t. over cor., 1 sl.st. in each st., taking up front thread only. **9th Row**—Taking up back thread. Same as 8th row, ch. 3, 1 d.t., ch. 3, 1 d.t., ch. 3 over cor. Don't work rib. **10th Row**—Same as 7th row, sk. 5 instead of 4. Add one figure at each end of each side, ch. 7 over cor. **11th Row**—Same as 8th row, 7 d.t., ch. 5, 7 d.t. over cor. Don't work rib. **12th Row**—5 d.t. over 7 d.t., ch. 3, 1 d.t. over 3rd ch.st., ch. 3, 5 d.t. over 7 d.t., ch. 3, 1 d.t., ch. 5, 1 d.t., ch. 3 over cor. **13th Row**—3 d.t. over 5 d.t., ch. 2, sk. 2, 1 d.t., ch. 3, sk. 3, 1 d.t., ch. 2, sk. 2, 3 d.t., ch. 4, 7 d.t. with 1 ch. bet. each over cor., ch. 4. **14th Row**—1 sl.st. over 2nd d.t., ch. 2, 5 d.t. with 1 p. bet. each over the 3 ch. sts., ch. 2, 1 sl.st., ch. 4, 8 d.t. with 1 p. bet. each over cor., ch. 4.

ILLUSTRATED ON FRONT COVER.

No. 608—Opera Bag.

1 Ball Size 40 Thread. **Filet Band 1st Row**—Ch. 38, 11 o.m. **2nd Row**—Same as 1st. **3rd Row**—Ch. 7, 1 d.c. over 1st d.c. bel. (this will add 1 o.m.), 11 o.m. over same. **4th Row**—8 o.m., 1 s.m., 3 o.m., ch. 2, 1 d.t. in same st. **5th Row**—Ch. 7, 1 d.c. over d.t., 3 o.m., 3 s.m., 7 o.m. **6th Row**—6 o.m., 2 s.m., 1 o.m., 2 s.m., 1 o.m., ch. 2, 1 d.t. in same st. **7th Row**—Ch. 7, 1 d.c. over d.t, 2 o.m., 1 s.m., 2 o.m., 3 s.m., 1 o.m., 1 s.m., 5 o.m. **8th Row**—5 o.m., 2 s.m., 1 o.m., 1 s.m., 1 o.m., 1 s.m., 4 o.m., ch. 2, 1 d.t. in same st. **9th Row**—Ch. 6, 1 d.c. over d.t (this gives center line) 1 o.m., 2 s.m., 3 o.m., 1 s.m., 3 o.m., 1 s.m., 1 o.m., 1 s.m., 2 o.m., 1 s.m., 4 o.m. **10th Row**—5 o.m., 2 s.m., 1 o.m., 1 s.m., 2 o.m., 1 s.m., 4 o.m., 1 d.t. in last d.c. bel. (this will omit 1 o.m.), ch. 4. Rep. in opp. direction. At end of center line of 2nd pt. work tr.t., ch. 4, tn. **Edging Over Points**—1 sl.st., 1 s.c., 2 s.c., 1 s.c. over each m., add 1 d.c. over m. at outer pt., 2 sl.st. in 1st m. bet. large pts., 3 sl.st. in 2nd and 3rd m., 2

sl.st. in 4th m. **Upper Edge. 1st Row**—1 pt.st. of 2 d.t. in every other m., ch. 3 bet. **2nd Row**—4 sl.st. over every 3 chs. **Bottom. 1st Row**—Ch. 10, form ring, ch. 3, 29 d.c. in ring, close. **2nd Row**—Ch. 5, 14 d.c. with 2 chs. bet. each, sk. 1. **3rd Row**—Ch. 3, 4 d.c. in every sp. **4th Row**—Ch. 5, sk. 1, 1 d.c., ch. 2, sk. 1, 1 d.c. **5th Row**—Ch. 3, 3 d.c. in 1st sp., 4 d.c. in 2nd sp. **6th Row**—Same as 4th r. **7th Row**—Ch. 3, 3 d.c. in each sp. **8th Row**—Ch. 4, sk. 1, 1 d.c., ch. 2, sk. 1, 1 d.c. **9th Row**—1 sl.st. over each st. **Ornaments. 1st Row**—Ch. 4, form ring, 2 sl.st. in each st. **2nd Row**—2 sl.st. in each st. **3rd Row**—1 sl.st. in 1st sl.st., 2 sl.st. in 2nd sl.st. bel. **4th Row**—1 sl.st. in each st. **5th Row**—Same. Place 2 together, fill out with cotton, put ends of cord between and sew all around. **Cord**—Ch. with 3 double threads.

No. 629—Infant's Bib.

Size 40, 1 Ball Cotton. Ch. 209, 68 o.m., 21 rows, follow design; 40 m. for 4 rows, following design, leaving 14 o.m. at each side. Edging—5 sl.st., 1 p. over each 2 o.m.

No 640—Laundry Bag.

Crochet Cotton, Size 20, 4 Balls. Lower panel is worked first, start at left side, ch. 120, 7 rows of 35 o.m., then follow design. Work upper panel over 46 meshes right in lower panel. This leaves 16 meshes between the 2 upper panels. Omit 1 o.m. at each side in each row for point. **Finishing Row**—3 sl.st. in each mesh.

No. 649—Three-Cornered Hand Bag.

Size 30 Crochet Cotton, 3 Balls. The 3 filet squares for bottom are worked first and each separately. Ch. 80, 25 o.m., following design for 19 rows. From 20th to 25th rows omit 1 o.m. in each row at one side only; this forms curve. 5 sl.st., 1 p. over each 2 meshes at 2 sides opp. curve. In working 2nd and 3rd parts connect each p. **Upper Part. 1st Row**—3 d.c. in each m., 4 d.c. in m. over curve. **2nd Row**—1 d.c., ch. 3, sk. 3, 1 d.c. (108 m.). **3rd Row**—1 kn.st. in every other m. 54 kn.st.), making 20 rows of kn.st. **Band 1st Row**—Ch. 21, 2 d.c. in 4th and 5th sts. from hook, ch. 3, 3 d.c. in next 3 sts., sk. 1, 1 sl.st., ch. 5, sk. 5, 3 d.c., ch. 3, 3 d.c., ch. 3, tn. **2nd Row**—3 d.c., ch. 3, 3 d.c. over same figure, 1 sl.st. in last d.c. bel., ch. 5, then same as 1st row. Continue until there are 89 rows. Connect 1 kn.st. in each one of the 1st 4 loops, connect 2 kn.sts. in every 5th loop. **Upper Edge. 1st Row**—2 sl.st. in loop, ch. 6 to next loop. **2nd Row**—4 sl.st., ch. 4, 2 sl.st., ch. 4, 2 sl.st., ch. 4, 4 sl.st. in every loop. Cord and Tassel same as Yoke Cord No. 647.

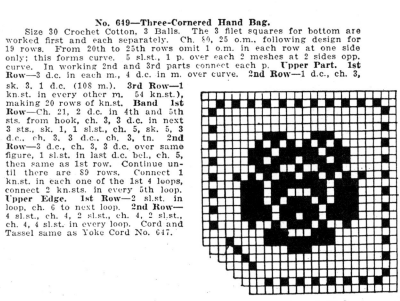

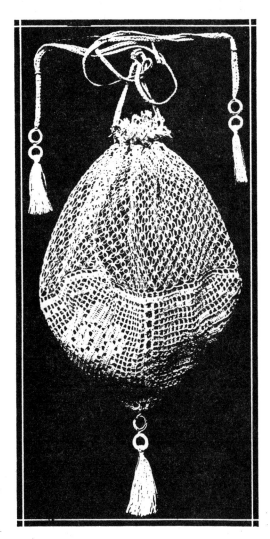

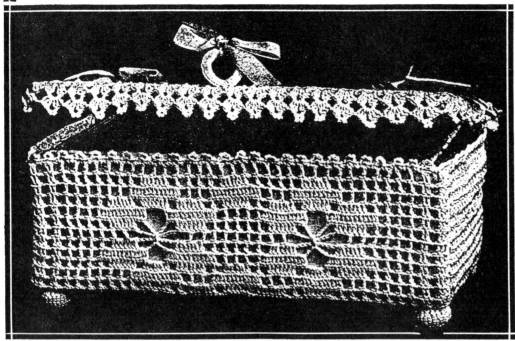

No. 627—Jewelry Case

2 Ball, Size 30 Cotton—**Insertion—1st Row**—Ch. 120, 2 d.c. start in 4th st. from hook, ch. 2, sk. 2, 2 d.c., 32 o.m., 2 d.c., ch. 2, sk. 2, 3 d.c., ch. 3 tn. **2nd Row**—2 d.c., ch. 2, 2 d.c. (this is the end and start of every r. for the whole design has to be worked in every row and will not be mentioned again in directions), 8 o.m., 2 s.m., 5 o.m., 2 s.m., 5 o.m., 2 s.m., 8 o.m. **3rd Row**—7 o.m., 3 s.m., 3 o.m., 3 s.m., 3 o.m., 3 s.m., 7 o.m. **4th Row**—5 o.m., 2 s.m., 1 o.m., 2 s.m., 1 o.m., 2 s.m., 2 o.m., 2 s.m., 2 o.m., 2 s.m., 1 o.m., 2 s.m., 1 o.m., 2 s.m., 5 o.m. **5th Row**—*4 o.m., 3 s.m., ch. 8 sk. 2 s.m., 3 s.m., 4 o.m.,* rep. in opp. direction. **6th Row**—*5 o.m., 2 s.m., ch. 10, (sk. 1 s.m. 8 chs. 1 s. m.), 2 s.m., 6 o.m., * rep. **7th Row**—* 6 o.m., ch. 14, (sk. 1 s.m., 10 chs. 1 s.m.), 8 o.m. **8th Row**—* 5 o.m., 2 s.m., ch. 5, 1 sl.st., taking up the 3 chs. bel., ch. 5, 2 s.m. over 2 last ch.sts. and 1st o.m. 6 o.m., rep. **9th Row**—* 4 o.m., 3 s.m. (that is last s.m. over 2 ch.sts.), ch. 4 3 sm., 4 o.m., * rep. **10th Row**—5 o.m., 2 s.m., 1 o.m., 2 s.m., 1 o.m., 2 s.m., 2 o.m., 2 s.m., 2 o.m., 2 s.m., 1 o.m., 2 s.m., 1 o.m., 2 s.m., 5 o.m. **11th Row**—Same as 3rd r. **12th Row**—8 o.m., 2 s.m., 2 o.m., 2 s.m., 1 o.m., 2 s.m., 1 o.m., 2 s.m., 2 o.m., 2 s.m., 8 o.m. This makes

2 rose designs and start for single one in center, this worked same. Start 2 rose designs in 18th r., worked same as 12th r. Side Parts. Ch. 56, work 4 rows of 17 o.m. **5th Row**—4 o.m., 1 s.m., 7 o.m., 1 s.m., 4 o.m. **6th Row**—3 o.m., 3 s.m., 2 o.m., 1 s.m., 2 o.m., 1 s.m., 3 s.m., 2 o.m. **7th Row**—4 o.m., 1 s.m., 2 o.m., 3 s.m., 2 o.m., 1 s.m., 4 o.m. **8th Row**—8 o.m., 1 s.m., 8 o.m.—Work 3 more rows of 17 o.m. Place over box and connect with insertion. **Edging on 3 sides of box:**—1 p., 1 sl.st. in each m. **Edging on Cover—1st Row**—3 d.c., ch. 3, 3 d.c. in every other m. **2nd Row**—3 d.c., 1 p., 3 d.c. in center 3 chs. **Balls for Feet.**—Ch. 4, form ring, 2 sl.st. in each st. Increase same way until there are 4 rows, then 2 rows without increasing; fill out with cotton, place tack in and omit same way as increasing is made. **Ring for Handle**—Wind thread over finger 6 times, 40 sl.st. over ring. Requires box about 6 inches long, 3 inches wide and 2 inches deep, 1-2 yd. lining, 1 yd. ribbon for ornamental bows, and 4 tacks for feet. Place lining over box and tack on. For inside of box cut cardboard exact size, cover with lining and place in box. Make cushion of lining for bottom.

No. 644—"My" Liberty

Size 30 Crochet Cotton—**1st Row**—Ch. 4, form ring, 2 sl.st. in each st. **2nd Row**—2 sl.st. in each st. **3rd Row**—3 sl.st. over 3 sl.st., 1 sl.st. in every 4th sl.st. **4th-5th-6th Rows**—1 sl.st. in each st. **7th Row**—3 sl.st. over 3 sl.st., 1 sl.st. in every 4th sl.st. **8th-9th-Rows**—Same as 7th r. **Knocker—1st Row**—Ch. 4, form ring. 1 sl.st. in 1st st., 2 sl.st. in 2nd st., 1 sl.st. in 3rd st. 2 sl.st. in 4th st. **2nd Row**—1 sl.st. in 1st st., sk. 2nd st., 1 sl.st. in 3rd st., sk. 4th st., 1 tight sl.st. in 5th st., sk. 6th st. **3rd Row**—1 tight sl.st. in center sl.st., ch. 10. Fasten in bell. ch. for hanger.

No. 607—Powder Bag

1st Row—Ch. 31, 3 d.t., start in 5th st. from hook, ch. 1 3 d.t., ch. 6, 16 d.t., ch. 6, 3 d.t., ch. 1, 3 d.t., ch. 4, tn. **2nd Row**—3 d.t. over 1 ch. ot previous r., ch. 1, 3 d.t. in same sp., ch. 6, 1 d.t. bet. 1st and 2nd d.t. of previous r., ch. 1 d.t. bet. 2nd and 3rd d.t. and so on until last d.t. is reached, ch. 6, 3 d.t. over 1 ch., 3 d.t. in same sp., ch. 4 tn. Always ch. 4 at end of each r. **3rd Row**—3 d.t. over 1 ch., ch. 1, 3 d.t. in same sp., ch. 6, d.t. bet. 1st and 2nd d.t. of previous r., ch. 2, d.t. bet. next d.t. and so on. Make 2 ch. bet. d.t. in this r., ch. 6, 3 d.t. over 1 ch., ch. 1, 3 d.t. in same sp., ch. 4 tn. **4th Row**—3 d.t. over 1 ch., ch. 1, 3 d.t. in same sp., ch. 6, sc. over 2 ch., ch. 4, s.c over next 2 ch., and so on. **5th Row**—3 d.t. over 1 ch., ch. 1, 3 d.t. in same sp. ch. 6, s.c. over 4 ch., ch. 4, s.c. over next 4 ch. and so on. **6th Row**—3 d.t. over 1 ch., ch. 1, 3 d.t. in same sp., ch. 6, s.c. over 3 ch., s.c. over next 3 ch., and so on. Continue in this way until pineapple comes to a point, which finishes the 16th r. **17th Row**—3 d.t. over 1 ch., ch. 6, s.c. over 3 ch., ch. 6, 3 d.t. over 1 ch., sl.st. in 1 ch. on other side of pineapple. Now 2 d.t. over 1 ch. that you have only 3 d.t. in ch. 3 and fasten with sl.st. in same sp. Make another pineapple like this. Take a piece of thin cashmere or flannel and make the bag the size of inside of pineapple and fill with talcum powder and put it between the two pineapples and lace together with ribbon.

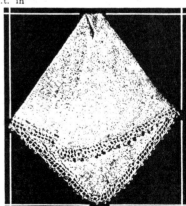

No. 630—Wash Rag.

No. 8 Pearle Cotton—**1st Row**—5 o.m. in material, 1 s.m., 1 o.m., 1 s.m. **2nd Row**—7 o.m., 1 s.m. over the o.m. bel. **3rd Row**—3 sl.st., 1p. over 1st o.m., 2 sl.st. in 2nd o.m., 3 sl.st., 1 p. in 3rd o.m., 3 sl.st., 1 p. in 4th o.m., 3 sl.st. in 5th o.m., 2 sl.st. 1 p. in 6th o.m., 3 sl.st. in 7th o.m., ch. 4 over s.m.

No. 613—Hair Receiver

1 Spool White and 1 spool Colored Silkateen. **1st Row**—Ch. 10 form r., ch. 3, 23 d.c. in r., close. **2nd Row**—24 d.c. with 1 ch. bet. each. **3rd Row**—48 d.c. (1 d.c. in each st.). **4th Row**—48 d.c. with 1 ch. bet. each. **5th Row**—2 d.c., ch. 2, sk. 2 sts. **6th Row**—2 d.c., ch. 1, 2 d.c., ch. 2 in sp. **7th Row**—2 d.c. in every sp., ch. 2. **8th Row**—Ch. 4 over every sp., making 24 of these ls. **9th Row**—3 d.c., ch. 2 in every l. Continue to work these 2 r. until there are 8 r. of each one. **Frill 1st Row**—1 d.c. in each st. **2nd Row**—2 d.c. in each st. **3rd Row**—1 d.c., ch. 1 in each st. **4th Row**—Ch. 3, 1 sl.st. over each st. **Band. 1st Row**—Ch. 165. **2nd Row**—1 X. start in 10th st. from hook, making 40 X., ch. 2, sk. 2. **3rd Row**—Ch. 4 over every 2 chs. **4th Row**—Same as 3rd Row. **Tassel**—Wind thread over 3 fingers about 28 times, draw last thread thru all with hook, leaving loop on top. Wind thread tightly about 5 times, 1-4 inch from top of tassel and cut.

No. 631—Combing Jacket.

Crochet Cotton, Size 20, 5 Balls. **Frog—1st Row**—Wind thread over finger 8 times, fasten with 1 sl.st., ch. 3, 65 d.c. over this ring, close. **2nd—Row**—1 sl.st. in each st. **3rd Row**—*ch. 6, sk. 4, 1 sl.st. * once, tn., 3 sl.st., 1 p., 8 sl.st. in 1st l., 6 sl.st. in 2nd l., ch. 6, tn., fasten over 1st l., tn., 3 sl.st., 1 p., 4 sl.st., 1 p., 1 p., 3 sl.st. in new l., 2 sl.st., 1 p., 4 sl.st. in remaining l., fasten. **4th Row**—Ch. 14, fasten with 1 sl.st. in center p., ch. 14, fasten in st. next to 1st small l., tn. **5th Row**—22 sl.st. in each of these larger l.'s, fasten, tn. **6th Row**—7 sl.st. over same, * 1 p., sk. 1, 4 sl.st. over same * twice, 3 p. over center. Rep. same over 2nd l., fasten, sl.st. over 3 sts. Start 2nd pt., making 3 altogether. Work 1st 6 rows of button for center. **Button—1st Row**—Ch. 4, 2 sl.st. in each st. **2nd—Row**—2 sl.st. in each st. **3rd Row**—1 sl.st. over same, 2 sl.st. in 2nd sl.st. **4th Row**—1 sl.st. in each one bel. **5th Row**—4 sl.st. over same, 2 sl.st. in every 5th sl.st. **6th Row**—Same. Increasing over 2nd of the 4 sl.st. **7th Row**—1 sl.st. in each st. Commence omitting, 2 sl.st. over same, sk. 3rd sl.st., work 3 of these rows, insert mold, work 2 more rows and fasten. **Edge on Pocket. 1st Row**—o.m. in material. **2nd Row**—3 sl.st. in each m. **3rd Row**—5 sl.st. over same, 1 p., sk. 1. **Edging. 1st Row**—Ch. 9, 2 d.c. in 4th and 5th st. from hook, ch. 3, 3 d.c., ch. 4, tn. **2nd Row**—3 d.c., ch. 3, 3 d.c. over 3 chs. in center of same figure, ch. 7, tn. **3rd Row**—3 d.c., ch. 3, 3 d.c. over same, ch. 4, tn. **4th Row**—3 d.c., ch. 3, 3 d.c. over same, 8 d.c., ch. 3, 8 d.c. over loop of 7 chs., fasten with 1 sl.st., tn. **5th Row**—Ch. 4, sk. 1, 1 sl.st., * ch. 3, sk. 1, 1 sl.st. * twice, ch. 4 in loop over center. Work same 4 loops over other side of pt., 1 sl.st., 3 d.c., ch. 3, 3 d.c. over same. Heading: 2 sl.st. in every loop, ch. 4 to next loop.

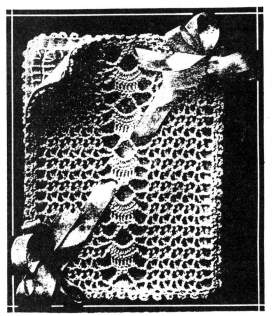

No. 611—Needle Case.

No. 30 Thread, 1 Ball. **1st Row**—Ch. 48, 1 d.c., ch. 2, 1 d.c. in 7th st. from hook, * sk. 2, 1 d.c., ch. 2, 1 d.c., * 3 times, ch. 6, sk. 5, 3 sl.st. in 3 sts., ch 6, sk. 5, * 1 d.c., ch. 2, 1 d.c. in 1st., * 4 times, ch. 2, 1 d.c., ch. 5, tn. **2nd Row**—* 1 d.c., ch. 2, 1 d.c. over 2 chs. in center, * 4 times, ch. 3, 1 sl.st. over 6 chs., ch. 6, 1 sl.st. over next 6 chs., ch. 3, rep. same figure at side, ch. 2, 1 d.c., ch. 5, tn. **3rd Row**—Same as r. above. Over center part: ch. 3, 11 d.c., ch. 3. **4th Row**—Same. Over center part: ch. 3, 7 d.c. over 11 d.c., ch. 3. **5th Row**—Same as 1st r. **Finishing Row**—1 p., 2 sl.st. all around. Make other side of case the same way, mount both sides on a double piece of silk, cut the size of the two crocheted parts. Turn edges in before mounting. Cut piece of flannel this size for leaves of Case, finish edge with buttonhole stitch. The addition of ribbon on the front beautifies the finished article.

No. 647—Cord

Size 30 Cotton. Ch. 2, 1 sl.st. in 1st ch.st., ch. 1, 1 sl.st. in 1st sl.st., that is sk. last ch.st., taking up side thread of sl.st., ch. 1. Continue to desired length, tn., ch. 1, 1 sl.st. going twice in last sl.st., ch. 1, 1 sl.st. in same thread on side until start is again reached; 36 sl.st. in ring. **Tassel**—Wind thread over 3 fingers 30 times, cut, place in ring and tie.

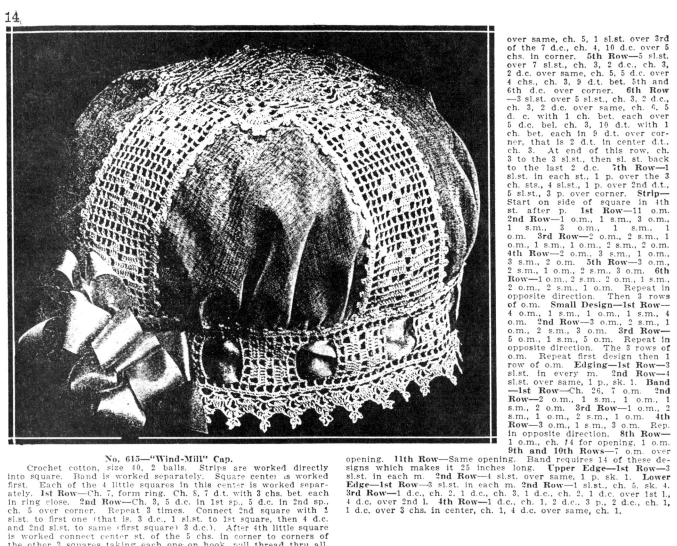

No. 615—"Wind-Mill" Cap.

Crochet cotton, size 40, 2 balls. Strips are worked directly into square. Band is worked separately. Square center is worked first. Each of the 4 little squares in this center is worked separately. **1st Row**—Ch. 7, form ring. Ch. 8, 7 d.t. with 3 chs. bet. each in ring close. **2nd Row**—Ch. 3, 5 d.c. in 1st sp., 5 d.c. in 2nd sp., ch. 5 over corner. Repeat 3 times. Connect 2nd square with 1 sl.st. to first one (that is, 3 d.c., 1 sl.st. to 1st square, then 4 d.c. and 2nd sl.st. to same (first square) 3 d.c.). After 4th little square is worked connect center st. of the 5 chs. in corner to corners of the other 3 squares taking each one on hook, pull thread thru all. Fasten thread. **1st Row Over Square**—Start over 8th d.c. on one side, 1 sl.st. in each st., 3 sl.st. in ch. st. on corner. This row will fasten all threads. **2nd Row**—11 d.c. over 11 sl.st., ch. 2, sk. 2, 1 d.c., ch. 3, 1 d.c. in next st., ch. 2, sk. 2, 1 sl.st., ch. 5 to corner. Repeat in opposite direction. **3rd Row**—9 sl.st. over 11 d.c., ch. 3, 2 d.c., ch. 3, 2 d.c. over 3 chs., ch. 3, 7 d.c. over 5 chs., ch. 5, 7 d.c. over next 5 chs. This makes corner. Repeat in opposite direction. **4th Row**—7 sl.st. over 9 sl.st., ch. 3, 2 d.c., ch. 3, 2 d.c.

over same, ch. 5, 1 sl.st. over 3rd of the 7 d.c., ch. 4, 10 d.c. over 5 chs. in corner. **5th Row**—5 sl.st. over 7 sl.st., ch. 3, 2 d.c., ch. 3, 2 d.c. over same, ch. 5, 5 d.c. over 4 chs., ch. 3, 9 d.t. bet. 5th and 6th d.c. over corner. **6th Row** —3 sl.st. over 5 sl.st., ch. 3, 2 d.c., ch. 3, 2 d.c. over same, ch. 6, 5 d. c. with 1 ch. bet. each over 5 d.c. bel. ch. 3, 10 d.t. with 1 ch. bet. each in 9 d.t. over corner, that is 2 d.t. in center d.t., ch. 3. At end of this row, ch. 3 to the 3 sl.st., then sl. st. back to the last 2 d.c. **7th Row**—1 sl.st. in each st., 1 p. over the 3 ch. sts., 4 sl.st., 1 p. over 2nd d.t., 5 sl.st., 3 p. over corner. **Strip**— Start on side of square in 4th st. after p. **1st Row**—11 o.m. **2nd Row**—1 o.m., 1 s.m., 3 o.m., 1 s.m., 3 o.m., 1 s.m., 1 o.m. **3rd Row**—2 o.m., 2 s.m., 1 o.m., 1 s.m., 1 o.m., 2 s.m., 2 o.m. **4th Row**—2 o.m., 3 s.m., 1 o.m., 3 s.m., 2 o.m. **5th Row**—3 o.m., 2 s.m., 1 o.m., 2 s.m., 3 o.m. **6th Row**—1 o.m., 2 s.m., 2 o.m., 1 s.m., 2 o.m., 2 s.m., 1 o.m. Repeat in opposite direction. Then 3 rows of o.m. **Small Design**—1st Row— 4 o.m., 1 s.m., 1 o.m., 1 s.m., 4 o.m. **2nd Row**—3 o.m., 2 s.m., 2 o.m., 2 s.m., 3 o.m. **3rd Row**— 5 o.m., 1 s.m., 5 o.m. Repeat in opposite direction. The 3 rows of o.m. Repeat first design then 1 row of o.m. **Edging**—1st Row—3 sl.st. in every m. **2nd Row**—4 sl.st. over same, 1 p., sk. 1. **Band** —1st Row—Ch. 26, 7 o.m. **2nd Row**—2 o.m., 1 s.m., 1 o.m., 1 s.m., 2 o.m. **3rd Row**—1 o.m., 2 s.m., 1 o.m., 2 s.m., 1 o.m. **4th Row**—3 o.m., 1 s.m., 3 o.m. Rep. in opposite direction. **8th Row**— 1 o.m., ch. 14 for opening, 1 o.m. **9th and 10th Rows**—7 o.m. over opening. **11th Row**—Same opening. Band requires 14 of these designs which makes it 25 inches long. **Upper Edge**—1st Row—3 sl.st. in each m. **2nd Row**—4 sl.st. over same, 1 p. sk. 1. **Lower Edge**—1st Row—3 sl.st. in each m. **2nd Row**—1 sl.st., ch. 5, sk. 4. **3rd Row**—1 d.c., ch. 2, 1 d.c., ch. 3, 1 d.c., ch. 2, 1 d.c. over 1st l., 4 d.c. over 2nd l. **4th Row**—1 d.c., ch. 1, 2 d.c., 3 p., 2 d.c., ch. 1, 1 d.c. over 3 chs. in center, ch. 1, 4 d.c. over same, ch. 1,

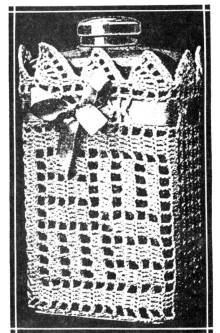

No. 638—Cover for Talcum Shaker.

Size 30 Cotton. **1st Row**—Ch. 61, 1 d.c. in 8th ch. from hook, 16 o.m., ch. 7, 1 d. c. in 7 chs., ch. 2, 6 d.c. in 3 chs., ch. 4, tn. **2nd Row**—1 d.c. over d.c., ch. 1, 1 d.c. over d.c., ch. 1, 1 d.c. over d.c., 1 d.c. over d.c. (4 o.m.), ch. 3, 1 sl.st. in 4 chs., ch. 3, 1 d.c. over d.c., ch. 2, 1 d.c. over d.c. to end, ch. 5, tn. **3rd Row**—Same as 2nd r., ch. 4, tn. **4th Row**—2 sl.st. in each o.m., 1 sl.st. over d.c., making 12 sl.st. in all in the 4 o.m. Follow design.

No. 645—Violet Shower Necktie.

Size 30 Crochet Cotton.—Make 1 lose ch. st. after leaving thread about 14 or 18 inches, ch. 3, 3 d.t. in loose ch.st., ch. 3, 1 tight sl.st. in loose ch.st., this makes 1 petal of leaf, ch. 3, work 3 more petals, fasten; ch. 6, fasten over center d.t., ch. 6 fasten in sl.st. bet. petals, rep. over each petal. Fasten with 1 tight sl.st., ch. 1, place hanging thread bet. hook and thread you are working with, ch. 1, place hanging thread same way; this will take the hanging thread up with the ch.sts. Continue to desired length.

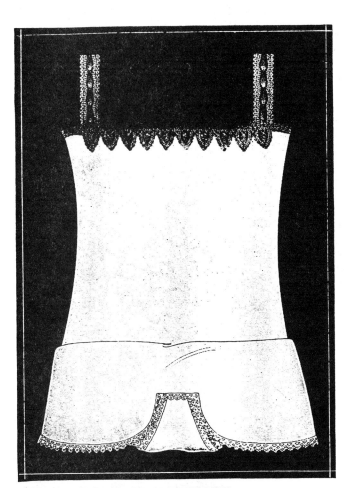

No. 618—Combination Yoke.

3 Balls, Size 40 Cotton. **1st Row**—Ch. 9, 3 d.c. start in 4th st. from hook, ch. 3, 3 d.c., ch. 3, tn., 3 d.c., ch. 3, 3 d.c. over 3 chs. in center. Rep. until there are 10 of these figures, ch. 4, tn. **2nd Row**—3 d.c., ch. 3, 3 d.c. in 1st l. on side going back, ch. 4, 2 d.c. in 2nd l., ch. 4, 2 d.c. in 3rd l., ch. 4, 3 d.c., ch. 3, 3 d.c. in 4th l., ch. 4 to starting pt., tn. **3rd Row**—6 sl.st. over 4 chs., 3 d.c., ch. 3, 3 d.c. over same, ch. 4, 7 d.t. over 2nd 4 chs. bel., ch. 4, 3 d.c., ch. 3, 3 d.c. over same, ch. 7, tn. **4th Row**—3 d.c., ch. 3, 3 d.c. over same, ch. 4, 1 sl.st. in 1st d.t., ch. 3, 1 sl.st. in every d.t., making 6 little loops, ch. 4, 3 d.c., ch. 3, 3 d.c., ch. 5, going back to scallop on side. Fasten. **5th Row**—11 sl.st. over this 5 chs., 3 d.c., ch. 3, 3 d.c. over same, ch. 4, 5 loops over 6 loops, ch. 4, 3 d.c., ch. 3, 3 d.c. over same, ch. 7, tn. Continue this way, omitting 1 little loop in every row until 9th row is finished. **10th Row**—Ch. 7, tn., 3 d.c., ch. 3, 3 d.c. over same, ch. 5, 1 sl.st. in last l., ch. 5, 3 d.c., ch. 3, 3 d.c. over same, ch. 5, fasten on last scallop, tn. **11th Row**—11 sl.st. over these 5 chs., 3 d.c. over 3 chs. in center, ch. 1, 3 d.c. over next 3 center chs., ch. 8, tn. **12th Row**—1 sl.st. over 1 ch.st., ch. 5, fasten on last scallop, tn. **13th Row**—11 sl.st. over these 5 chs., 5 sl.st. over half of the 8 chs., ch. 5, tn., fasten over scallop just made, 11 sl.st. in this outer l., 6 sl.st. in remaining l., 11 sl.st. over each of the 7 chs., drawing scallops together and working thread up again, 6 sl.st. in last small scallop, 3 d.c., ch. 3, 3 d.c. over same, starting a new large pt. Connect pts. with 2nd and 2nd last scallop. Making 10 pts. for front and 10 for back. **Upper Row**—**1st Row**—3 d.c., ch. 3, 3 d.c. in each l. **2nd Row**—Same as 1st r. **Shoulder Strap**—**1st Row**—3 d.c., ch. 3, 3 d.c. in 1st l. of front, ch. 4, 2 d.c. in 2nd l., ch. 5, 2 d.c. in 3rd l., ch. 4, 3 d.c., ch. 3, 3 d.c. in 4th l., ch. 3, tn. **2nd Row**—*3 d.c., ch. 3, 3 d.c. over same, ch. 3, 7 d.t. over 5 chs. * Rep. **3rd Row**—*3 d.c., ch. 3, 3 d.c. over same, ch. 3, 6 l.'s of 4 chs. each over 7 d.t. * rep. **4th Row**—*3 d.c., ch. 3, 3 d.c. over same, ch. 3, 5 l.'s of 4 chs. each over 6 l.'s, * rep. Continue until there are 7 rows. **8th Row**—*3 d.c., ch. 3, 3 d.c. over same, ch. 4, 1 l. over 2 l.'s, ch. 4, * rep. **9th Row**—*3 d.c., ch. 3, 3 d.c. over same, ch. 5, 1 sl.st. in last l., ch. 5, * rep. **10th Row**—3 d.c., ch. 3, 3 d.c. over same, ch. 4, 1 tr.t., keeping last 2 l.'s of thread on hook over first 5 chs., 1 d.t. over 2nd 5 chs. Working thread off 2 by 2, ch. 4. Start 2nd design with 2nd r. 8 designs for each shoulder strap. Sew to back. **Edging on Neck and Shoulder Strap**—**1st Row**—3 d.c., ch. 3, 3 d.c. in each l. **2nd Row**—1 sl.st. bet. figures, ch. 3, 1 sl.st., ch. 4, 1 sl.st., 1 p., 1 sl.st., ch. 4, 1 sl.st. over 3 chs. in center, ch. 3. **Narrow Edge.**—Ch. 9, 3 d.c., start in 4th st. from hook, ch. 3, 3 d.c., ch. 3, tn. Continue until desired length. 1st and 2nd rows on lower edge same as 1st and 2nd rows on neck. **Row on Upper Edge**—2 sl.st. in each l., ch. 5.

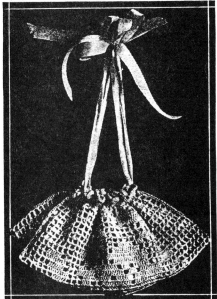
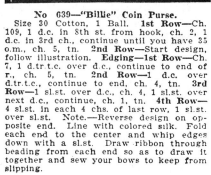
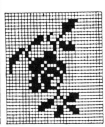

No 639—"Billie" Coin Purse.

Size 30 Cotton, 1 Ball. **1st Row**—Ch. 109, 1 d.c. in 8th st. from hook, ch. 2, 1 d.c. in 3rd ch., continue until you have 35 o.m., ch. 5, tn. **2nd Row**—Start design, follow illustration. **Edging**—**1st Row**—Ch. 7, 1 d.tr.t.c. over d.c., continue to end of r., ch. 5, tn. **2nd Row**—1 d.c. over d.tr.t.c., continue to end, ch. 4, tn. **3rd Row**—1 sl.st. over d.c., ch. 4, 1 sl.st. over next d.c., continue, ch. 1, tn. **4th Row**—4 sl.st. in each 4 chs. of last row, 1 sl.st. over sl.st. **Note.**—Reverse design on opposite end. Line with colored silk. Fold each end to the center and whip edges down with a sl.st. Draw ribbon through beading from each end so as to draw it together and sew your bows to keep from slipping.

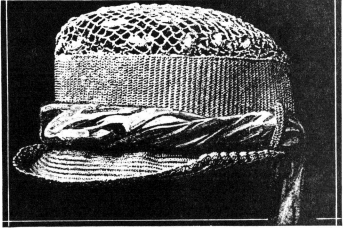

No. 628—Auto Bonnet.

5 Balls No. 10. Cotton. **Crown**—**1st Row**—Ch. 150, 1 sl.st. in 10th st. from hook, * ch. 7, sk. 6, 1 sl.st., * 19 times. **2nd Row**—Ch. 8, 1 sl.st. over 1st l., same as r. above (work center ch.st. loose, this holds sh.st.), 1 sl.st. in last l., ch. 8, tn. **3rd Row**—1 sl.st. in 1st l., ch. 4, * 1 sh.st. of 7 d.c. in center ch.st. of 2nd l., 1 loose ch.st., 1 sh.st. in center ch.st. of 3rd l., ch. 4, 1 sl.st. in 4th l., ch. 7, 1 sl.st. in 5th l., ch. 4 * 4 times, ch. 8, tn. **4th Row**—*1 sl.st. in 1st l., ch. 7, 1 sl.st. in 1st d.c. of sh.st., ch. 4, 1 sh.st. in loose ch.st., ch. 7, 1 sl.st. in 1st d.c. of sh.st. bel., ch. 7, * 4 times. **5th Row**—Same as first r. **6th Row**—Same as 2nd r., ch. 8, tn. **7th Row**—1 sl.st. in 1st l., 2 l.'s of 7 chs., ch. 4, sh.st. over next l. (this places 3 sh.sts. in center of same bel.) Continue until it is about 11 1-2 in. long. Place over crown, turn corners down to fit. Draw a thread thru every other ch.st. of brim and thru this you can give brim desired shape. **Band**—**1st Row**—Ch. 35, 1 sl.st. in each st., start in 2nd st. from hook, tn. **2nd Row**—Ch. 1, 1 sl.st. in each st., taking up back thread only. Continue until band is 25 1-2 inches long. **Brim**—**1st Row**—Ch. 200, 1 sl.st. in each st., ch. 1, tn. **2nd Row**—Work tight sl.st. over 1st 5 sl.st., ch. 1, sl.st. over each bel., leaving last 5 sl.st., take up back thread only, ch. 1, tn. **3rd Row**—1 sl.st. over same, leaving last 3 sl.st., ch. 1, tn. **4th Row**—sk. 1st sl.st., 1 sl.st. over each bel., leaving last 3 sl.st., tn. **5th Row**—Sk. 1st sl.st., 1 sl.st. over each bel., leaving last 2 sl.st., ch. 1, tn. This omits 3 sl.st. at end of each r. Continue to work 5th r. until there are 25 rows. **Edging**—**1st Row**—1 sl.st. over each st. over outer edge. **2nd Row**—1 sh.st. of 7 d.c. in 1 sl.st., sk. 4.

DESCRIPTION OF TERMS USED IN CROCHET.

Chain Stitch.—Make a loop of twine, and draw the twine through each loop thus made, until the chain is of the required length.

Close Chain Stitch.—Insert the hook in loop of preceding row, and draw twine through both this loop and the loop on the needle at the same time.

Single Crochet.—Pass the hook through a loop of the last row, bring twine through, throw the twine around the needle and draw it through the two loops on the needle.

Double Crochet.—Turn the twine around the needle once, pass the hook through a loop of preceding row, bring twine through, throw the twine around the needle and draw it through two loops, turn the twine again around the needle and draw it through the two next loops.

Treble.—Turn the twine twice around the needle, work as double crochet, bringing twine through two loops three times.

Double Double Crochet.—Turn twine three times around the needle, work as double crochet, bringing twine through two loops four times.

Slip Stitch.—This stitch is used in joining. Take the hook from the last loop worked, pass it through the loop where the work has to be joined; then take the first loop spoken of and draw it through.

* The above are the primitive or foundation stitches, of which all fancy stitches are modifications or combinations.

TWINE CROCHET WORK.

The use of twine in fancy work has introduced a material that can be employed extensively in household decoration, and has brought the crochet needle into greater requisition than ever before. Many of those articles that contribute so much to the attractiveness of a home can be made of twine at comparatively little cost. It can be made in colors and of different sizes, and on account of its durability, cheapness and beauty, is considered by many superior to macramé work. By a judicious selection of shades, and a tasteful combination of trimmings, a large assortment of which are sold for that purpose, consisting of silk and plush balls of various shapes and colors, ribbon, etc., a great variety of articles may be fashioned which are at once both beautiful and effective, such as, for instance, window, mantel, table and bracket labrequins, scarfs for chairs and tables, covers for sofa pillows and ottomans, toilet and dinner mats, hand-bags, etc., etc.

LAMBREQUIN DESIGN No. 1.

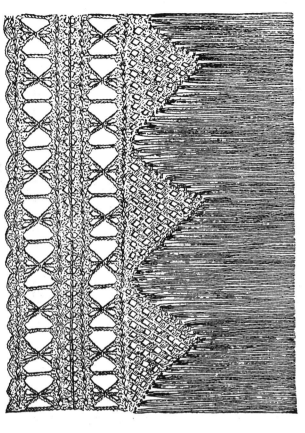

DIRECTIONS.

Make a chain of 43 stitches.

1st row.—3 d.c. in 4th ch.st., 3 ch.st., miss 1 ch. st., 3 d.c. in next ch.st., 9 ch.st., miss 11, 3 d.c. in 12th, 3 ch.st., miss 1, 3 d.c. in next ch.st., miss 3, 1 d.c. in 4th, miss next 3, 3 d.c. in 4th, 3 ch.st., miss 1, 3 d.c. in next ch.st., 9 ch.st., miss 11, 3 d. c. in 12th, 3 ch.st., miss 1, 3 d.c. in next ch.st. Turn.

2d row.—3 ch.st., 3 d.c. around chain of 3 be-tween the two 3 d.c. of last row, 3 ch.st., 3 d.c. around same chain, 9 ch.st., 3 d.c., 3 ch.st., 3 d.c. around next ch. of 3, 1 d.c. in d.c. of last row, 3 d. c., 3 ch.st., 3 d.c. around next ch. of 3, 9 ch.st., 3 d.c., 3 ch.st., 3 d.c. around following ch. of 3. Turn.

TWINE.

The best twine for crocheting is what is known as seine or macramé cotton twine, and is sold by num-bers; 6 and 9, the finer numbers, are used for tidies, etc.; 12, 16 and 20 for lambrequins. Care should be taken in purchasing the twine, to get the best quali-ty, as there are several grades made; that having a cream color, bordering on écru, makes the best work.

NEEDLES.

A five-inch bone needle, even and smooth, is con-sidered the best for crocheting with twine.

ABBREVIATIONS USED IN DIRECTIONS.

st............................Stitch.
ch. st......................Chain Stitch.
cl. ch. st.................Close Chain Stitch.
s. c.........................Single Crochet.
d. c........................Double Crochet.
t............................Treble.
d. d. c....................Double Double Crochet.
sl. st......................Slip Stitch.

—— means to repeat the directions between the stars as often as told, as, for example: * 1 s.c., 1 ch.st. * 5 times. means to crochet 1 single crochet and 1 chain stitch until you have 5 alternate single crochet stitches and 5 chain stitches.

6   7

[79]

3d. row.—3 ch.st., 2 d.c. in last d. crochet of 2d row, 3 ch.st., 3 d.c. around next ch. of 3, 3 ch.st., 3 d.c. around same ch., 4 ch.st., fasten in 5th ch.st. of chains of 2d and 1st rows, 4 ch.st., 3 d.c. around next ch. of 3, 3 ch.st., 3 d.c. around same ch., 1 d. c. in d.c. of last row, 3 d.c., 3 ch.st., 3 d.c. around following ch. of 3, 4 ch.st., fasten in 5th ch.st of chains of 2d and 1st rows, 4 ch.st., 3 d.c. around next ch. of 3, 3 ch.st., 3 d.c. around same chain. Turn

4th row.—3 ch.st., 3 d.c. around ch. of 3 of 3d row, 3 ch.st., 3 d.c. around same ch., 9 ch.st., 3 d. c. around next ch. of 3, 3 ch.st., 3 d.c. around same chain, 1 d.c. in d.c. of last row, 3 d.c., 3 ch. st., 3 d.c. around ch. of 3, 9 ch.st., 3 d.c. around next ch. of 3, 3 ch.st., 3 d.c. around same ch., then 3 ch.st., 3 d.c. around next ch. of 3. Turn.

5th row.—3 ch.st., 2 d.c. in last d.c. of preceding row (4th row), 3 ch.st., 3 d.c. around next ch. of 3, 3 ch.st., 3 d.c. around next ch. of 3, 3 ch.st.; 3 d. c. around same ch., 9 ch.st., 3 d.c., 3 ch.st., 3 d. c., 1 d.c., 3 d.c., 3 ch.st., 3 d.c., 9 ch.st., 3 d.c., 3 ch.st., 3 d.c. Turn.

6th row.—3 ch.st., 3 d.c. around next ch. of 3, 3 ch.st., 3 d.c. around same, 9 ch.st., 3 d.c., 3 ch.st., 3 d.c., 1 d.c., 3 d.c., then 3 ch.st., 3 d.c. around next ch. of 3, 3 ch.st., 3 d.c. around next ch. of 3. Turn.

7th row.—3 ch.st., 2 d.c. in last d.c. of last row, 3 ch.st., 3 d.c. around ch. of 3, 3 ch.st., 3 d.c. around next ch. of 3, 3 ch.st., †3 d.c. around next ch. of 3, 3 ch.st., 3 d.c. around same, 4 ch.st., fasten in 5th ch.st. of chains of two last rows, 4 ch.

st., 3 d.c. around next ch. of 3, 3 ch.st., 3 d.c. around same ch., 1 d.c. in d.c. of 3, 4 ch.st., fasten in 5th ch. st. of chains of 2 last rows, 4 ch.st., 3 d.c., 3 ch.st., 3 d.c. around next ch. of 3. Turn.

8th row.—3 ch.st., 3 d.c. around ch. of 3, 3 ch.st., 3 d.c. around same, 9 ch.st., etc., as before. Then at the point work 3 ch.st., 3 d.c. around next ch. of 3, 3 ch.st., 3 d.c. around next ch. of 3, 3 ch.st., 3 d.c. around last ch. Turn

9th row.—3 ch.st., 2 d.c. in last double crochet of last row, 3 ch.st., 3 d.c. around next ch. of 3, 3 ch. st., 3 d.c. around next ch. of 3, 3 ch.st., 3 d.c. around next ch. of 3, 3 ch.st. Crochet to the end of the row, as before.

10th row.—3 ch.st., 3 d.c., 3 d.c., 3 d.c., 9 ch. st., etc. Then, at beginning of point, work 3 ch.st., 3 d.c. around next ch. of 3, 3 ch.st., 3 d.c. around next ch., 3 ch.st., 3 d.c. around following ch., 3 ch. st., 3 d.c. around next ch. Turn.

11th row.—3 ch.st., 2 d.c. in last d.c. of preceding row, 3 ch.st., 3 d. c., 3 ch.st., 3 d.c., 9 ch. c., 3 ch.st., 3 d.c., 3 ch.st., then continue working like 7th row from † to end of the row.

12th row.—3 ch.st., 3 d.c. around ch. of 3, 3 ch. st., 3 d. c. around same ch., 9 ch.st., etc., as before, to beginning of point. Then * 3 ch.st., 3 d.c. around next ch. of 3*. Repeat 4 times.

13th row.—3 ch.st., 3 d.c. in last d.c. of last row. * 1 s.c., 1 h.d.c., 3 d.c. around next ch. of 3*. Repeat 4 times, then work as usual to the end, making it the required length.

Fasten the fringe in every other stitch around the points of the lambrequin.

LAMBREQUIN DESIGN No. 2.

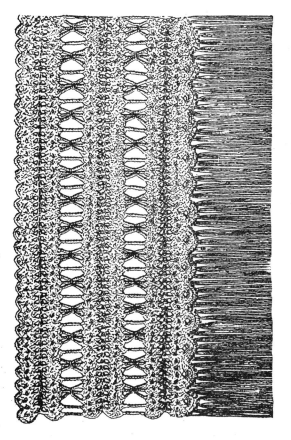

DIRECTIONS.

Make a chain of 49 stitches.

1st row.—4 d.c. in 3d ch.st., 1 ch.st., 3 d.c. in same, miss next 4 ch.st., 2 d.c. in 5th, miss 2 ch. st., 4 d.c. in 3d, make 1 ch.st., 3 d.c. in same 3d ch.st., 7 ch.st., miss 10, 4 d.c. in 11th, 1 ch.st., 3 d.c. in same, miss 4 ch.st., 2 d.c. in 5th, miss next 2, 4 d.c. in 3d, 1 ch.st., 3 d.c. in same, 7 ch.st., miss 10, 4 d.c. in 11th, 1 ch.st., 3 d.c. in same, miss next 4 ch.st., 2 d.c. in 5th, miss next 2, 4 d.c. in 3d, 1 ch.st. 3 d.c. in same. Turn.

2d row.—3 ch.st., * 4 d.c. around next ch. of 1, 1 ch.st., 3 d.c. around same ch., 2 d.c. between next 2 d.c. of last row, 4 d.c. around next ch. of 1, 1 ch.st., 3 d.c. around same ch., 7 ch.st.; * repeat once; then 4 d.c. around next ch. of 1, 1 ch.st., 3 d.c. around same ch., 2 d.c. between next 2 d.c., 4 d.c. around next ch. of 1, 1 ch.st., 3 d.c. around same ch. Turn.

3d row.—3 ch.st., 3 d.c. around same ch., 2 d.c. between next 2 d.c., 4 d.c. around next ch. of 1, 1 ch.st., 3 d.c. around same ch., 4 ch.st., fasten to chains of 2d and 1st rows by passing the hook through 4th ch.st. of ch. of 1st row, making at the same time a s.c.; 3 ch.st.; * repeat once; then 4 d.c. around next chain of 1, 1 ch.st., 3 d.c. around same ch., 2 d.c. between 2 d.c., 4 d.c. around next ch. of 1, 1 ch.st., 3 d.c. around same ch. Turn.

4th row.—3 ch.st., 4 d.c., 1 ch.st., 3 d.c., 2 d.c., 4 d.c., 1 ch.st., 3 d.c., 7 ch.st., 4 d.c. around next ch. of 1, 1 ch.st., 3 d.c. around same ch., 2 d.c., 4 d.c., 1 ch.st., 3 d.c., 7 ch.st., 4 d.c., 1 ch.st., 3 d. c., 2 d.c., 4 d.c., 1 ch.st., 3 d.c.; then 10 d.c. around the ch. of 3, which is at the bottom edge of the work; fasten in 1st d.c. of 1st row. Turn.

5th row.—1 cl.ch.st., 3 ch.st. in every other d.c. of the 10 d.c. last made, * 4 d.c. around next ch. of 1, 1 ch.st., 3 d.c. around same ch., 2 d.c. between next 2 d.c., 4 d.c. around next ch. of 1, 1 ch.st., 3 d.c. around same ch., 7 ch.st.; * repeat, but at the last repetition stop at 7 ch.st.

The work is continued by always repeating the rows described, from 2d row.

Fasten the fringe in every other stitch at the bottom edge of the work.

4th row.—3 ch.st., * 1 d.c. around ch. of 1 of last row, 2 ch.st.* Repeat 9 times. Then 3 d.c., 3 ch.st., 3 d.c. around next ch. of 3, etc. Work to the end as in 2d row. Turn.

5th row.—2 ch.st., 3 d.c., 3 ch.st., 3 d.c., 9 ch.st., 3 d.c., 3 ch.st., 3 d.c., 9 ch.st. 3 d.c., 3 ch.st., 3 d.c.; then 1 ch.st., * 1 d.c. around next ch. of 2, 3 ch.st.*; repeat 9 times. Turn.

6th row.—* 5 ch.st., 1 s.c. around next ch. of 3 *; repeat 8 times; then 5 ch.st., 1 s.c. around next ch. of 1, 3 d.c., 3 ch.st., 3 d.c. around next ch. of 3, 4 ch.st., etc., like 4th row. Turn.

7th row.—2 ch.st., 3 d.c., 3 ch.st., 3 d.c., 9 ch. st., 3 d.c., 3 ch.st., 3 d.c., 9 ch.st., 3 d.c., 3 ch.st., 3 d.c.; then 7 ch.st., fasten around 2d chain of 5 of 6th row. Turn.

8th row.—3 ch.st., 12 d.c. around last ch. of 7; go on working like 2d row. Turn.

9th row.—Work up to scallop like 3d row; then make * 1 d.c. in next d.c., 1 ch.st.; * repeat 11 times, then fasten around 3d ch. of 5 of 6th row. Turn.

10th row.—3 ch.st., * 1 d.c. around next ch. of 1 of last row, 2 ch.st.*; repeat ten times; work to the end of row, like 4th row.

11th row.—Work up to the scallop like 5th row, then 1 ch.st., * 1 d.c. around next ch. of 2, 3 ch.st., * repeat 11 times, fasten in 4th ch. of 5 of 6th row. Turn.

12th row.—* 5 ch.st., 1 s.c. around next ch. of 3 *; repeat 10 times; then continue to work 5 ch.

LAMBREQUIN DESIGN No. 3.

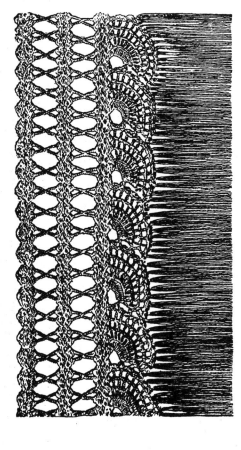

DIRECTIONS.

Make a chain of 43 stitches.

1st row.—3 d.c. in the 5th ch.st.; 3 ch.st.; 3 d.c. in same 5th ch.st.; 9 ch.st.; miss 12; 3 d.c. in 13th; 3 ch.st., 3 d.c. in same, 9 ch.st., miss 12, 3 d.c. in 13th, 3 ch.st., 3 d.c. in next stitch, 7 ch.st., miss 4, fasten in 5th with a s.c. Turn.

2d row.—3 ch st., 12 d.c. around last chain of 7, * 3 d.c., 3 ch.st., 3 d.c. around next ch. of 3, 4 ch.st., fasten in 5th ch.st. of ch. of last row, 4 ch.st.; * repeat once, then make 3 d.c., 3 ch.st., 3 d.c. around last chain of 3. Turn.

3d row.—2 ch.st., 3 d.c., 3 ch.st., 3 d.c. around next chain of 3, 9 ch.st., 3 d.c., 3 ch.st., 3 d.c. around next ch. of 3, 9 ch.st., 3 d.c., 3 ch.st., 3 d. c. around next ch. of 3, * 1 d.c. in next d.c., 1 ch. st. * Repeat 10 times; at the end fasten in 1st st. of foundation chain. Turn.

st., 1 s.c. around next ch. of 1, 3 d.c., etc., like 6th row

The following scallops are worked after directions of 2d scallop, as the foundation chain make a difference in the number of stitches of the 1st.

Fasten fringe in the chains of 5 on the edge of every scallop.

LAMBREQUIN DESIGN No. 4.

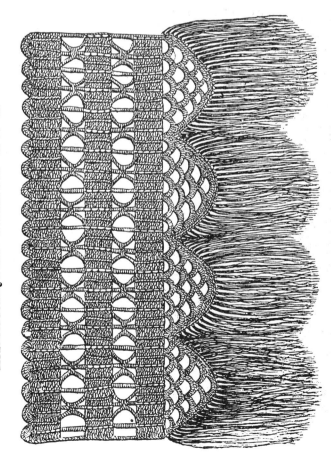

DIRECTIONS.

Make a chain of 44.

1st row.—Miss 4 ch.st., make 1 d.c. in each of the next 7 ch.st., 8 ch.st., miss 8, 1 d.c. in the following 8 ch.st., 8 ch.st., miss 8, 1 d.c. in the following 8 ch.st. Turn.

2d row.—3 ch.st., miss 1 d.c., make 1 d.c. in the next 7 d.c. of last row, 8 ch.st., 1 d.c. in the next 8 d.c., 8 ch.st.; 1 d.c. in the next 8 d.c., 7 ch.st., fasten in last stitch of foundation. Turn.

3d. row.—13 s.c. around ch. of 7 of last row ; 1 ch.st., * 1 d.c. in next 8 d.c., 4 ch.st., fasten in middle st. of both preceding chains, 4 ch.st.; * repeat once, then 1 d.c. in next 8 d.c. Turn.

4th row.—3 ch.st., 1 d.c. in next 7 d.c., 8 ch.st., 1 d.c. in next 8 d.c., 8 ch.st., 1 d.c. in next 8 d.c., 7 ch.st., fasten on end of 3d in the 1 ch.st. Turn.

5th row.—13 s.c. around ch. of 7 of last row, 1 ch.st., 8 d.c., 8 ch.st., 8 d.c., 8 ch.st., 8 d.c. Turn.

6th row.—3 ch.st., 7 d.c., 8 ch.st., 8 d.c., 8 ch.st., 8 d.c., 7 ch.st., fasten on end of 5th row in the 1 ch.st. Turn.

7th row.—13 s.c. around ch. of 7, 1 ch.st., 8 s.c., 4 ch.st., fasten in middle st. of 2 preceding chains, 4 ch.st., 8 d.c., 4 ch.st., fasten as before, 4 ch.st., 8 d.c. Turn.

8th row.—3 ch.st., 7 d.c., 8 ch.st., 8 d.c., 8 ch.st., 8 d.c., 7 ch.st., fasten in the 1 ch.st. Turn.

9th row.—13 s.c. around chain of 7, 1 ch.st., 8 d.c., 8 ch.st., 8 d.c., 8 ch.st., 8 d.c. Turn.

10th row.—3 ch.st., 7 d.c., 8 ch.st., 8 d.c., 8 ch.st., 8 ch. st., 8 d.c.; then 7 ch.st.; fasten in chain of 1. Turn. 7 s.c. around half of ch. of 7, turn, * 7 ch.st., fasten in 7th s.c. of next scallop * ; repeat 3 times, turn * 13 s.c. around ch. of 7 * ; repeat twice, then 7 s.c. around half of next ch. of 7, turn, * 7 ch.st., fasten in 7th s.c. of next scallop * ; repeat twice, turn, * 14 s.c. around next ch. of 7 ; * repeat once, turn, 7 s.c. around half of next ch. of 7, turn, * 8 ch.st., fasten in 7th s.c. of next scallop * ; repeat once, turn, 15 s.c. around ch. of 8 last worked, 8 s.c. around half of next ch. of 8, turn, 9 ch.st., fasten in 8th s.c. of next scallop, turn, 16 s.c. around ch. last worked, 7 s.c. around remaining half of next ch. of 8, 7 s.c. around remaining half of next ch. of 7, 6 s.c. around the remaining half of the next ch. of 7, 6 s.c. around the remaining half of the next ch. of 7.

11th row.—1 ch.st., 8 d.c., 4 ch.st., fasten as before, 4 ch.st., 8 d.c., 4 ch.st., fasten, 4 ch.st., 8 d.c.

Repeat entire work from second row.

After having reached the entire length of the lambrequin, work 8 d.c. in the end of every other row on the upper edge of the lambrequin, fastening by 1 s.c. in the intervening rows.

FRINGE.

All the Lambrequin designs given are finished with a fringe, which is easily made, and the following directions will apply to all : Cut the twine twice the required length, double in center ; take two pieces together, put the needle through the stitch nearest the edge, and with the hook catch the twines in center and draw through until a loop is formed on the opposite side ; pass the needle through the loop and draw the four ends through, then pull tight.

LAMBREQUIN DESIGN No. 5.

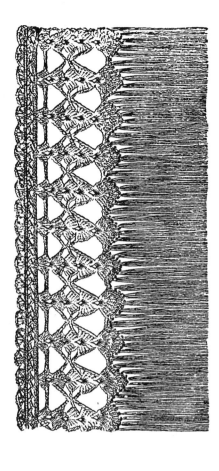

DIRECTIONS.

Make a chain of the required length.

1st row.—4 ch.st., 3 t. in last st. of foundation chain, 2 ch.st., 3 t. in same ch.st., * 6 ch.st., miss 8, 3 t., 3 ch.st., 3 t. in 9th * ; repeat to the end of row ; turn with 2 cl.ch.st. in last 2 t.

2d row.—2 ch.st., 4 t., 2 ch.st., 4 t. around next ch. of 2, separating the two 3 t. of last row, * 7 ch. st., 4 t., 2 ch.st., 4 t. around next 2 ch.st.* ; repeat to end of row ; turn with 3 cl.ch.st. in last 3 t.

3d row.—5 t., 3 ch.st., 5 t. around next chain of 2, * 7 ch.st., 5 t., 3 ch.st., 5 t. around next ch. of 3 * ; repeat to end of row. Turn, with 4 cl.ch.st. in last 4 t.

4th row.—2 ch.st., 6 t., 3 ch.st., 6 t. around next chain of 3, * 4 ch.st., fasten in the middle of the chains of two preceding rows, 3 ch.st., 6 t., 3 ch. st., 6 t. around next ch. of 3 * ; repeat to end of row. Turn, with 3 cl.ch.st.

LAMBREQUIN DESIGN No. 6.

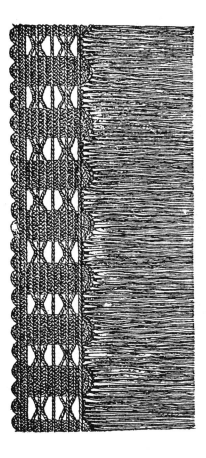

5th row.—1 ch.st., 11 t. around next ch. of 3, * 4 ch.st., 11 t. around next ch. of 3 *; repeat to end of row. Turn.

6th row.—3 ch.st., miss 1 t., 1 d.c., followed by 1 ch.st. in each of next 9 t., *1 s.c. in last t. of scallop, 4 cl.ch.st. in next 4 ch.st., 1 s.c. in next t., 1 d.c., followed by 1 ch.st. in each of next 9 t.*; repeat to end of row.

Heading.—1 s.c. in each st. of foundation chain. Turn.

2d row.—3 ch.st., fasten in every other s.c. of last row. Turn.

3d row.—*3 ch.st., fasten in middle stitch of chain of 3 of last row *; repeat to end of row. Turn, with 1 ch.st.

4th row.—1 s.c. in every stitch of last row.

5th row.—1 ch.st., 1 d.c., 1 ch.st., 1 d.c., 1 ch. st., 1 d.c., all worked in next 2d st. of last row, 1 ch.st., miss next s.c., 1 s.c. in next s.c. *; repeat to end of row.

DIRECTIONS.

Make any number of chain stitches divisible by 9, half as long again as desired when finished, as it takes up in working.

1st row.—*1 d.c. in each of first 9 ch.st.; 9 ch. st.; miss 8; 1 d.c. in next 9 ch.st.* Repeat to end of row, finishing with 9 d.c.

Every row has to be worked on the right side of the work; consequently the twine has to be broken at the end of every row.

2d row.—*9 d.c.; 9 ch.st.* Repeat to the end of the row, finishing with 9 d.c.

3d row.—*9 d.c.; 4 ch.st.; 1 s.c. through 5th ch. st. of 2d and 3d rows, drawing tightly together; 4 ch.st.* Repeat.

4th row.—*9 d.c.; 9 ch.st.* Repeat.
5th row.—*9 d.c.; 9 ch.st.* Repeat.
6th row.—*9 d.c.; 9 ch.st.* Repeat.
7th row.—*9 d.c.; 4 ch.st.; 1 s.c. through 5th ch.st. of chain of 5th and 6th rows; 4 ch.st.* Repeat.

8th row.—Repeat 5th row.

9th row.—d.c. to end of row.

Heading.—* 6 d.c. in 3d d.c.; miss 2; fasten on 3d by 1 s.c.* Repeat.

To finish it off on the bottom, work * 10 t. in 5th d.c.; 1 s.c. in 9th d.c.; 4 ch.st.; 1 s.c. in 5th ch.st. of chain of the last row; 4 ch.st.; 1 s.c. in first of the next 9 d.c.* Repeat.

The fringe is put in every other loop of the edge of this last described row.

LAMBREQUIN DESIGN No. 7

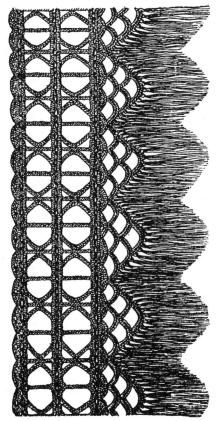

DIRECTIONS.

Make a chain of 28 stitches.

1st row.—3 d.c. in 4th ch.st.; 3 ch.st.; 3 d.c. in next ch.st.; 7 ch.st.; miss 9 ch.st.; make 3 d.c. in the 10th; 3 ch.st.; 3 d.c. in next ch.st.; 7 ch.st.; miss 9 ch.st.; work 3 d.c. in the 10th; 3 ch.st.; 3 d.c. in the next ch.st., which should be the last st. of foundation chain.

2d row.—Turn; 3 ch.st.; 3 d.c. around chain made by 3 ch.st. in last row; 3 ch.st.; 3 d.c. around same chain; 7 ch.st.; 3 d.c. around the next chain of 3; 3 ch.st.; 3 d.c. around the same chain; 7 ch.st.; 3 d.c. around the next chain of 3; 3 ch.st.; 3 d.c. round the same chain; 7 ch.st.; fasten to end of 1st row; 12 s.c. in chain made by 7 ch.st.

3d row.—1 ch.st.; 3 d.c. around last chain of 3 in 2d row; 3 ch.st.; 3 d.c. around the same chain; 3 ch.st.; 1 s.c. through the middle stitch of ch. of 7 of 1st and 2d rows; 3 ch.st.; 3 d.c. around next chain of 3; 3 ch.st.; 3 d.c. around same chain; 3 ch.st.; 1 s.c. through middle stitch of next ch. of 7 of 1st and 2d rows; 3 ch.st.; 3 d.c. around the next chain of 3; 3 ch.st.; 3 d.c. around the same chain.

4th row.—Turn the work; 3 ch.st.; 3 d.c. around 3 ch. of 3; 3 ch.st.; 3 d.c. around same chain; 7 ch.st.; 3 d.c. around next ch. of 3; 3 ch.st.; 3 d.c. around same chain; 7 ch.st.; 3 d.c. around next ch. of 3; 3 ch.st.; 3 d.c. around same chain; 7 ch. st.; fasten to loop made by the 1 ch.st. at beginning of 3d row; 12 s.c. around 2d scallop.

5th row.—1 ch.st.; 3 d.c. around chain of 3; 3 ch.st.; 3 d.c. around same; 7 ch.st.; 3 d.c. around next chain of 3; 3 ch.st.; 3 d.c. around the same; 7 ch.st.; 3 d.c. around next chain of 3; 3 ch.st.; 3 d.c. around same.

6th row.—Turn the work; 3 ch.st.; 3 d.c. around chain of 3; 3ch.st.; 3 d.c. around same chain; 7 ch. st.; 3 d.c.; 3 ch.st.; 3 d.c.; 7 ch.st.; 3 d.c.; 3 d.c.; 7 ch.st.: fasten to loop made by the 1 ch.st. at beginning of 5th row; turn; 6 s.c.; turn 7 ch.st.;

fasten in middle of 2d scallop at bottom of work; 7 ch.st.; fasten in middle of next scal.; turn; 12 s.c. around chain of 7; 6 s.c. around next 7 ch.st.; turn; 7 ch.st.; fasten in scal.; turn; 12 s.c. around 7 ch.st.; 6 s.c. around half finished scal.; 6 s.c. around next half scal.; 1 ch.st.; 3 d.c. around chain of 3 of preceding row; 3 ch.st.; 3 d.c. around same chain; 3 ch.st.; 1 s.c. through middle stitch of ch. of 5th and 6th rows; 3 ch.st.; 3 d.c. around next chain of 3; 3 ch.st.; 3 d.c. around same chain; 3 ch.st.; 1 s.c. in middle stitch of ch. of 5th and 6th rows; 3 ch.st.; 3 d.c. around next chain of 3 · 3 ch.

Fasten fringe in every other stitch of the bottom edge.

LAMBREQUIN DESIGN No. 8.

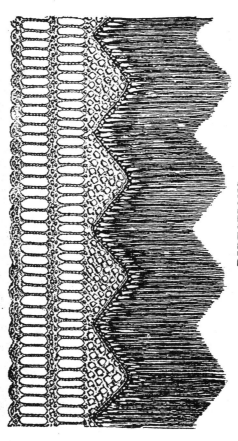

DIRECTIONS.

Make a chain of 30 stitches.

1st row.—3 d.c. in 4th st. of chain ; 3 ch.st.; 3 d. c. in same (4th) st.; 7 ch.st.; miss 10 ch.st.; put 3

d.c. in 11th; 3 ch.st.; 3 d.c. in same ; miss 3 ch.st.; put 3 d.c. in 4th; 3 ch.st.; 3 d.c. in same ; 7 ch.st.; 3 d.c. in last of foundation chain ; 3 ch.st.; 3 d.c. in same.

2d row.—Turn ; 3 ch.st.; 3 d.c. around chain of 3 of last row ; 3 ch.st.; 3 d.c. around same chain ; 7 ch.st.; 3 d.c. around next chain of 3 ; 3 ch.st.; 3 d.c. around same chain ; 3 d.c. around next chain of 3 ; 3 ch.st.; 3 d.c. around same chain ; 7 ch.st.; 3 d.c. around next chain of 3 ; 3 ch.st.; 3 d.c. around same chain ; 3 ch.st.

3d row.—Turn ; crochet to end of row as before, then 3 ch.st.; 3 d.c. around chain of 3 of last row.

4th row.—3 ch.st.; 3 d.c. in chain of 3 of 3d row ; 3 ch.st.; then 3 d.c. in next chain of 3 ; 3 ch.st., etc. Crochet to end of, as before.

5th row.—3 ch.st.; 3 d.c. around chain of 3 of preceding row ; 3 ch.st.; 3 d.c. around same ; 7 ch. st.; 3 d.c. around next ; 3 ch.st.; 3 d.c. around same ; 3 d.c. around next ; 3 ch.st.; 3 d.c. around same ; 3 ch.st.; 3 d.c. around next ch. of 3, which is in the point ; 3 ch.st.; 3 d.c. around next ch.

6th row.—3 ch.st.; 3 d.c.; 3 ch.st.; 3 d.c.; 3 ch. st.; finish to the end of row, as usual.

7th row.—Crochet as usual to beginning of point, then 3 ch.st.; 3 d.c.; 3 ch.st.; 3d.c.; 3 ch.st.; 3 d.c.

8th row.—3 ch.st.; 3 d.c., etc.

9th row.—Crochet as usual to beginning of point, then 3 ch.st.; 3 d.c.; 3 ch.st.; 3 d.c.; 3 ch.st.; 3 d. c.; 3 ch.st.; 3 d.c.

10th row.—3 ch.st.; 3 d.c.; 3 ch.st.; 3 d.c.; 3 ch. st.; 3 d.c.; 3 ch.st.; 3 d.c.; then as usual to the end,

2d row.—4 d.c. around last 1 ch.st. of 1st row; 2 ch.st.; 4 d.c. around next 3 ch.st.; 2 ch.st.; miss next 2 d.c.; make 1 d.c. in following 10 d.c. of 1st row; 1 ch.st.; miss 1 ch.st.; 2 d.c. around next chain of 1, which separates the 4 d.c. coming together in last row; 1 ch.st.; 2 d.c. around same chain of 1; 2 d.c. around next chain of 1; 1 ch.st.; 2 d.c. in same chain; 7 ch.st.; 2 d.c. around next chain of 1; 1 ch.st.; 2 d.c. around same chain; 2 d.c. around next chain of 1; 1 ch.st.; 2 d.c. in same chain; 3 ch.st.; turn.

3d row.—2 d.c. around 1st chain of 1 of 2d row; 1 ch.st.; 2 d.c. around same chain; 2 d.c.; 1 ch.st.; 2 d.c. around next chain of 1; 3 ch.st.; 1 s.c. through 4th st. of chain of 1st and 2d row, drawing tightly together; 3 ch.st.; 2 d.c. around next chain of 1; 1 ch.st.; 2 d.c. around same chain; 2 d.c. around next chain of 1; 1 ch.st.; 2 d.c. around same chain; 1 ch.st.; 1 d.c. in 8 d.c. of preceding row; 2 ch.st.; 4 d.c. around 2 ch.st. of preceding row; 2 ch.st.; 4 d.c.; 2 ch.st.; 4 d.c.; 1 ch.st.; 1 t.; 4 ch.st.

4th row.—4 d.c. around last t. and d.c. of 3d row; 2 ch.st.; 4 d.c.; 2 ch.st.; 4 d.c.; 2 ch.st.; 4 d.c.; 2 ch.st.; miss 2; 1 d.c. in next 6 d.c. of 3d row; 1 ch. st.; 2 d.c. around next chain of 1; 1 ch.st.; 2 d.c. around same chain; 2 d.c. around next chain of 1; 1 ch.st.; 2 d.c. around same chain; 7 ch.st.; 2 d.c. around next chain of 1; 1 ch.st.; 2 d.c. around same chain; 2 d.c. around next chain of 1; 1 ch.st.; 2 d. c. in same chain; 3 ch.st.

5th row.—2 d.c.; 1 ch.st.; 2 d.c., as before; 2 d. c.; 1 ch.st.; 2 d.c. in next chain of 1; 7 ch.st.; 2 d.

---

making it the required length. Crochet as a heading, 7 d.c. around 3 ch.st. at the top, fastening each one down before another.

The fringe must be fastened in every other stitch of the bottom edge.

LAMBREQUIN DESIGN No. 9.

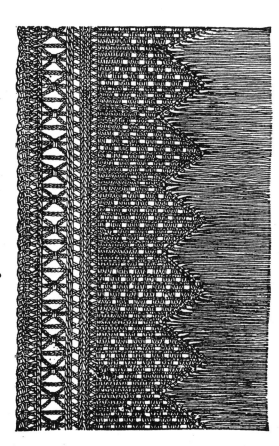

DIRECTIONS.

Make a chain of 39 stitches.

1st row.—2 d.c. in 4th st. of ch.; 1 ch.st.; 2 d. c. in same (4th) st.; miss 2 ch.st.; put 2 d.c. in 3d ch. st.; 1 ch.st.; 2 d.c. in same 3d ch.st.; 7 ch.st.; miss 8 ch.st.; put 2 d.c. in 9th ch.st.; 1 ch.st.; 2 d.c. in same; miss 3 ch.st.; put 2 d.c. in 4th; 1 ch.st.; 2 d.c. in same 1 ch.st.; miss 2 ch.st.; put 1 d.c. in next 12 ch.st.; 3 ch.st.; 3 d.c. in last stitch of chain; 1 ch.st.; 1 t.c. in 1 last st. of chain; 4 ch.st. and turn.

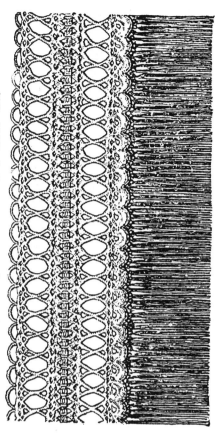

c.; 1 ch.st.; 2 d.c.; 2 d.c.; 1 ch.st.; 2 d.c.; 1 ch.st.; 1 d.c. in 4 d.c. of preceding row; 2 ch.st.; 4 d.c.; 2 ch.st.; 4 d.c.; 2 ch.st.; 4 d.c.; 4 d.c.; 1 t.; 4 ch.st.

6th row.—4 d.c. around last t. and d.c. of 5th row; 2 ch.st.; 4 d.c.; 2 ch.st.; 4 d.c.; 2 ch.st.; 4 d.c.; 2 ch.st.; miss next 2 d.c.; 1 d.c. in next 2 d.c. of 5th row; 1 ch.st.; 2 d. c. around next chain of 1; 1 ch.st.; 2 d.c. in same chain; 2 d.c. in next chain of 1; 1 ch.st.; 2 d.c. in same chain; 7 ch.st.; 2 d.c. around next chain of 1; 1 ch.st.; 2 d.c. around same chain; 2 d.c.'around same chain; 3 ch.st.

7th row.—2 d.c. around chain of 1; 1 ch.st.; 2 d. c. around same chain; 2 d.c. around next chain of 1; 1 ch.st.; 2 d.c. around same chain; 3 ch.st.; 1 s.c. through 4th st. of last 2 chains, drawing tightly together; 3 ch.st.; 2 d.c. around next chain of 1; 1 ch.st.; 2 d.c. around same chain; 2 d.c. around next chain of 1; 1 ch.st.; 2 d.c. around same chain; 1 ch.st.; 1 d.c. in next 4 st. of last row; 2 ch.st.; 4 d.c.; 2 ch.st.; 4 d.c.; 2 ch.st.; 4 d.c.· 1 s.c. in d.c. of 6th row; turn.

8th row.—1 s.c. in each of 4 d.c. of preceding row; 4 d.c. around 3 ch.st. of 7th row; 2 ch. st.; 4 d.c.; 2 ch.st.; 4 d.c.; 2 ch.st.; 4 d.c.; 2 ch.st.; miss next 4 d.c.; 1 d.c. in next 6 st.; 1 ch.st.; 2 d.c. around chain of 1; 1 ch.st.; 2 d.c. around same chain; 2 d.c. around next chain of 1; 1 ch.st.; 2 d.c. around next chain of 1; 1 ch.st.; 2 d.c. around same; 7 ch.st.; 2 d.c. around same chain; 2 d.c. around next chain of 1; 1 ch.st.; 2 d.c. around same chain; 3 ch.st.

9th row.—2 d.c.; 1 ch.st.; 2 d.c. around chain of 1; 2 d.c.; 1 ch.st.; 2 d.c. around next chain of 1; 7 ch.st.; 2 d.c.; 1 ch.st.; 2 d.c. around chain of 1; 2 d.c. around next chain of 1; 1 ch.st.; 2 d.c. around same chain; 1 ch.st.; 1 d.c. in next 8 d.c.; 2 ch.st.; 4 d.c.; 2 ch.st.; 4 d.c.; 2 ch.st.; 4 d.c.; 1 s.c. in d.c. of 6th row; turn.

10th row.—1 s.c. in each of 4 d.c. of preceding row; 4 d.c. around next chain of 3 of 9th row; 2 ch.st.; 4 d.c.; 2 ch.st.; miss next 4 d.c.; make 10 d.c.; 1 ch.st.; 2 d.c.; 1 ch.st.; 2 d. c. around chain of 1; 2 d.c.; 1 ch.st.; 2 d.c. around next chain of 1; 7 ch.st.; 2 d.c.; 1 ch.st.; 2 d.c. around chain of 1; 2 d.c.; 1 ch.st.; 2 d.c. around last chain of 1; 3 ch.st.

These 10 rows are continually repeated, until the length of the lambrequin is reached.

LAMBREQUIN DESIGN No. 10.

DIRECTIONS.

Make a chain of 41 stitches.
1st row.—3 d.c. in 4th ch.st.; 3 ch.st.; 3 d.c. in

LAMBREQUIN DESIGN No. 11.

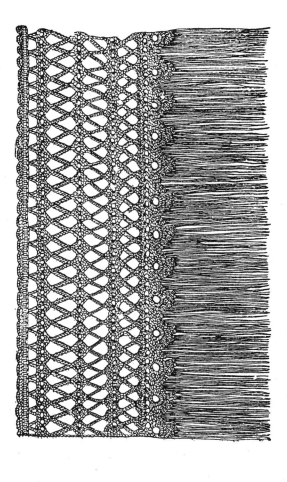

DIRECTIONS.

Make a chain of 35 stitches.

1st row.—3 d.c. in 4th ch.st., 3 ch.st., 3 d.c. in same st., fasten to next 3d st. of ch., 6 ch.st., miss 6 ch.st., 3 d.c. in 7th, 3 ch.st., 3ʹ d.c. in same, fasten to next 3d ch.st., 6 ch.st., miss 6, put 3 d.c. in 7th, 3 ch.st., 3 d.c. in same, fasten to next 3d st., 6 ch.st., miss 6, 3 d.c. in' 7th st. of ch., 3 ch.st., 3 d.c. in next ch.st., 5 ch.st., and turn.

2d row.—3 d.c. around next chain of 3, worked between the last 3 d.c. in preceding row, 3 ch.st., 3 d.c. around same, fasten around 1st st. of next chain of 6, 6 ch.st., 3 d.c. around next chain of 3, 3 ch.st., 3 d.c. around same ch., fasten, 6 ch.st., 3 d.c. around next chain of 3, 3 ch.st., 3 d.c. around

next st.; 9 ch.st.; miss 11; put 3 d.c. in 12th ch.st.; 3 ch.st.; 3 d.c. in next; miss 3 ch.st.; put 1 d.c. in each of next 3 ch.st.; miss 3 ch.st.; put 3 d.c. in 4th; 3 ch.st.; 3 d.c. in next; 9 ch.st.; miss 11; 3 d.c. in 12th ch.st. ; 3 ch.st.; 3 d.c. in same st. of chain ; 3 ch.st.

2d row.—3 d.c. around 1st chain of 3 between the two 3 d.c. of 1st row ; 3 ch.st.; 3 d.c around same; 4 ch.st.; 1 cl.ch.st. through 5th st. of chain in 1st row; 4 ch.st.; 3 d.c. around next chain of 3; 3 ch. st.; 3 d.c. around same ; 1 d.c. in each of the d.c. of 1st row ; 3 d.c. around next chain of 3 ; 3 ch.st.; 3 d.c. around same ; 4 ch.st.; 1 cl.ch.st. through 5th st. of ch. of 1st row ; 4 ch.st.; 3 d.c. around next chain of 3 ; 3 ch.st.; 3 d.c. around same ; 5 ch.st.; fasten to beginning of preceding row. Turn 10 s.c. around last chain of 5.

Repeat these two rows until the desired length, then finish off the bottom with 12 trebles around chain of 3 at end of rows, always fastening before beginning the next one.

same chain, fasten, 6 ch.st., 3 d.c. around next chain of 3, 3 ch.st., 3 d.c. around same, work 6 ch. st., turn.

3d row—3 d.c. around next chain of 3 of 2d row, 3 ch.st., 3 d.c. around same chain, fasten, 6 ch.st., 3 d.c., around next ch. of 3, 3 ch.st., 3 d.c. around same ch., fasten, 6 ch.st., 3 d.c. around next ch. of 3, 3 ch.st., 3 d.c. around same, fasten, 6 ch.st., 3 d.c. around next ch. of 3, 3 ch.st., 3 d.c. around same, fasten in 1st st. of chain of 5 of last row.

4th row—5 ch.st., 3 d.c. around next chain of 3 of 3d row, 3 ch.st., 3 d.c. around same, fasten, 6 ch.st., 3 d.c. around next ch. of 3, 3 ch.st., 3 d.c. around same, fasten, 6 ch.st., 3 d.c. around next ch. of 3, 3 ch.st., 3 d.c. around same, fasten, 6 ch. st., 3 d.c. around next ch. of 3, 3 ch.st., 3 d.c. around same; work around next chain of 6, *2 d. c., 3 ch.st.* Repeat 5 times, stopping before 3 ch. st., fasten by 1 s.c. in last 3d d.c. of 1st row.

5th row.—Turn, * 1 s.c., 3 d.c., 1 s.c. around chain of 3.* Repeat 4 times ; 3 ch.st., 3 d.c. around next ch. of 3 of last row, *3 ch.st., 3 d.c. around same, fasten, 6 ch.st., 3 d.c. around next chain of 3*, repeat to the end of the row. Finally, make 5 ch.st. instead of 3.

Begin again from 2d row.

For the heading, fasten the twine to end of work, then crochet 1 s.c. in every stitch of the edge.

The second row of heading is worked as follows :

Turn, *3 d.c in next s.c. of last row, miss next s.c., fasten in following s.c., miss 1, * repeat to end of the row.

4

No. 488—ELECTRIC SHADE

To Make Shade.

This shade is made by mounting the crochet over four circles of cardboard, which are held in place by drawstrings. After the circles are covered, place square cardboard inside and fasten with a stitch through each corner.

ROYAL SOCIETY Pink CORDICHET, No. 3015, size 30, 2 balls, crochet hook size 11.

Round with Rose.

1st row.—Ch. 6, join to ring, ch. 4, 7 d.c. into first ch. of ch. 4, 1 sl.st. into top of first d.c., 1 sl.st. into 3rd ch. of ring.

2nd row.—Ch. 5, 1 s.c. into ring, ch. 5, 1 s.c. into ring, ch. 5, 1 s.c. into same st. as 7 d.c., ch. 5, 1 s.c. into other side of ring, ch. 5, 1 s.c. into ring.

3rd row.—Into each loop, 1 s.c., 1 h.d.c., 4 d.c., 1 h.d.c., 1 s.c., join with sl.st.

4th row.—1 s.c. around s.c. of 2nd row, ch. 6, 1 s.c. around next s.c. of 2nd row, repeat 3 times more, join with sl.st.

5th row.—Into each loop, 1 s.c., 1 h.d.c., 8 d.c., 1 h.d.c., 1 s.c., join with sl.st.

6th row.—1 s.c. around s.c. of 4th row, ch. 7, repeat 4 times more, join with sl.st.

7th row.—Into each loop, 1 s.c., 1 h.d.c., 12 d.c., 1 h.d.c., 1 s.c., join with sl.st.

8th row.—1 s.c. around s.c. of 6th row, ch. 9, continue around, join with sl.st.

9th row.—Into each loop, 1 s.c., 1 h.d.c., 15 d.c., 1 h.d.c., 1 s.c., join with sl.st.

10th row.—3 sl.sts. into 3 following sts. of scallop, ch. 9, sk. 2, 1 s.c., repeat this 4 times more into same scallop, ch. 9, sk. 3, of next scallop, 1 s.c., ch. 9, sk. 2, 1 s.c., repeat until 5 s.c. into scallops are made, continue around. To finish row ch. 4, 1 tr.c. into 3rd sl.st. from beginning of row.

11th row.—Ch. 9, 1 s.c. into 5th ch. of loop of previous row, ch. 9, 1 s.c. into 5th ch. of next loop, and repeat around. Finish row with ch. 4, and 1 tr.c.

12th row.—Same as eleventh row.

13th row.—Ch. 7, 1 s.c. into 5th ch. of next loop, ch. 7, 1 s.c. into next loop, continue around.

14th row.—Ch. 3, 1 d.c. into each st., join with sl.st.

15th row.—Ch. 3, 1 d.c. into each st., taking up back rib, join with sl.st., finish off.

Pull cotton through every other back rib of last row made, stretch over cardboard and fasten draw string on back. The last row of d.c. is to serve as turnover at inside of cardboard.

Make 3 more rounds this way, join them at front rib between last two rows of d.c. with 20 sl.sts. To join next 2 rounds, leave 56 sts. for top of shade, then make 20 sl.sts., working downwards.

Tassel.

Trim bottom of shade with small tassels.

Wind cotton 50 times around cardboard 1¼ inches long, cut off, tie in center, work with same thread, ch. 1, 1 s.c., ch. 1, and repeat until 8 s.c. are made, tie again ¼ of an inch from top. Attach this tassel in between rounds to joining. Make one other tassel the same way, with only 6 s.c. for string, sk. 17 sts. from joining and attach. 1 tassel with 4 s.c. for string, sk. 15 sts. from last tassel and attach.

One tassel with 2 s.c. for string, sk. 15 sts. and attach. This last tassel must be in the center of bottom of round. Finish other side of round the same way reversing, and continue all around shade.

No. 489—WORK BASKET

The basket is made by mounting the crochet over a cardboard foundation and is held in place by draw strings.

This basket may be used on the table for bread, cakes or rolls as it is very easily laundered by simply loosening the draw strings and removing the cardboards. It may also be used in the boudoir as a work basket by substituting colored cardboards to carry out the color scheme of the room.

ROYAL SOCIETY White CORDICHET, size 30, 2 balls, Crochet hook size 11.

Center of Basket.

1st row.—Ch. 6, join to ring, ch. 3, 15 d.c. into ring, join with sl.st.

2nd row.—Ch. 5, 1 d.c. into next, ch. 2, 1 d.c. into next, continue around, at end of row, join to 3rd ch. from beginning (this row has 15 holes).

3rd row.—1 s.c. into first hole, ch. 10, 1 tr.c. into same, 1 tr.c. into next hole, ch. 5, 1 tr.c. into same, continue all around. Join to 5th ch. from beginning.

4th row.—1 s.c. into first space, ch. 5, 1 tr.c. into same, ch. 5, 2 tr.c. into same, 2 tr.c. into next space, ch. 5, 2 tr.c. into same. Continue around. Join to 5th ch. from beginning of row.

5th row.—Into every space of ch. 5, 1 s.c., 1 h.d.c., 1 d.c., 5 tr.c., 1 d.c., 1 h.d.c., 1 s.c. Join with sl.st.

6th row.—5 sl.sts. to center of first scallop, 1 s.c. into next st., ch. 9, 1 s.c. into center of next scallop, ch. 9, and continue around.

Continued on page 45.

No. 6208—FILET SCARF

ROYAL SOCIETY Ecru CORDICHET, size 20, 9 balls. Crochet hook size 11.

Description of Filet.

Open Mesh.—1 d.c., ch. 2, sk. 2, 1 d.c. into next st.

Closed Mesh.—1 d.c. into d.c. taking up both loops, 2 d.c. into chs. not around chs., 1 d.c. into next d.c.

For foundation chs. make three times as many chs. as m. Always make 5 chs. to turn.

For Filet parts follow black and white drawings. Around big center Medallion work 3 s.c. into one, 2 s.c. into the next m., 7 s.c. into the corners. Make one other row of 5 s.c., 1 p., 5 s.c. all around.

Around side panels, work 1 row of 5 s.c., 1 p., 5 s.c. At side which is to be joined to center Medallion, begin after 9th row from top of band. Catch into corner p. of center Medallion instead of making a p. At side band, 5 s.c. joined to next p. and continue.

Around pointed edge work 3 s.c. into each m., 9 s.c. into m. at point. (Make one other row of 3 s.c., one p., 3 s.c., the edge must have 5 points. At straight side of edge make one row of one d.c. into each st. Make one row of s.c. After every 5th s.c. catch into p. of center Medallion to join.

Sew a tassel at each point and one tassel between points.

At each point of side panel fasten a longer tassel.

Tassel.

Wind the cotton 80 times around cardboard one and three-quarter inches long, tie in center, tie again one-half inch from top and sew on.

For longer tassel take cardboard two and a half inches long.

Place on stamped lines and cut linen away underneath.

No. 5955—PILLOW

ROYAL SOCIETY Ecru CORDICHET, size 20, 9 balls. Crochet hook size 11.

For oval center follow black and white drawing. Work 3 s.c. into each m. all around. Make one other row of 5 s.c., one p., 5 s.c.

For pointed edge follow black and white drawing long enough to go around stamped line on pillow, then work around points 2 s.c., 1 p., 2 s.c. into each m.

At straight edge of same one row of d.c. around, one row of m., and 2 rows of d.c. To finish make one row of 5 s.c., 1 p., 5 s.c.

24

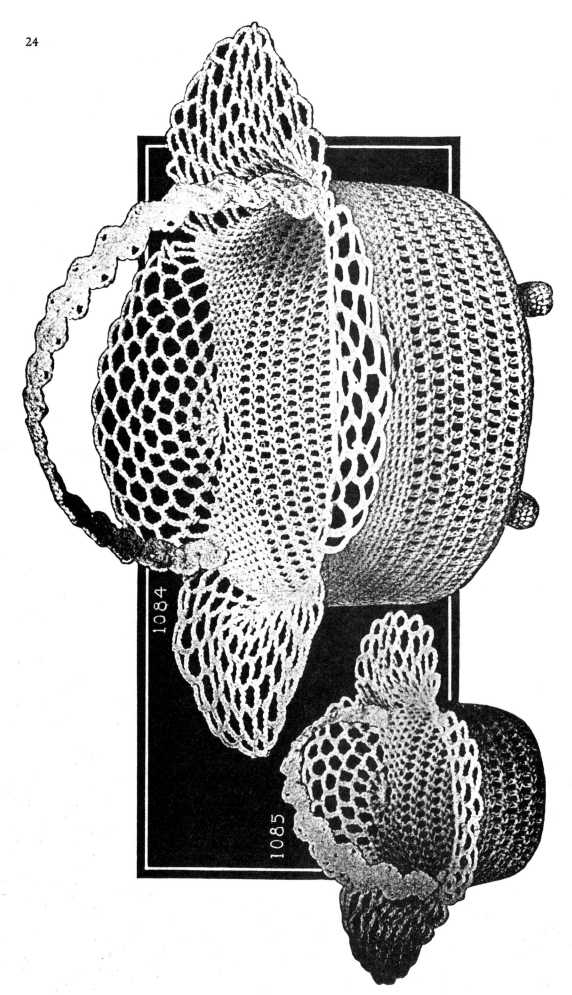

1084

1085

No. 1084—LARGE BASKET

ROYAL SOCIETY White Cordichet size 30—1 ball.

1st row.—Ch. 5, join to ring, 8 s.c. into ring, join with sl. st.

2nd row.—2 s.c. into each st., join.

3rd row.—2 s.c. into first st., 1 s.c. into next, 2 s.c. into 3rd st., 1 s.c. into next, continue around, join.

4th row.—2 s.c. into first st., 1 s.c. into each of 2 following sts., 2 s.c. into 4th st., 2 s.c. into each of 2 following sts., continue around, join.

5th row.—2 s.c. into first st., 1 s.c. into each of 3 following sts., continue around, join.

6th row.—2 s.c. into first st., 1 s.c. into each of 4 following sts., continue around, join.

7th row.—1 s.c. into each st. all around, join.

8th row.—2 s.c. into first st., 1 s.c. into each of 5 following sts., continue around, join.

9th row.—1 s.c. into each st. all around, join.

10th row.—2 s.c. into first st., 1 s.c. into each of 6 following sts., join.

11th row.—1 s.c. into each st. all around, join.

12th row.—2 s.c. into first st., 1 s.c. into each of 7 following sts., join.

13th row.—1 s.c. into each st., all around, join.

14th row.—2 s.c. into first st., 1 s.c. into each of 8 following sts., join.

15th row.—1 s.c. into each st. all around, join.

16th row.—2 s.c. into first st., 1 s.c. into each of 9 following sts., join.

17th row.—1 s.c. into each st., all around, join.

18th row.—2 s.c. into first st., 1 s.c. into each of 10 following sts., join.

19th row.—1 s.c. into each st. all around, join.

20th row.—2 s.c. into first, 1 s.c. into each of 7 following sts., join.

21st row.—1 s.c. into each st. all around, join. This row has 108 sts.

22nd row, 23rd, 24th, 25th, 26th row are the same as 21st row.

27th row.—Ch. 3, 1 d.c. into each st. all around, join.

28th row, 29th, 30th, 31st, 32nd rows same as 27th row.

33rd row.—1 s.c. into each st., join.

34th row.—Ch. 3, * sk. 1, 26 s.c., ch. 2, repeat from * 3 times more, join.

35th row.—Ch. 2, * 6 d.c., with always ch. 1 between, into space of ch. 2 ch. 1, sk. 1, 24 s.c. into following sts., ch. 1. Repeat from * 3 times more, at end of row after 24 s.c. are made join to first ch. from beginning.

36th row.—Ch. 3, * 1 d.c. into space before first d.c., ch. 2, 1 d.c. into next space, continue until 7 d.c. with always ch. 2 between are made, ch. 2, sk. 2, 20 s.c. into following sts., ch. 2, repeat from * 3 times more. At end of row after last 20 s.c. are made join to first ch. from beginning.

37th row.—Ch. 4, * 1 d.c. into first space before first d.c., ch. 3, 1 d.c. into next space, ch. 3, continue with 8 d.c. with ch. 3. Between are made ch. 3, sk. 2, 16 s.c., ch. 3. Repeat from * 3 times more. After last 16 s.c. are made join to first ch. from beginning of row.

38th row.—Ch. 5, * 1 d.c. into first space before d.c., ch. 4, 1 d.c. into next space, ch. 4, continue until 9 d.c. are made, ch. 4, sk. 1, 14 s.c. ch. 4. Repeat from * 3 times more. After last 14 s.c. join to first ch. from beginning.

39th row.—Ch. 6, * 1 d.c. into first space, ch. 5, 1 d.c. into next space, continue until 10 d.c. are made, ch. 5, sk. 2, 10 s.c., ch. 5. Repeat from 3 times more. After last 10 s.c. join to first ch. from beginning.

40th row.—Ch. 7, * 1 d.c. into first space, ch. 6, 1 d.c. into next space, continue until 11 d.c. are made, ch. 6, sk. 1, 8 s.c., ch. 6. Repeat from * 3 times more, after last 8 s.c. join to first ch. from beginning.

41st row.—Ch. 8, * 1 d.c. into first space, ch. 7, 1 d.c. into next space, continue until 12 d.c. are made, ch. 7, sk. 2, 4 s.c., ch. 7. Repeat from 3 times more. After last 4 s.c. are made join to first ch. from beginning.

42nd row.—Ch. 9, * 1 d.c. into first space, ch. 8, 1 d.c. into next space, continue until 12 d.c. are made, ch. 7, sk. 2, 4 s.c., ch. 7. Repeat from * 3 times more. After After last 3 s.c. join to first ch. from beginning.

43rd row.—Ch. 9, * 1 s.c. into first space, ch. 8, 1 s.c. into next space, continue into each space, ch. 8, sk. 1, 2 s.c. Repeat from * 3 times more after last 2 s.c. Join to first ch. from beginning, finish off.

Handle.

Ch. 5, join to ring, 4 d.c., ch. 2, 3 d.c. into ring, turn, * ch. 3, 4 d.c., ch. 2, 3 d.c. into space of ch. 2, turn, repeat from * for 7½ inches. Sew to basket between 2 scallops on opposite sides.

Feet.

Ch. 9, sk. 1, 2 s.c. into each ch., turn 1 s.c. into each st., turn, make 10 more rows of 12 s.c., fill with cotton, sew together along side, sew to bottom of basket, make 3 more feet the same way.

No. 1085—SMALL BASKET

ROYAL SOCIETY White Cordichet, size 30, 1 ball.

1st row.—Ch. 5, join to ring, 8 s.c. into ring, join with sl. st.

2nd row.—2 s.c. into each st. all around, join with sl. st.

3rd row.—2 s.c. into first st., 1 s.c. into next st., 2 s.c. into 3rd st., continue around, join.

4th row.—2 s.c. into first st., 1 s.c. into each of 2 following sts., 2 s.c. into 4th st., continue around, join.

5th row.—1 s.c. into each st. all around, join.

6th row.—2 s.c. into first st., 1 s.c. into each of 3 following sts., 2 s.c. into next, continue around, join.

7th row.—1 s.c. into each st. all around, join.

8th row.—2 s.c. into first st., 1 s.c. into each of 4 following sts., continue around, join.

9th row.—1 s.c. into each st. all around, join.

MOTIFS FOR THIS SET
Illustrated on Pages 30 and 32.

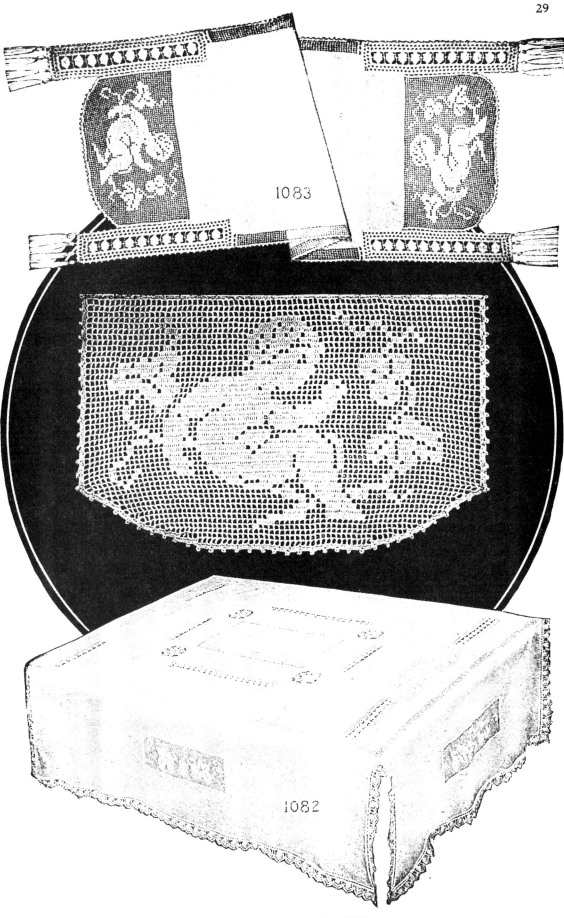

1083

1082

MOTIF FOR THIS SET
Illustrated on pages 34, 36, 38.

MOTIFS FROM SET

Illustrated on page 28

Filet and Venetian Lace.

For Filet use White CORDICHET, size 20, 9 balls.
For Venetian Lace use White CORDICHET, size 10, 22 balls.

Filet Explanation.

Open Mesh.—1 d.c., ch. 2, sk. 2, 1 d.c. into next st.
Closed Mesh.—1 d.c. into d.c., 2 d.c. into 2 chs., 1 d.c. into next d.c. For foundation chain make three times as many chains as meshes and add 1 ch., always ch. 5 to turn. At top of d.c. take up both loops, and over open loop. If closed loop is indicated work into chains, not around.

Centre Filet Oblong.

To make this center, ch. 300, sk. 7, 1 d.c., ch. 2, sk. 2, 1 d.c., continue until 59 m. are made. This is first row of Filet, then follow cut which shows clearly the stitches.
When Filet part is completed work around 3 s.c. into one m., 2 s.c. into next, continue all around, into corner holes 7 s.c. Join.
Ch. 3, 1 d.c. into next st., ch. 3, sk. 3, 2 d.c., ch. 3, sk. 3, 2 d.c., continue around. At corners ch. 5, 2 d.c. into next 2 sts. At end of row join to 3rd ch. from beginning.
1 s.c. into next st., 3 s.c. into space, 2 s.c. into next 2 sts., 3 s.c. into space, continue around. Into corner hole 7 s.c., 1 row of 5 s.c., 1 p., 5 s.c., 1 p., continue all around.

Small Filet Oblong.

Ch. 101, sk. 7, 1 d.c., ch. 2, sk. 2, 1 d.c., continue until 32 m. are made, this is first row of oblong. Now follow cut which shows plainly the stitches.
When the Filet part is completed work around oblong, 3 s.c. into one hole, 2 s.c. into next, continue around. Into corner holes 7 s.c. Join with sl.st. 1 row of 5 s.c., 1 p., 5 s.c. all around.
Four more oblongs like this are required for the design of Bedspread.

Venetian Medallion.

1st row.—Ch. 5, join to ring, 1 s.c. into ring, ch. 8, 1 tr.c. into ring, ch. 3, 1 tr.c. into ring, ch. 3, continue until 7 tr.c. are made, ch. 3, join to 4th ch. from beginning.
2nd row.—5 s.c. into each hole, join.
3rd row.—Ch. 3, 1 d.c. into next st., ch. 2, sk. 1, 2 d.c., ch. 2, sk. 1, 2 d.c., continue all around. Join to 3rd ch. from beginning.
4th row.—1 s.c. into next st., 3 s.c. into next hole, 2 s.c. into 2 next sts., continue around. Join.
5th row.—1 s.c. into next st., * ch. 10, sk. 1, 6 s.c., ch. 1, work upwards, 6 s.c. into same sts., 3 s.c. into next st., continue working around, 6 s.c. into following sts., 3 s.c. into next st., 7 s.c. into following sts., 3 s.c. into next st., 8 s.c. into next sts., 3 s.c. into next st., 3 s.c. into following sts., 1 p., 3 s.c. into next st., 1 p., 2 s.c. into next sts., 3 s.c. into next st., 3 s.c., 1 p., 3 s.c., 1 p., 3 s.c., 1 sl. st. into next st., 1 sl. st. into top of s.c., 8 s.c. into following sts. Repeat from * seven times more.
6th row.—Sl. sts. into center up the back of small oval, 1 s.c. into point of oval, * ch. 6, cotton 3 times around needle, insert into st. between 2 p. of same oval, pull through 2 loops, cotton once over needle, insert into st. between 2 p. of next oval, pull 5 times through 2 loops, ch. 6, 1 s.c. into top of same oval. Repeat from * all around. Join into first s.c. from beginning.
7th row.—* 9 s.c. into first hole, 4 s.c. into next hole, 4 s.c. into 4 last chs. of same hole, 1 s.c. into s.c., 4 s.c. into 4 following chs., turn, sk. 1, 7 s.c., turn, sk. 1, 5 s.c., turn, sk. 1, 3 s.c., turn, sk. 1, 1 s.c., 4 sl. sts. down the side of triangle, 4 s.c. into same hole, 9 s.c. into following hole. Repeat from * three times more. Join.
8th row.—1 s.c. into each st. all around, 3 s.c. into each corner st. Join.
9th row.—Ch. 3, 1 d.c. into first st., ch. 2, sk. 2, 2 d.c., ch. 2, sk. 2, 2 d.c., continue to corner. At corner 2 d.c. into one st., ch. 5, 2 d.c. into next st., ch. 2, sk. 2, 2 d.c., continue all around. Join to 3rd ch. from beginning.
10th row.—1 s.c. into first d.c., 2 s.c. into space, 2 s.c. into next, 2 d.c., continue to corner. Into corner hole 7 s.c., continue all around. Join.
11th row.—1 s.c. into each st. all around. Into center st. at corners, 3 s.c. Join
12th row.—5 s.c., 1 p., 5 s.c., 1 p., continue all around.
Make 3 more medallions the same way. Place one at each corner of center oblong.

Bands of Insertion.

Ch. 109, sk. 1, 6 s.c., ch. 10, sk. 1, 6 s.c., ch. 1, 6 s.c. into same chs., working upwards, 3 s.c. into next st., work around, 6 s.c. into next sts., 3 s.c. into ch., 7 s.c. into next sts., 3 s.c. into following st., 8 s.c. into next sts., 3 s.c. into following st., 3 s.c. into next sts., 1 p., continue around, 3 s.c., 1 p., 3 s.c., 3 s.c. into center st., 3 s.c., 1 p., 3 s.c., 1 p., 3 s.c., 1 sl. st into next st., 1 sl. st. on top of last s.c. of foundation ch., 12 s.c. into following sts. of foundation ch. Repeat from * 8 times more (9 ovals in all), finish with 6 s.c. Turn.
Ch. 6, 1 s.c. into st. between 2 p. of last oval made, ch. 11, 1 s.c. into center st. of top of same oval, * ch. 5, cotton 4 times around needle, insert into st. between 2 p. at other side of same oval, pull once through 2 loops, cotton 3 times around needle, insert into 6th st. between ovals, pull three times through 2 loops, cotton once around needle, insert into center st. between 2 p. of next oval, pull through all loops on needle 2 at a time. Ch. 5, 1 s.c. into top of same oval. Repeat from * to top of last oval, ch. 11, 1 s.c. into center st. between 2 p. at side of last oval, ch. 6, 1 s.c. into last s.c. of foundation ch., turn, 7 s.c. into first hole, 13 s.c. into next hole, which is the corner, 6 s.c. into each of following holes. Finish other end the same way and join to foundation ch.
Work all around band, 1 s.c. into each st., 3 s.c. into corner st. After 3 s.c. into last corner are made, join with sl. st.
Ch. 3, 1 d.c. into next st., ch. 2, sk. 2, 2 d.c., ch. 2, sk. 2, 2 d.c., continue to corner, 2 d.c., ch. 5, 1 d.c. into same, 1 d.c. into next st., continue around. Join.
1 s.c. into next st., 2 s.c. into space, 2 s.c. into next sts., continue around. Into corner holes 7 s.c. Join. *Continued on page 33.*

MOTIFS FROM SET
Illustrated on page 28

2 sl. st. into next sts., ch. 3, 1 d.c. into following st., ch. 2, sk. 2, 2 d.c., continue around. At corner sk. 1, 2 d.c. into center st., ch. 3, 2 d.c. into same, ch. 2, sk. 1, 2 d.c., continue. At end of row join to 3rd ch. from beginning.

1 s.c. into next st., 2 s.c. into next hole, 2 s.c. into next sts., continue around. Into corner holes 5 s.c., 1 row of 5 s.c., 1 p., 5 s.c. all around.

Make one other band the same way. These two bands are placed at top and bottom of center medallion, joining corners of square venetian medallions.

Make two other bands the same way, but starting with 217 chs., which gives 18 ovals. These 2 bands are placed to opposite point of square medallion running parallel with center medallion.

At top and bottom of spread about 7 inches from insertion place filet oblongs. At center of end of this medallion place a band of insertion, for which ch. 121, which gives 10 ovals. Make 3 more bands the same way.

To join flouncing to spread make narrow insertion, with size 10 CORDICHET.

Narrow Insertion.

Ch. 21, sk. 3, 2 d.c., ch. 2, sk. 2, 1 d.c., ch. 2, sk. 2, 1 d.c., 3 more m., 1 d.c. into last st., turn. * ch. 3, 2 d.c. 1 m., 4 d.c., 1 m., 4 d.c., 1 m., 2 d.c., turn, ch. 3, 2 d.c., 2 m., 4 d.c., 2 m., 2 d.c., turn, ch. 3, 2 d.c., 1 m., 4 d.c., 1 m., 4 d.c., 1 m., 2 d.c., turn, ch. 3, 2 d.c., 5 m., 2 d.c., repeat from * for length of bedspread.

Corner.—For corner work 5 rows the same way but having on one side of band only 1 d.c. to finish m. Work into this 5 m., starting with 2 d.c., 1 m., 4 d.c., 1 m., 4 d.c., 1 m., 2 d.c. and continue again as before for width of spread and finish other half the same way.

At each side put a flouncing 2 yards long, ½ yard wide. At bottom of spread a flouncing 40 inches long, ½ yard wide. Into center of each of 3 flouncing place a filet oblong.

Make 9 yards of edging to go all around flouncing.

Edging.

Make chs. for length required, sk. 1, 7 s.c., * ch. 7, sk. 1. 4 s.c., ch. 1, 4 s.c. into same sts., working upwards, 3 s.c. into next st., work around, 4 s.c. into next st., 3 s.c. into ch., 5 s.c. into next sts., 3 s.c. into next st., 6 s.c. into next sts., 3 s.c. into next st., 2 s.c., 1 p., 3 s.c., 1 p., 2 sc., 3 s.c. into next st., 2 s.c., 1 p., 3 s.c., 1 p., 2 s.c., 1 sl. st. into next st., 1 sl. st. into top of last s.c. of foundation ch., 6 s.c. into following sts., turn, ch. 6, 1 d.c. into center st. between 2 p. of oval, ch. 6, 1 d.c. into point of oval, ch. 5, 1 d.c. into same, ch. 6, 1 d.c. into center st. between 2 p. at other side of oval, ch. 6, 1 s.c. into last s.c. of foundation ch., turn, 1 s.c. into each of 16 following sts., 3 s.c. into next, 16 s.c. into next sts., 10 s.c. into following sts. of foundation ch. Repeat from * across. Turn, 7 s.c., 1 h.d.c., 1 d.c., * ch. 2, sk. 2, 1 d.c., ch. 2, sk. 2, 1 d.c., ch. 2, sk. 1, 1 d.c., ch. 3, 1 d.c. into same, ch. 2, sk. 1, 1 d.c., ch. 2 sk. 2, 1 d.c., ch. 2, sk. 2, 1 d.c., 1 h.d.c., 1 s.c., 1 s.c. into the 8th st. from other scallop, 1 h.d.c., 1 d.c. Repeat from * across, turn, * 1 s.c. on top of h.d.c., 1 p., 3 s.c. into next space, 1 p., 3 s.c. into 2nd space, 1 p., 3 s.c. into 3rd space, 1 p., 2 s.c., 1 p., 2 s.c. into center space, 1 p., continue the same way for other side of scallop. After last p. and 1 s.c. into h.d.c. Repeat from * across.

At other side of foundation ch. 1 s.c. into each st., turn, ch. 3, 1 d.c., ch. 2, sk. 2, 2 d.c., ch. 2, sk. 2, 2 d.c., continue across, turn, 2 s.c. into 2 sts., 2 s.c. into next hole, 2 s.c. into next sts., continue across.

No. 1083—WHITE SCARF

For filet medallion at end of scarf ch. 107, sk. 7, 1 d.c., ch. 2, sk. 2, 1 d.c., continue for 34 m. in all, turn, ch. 16, sk. 7, 1 d.c., ch. 2, sk. 2, 1 d.c., 2 more m., continue with m. across previous row, ch. 5, 1 d.c. into same as last d.c., turn, ch. 5, 1 d.c. into 3rd ch. of previous hole, make 2 more m. the same way, ch. 13, sk. 7, 1 d.c., 3 more m., continue with m. over previous row, ch. 5, 1 d.c. into same as last d.c., turn, ch. 5, 1 d.c. into 3rd ch. of previous hole, turn, ch. 5, 1 d.c. into 3rd ch. of previous hole, turn, 3 sl. sts. into 3 last sts. made, ch. 10, sk. 7, 1 d.c., continue increasing the same way by following cut, which shows plainly the sts., then work around 3 s.c. into one hole, 2 s.c. into next, into corner hole at top 5 s.c., into corner holes for increasing at bottom 3 s.c.

1 row of 5 s.c., 1 p., 5 s.c. all around.

At each side of the filet medallion place a band of insertion in venetian crochet, for which follow directions of bands of insertion given in Bedspread, but start with 133 chs., which gives 11 ovals.

Finish band the same way, make 3 more bands and place them 4 inches higher than filet medallion. Connect the bands with a plain filet insertion worked in size 20 CORDICHET.

Filet Insertion.

Ch. 23, sk. 7, 1 d.c., ch. 2, sk. 2, 1 d.c., 3 more m., turn, ch. 5, 5 m., continue for length of scarf to venetian band at other end. Work all around insertion, 2 s.c. into one m., 3 s.c. into next, into corners 5 s.c.

1 row of 5 s.c., 1 p., 5 s.c. Make one other insertion the same way for other side. At end of venetian bands attach 4 tassels to every other p. on each band.

Tassels.

Wind size 10 CORDICHET 60 times around cardboard 5 inches long, cut off, tie in center, tie again ½ inch from top.

BOUDOIR SET

No. 1071—ECRU BEDSPREAD

Use ROYAL SOCIETY Ecru CORDICHET, size 5, 38 balls.

Large Center Medallion.

1st row.—Ch. 5, join to ring, 8 s.c. into ring, join with sl. st.

2nd row.—2 s.c. into each st. until 16 s.c. are made, join.

3rd row.—2 s.c. into first st., 1 s.c. into next st., 2 s.c. into next, continue until 24 s.c. are made, join.

4th row.—2 s.c. into first st., 1 s.c. into each of 2 following sts., 2 s.c. into 4th st., continue around until 32 s.c. are made, join.

Continued on page 35.

34

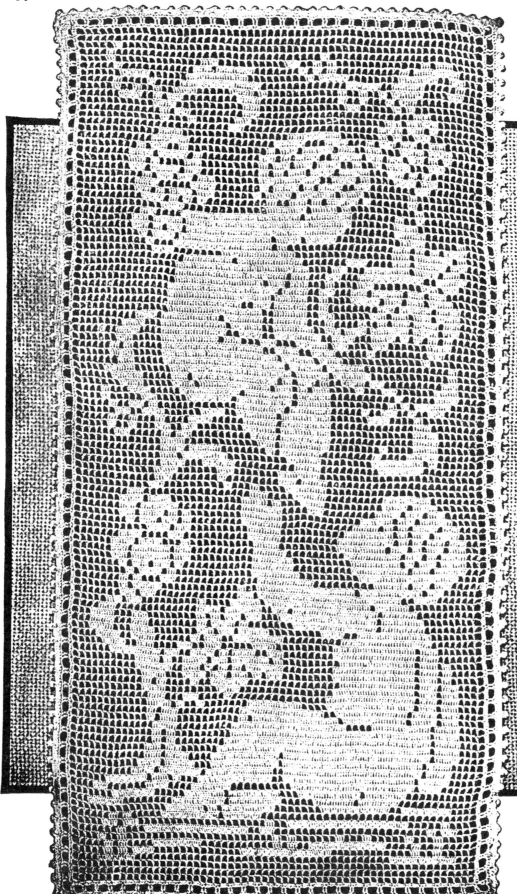

FILET MOTIF FROM CENTER OF BEDSPREAD
Illustrated on page 29

[104]

5th row.—1 s.c. into each st. all around, join.

6th row.—Ch. 12, sk. 3, 1 tr.c., ch. 8, sk. 3, 1 tr.c., continue around at end of row. join to 4th ch. from beginning.

7th row.—1 s.c. into each st. all around, join.

8th row.—2 s.c., ch. 2, sk. 1, 2 s.c., ch. 2, sk. 1, continue all around, join.

9th row.—Ch. 3, sk. 2, 2 s.c. into space, ch. 2, sk. 2, 2 s.c. into next space, continue around, at end of row, join to first ch. from beginning.

10th row.—2 s.c. into first space, 2 s.c. into 2 next sts., 2 s.c. into next space, continue around, join.

11th row.—Ch. 11, sk. 5, 1 tr.c., ch. 7, sk. 5, 1 tr.c., ch. 7, continue around 16 holes in all, join to 4th ch. from beginning.

12th row.—2 s.c. into first 2 sts., 1 p., * 3 s.c. into next 3 sts., 1 p., 5 s.c. into 5 following sts., 1 p. Repeat from * all around, join.

13th row.—Ch. 14, 1 tr.c. into 3rd st. after 2nd p. on top of sp., ch. 10, 1 tr.c. on top of next sp., continue around, join to 4th ch. from beginning.

14th row.—1 s.c. into each st. all around, join.

15th row.—2 s.c., * ch. 2, sk. 2, 2 s.c., ch. 2, sk. 2, 2 s.c., continue until 6 times 2 s.c. with a space between are made, turn, ch. 1, sk. 1, 1 s.c., 2 s.c. into next space, ch. 2, sk. 2, 2 s.c. into next space, continue until 2 s.c. into the last space, 1 s.c. into next st., turn, ch. 3, 2 s.c. into first space, ch. 2, 2 s.c. into next space, ch. 2, 2 s.c. into third space,, ch. 2, 2 s.c. into fourth space, ch. 2, 1 s.c. into last st., turn, 2 s.c. into first space, ch. 2, 2 s.c. into next space, continue until 2 s.c. into last space, turn, sk. 1, 1 s.c. into next st., 2 s.c. into next space, ch. 2, 2 s.c. into 2nd space, continue, after 2 s.c. into last space are made, 1 s.c. into next st., turn, ch. 3, 2 s.c. into first space, ch. 2, continue after 2 s.c. into last space, ch. 2, 1 s.c. into last st., turn, 2 s.c. into first space, ch. 2, continue, turn, sk. 1, 1 s.c., 2 s.c. into space, ch. 2, 2 s.c. into next space, ch. 2, 2 s.c. into last space, 1 s.c. into next st., turn, ch. 3, 2 s.c. into space, ch. 2, 2 s.c. into next space, ch. 2, 1 s.c. into last st., turn, 2 s.c. into space, ch. 2, 2 s.c. into next space, ch. 2, 2 s.c. into last space, turn, sk. 1, 1 s.c., 2 s.c. into space, ch. 2, 2 s.c. into next space, 1 s.c. into next st., turn, ch. 3, 2 s.c. into space, ch. 2, 1 s.c. into last st., turn, 2 s.c. into space, ch. 2, 2 s.c. into next space, turn, sk. 1, 1 s.c. into next st., 2 s.c. into space, 1 s.c. into next st., turn, sk. 1, 2 s.c., turn, 14 sl. sts., down the side of triangle, 19 s.c. into following sts., turn, ch. 12, sk. 7, 1 s.c., ch. 12, sk. 7, 1 s.c., turn, 21 s.c. into first loop, 10 s.c. into next, turn, ch. 12, 1 s.c. into 11th st. of loop, turn, 21 s.c. into loop, 10 s.c. into unfinished loop, 2 s.c. into 2 following sts., turn, ch. 2, sk. 2 sts. of scallop, 2 s.c., ch. 2, sk. 2, 2 s.c., continue. At center of scallop sk. only 1 st., 2 s.c. into 2 following sts., turn, 2 s.c. into first space of scallop, ch. 2, 2 s.c. into next space, continue, into center space 3 s.c. After 2 s.c. into last space are made, 3 s.c. into round and repeat from * three times more.

16th row.—14 sl. sts. up to point of first triangle, 1 s.c. into each st. down the side of same triangle, 1 s.c. into each st. up the side of scallop until 2 s.c. into 3rd space are made, turn, ch. 13, 1 s.c. into 7th st. from point of triangle, turn, 17 s.c. around ch., 1 s.c. into each st. around scallop, 9 s.c. into sts. of triangle, turn, ch. 13, 1 s.c. into 10th st. from bottom of scallop, turn, 17 s.c. around ch., continue with s.c. around triangle and repeat from * 3 times more and continue with s.c. to top of first triangle.

17th row.—* ch. 11, 1 d.tr.c. into 2nd st. of bar, ch. 11, 1 d.tr.c. into st. before last of bar, ch. 11, 3 s.c. into 3 center sts. of scallop, ch. 11, 1 d.tr.c. into 2nd st. of next bar, ch. 11, 1 d.tr.c. into st. before last of bar, ch. 11, 1 s.c. into top of triangle. Repeat from * 3 times more.

18th row.—1 s.c. into each st. all around, join.

19th row.—1 s.c. into each st. all around, join.

20th row.—17 s.c., * turn, sk. 1, 12 s.c., turn, sk. 1, 11 s.c., turn, sk. 1, 10 s.c., continue until 1 s.c. is left, 12 sl. sts. down the side of triangle, 14 s.c. into following sts. turn, sk. 1, 12 s.c., turn, sk. 1, 11 s.c., continue for one other triangle, 12 sl. sts. down the side, 12 s.c. into following sts., turn, ch. 13, sk. 5, cotton 8 times around needle, pull always through 2 loops, ch. 13, sk. 4, 2 s.c., turn, 17 s.c. around ch. to sp., 3 s.c. into sp., 17 s.c. around other ch., 14 s.c. into following sts., turn, sk. 1, 12 s.c., turn, sk. 1, 11 s.c., turn and continue until 1 s.c. is left, 12 sl. sts. down the side of triangle, 14 s.c. into following sts., turn, repeat triangle, 12 sl. sts. down the side of triangle, 20 s.c. into following st. Repeat from * 3 times more, at end of row, 3 s.c. into 3 remaining sts. Join.

21st row.—Sl. sts. into sts. up to point of first triangle, * ch. 15, 1 s.c. into point of next triangle, ch. 15, 1 s.c. into center st. of next scallop, ch. 15, 1 s.c. into point of next triangle, ch. 15, 1 s.c. into point of following triangle, ch. 15, cotton 6 times around needle insert into center of side of same triangle, pull always through 2 loops until 2 loops are left, cotton 6 times around needle, insert into center of side of other triangle, pull again always through 2 loops, and finish pulling through last three loops, ch. 12, 1 s.c. into point of same triangle. Repeat from * three times more.

22nd row.—1 s.c. into each st. all around, join.

23rd row.—2 s.c. into 2 next sts., ch. 2, sk. 2, 2 s.c., ch. 2, sk. 2, 2 s.c., continue all around, join.

24th row.—Ch. 3, 2 s.c. into first space, ch. 2, 2 s.c. into next space, ch. 2, and continue around, join to first ch. from beginning.

25th row.—2 s.c. into first space, 2 s.c. into 2 sts., 2 s.c. into next space, 2 s.c. into sts., continue around, join.

26th row.—25 sl. sts. into following sts., 13 s.c. into next sts., * ch. 6, sk. 5, 1 d.c., ch. 6, sk. 6, 1 tr.c., ch. 6, sk. 6, 1 tr.c., ch. 6, sk. 6, 1 tr.c., ch. 8, sk. 6, 4 s.c., ch. 39, 1 s.c., into next st., turn, 19 s.c. into chs., 3 s.c. into center ch., 19 s.c. into other chs., 2 s.c. into 2 next sts., turn, ch. 2, sk. 2, of loop, 2 s.c. into next 2 sts., ch. 2, sk. 2, 2 s.c., continue to center, ch. 2, 1 s.c. into center st., ch. 2, 2 s.c. into next sts., ch. 2, sk. 2, 2 s.c., continue, 2 s.c. into 2 next sts., turn, 2 s.c. into first space, ch. 2, 2 s.c. into next space, continue all around, 1 s.c. into next st., turn 1 s.c. into each s.c., 2 s.c. into each space, until third space is reached, turn, ch. 14, 1 s.c. into next tr.c. after ch. 8, turn, 19 s.c. around chs., continue with s.c. until center space is reached, turn, ch. 15, 1 s.c. into center st. of last bar made, ch. 10, 1 s.c. into next tr.c., turn, 13 s.c. around ch. 10, 19 s.c. around ch. 19, 3 s.c. into center space of point, and continue at other side of scallop with s.c., 1 s.c. into next st., ch. 8, sk. 6, 1 tr.c., ch. 6, sk. 6, 1 tr.c., turn, ch. 17, 1 s.c. into next tr.c., turn, 10 s.c. around ch., turn, ch. 7, 1 s.c. into 12th st. from point of scallop, turn, 10 s.c. around ch., turn, ch. 15, 1 s.c. into st. next to

Continued on page 37.

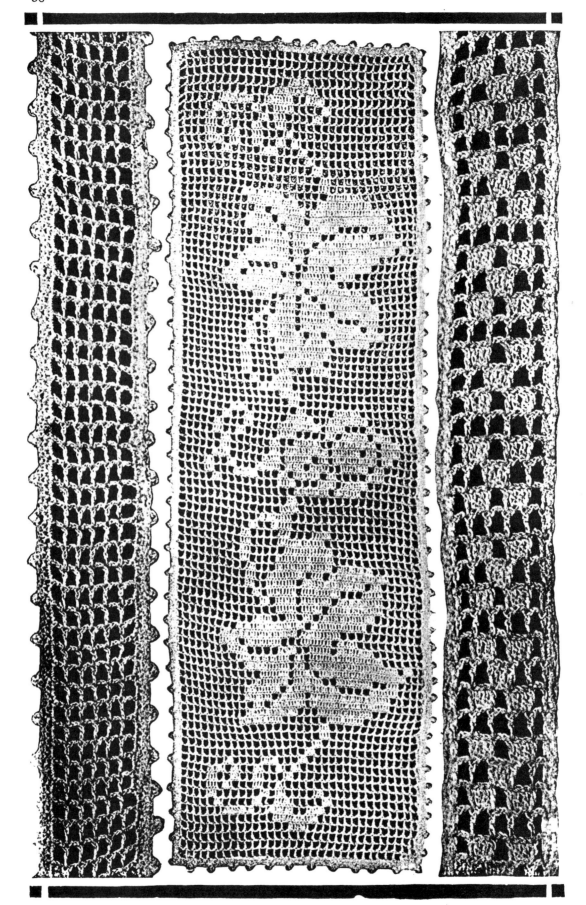

MOTIF FROM SET

Illustrated on page 29

center st., turn, 19 s.c. around ch., 12 s.c. around next ch., ch. 6, sk. 6, 1 tr.c., ch. 6, sk. 6, 1 d.c., ch. 6, sk. 6, 13 s.c. Repeat from * three times more and join to first s.c. of row.

27th row.—1 s.c. into each st., 7 s.c. into each hole, 3 s.c. into corner st. Join.

28th row.—1 s.c. into each st. all around, 3 s.c. into corner st.

29th row.—Same as 28th row.

30th row.—5 s.c., 1 p., sk. 1, 5 s.c., 1 p. Continue around, have 1 p. at each corner.

Triangle for Corners.

Center.—Ch. 23, sk. 2, 1 s.c., ch. 2, sk. 2, 2 s.c. into next 2 sts., ch. 2, sk. 2, 2 s.c. into next 2 sts., continue to end of chs., turn, ch. 1, sk. 2 first sts., 2 s.c. into first space, ch. 2, 2 s.c. into next space, repeat 3 times more, turn, ch. 1, 2 s.c. into first space, ch. 2, 2 s.c. into next space, repeat twice, 1 s.c. into last st., turn, ch. 2, 2 s.c. into first space, ch. 2, repeat twice, 1 s.c. into last st., turn, ch. 2, 2 s.c. into first space, ch. 2, 2 s.c. into next space, ch. 2, 1 s.c. into last space, turn, 2 s.c. into first space, ch. 2, 2 s.c. into next space, ch. 2, 1 s.c. into last space, turn, 2 s.c. into first space, ch. 2, 2 s.c. into next space, turn, ch. 2, work down the side 12 s.c. Into corner 3 s.c.. Across bottom of triangle 20 s.c. Into corner 3 s.c., up to point 12 s.c. Into point 5 s.c., join with sl. st.

1st row.—Ch. 10, sk. 5, 1 tr.c., ch. 6, 1 tr.c. into corner, ch. 8, cotton 6 times around needle, insert into same, always pull through 2 loops, ch. 8, 1 tr.c. into same, ch. 6, sk. 5, 1 tr.c., ch. 6, sk. 4, 1 tr.c., ch. 6, 1 tr.c. into corner and continue for point as on other side, ch. 8, join to 4th ch. from beginning.

2nd row.—3 s.c. into sts., 1 p., 7 s.c. into next sts., 1 p., 7 s.c., 1 p., 5 s.c. to corner, 5 s.c. into point, 5 s.c. into next sts., 1 p., 7 s.c., 1 p., continue around. Into chs. at point of triangle 5 s.c.. Into center st. 1 s.c., 1 p., 1 s.c. Into next sts. 5 s.c., join with sl. st.

3rd row.—Ch. 10, 1 tr.c. in the center st. between next 2 p., ch. 6, 1 tr.c. between next 2 p., ch. 6, 1 tr.c. into 3rd st. after next p., ch. 6, 1 tr.c. into point, ch. 9, 1 tr.c. into same, ch. 6, sk. 3, 1 tr.c., ch. 6, 1 tr.c. between next 2 p., continue around. For point ch. 6, 1 tr.c. into st. before p. of point, ch. 7, 1 tr.c. into st. after same p., ch. 6, join to 4th ch. from beginning.

4th row.—1 s.c. into each st. Into corners 5 s.c., into point 3 s.c., join with sl. st.

5th row.—11 s.c., turn, sk. 1, 10 s.c., turn, sk. 1, 9 s.c., continue until 1 s.c. is left, 10 sl. sts. down to side, 14 s.c. into following sts., turn, sk. 1, 10 s.c., continue again until 1 s.c. is left, 10 sl. sts. down the side, 9 s.c. into sts. to corner, 3 s.c. into corner st., 5 s.c. into following sts., turn, ch. 9, 1 s.c. into corner st., ch. 9, sk. 4, 1 s.c., turn, 13 s.c. into first loop, 5 s.c. into next, turn, ch. 9, sk. 4 sts. of first loop, 1 s.c., turn, 13 s.c. into loop, 9 s.c. into unfinished loop, 1 s.c. into next st., turn, ch. 2, sk. 3, * 2 s.c., ch. 2, sk. 2, repeat twice more from *. 2 s.c. into center st., ch. 2, 2 s.c. into same, repeat the same at other side of scallop. 1 s.c. into next st., turn, 2 s.c. into all spaces with 2 ch. between. Into center space of corner, 2 s.c., ch. 2, 2 s.c. into same, 13 s.c. into following sts., turn, sk. 1, 10 s.c., turn, sk. 1, 9 s.c., continue until 1 s.c. is left, 10 sl. sts. down the side of triangle, 14 s.c. into following sts., turn, make 3 more triangles the same way, 1 s.c. into each st. to corner, 3 s.c. into corner st., 5 s.c. into next sts., repeat the same as on other corner and the two triangles up the side, then make s.c. into sts. to point, 3 s.c. into point, 5 s.c. into next sts., turn, ch. 9, 1 s.c. into center st. of point, ch. 9, sk. 5, 1 s.c., turn, 13 s.c. into first loop, 5 s.c. into next, turn, ch. 9, 1 s.c. into 6th st. of first loop, turn, 13 s.c. into loop, 8 s.c. into unfinished loop, 1 s.c. into next st., finish scallop the same way as at corners, then 1 s.c. into each of 4 s.c. to first triangle.

6th row.—1 sl. st. into every st. up and down triangle to scallop, 2 s.c. into 2 first sts. of scallop, 2 s.c. into space, continue around. Into center space, 3 s.c., repeat the sl. sts. to other scallop, and finish row the same way. Make again sl. sts. up to point of first triangle.

7th row.—Turn, ch. 10, 1 s.c. into center of side of same triangle, turn, 7 s.c. around ch., turn, ch. 6, 1 s.c. into 6th st. of scallop, turn, 7 s.c. around ch., turn, ch. 10, 1 s.c. into 7th following st. of scallop, turn, 7 s.c. around ch., turn, ch. 10, 1 s.c. into point, turn, 7 s.c. around ch., turn, ch. 10, 1 s.c. into same, turn, 7 s.c., turn, ch. 10, sk. 5, 1 s.c., turn, 7 s.c., turn, ch. 10, sk. 6, 1 s.c. into center of side of next triangle, turn, 7 s.c., turn, ch. 5, 1 s.c. into point of triangle, turn, ch. 10, 1 s.c. into center of other side of same triangle, turn, 7 s.c., turn, ch. 6, 1 s.c. into center of side of next triangle, turn, 7 s.c., turn, ch. 5, 1 s.c. into same triangle, turn, ch. 10, 1 s.c. into other side of triangle, turn, 7 s.c., turn, ch. 6, 1 s.c. into 5th st. of scallop, turn, 7 s.c., turn, ch. 10, sk. 4, 1 s.c., turn, 7 s.c., turn, ch. 10, 1 s.c. into same, turn, 7 s.c., turn, ch. 6, sk. 4, 1 s.c., turn, 7 s.c., turn, ch. 15, 1 s.c. into point of scallop, turn, 15 s.c., turn, ch. 10, 1 s.c. into center stitch of bar of 15 s.c., turn, 7 s.c., turn, ch. 12, 1 s.c. into same, turn, 7 s.c., turn, ch. 14, 1 s.c. into point of scallop, turn, 10 s.c., turn, ch. 12, sk. 5 from point, 1 s.c., turn, 7 s.c., turn, ch. 10, 1 s.c. into same, turn, 7 s.c., turn, ch. 6, sk. 4, 1 s.c., turn, 7 s.c., turn, ch. 10, 1 s.c. into same, turn, 7 s.c., turn, ch. 3, 1 s.c. into point of next triangle, ch. 10, 1 s.c. into side of same triangle, turn, 7 s.c., turn, ch. 6, 1 s.c. into side of next triangle, turn, 7 s.c., turn, ch. 5, 1 s.c. into point of same triangle, ch. 10, and repeat twice between following triangles.

After point of last triangle is reached, ch. 8, 1 s.c. into 5th st. of scallop, turn, 7 s.c., turn, ch. 10, 1 s.c. into same, turn, 7 s.c., turn, ch. 6, sk. 5, 1 s.c., turn, 7 s.c., turn, ch. 10, 1 s.c. into same, turn, 7 s.c., turn, ch. 12, 1 s.c. into point, turn, 10 s.c., turn, ch. 17, 1 s.c. into same st. of point, turn, 15 s.c., turn, ch. 12, 1 s.c. into 8th st. of bar just made, turn, 8 s.c., turn, ch. 12, 1 s.c. into same as last s.c., turn, 8 s.c., turn, ch. 12, 1 s.c. into 6th st. from point of scallop, turn, 8 s.c., turn, ch. 6, sk. 5, 1 s.c., turn, 7 s.c., turn, ch. 10, 1 s.c. into same, turn, 7 s.c., turn, ch. 10, sk. 4, 1 s.c., turn, 7 s.c., turn, ch. 6, 1 s.c. into side of next triangle, turn, 7 s.c., turn, ch. 5, 1 s.c. into point of triangle, continue as at other side, join with sl. st., turn.

8th row.—7 s.c. into each of 7 holes to corner, into corner hole 13 s.c., 7 s.c. into each of 4 next holes, 4 s.c. into following hole, 7 s.c. into next 6 holes, 4 s.c. into following hole, continue row, join with sl. st.

9th row.—Ch. 10, sk. 5, 1 tr.c., ch. 6, sk. 5, 1 tr.c., ch. 6, continue around. Join ner after 2 s.c. ch. 2, 1 s.c. into same, 1 s.c. into next and continue around. Join with sl. st.

Continued on page 39.

MOTIFS FROM SET

Illustrated on page 29

10th row.—Ch. 2, sk. 2, 2 s.c. into space, ch. 2, continue around. Into corner spaces 2 s.c., ch. 2, 2 s.c.

11th row.—2 s.c. into space, 2 s.c. into next sts., 2 s.c. into space, continue around. Into corner spaces 5 s.c. Into space at point 3 s.c. Join with sl. st.

12th row.—15 s.c., * turn, ch. 9, sk. 6, 1 s.c., ch. 9, sk. 6, 1 s.c., turn, 13 s.c. into first loop, 6 s.c. into next loop, turn, ch. 9, 1 s.c. into center of first loop, turn, 13 s.c. into loop, 6 s.c. into unfinished loop, 20 s.c. into following sts., repeat from * twice, 5 s.c. into next sts. to corner, 5 s.c. into corner st., 5 s.c. into following sts., turn, ch. 9, 1 s.c. into corner, ch. 9, sk. 6, 1 s.c., turn, 9 s.c. into first loop, 5 s.c. into next, turn, ch. 11, 1 s.c. into 5th st. of next loop, turn, 15 s.c. into loop, 8 s.c. into unfinished loop, 15 s.c., turn, ch. 9, sk. 6, 1 s.c., ch. 9, sk. 6, 1 s.c., turn, 13 s.c. into first loop, 6 s.c. into next loop, turn, ch. 9, 1 s.c. into center st. of next loop, turn, 13 s.c. into loop, 6 s.c. into unfinished loop, 17 s.c., turn, repeat from * 6 times more, then 5 s.c. into sts. to corner, 5 s.c. into corner st., 5 s.c. into next sts., turn and repeat scallop as on other corner, then 15 s.c., turn, repeat scallop, 20 s.c. and make three more scallops. 12 s.c. to point, turn, ch. 9, sk. 5, 1 s.c., ch. 9, sk. 5, 1 s.c., turn, finish scallop as before, 3 s.c. to point, 12 s.c. at other side, repeat scallop, 15 s.c., repeat scallop, 7 s.c. to first scallop, join with sl. st.

13th row—Sl. sts. to center st. of first scallop, * ch. 9, 1 d.tr.tr.c. into center st. of side of scallop. Keep two last loops on needle, 1 d.tr.tr.c. into center st. of side of other scallop, finish 3 last loops on needle together, ch. 9, 1 s.c. into center st. of same scallop, repeat from *. Make ch. 9, and 2 d.tr.tr.c. the same way into side of 3rd scallop, and into 4th st. of corner scallop, ch. 9, sk. 3, 1 d.tr.tr.c., ch. 9, 1 d.tr.tr.c. into center st. of corner, ch. 11, 1 d.tr.tr.c. into same, ch. 9, sk. 6, 1 d.tr.tr.c., ch. 9, sk. 3, 1 d.tr.tr.c. and 1 d.tr.tr.c. into center of side of next scallop, finish them together, ch. 9, 1 s.c. into same scallop. Continue across bottom and other side of triangle. Between 2 scallops of point of triangle work the same way as between other scallops. Continue to starting point and join with sl. st.

14th row.—10 s.c. into each hole, 19 s.c. into corner holes, 3 s.c. into st. at point. Join with sl. st.

15th row.—1 s.c. into each st. Into center st. of corner loop, 3 s.c. Into center st. of point, 3 s.c. Join with sl. st.

16th row.—5 s.c., 1 p., sk. 1, 5 s.c., 1 p., sk. 1, 5 s.c. Continue around. Have 1 p. at each point.

Medium Medallion.

1st row.—Ch. 5, join to ring, 8 s.c. into ring, join with sl. st.

2nd row.—2 s.c. into each st. all around, join.

3rd row.—2 s.c. into one, 1 s.c. into next st., 2 s.c. into 3rd st., continue around, join.

4th row.—Ch. 10, sk. 2, 1 tr.c., ch. 6, sk. 2, 1 tr.c., continue around 8 holes in all, at end of row, join to 4th ch. from beginning.

5th row.—7 s.c. into each hole, join.

6th row.—2 s.c., ch. 2, sk. 1, 2 s.c., ch. 2, sk. 1, 2 s.c., continue all around, join.

7th row.—Ch. 3, 2 s.c. into first space, ch. 2, 2 s.c. into next space, continue around, join to first ch. from beginning.

8th row.—3 s.c. into each space, 1 s.c. into each s.c., join.

9th row.—Ch. 10, sk. 5, 1 tr.c., ch. 6, sk. 5, 1 tr.c., ch. 6, continue around. Join to 4th ch. from beginning.

10th row.—1 s.c. into each st. all around, join.

11th row.—13 s.c., turn, * 1 s.c. into each until 12 s.c. are made, turn, 12 s.c., turn, 2 more rows of 12 s.c., 4 sl. sts. down the side, 13 s.c. into following sts., turn, ch. 10, sk. 4, 1 s.c., ch. 10, sk. 4, 1 s.c., turn, 15 s.c. into first loop, 7 s.c. into next loop, turn, ch. 10, 1 s.c. into center st. of previous loop, turn, 15 s.c. into loop, 8 s.c. into unfinished loop, 1 s.c. into next st., turn, ch. 2, sk. 2, 2 s.c., ch. 2, sk. 2, 2 s.c., continue to center of scallop, 3 s.c. into center st., ch. 2, sk. 2, 2 s.c., continue for other side, 1 s.c. into next st., turn, ch. 3, 2 s.c. into first space, ch. 2, 2 s.c. into next space, continue to center, ch. 2, 3 s.c. into center st., ch. 2, 2 s.c. into next space, continue for other side, 14 s.c. into following sts., turn and repeat from * 3 times more. At end join with sl. st.

12th row.—* sl. sts. into each st. of oblong to scallop, 2 s.c. into first space, 2 s.c. into sts., 2 s.c. into next space, continue around scallop, into center st., 3 s.c. Repeat from * three times more.

13th row.—Sl. sts. up the side of oblong, ch. 11, 1 d.c. into last st. of top of oblong, * ch. 8, 1 tr.c. into center of sides of scallop, ch. 10, 1 d.c. into center st. of scallop, ch. 5, 1 d.c. into same, ch. 10, 1 tr.c. into center of other side of same scallop, ch. 8, 1 d.c. into first st. of next oblong, ch. 8, 1 d.c. into last st. of oblong. Repeat from * three times more. Join to 3rd st. from beginning.

14th row.—1 s.c. into each st. all around, 3 s.c. into corner sts. Join.

15th row.—5 s.c., 1 p., sk. 1, 5 s.c., 1 p., sk. 1, 5 s.c., continue all around. Have 1 p. at each of three corners, at 4th corner have 3 p. together, which are needed for joining. Make one more medallion the same way.

Small Medallion.

1st row.—Ch. 5, join to ring, 8 s.c. into ring. Join with sl. st.

2nd row.—2 s.c. into each st. Join.

3rd row.—Ch. 7, sk. 1, 1 d.c., ch. 4, sk. 1, 1 d.c., ch. 4, continue around. Join to 3rd ch. from beginning.

4th row.—2 s.c., ch. 2, sk. 1, 2 s.c., ch. 2, sk. 1, and continue around. Join.

5th row.—2 s.c. into sts., 2 s.c. into space, continue until 11 s.c. are made, turn, * Ch. 9, sk. 4, 1 p.c. ch. 9, sk. 4, 1 s.c., turn, 13 s.c. into first loop, 6 s.c. into next loop, turn, ch. 9, 1 s.c. into center of previous loop, turn, 13 s.c. into loop, 6 s.c. into unfinished loop, 14 s.c. into following sts. and spaces, turn, and repeat from * three times more, 2 s.c. into two remaining sts.

6th row.—Sl. sts. up to center of first scallop, ch. 6, 1 d.c. into same, * ch. 6, 1 tr.c. into center of side of same scallop, ch. 6, 1 d.tr.tr.c. into center st. in between scallops, ch. 6, 1 tr.c. into center of side of next scallop, ch. 6, 1 d.c. into center st. of same scallop, ch. 3, 1 d.c. into same. Repeat from * three times more. Join to 3rd ch. from beginning.

7th row.—1 s.c. into each st. all around, 3 s.c. into corner st.

[109]

Continued on page 52.

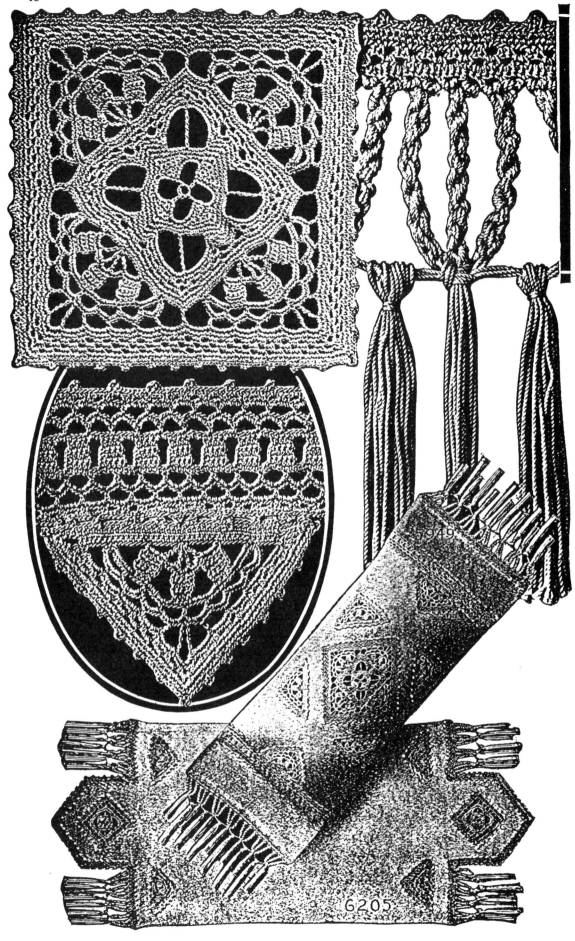

No. 5949—PILLOW

ROYAL SOCIETY ECRU CORDICHET, 6 balls, size 3, 5 balls, size 1, for fringes.

Center Medallion.

1st row—Ch. 6, join to ring, ch. 12, 1 d.c. into ring, ch. 9, 1 d.c. into ring. ch. 9, 1 d.c. into ring, ch. 9, join to 3rd ch. at beginning.

2nd row—2 s.c. into first loop, turn, * 2 s.c. into sts, 2 s.c. into next loop, turn, 4 s.c. into sts., 2 s.c. into loop, turn, 6 s.c. into sts., 2 s.c. into loop, turn, 8 s.c. into sts., 2 s.c. into loop, turn, 5 s.c. into sts., 3 s.c. into next st., 4 s.c. into following sts., 2 s.c. into loop, turn, 7 s.c. into sts., 3 s.c. into next st., 6 s.c. into following sts., 6 s.c. into loop, 2 s.c. into following loop, repeat from * 3 times, join with sl. st.

3rd row—1 s.c. into each st. all around, 3 s.c. into corner sts., join with sl. st.

4th row—5 more sl. sts., 5 s.c. to corner, 3 s.c. into corner, 5 s.c. into following sts., * ch. 11, sk. 5, cotton 5 times around needle, pull through loop, 2 at the time, ch. 11, sk. 5, 5 s.c., 3 s.c. into corner, 5 s.c. into following sts., repeat from * three times.

5th row—sk. 2, sts., * 11 s.c. into following sts., 18 s.c. into each hole of ch. 11, repeat from * around.

6th row—* sk. 2 sts., 1 s.c., ch. 2, sk. 2, 2 s.c., ch. 2, sk. 2, 1 s.c., sk. 2, 1 s.c. into first st. of loop, ch. 2, sk. 2, 2 s.c., continue around big scallop and repeat from * three times.

7th row—2 s.c. into first space after big scallop, ch. 2, 2 s.c. into next space, 2 s.c. into following space, ch. 2, and repeat around. Into center space on top of big scallop, 2 s.c., ch. 2, 2 s.c. into same.

8th row—Same as 7th row, but into center space at point 3 s.c..

9th row—2 s.c. into sts., 2 s.c. into spaces, at corners, 3 s.c.

10th row—8 s.c., turn, * ch. 3, sk. 8, 1 tr.c., ch. 3, 1 tr.c., ch. 3, 1 tr.c., ch. 3, 1 tr.c. all into same, ch. 3, sk. 8, 1 s.c., turn, 4 s.c. into first loop, turn, 4 s.c., turn, 3 more rows of 4 s.c., 4 sl. sts. down the side, 4 s.c. into next loop, 4 s.c. into following loop, turn, 4 more rows of 4 s.c., 4 sl. sts. down the side, 4 s.c. into next loop, 4 s.c. into following loop, repeat solid square, 7 s.c. into following sts., turn, ch. 5, 4 s.c. into solid square, ch. 5, 4 s.c., ch. 5, 4 s.c. ch. 5, sk. 6, 1 s.c., turn, 6 s.c. into each space of ch. 5, and 4 s.c. into solid squares, 1 s.c. into next st., turn, ch. 5, sk. 4, 1 s.c. Repeat twice, ch. 5, sk. 3, 1 s.c., repeat, reversing, 1 s.c. into following st., turn, 7 s.c. into each loop, 1 s.c. into remaining sts. to corner, 3 s.c. into corner st., 31 s.c. into following sts., turn. Repeat from * three times.

11th row—When corner st. is reached, ch. 9, * 1 d.c. into center st. of first loop, ch. 5, 1 s.c. into center st. of second loop, ch. 5, 1 s.c. into third loop, ch. 5, 1 d.c. into fourth loop, ch. 5, 1 d.tr.c., ch. 5, 1 d.tr.c. all in between two following loops. Ch. 5, and repeat, reversing. At point of square 1 tr.c., ch. 5, and repeat from * three times.

12th row—6 s.c. into each hole, 7 s.c. into corner holes.

13th row—1 s.c. into each st., 3 s.c. into corner sts.

14th row—2 s.c., ch. 2, sk. 2, 2 s.c., continue all around. At corners 2 s.c., ch. 2, 2 s.c. into following sts. At end join with sl. st.

15th row—ch. 3, 2 s.c. into first space, ch. 2, continue around, at corners, 3 s.c.

16th row—Same as previous row, at corner ch. 2, 3 s.c. into center st., ch. 2.

17th row—1 s.c. into each st., 2 s.c. into each space, 3 s.c. into corner st.

18th row—5 s.c., 1 p., 5 s.c. all around.

Insertion for End of Pillow.

Make a ch. 16 inches long, sk. 1, 4 s.c., turn, * 4 s.c., turn, 3 more rows of 4 s.c., 4 sl. sts. down the side, 7 s.c. into following sts., turn and repeat from * across.

After last solid square is made, turn, 4 s.c. into square, ch. 3, 4 s.c. into following square, ch. 3, continue across, turn, 1 s.c. into each st. across, turn, ** 1 s.c. into first st., ch. 5, sk. 4, 1 s.c., ch. 5, sk. 4, 1 s.c., continue across, turn, 7 s.c. into each loop, turn, ch. 3, 1 s.c. into center of first loop, ch. 4, 1 s.c. into center of next loop, ch. 4, 1 s.c. with center of following loop, continue across, at end, ch. 2, 1 d.c. into last st., turn, 3 s.c. into first hole, 5 s.c. into each of following holes, 3 s.c. into last hole, turn, 2 s.c., ch. 2, sk. 2, 2 s.c., continue across, turn, 5 s.c., 1 p., 5 s.c. across.

Repeat from ** on other side of foundation ch.

Make on other insertion for other end of pillow.

For the 6 triangles follow instructions as for triangles given for scarf.

To make border with fringes follow instructions of scarf, but ch. 129 instead of ch. 75.

Place crochet pieces on stamped linen, cut linen away underneath, put over silk covered form 30 inches long.

No. 6205—SCARF

ROYAL SOCIETY ECRU CORDICHET, 5 balls, size 3, 5 balls, size 1 for fringes.

Center Medallion.

1st row—Ch. 5, join to ring, ch. 10, 1 d.c. into ring, ch. 7, 1 d.c. into ring, ch. 7, 1 d.c. into ring, ch. 7, join to 3rd ch. at beginning.

2nd row—2 s.c. into first loop, turn, * 2 s.c. into sts., 2 s.c. into next loop, turn, 4 s.c. into sts,, 2 s.c. into loop, turn, 3 s.c. into sts., 3 s.c. into next st., 2 s.c. into

Continued on page 54.

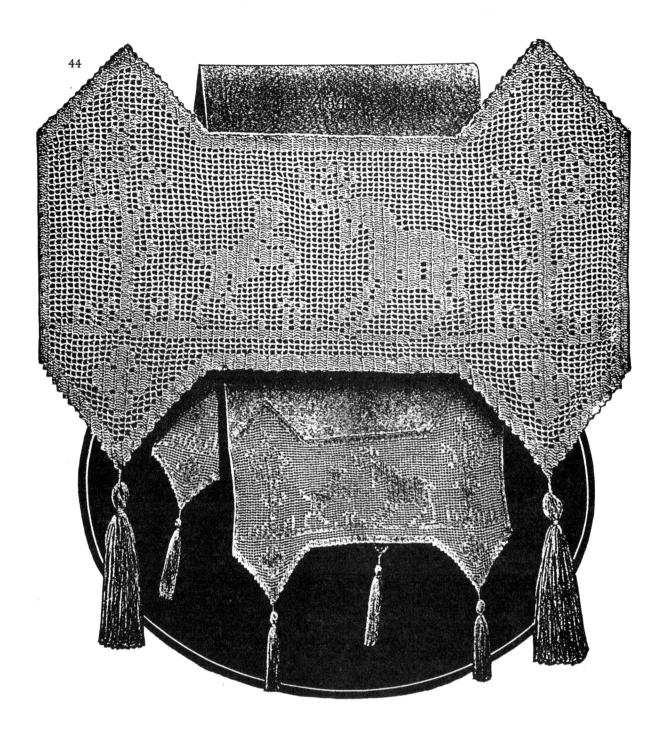

No. 484—18x54 SCARF

To Make Scarf.

After Crochet has been completed, baste in place along stamped lines, then stitch firmly. Cut away extra material under crochet.

ROYAL SOCIETY CORDICHET, size 30, No. 3040, 6 balls, crochet hook size 11.

Explanation for Filet.

Open Mesh.—1 d.c., ch. 2, sk. 2, 1 d.c. into next st.

Closed Mesh.—1 d.c. into d.c., 2 d.c. into 2 chs., 1 d.c. into next d.c. For foundation chain make 3 times as many chains as meshes and add 1 ch. Always make ch. 5 to turn. At top of d.c. take up both loops, and over open loop. If closed loop is indicated, work with chains, not around.

Follow black and white drawing for Filet ends, starting at one side and working up and down.

Tassels.

Wind cotton 100 times around cardboard 5 inches long. Cut and tie in center. With same thread make 2 ch., 1 s.c. into first ch., ch. 1, 1 s.c. into s.c., repeat twice more. Tie again one-half inch from top. Attach a tassel to each point on bottom of crochet.

7th row.—Ch. 10, 1 tr.c. into first s.c. of previous row, sk. 4, 1 tr.c., ch. 5, 1 tr.c. into same, sk. 4, 1 tr.c., ch. 5, 1 tr.c. into same, continue all around. Join to 5th ch. from beginning of row.

8th row.—1 s.c. into first space, ch. 5, 1 tr.c. into same, ch. 5, 2 tr.c. into same, 2 tr.c. into next space, ch. 5, 2 tr.c. into same. Continue around. Join to 5th ch. from beginning of row.

9th row.—Into each space of ch. 5, 1 s.c., 1 h.d.c., 1 d.c., 5 tr.c., 1 d.c., 1 h.d.c., 1 s.c.

10th row.—5 sl.sts. to center of scallop * 1 s.c. into next st., ch. 7, 1 s.c. into center of next scallop, ch. 7, 1 d.c. into center of next scallop, ch. 7 1 d.c. into center of following scallop, ch. 5, 1 d.c. into same, ch. 7, 1 d.c. into next scallop, ch. 7, 1 s.c. into next scallop, ch. 7, and repeat from * three times more, finish with 1 sl.st. into first s.c. of row.

11th row.—Ch. 4, sk. 1, 1 d.c., ch. 1, sk. 1, 1 d.c., continue to corner. For corner, ch. 3, 1 d.c. into same, continue ch. 1, sk. 1, 1 d.c. Join to 3rd ch. from beginning of row.

12th row.—1 d.c. into each st., 5 d.c. into corner st.

13th row.—Taking up back rib, 1 d.c. into each st. At corners finish 5 d.c. together. Join with sl.st.

14th row.—Ch. 5, sk. 5, 1 s.c., ch. 5, sk. 5, 1 s.c. Continue all around, finish off. Pull thread through last row of loops for draw string.

Side of Basket.

Ch. 44, sk. 3, 1 d.c., ch. 5, sk. 3, 1 d.c., continue for 9 more holes, turn * ch. 8, 1 d.c. into first hole, ch. 5, 1 d.c. into next hole, continue across, turn, repeat from * once, turn, * ch. 9, 1 d.c. into first hole, ch. 6, 1 d.c. into next hole, continue across, turn, repeat from * twice, (6 rows of holes in all).

Work down the side, ch. 4, sk. 1, 1 d.c., ch. 1, sk. 1, 1 d.c., continue for 12 spaces, for corner ch. 3, 1 d.c. into same. Ch. 1, sk. 1, 1 d.c., continue across bottom, at corner, ch. 3, 1 d.c. into same. Repeat up the side for 13 spaces at corner of top, ch. 5, 1 d.c. into same, ch. 1, sk. 1, 1 d.c. across top, at corner ch. 5, 1 d.c. into same, ch. 1, join with sl.st. to 3rd ch. from beginning of row.

Ch. 4, 1 d.c. into first sp., ch. 1, sk. 1, 1 d.c. into next sp. Continue around the same as previous row, but at corners of top into the ch. 5, ch. 1, sk. 1, 1 d.c., ch. 1, 1 d.c. into next, ch. 3, 1 d.c. into same, ch. 1, 1 d.c. into next, ch. 1, 1 d.c. into following sp. At end of row, join with sl.st., ch. 3, 1 d.c. into each st., 5 d.c. into corner sts.

Make one other row of 1 d.c. into each st., taking up back rib, at corners, finish 5 d.c. together. Join with sl.st.

Ch. 4, sk. 1, 1 d.c., ch. 1, sk. 1, 1 d.c., continue all around. At corners, ch. 1, 1 d.c., pull thread once through 2 loops, sk. 1, 1 d.c., pull thread once through 2 loops, sk. 1, 1 d.c. Finish all 3 together. Finish off.

With sewing needle pull a thread through last row of spaces for draw string.

Make 4 more sides the same way. Crochet them together, having turnover to hold cardboard in place at outside of basket on which side they are joined with s.c., taking up front rib between two rows of d.c.

Then join the 5 sides to the bottom the same way.

Stretch crochet over cardboards, draw up strings and tie securely.

Trim each of the 5 upper corners with a small medallion and tassel.

Medallion.

Ch. 5, join to ring, 9 s.c., into ring, join with sl.st., 1 s.c. into first st. * ch. 4, 1 Bullion st. (cotton 12 times around needle, pull through all loops at once), ch. 1, 2 Bullion sts. into next st., always ch. 1 between, 1 Bullion st. into following st., ch. 4, 1 s.c. into same, 3 s.c. into 3 following sts. Repeat from *.

* 4 s.c. into space of ch. 4, 1 p., 2 s.c. between 2 first Bullion sts., 1 p., 2 s.c. between 2 next Bullion sts., 1 p., 2 s.c. between 2 following Bullion sts, 1 p., 4 s.c. into space of ch. 4, 3 s.c. into next sts. Repeat from *. Finish off.

Tassel.

Wind cotton 100 times around cardboard 1¾ inches long, tie in center, work with same thread, ch. 1, 1 s.c. into first ch., ch. 1, 1 s.c. into first s.c., repeat this until 6 s.c. are made, tie tassel again ¼ of an inch from top, and fasten to center of medallion.

46

5954

5951

No. 5951—PILLOW

This pillow consists of a filet medallion showing the head of Marie Antoinette, and surrounded with a Venetian Crochet edge. A wreath of pink roses is embroidered on crochet just outside the medallion. Mount crochet on a pale blue satin cushion with puffing around the edge.

ROYAL SOCIETY White CORDICHET size 40 for filet. Crochet hook size 12. Size 15 for pointed edge. Cochet hook size 8.

DESCRIPTION OF FILET.

Open Mesh.—1 d.c., ch. 2, sk. 2, 1 d.c. into next st.

Closed Mesh.—1 d.c. into d.c. taking up both loops, 2 d.c. into chs. not around chs., 1 d.c. into next d.c.

For foundation chs. make three times as many chs. as m. Always make 5 chs. to turn.

For round filet center follow black and white drawing.

First Row.—With size 15, CORDICHET, work around one 3 s.c. into one, 2 s.c. into next m.

Second Row.—1 s.c. into each st.

Third Row.—5 s.c., 1 p., 9 s.c., 1 p., 9 s.c., continue around.

Fourth Row.—4 s.c., ch. 9, * 1 s.c. into 2nd st. after 1 st. p., 1 s.c. into next st. turn, 15 s.c. into loop, 2 s.c. into 2 following sts. turn, 1 s.c. into each of 15 s.c., 4 s.c. into following sts. of previous row, ch. 9, and repeat from * around.

Fifth Row.—3 sl. sts. into 3 1st sts. of 1st scallop, ch. 10, 1 s.c. into center st. of scallop, * ch. 5, sk. 5, 1 trc. and 1 trc. into 4th st. of following scallop, finish both together, ch. 5, 1 s.c. into center of 2nd scallop, repeat from * around. At end of row 1 sl. st. into 5th ch. from beginning.

Sixth Row.—6 s.c. into each hole.

Seventh Row.—24 s.c., ** ch. 6, turn, sk. 5, 1 d. trc., ch. 9, 1 d. trc. into top of d. trc., 1 d. tr.c. into same of previous row, ch. 6, sk. 5, 2 s.c., turn, 7 s.c. into 1st loop, 11 s.c. into center loop, 7 s.c. into 1st loop, 11 s.c. into center loop, 7 s.c. into last loop, 2 s.c. into following sts., turn, sk. 2, 12 s.c., 3 s.c. into center st., 12 s.c., 2 s.c. into following sts., turn, sk. 2, 13 s.c., 3 s.c. into center st., 13 s.c., 4 s.c. into following st. turn, sk. 5, sk. 6, 1 s.c., ch. 5, sk. 3, 1 s.c., ch. 5, sk. 2, 1 s.c., ch. 5, sk. 2, 1 s.c., ch. 5, sk. 1, 1 s.c. into center of point. Make other side the same way reversing, 1 s.c. into following st., turn, 4 s.c. into 1st loop, turn, sk. last 4 and 3 sts. on other side of angle, 2 s.c. turn, 5 s.c. into loop of ch. 3, * 4 s.c. into unfinished loop, 4 s.c. into next loop, turn, ch. 5, 1 s.c. into center of previous loop, turn, 7 s.c. into loop. Repeat from * around point. Into center loop 9 s.c., finish with loop of ch. 3, as in beginning, 36 s.c. and repeat from **.

Eighth Row.—Sk. 1st. st. of loop, 3 s.c., * sk. 1st of same loop and 1st of next loop, 3 s.c., 1 p., 1 s.c. into same, 2 s.c. into following 2 sts., repeat from * across point, between points 5 s.c., 1 p., 5 s.c. and repeat around.

A wreath of colored embroidery may be worked on solid band just outside filet center. The roses are raised and worked in rows of Outline st. in two shades of pink, one rose opposite each point. The vine is worked in loop stitch in green with pink and purple French Knots between the roses as desired.

MATERIALS REQUIRED FOR EMBROIDERY

1312 Pink Celesta, 2 skeins	1183 Green Celesta, 2 skeins
1212 Purple Celesta, 1 skein	1314 Green Celesta, 1 skein

Description of Bolster No. 5954 on Page 48

No. 5954—BOLSTER

ROYAL SOCIETY White Crochet Cotton, size 3, 5 balls.

Center Strip.

Ch. 17, sk. 1, * 16 s.c., turn, sk. 1, 2 s.c., ch. 2, sk. 2, 2 s.c., ch. 2, sk. 2, 2 s.c., ch. 2, sk. 2, 1 s.c., sk. 1, 1 s.c., turn, sk. 1, 1 s.c., 2 s.c. into space, 2 s.c. into st., continue across, always skipping first and last stitch, turn, 2 s.c., ch. 2, sk. 2, 2 s.c., ch. 2, sk. 2, 2 s.c., turn, 1 s.c., 2 s.c. into space, 2 s.c. into sts., 2 s.c. into next space, 1 s.c. turn, 2 s.c., ch. 2, sk. 2, 2 s.c., turn, 1 s.c., 2 s.c. into space, 1 s.c., turn, 2 s.c turn, 1 sc.

Ch. 16, sk. 1, 1 s.c., 1 h.d.c., 1 d.c., 4 tr.c., 1 d.c., 1 h.d.c., 1 s.c. This is for one petal.

Ch. 11 and repeat the same for other petal, 1 s.c. into loop formed at beginning of petals, turn, ch. 11, and make 2 more petals for other side, after each petal, 1 s.c. into loop at beginning.

Ch. 7, sk. 1, 1 s.c., turn, 2 s.c., turn, 2 s.c. into each st., turn, 2 s.c. into first, ch. 2, sk. 2, 2 s.c. into last st., turn, 2 s.c. into first and last st., 1 s.c. into st., 2 s.c. into space, turn, 2 s.c. into first st., ch. 2, sk. 2, 2 s.c., ch. 2, 2 s.c. into last st., turn, 2 s.c. into first and last st., 1 s.c. into sts., 2 s.c. into spaces, turn, 2 s.c. into first, ch. 2, sk. 2, 2 s.c., ch. 2, sk. 2, 2 s.c., ch. 2, sk. 2, 2 s.c. into last st., turn, 1 s.c. into first st., 2 s.c. into spaces, 1 s.c. into each st., 2 s.c. into last st. This row has 16 s.c., repeat from *. The band must have 5 diamonds and a half diamond at each end.

Work along side of band, starting on first half diamond, 1 d.c. into point of diamond, * ch. 6, 1 d.tr.c. into center of side of diamond, ch. 6, 1 s.c. into point of petal, ch. 8, 1 s.c. into point of next petal, ch. 6, 1 d.tr.c. into center of side of next diamond, ch. 6, 2 d.c. into point of same diamond, repeat from * across, turn.

7 s.c. into spaces of ch. 6, 9 s.c. into spaces of ch. 8, turn, 1 s.c. into each st., turn, 7 s.c., * turn, 2 s.c., ch. 3, sk. 3, 2 s.c., turn, 2 s.c., 3 s.c. into space, 2 s.c., turn, 2 s.c., ch. 3, sk. 3, 2 s.c., turn, 2 s.c., 3 s.c. into space, 2 s.c., 4 sl. sts. down the side, 17 s.c., repeat from * across, turn, 7 s.c. into square, * ch. 2, sk. 2, 1 d.tr.c., pull twice through 2 loops, sk. 4, 1 tr.c., pull through all loops on needle, 2 at the time, ch. 4, 1 tr.c. into center of sps., ch. 2, 7 s.c. into square, repeat from * across, turn, 1 s.c. into each st. across, turn, 5 s.c., 1 p., 5 s.c. across.

Repeat the same on other side of band.

Scalloped Edge.

Ch. 17, * sk. 1, 16 s.c., turn, sk. 1, 2 s.c., ch. 2, sk. 2, 2 s.c., ch. 2, sk. 2, 2 s.c., ch. 2, sk. 2, 2 s.c., sk. 1 at end of row, turn, sk. 1, 1 s.c., 2 s.c. into spaces, 1 s.c. into each st., sk. 1 at end of row, turn, sk. 1, 2 s.c., ch. 2, sk. 2, 2 s.c., ch. 2, sk. 2, 2 s.c., turn, sk. 1, 1 s.c., 2 s.c. into spaces, 1 s.c. into each st., turn, sk. 1, 2 s.c., ch. 2, sk. 2, 2 s.c., turn, sk. 1, 4 s.c., turn, sk. 1, 3 s.c., turn, sk. 1, 2 s.c., turn, sk. 1, 1 s.c., 10 sl. sts. down the side, ch. 20, sk. 1, 1 h.d.c., 1 h.d.c., 1 tr.c., 1 d.c., 1 h.d.c., 1 s.c. 1 sl. st. into next ch., ch. 11, sk. 1, 1 s.c., 1 h.d.c., 1 d.c., 4 tr.c., 1 d.c., 1 h.d.c., 1 s.c., 1 sl. st. at beginning of petal, ch. 8, repeat small petal, 1 sl. st. at beginning, ch. 28, repeat from * for 5 triangles and 5 sets of petals. Finish with the 3 petals, then ch. 11, 1 s.c. into point of last petal made, * ch. 6, 1 tr.c. into center of side of large petal, ch. 5, 1 d.c. into point of same petal, ch. 5, 1 d.c. into same, ch. 5, 1 tr.c. into center of side of same petal, ch. 5, 1 s.c. into point of next petal, ch. 5, sk. 7 chs. of foundation ch., 2 s.c., ch. 2, 1 d.c. into second st. of triangle, ch. 2, sk. 1, 1 d.c., make 3 more d.c. with ch. 2, sk. 1 between, last d.c. must be into point of triangle, ch. 5, 1 d.c. into same, ch. 2, sk. 1, make 4 more d.c. with ch. 2, sk. 1 between ch. 2, sk. 3 sts. of foundation ch., 2 s.c., ch. 5, 1 s.c. into point of next petal, repeat from * across, turn.

* 3 s.c. into each of 5 holes at side of triangle, 7 s.c. into center hole, 3 s.c. into each of 5 holes at other side of triangle, 5 s.c. into each of 3 holes at side of petal, 7 s.c. into center hole, 5 s.c. into each of 3 holes at other side of petal, repeat from * turn.

5 s.c., * 1 p., sk. 1, 5 s.c., 1 p., sk. 1, 5 s.c., 1 p., 2 s.c., 1 p., 1 s.c. into same, 1 s.c. into next, 1 p., 5 s.c., 1 p., sk. 1, 5 s.c., 1 p., sk. 1, 4 s.c., sk. 2 sts. at angle, 4 s.c. Repeat from * across. At other side of foundation chain, 1 s.c. into each st. across, turn, 1 row of 1 s.c. into each st. across, turn, 16 s.c., turn, * 2 s.c., ch. 3, sk. 3, 2 s.c., turn, 2 s.c. into sts., 3 s.c. into space, 2 s.c., turn, 2 s.c., ch. 3, sk. 3, 2 s.c., turn, 2 s.c. into sts., 3 s.c. into space, 2 s.c., 4 sl. sts. down the side, 20 s.c. into following sts., turn. Repeat from * across. Turn, ch. 9, cotton twice around the needle, insert into 6th ch. from needle, sk. 2 s.c., 1 tr.c., pull through all loops on needle, 2 at a time, ch. 2, * 7 s.c. into square, ch. 2, 1 d.tr.c., pull twice through 2 loops, sk. 2, 1 tr.c., pull through all loops on needle, 2 at a time, 1 tr.c. into center of sps. (this forms a cross), ch. 1, sk. 1, repeat the cross, ch. 2, sk. 2, repeat from * across. After last cross, ch. 1, 1 d.tr.c., turn, 1 s.c. into each st. across, turn, 5 s.c., 1 p., 5 s.c., continue across. Make the other edge the same way. Attach a narrow strip to each point of edge and sew to center band as shown in cut.

Narrow Strip.

Ch. 6, sk. 3, 3 d.c., turn, ch. 3, 3 d.c., turn, ch. 3, continue for 6¼ inches.

Buttons for End of Bolster.

Ch. 5, join to ring, 12 s.c. into ring, join with sl. st., 2 s.c., * turn, ch. 3, sk. 1, 1 s.c., turn, 3 s.c., 1 p., 3 s.c. into loop, repeat from * 5 times, join with sl. st., ch. 6, 1 s.c. into p., ch. 2, 1 tr.c. between loops, ch. 2, 1 s.c. into next p., continue around, join to 4th ch. from beginning.

3 s.c. into each hole all around. Put over silk covered mold 1¾ inches in diameter, decrease 1 s.c., sk. 1, 1 s.c. until closed.

Place crochet pieces on stamped lines, cut linen away underneath.

Mount on bolster form 25 inches long which has first been covered with white satin.

8th row.—3 s.c. to corner, 1 p., 1 s.c. into same, 4 s.c. into following sts, 1 p., sk. 1, 5 s.c., continue all around. At one of 4 corners have 3 p. together, which are needed for joining to band. Make 1 other medallion the same way.

The two medium and two small medallions are used together with 4 strips of insertion to form center of bedspread.

Insertion.

Oval Medallion.

Ch. 15, sk. 1, 2 s.c., ch. 2, sk. 2, 2 s.c., ch. 2, sk. 2, 2 s.c., ch. 2, sk. 2, 2 s.c., turn, ch. 3, 2 s.c. into first space, ch. 2, 2 s.c. into next space, ch. 2, 2 s.c. into 3rd space, ch. 2, 1 s.c. into last st., turn, 2 s.c. into first space, ch. 2, continue row, turn, ch. 2, 2 s.c. into first space, ch. 2, continue row, turn, 2 s.c. into first space, 2 s.c. into sts., continue until 1 s.c. into last space is made, turn, * ch. 9, sk. 6, 1 s.c., ch. 9, sk. 6, 1 s.c., turn, 13 s.c. into first loop, 6 s.c. into next loop, turn, ch. 9, 1 s.c. into center st. of loop, turn, 13 s.c. into loop, 6 s.c. into unfinished loop.

2 s.c. into next space, 3 s.c. into next 4 sts., 3 s.c. into next corner, 13 s.c. on this side, turn. Repeat from *, finish off. Make 6 more oval medallions the same way and join them into center st. at side.

Work around these 7 medallions starting on top of oblong of first medallion ch. 8, 1 d.c. into last st. of top of oblong, ch. 5, 1 tr.c. into 7th following st. ch. 8, 1 tr.c. into 7th st. of following medallion, ch. 5, 1 d.c. into 7th following st. ch. 5, sk. 5, 1 d.c. continue across band. For end of band after tr.c. ch. 14, 1 s.c. into center st. of last medallion, ch. 14, 1 tr.c. into 7th following st. Continue all around. Join to 3rd ch. from beginning. 1 s.c. into each st. across band, into 4th st. of 14 chs. for end, 3 s.c. to form corner. Continue with 1 s.c. into each st. 3 s.c. into 4th st. before first tr.c. at other side of band, 1 s.c. into following sts. continue around, join, 5 s.c. 1 p. 5 s.c. 1 p. continue across band to corner. ch. 2, join to medium size medallion to one of 3 p. at one corner. Ch. 2, finish like p. 5 s.c. into following sts. ch. 2, join to next p. of side of medallion, finish p., sk. 1, 5 s.c., join again to next p., sk. 1, 5 s.c., join to next p., sk. 1, 5 s.c., join to next p. and continue across band with 5 s.c., 1 p., 5 s.c. When other end is reached ch. 2, join to small medallion to 4th p. from corner with 3 ps. Join 5 times, the last must be into one of 3 ps. of corner. Finish row.

Make other 3 bands the same way, join them always to sides near 3 p., one of the 3 p. must remain in center.

After large medallion is placed in center of spread, place insertion around it as shown in cut. Place 1 triangle medallion into each corner of spread.

If spread is to be for single bed make 2 pieces of insertion each two yards long, and 2 pieces of insertion each 1 yard long, join them to last 5 p. at inside of 2 yard insertion and place to scrim.

At two long sides at end of spread attach to insertion a flouncing ½ yard wide of scrim. Make edging long enough to go all around spread.

Edging.

Make ch. for length required, sk. 1, 2 s.c., ch. 2, sk. 2, 2 s.c. continue across, turn, ch. 3, 2 s.c. into next space, ch. 2, 2 s.c. into following space, continue across, turn, 2 s.c. into spaces, 1 s.c. into each s.c., continue across, turn, ch. 8, sk. 5, 1 d.tr.tr.c., ch. 8, sk. 5, 1 s.c., ch. 8, sk. 5, continue across, turn, 13 s.c. into first hole, * 4 s.c. into next hole, turn, ch. 7, sk. 4, 1 s.c., ch. 7, sk. 4, 1 s.c., turn, 3 s.c., 1 p., 6 s.c. into first loop, 4 s.c. into next loop, turn, ch. 5, 1 s.c. into 5th st. of next loop, turn, 3 s.c., 1 p., 2 s.c., 1 p., 2 s.c., 1 p., 3 s.c. into loop, 2 s.c., 1 p., 3 s.c. into unfinished loop, 9 s.c. into next hole, 8 s.c. into following hole, turn, ch. 2, join to 9th s.c. of previous scallop, ch. 2, turn, finish p., 5 s.c. into same hole. Repeat from * across.

At other side of foundation ch., 2 s.c. into each space, 1 s.c. into each st. Cut away scrim under crocheted pieces.

No. 1080—BOLSTER

Size 5, Ecru CORDICHET, 10 balls.

For Bolster use scrim 1 yard long and 40 inches wide.

At center of scrim place medium sized square medallion with 1 p. at each corner.

Make 4 small medallions and 4 bands of insertions each of 4 oval medallions, and join them together the same way as described for Bedspread.

Place this on scrim around center medallion.

Make 2 bands of insertion each 1 yard long, place them at each side, about 6 inches from ends. Then make 2 pieces of edging the same length and place them at each end, cut away scrim under crocheted piece.

No. 1076—PILLOW

Size of Pillow 16 x 30.

Size 5, Ecru CORDICHET, 10 balls.

For center of pillow make 1 medium size medallion and two small medallions. Place the two small medallions about 1½ inches from center medallion at each side.

Make 4 small medallions for each corner of pillow, 2 bands of insertion each of 4 oval medallions for ends, and 2 bands of insertion each of 10 oval medallions for length of pillow, join one long band of insertion to square medallion on 5 1st p. of one side, leaving 1 p. and corner p. free; join one short band to other side of medallion so that the outer sides of medallion run on a straight line with the insertion. Finish other 3 corners the same way. Place this insertion to scrim. Make edging long enough to go around pillow, allowing enough for gathering at corners and place next insertion around pillow. Cut away scrim under crochet pieces and place over silk or satin covered form.

Continued on page 53.

NO. 1078—LAUNDRY BAG

Size 5, Ecru CORDICHET, 10 balls.

For center of Laundry Bag make 1 medium size Medallion.

For corners make 2 small medallions, for lower part of bag 1 piece of insertion of 4 oval medallions, for sides of bag two pieces of insertion each of 9 oval medallions, join to small square medallions, as described in Pillow and place to scrim.

Make edging long enough to go all around bag and around flaps of front and back. Allow enough edging for gathering at corners.

NO. 1075—SCARF

Size 5, Ecru CORDICHET, 12 balls.

For scarf a piece of scrim is required, 20" x 54".

About 4 inches from each end place at triangle medallion as shown in cut for which follow instructions of triangle medallion for Bedspread to 11th row, then finish with 5 s.c., 1 p., 5 s.c. all around.

Make 4 small medallions for each corner, 2 bands of insertion each of 4 oval medallions for each end, 2 bands of insertion each of 17 oval medallions for length of scarf. Join as described in pillow. Place to scrim.

Make edging long enough to go around sides and front of scarf. Allow enough for gathering at corners. Place edging next insertion.

NO. 1079—PIN CUSHION, 5 x 24

Size 5 Ecru CORDICHET—4 Balls.

Make 3 small medallions the same way as described in bedspread to 6th row, then finish with 1 row of * 5 s.c., 1 p., 5 s.c., 1 p., 5 s.c., 1 p., this last p. is to be in center of first scallop. Finish other side of scallop the same way. Repeat from * three times more. Place them to scrim as shown in cut.

Make a band of insertion of 22 oval medallions, join.

Work side of band the same way over 9 medallions, after 2nd d.c. into oblong of 9th medallion * ch. 3, 1 tr.c. into 7th following st. Pull twice through 2 loops, 1 tr.c. into 7th following st. of next medallions, pull twice through 2 loops, once through 3 loops, ch. 3, 1 d.c. into 7th following st. This forms a corner. Work over 2 medallions. Repeat from * to form other corner, work over 9 medallions and finish other end the same way.

At other side of insertion repeat the same. Place to scrim around cushion.

NO. 1077—LAMP SHADE

Size 5 Ecru CORDICHET—4 Balls.

Make a band of insertion of 15 oval medallions, join. Finish at side the same way as described in bedspread. This band is to go around bottom of shade. For top of shade, make a narrow band, ch. 9, sk. 1, 8 s.c., turn, ch. 10, sk. 6, 1 s.c., turn, 13 s.c. into loop, 1 s.c. into next st., 2 s.c. into first st. of foundation ch., 7 s.c. into following st., turn, ch. 10, sk. 6, 1 s.c., turn, 13 s.c. into loop, 3 s.c. into side to next loop, finish off. Make 23 more small ovals, join them together into center st. of loop, and join. Work around beginning into center of first oval, 3 s.c., ch. 10, 3 s.c. into center of next oval, continue around, join.

1 row of s.c. into each st. Join 1 row of 5 s.c., 1 p., 5 s.c. all around. Finish other side of band the same way.

Dividing Bands.

Ch. 46, sk. 9, 1 tr.c., ch. 2, sk. 2, 1 tr.c., continue to end of ch. (13 holes in all), 8 s.c. into first hole, 1 s.c. into 11 following holes, 11 s.c. into last hole, finish other side the same way. Join, 5 s.c., 1 p., 5 s.c., continue all around. Make 5 more bands the same way.

Into center of each 6 sides place an oval medallion made the same way as the oval for wide insertion but work all around 1 row of 5 s.c., 1 p., 5 s.c.

NO. 1085—SMALL BASKET—*Continued from page 25.*

10th row.—2 s.c. into first st., 1 s.c. into each of 11 following st., continue around, join.

11th row.—1 s.c. into each st. all around, join (this row has 52 sts.).

12th row.—Ch. 3, 1 d.c. into each st. all around, join.

13th row, 14th, 15th row same as 12th.

16th row.—1 s.c. into each st. all around, join.

17th row.—Ch. 3, sk. 1, 12 s.c., * ch. 2, sk. 1, 12 s.c. Repeat from * twice more. At end join to first ch. from beginning.

18th row.—Ch. 2, * 5 d.c. with always ch. 1 between into space of ch. 2, ch. 1, sk. 2 sts., 8 s.c., ch. 1. Repeat from * 3 times more. After last 8 s.c. are made, join to first ch. from beginning.

19th row.—Ch. 3, * 1 d.c. into first space before first d.c., ch. 2, 1 d.c. into next space, ch. 2, continue until 6 d.c. are made, ch. 2, sk. 1, 6 s.c., ch. 2. Repeat from * 3 times more. After last 6 s.c. are made, join to first ch. from beginning.

20th row.—Ch. 4, * 1 d.c. into first space, ch. 3, 1 d.c. into next space, ch. 3, continue until 7 d.c. are made, ch. 3, sk. 1, 5 s.c., ch. 3. Repeat from * 3 times more. After last 5 s.c. are made join to first ch. from beginning.

21st row.—Ch. 5, * 1 d.c. into first space, ch. 4, 1 d.c. into next space, continue until 8 d.c. are made, ch. 4, sk. 1, 4 s.c., ch. 4. Repeat from * 3 times more. After last 4 s.c. join to first ch. from beginning.

22nd row.—Ch. 6, * 1 d.c. into first space, ch. 5, 1 d.c. into next space, continue until 9 d.c. are made, ch. 5, sk. 1, 3 s.c., ch. 5. Repeat from * 3 times more. After last 3 s.c. are made join to first ch. from beginning.

23rd row.—Ch. 6, * 1 s.c. into first space, ch. 5, 1 s.c. into next space, ch. 5, continue into each space, ch. 5, sk. 1, 2 s.c., ch. 5. Repeat from * 3 times more. After last 2 s.c. join to first ch. from beginning. Finish off.

Handle.

Ch. 5, join to ring, ch. 3, 3 d.c., ch. 2, 2 d.c. into ring, turn, ch. 3, 3 d.c., ch. 2, 2 d.c. into space, turn, ch. 3, and continue until 4½ inches long, sew to basket in between two scallops on opposite sides.

following sts, 2 s.c. into loop, turn, 5 s.c. into sts., 3 s.c. into next st., 4 s.c. into following sts., 4 s.c. into loop, 2 s.c. into following loop. Repeat from * three times, join with sl. st.

3rd row—Work around, 1 s.c. into each st., 3 s.c. into corner sts., 4 sl. sts. into next sts.

4th row—3 s.c. into 3 corner sts., ch. 7, 1 tr.c. into center at side, 3 s.c. into 3 corner sts., repeat around. Join to first st. of row.

5th row—3 s.c. into sts., * 8 s.c. into hole, 3 s.c. into sp., 8 s.c. into next hole, 3 s.c. into sts. Repeat from * 3 times, join with sl. st.

6th row—2 s.c., ch. 2, sk. 2, 2 s.c., continue around. At corners, 2 s.c., ch. 2, 2 s.c. into following sts., join with sl. st.

7th row—1 s.c. into each st., 2 s.c. into space, 3 s.c. into corner spaces. Join with sl. st.

8th row—Ch. 7, sk. 3, 1 tr.c., ch. 3, sk. 3, 1 tr.c. continue around. For hole before and after corner, sk. only 2 sts, 1 tr.c. into corner st., ch. 5, 1 tr.c. into same. Join to 3rd ch. at beginning.

9th row—4 s.c. into each hole, 7 s.c. into corner holes, join with sl. st.

10th row—2 s.c., ch. 2, sk. 2, 2 s.c., ch. 2, continue around, 3 s.c. into corner sts.

11th row—1 s.c. into each st., 2 s.c. into each space, 3 s.c. into corner st.

12th row—5 s.c., 1 p., 5 s.c., all around.

Triangle.

Ch. 50, turn, sk. 1, 42 s.c., turn, 29 s.c., turn, ch. 3, sk. 7, 1 d. tr.c., ch. 3, 1 d. tr.c.; ch. 3, 1 d. tr.c., ch. 3, 1 d. tr.c., all into next st., ch. 3, sk. 7, 1 s.c., turn, 4 s.c. into first hole, turn, * four more rows of 4 s.c., 4 sl. sts. down the side, 4 s.c. into next hole, 4 s.c. into following hole, turn, and repeat from * twice, 6 s.c. into following sts., turn, * ch. 6, 4 s.c. into top of solid square, repeat from * twice, ch. 6, sk. 5, 1 s.c., turn, 6 s.c. into first hole, 4 s.c. into sts., 6 s.c. into next hole, repeat across, 1 s.c. into next st., turn, ch. 5, sk. 4, 1 s.c., ch. 5, and repeat for 8 loops in all, 1 s.c. into next st., turn.

6 s.c. into each loop, 6 s.c. into following sts., turn, ch. 5, 1 s.c. into center of 1st loop, ch. 5, 1 s.c. into center of 2nd loop, ch. 5, 1 s.c. into center of 3rd loop, ch. 5, 1 d.c. into center of next loop, ch. 5, 1 d. tr.c., into st. between 2 loops, ch. 5, 1 d. tr.c. into same, ch. 5, 1 d.c. into center of next loop, repeat this side the same as other side, 1 s.c. into last st., turn.

6 s.c. into each of 5 following loops, 7 s.c. into center loop, continue for other side with 6 s.c. into each of 5 loops, turn, 2 s.c. into 2 first sts., ch. 2, sk. 2, 2 s.c. continue to center st., ch. 2, 1 s.c. into same, 1 s.c. into next, repeat at other side, turn, ch. 3, sk. 2, 2 s.c. into space of ch. 2, ch. 2, sk. 2, and repeat into center space, 3 s.c., repeat at other side. After last ch. 2, work around triangle, 1 d.c. into last st. of previous row, 2 tr.c. into 2 rows of beginning, ch. 6, 1 s.c. into each st. at other side of foundation ch., 1 s.c. into each of 5 ch.s. left, 2 tr.c. into 2 first row, 1 d.c. into next, 2 s.c. into first space, 1 s.c. into each stitch, continue around 2 sides, into a point 3 s.c., 1 s.c. into each sp., 6 s.c. into 6 chs., join with sl. st.

1 row of 5 s.c., 1 p., 5 s.c. all around having 1 p. at each of 3 points. Make three more triangles.

Border With Fringes.

Ch. 75, sk. 5, 2 s.c., ch. 2, sk. 2, 2 s.c., continue across, turn, ch. 3, sk. 2, 2 s.c. into 1st space, ch. 2, sk. 2, and continue across, turn, 1 s.c. into each st., 2 s.c. into each space, turn, 5 s.c., 1 p., 5 s.c. continue across.

At other side of foundation ch., 1 s.c. into each st., 2 s.c. into each space, turn, 1 s.c. into first st., ch. 2, sk. 2, 1 s.c., ch. 2, sk. 2, 1 s.c. continue across.

Fringes.

Size 1 CORDICHET, cut 2 threads each 22 inches long, fold in center, pull through small loop of last row from top to bottom, make ch., pull out. Repeat into each small loop.

Knotting.

Take strands of 2 first loops, make a buttonhole stitch with right hand strands, then repeat with left hand strands, continue alternating until solid bar is 2 inches long. When all the strands are knotted, take half of first and half of 3rd knotted bar, and work solomon knot over strands in between.

Solomon Knot.

Hold the center strand down straight between 2nd and 3rd fingers of left hand, bring left hand strand around over the middle strand, take right hand strand, bring it down over the left hand strand, across back of the middle one, up through the loop on left hand side. Repeat, starting with the right hand strand, bring the left hand strand up through the loop on the right hand side, holding the center one firmly, pull the two side strands to form a firm knot.

Repeat with every three knotted bars, then tie inside strand of first solomon knot to next strand of following, and make a small tassel over each knot. Wind cotton 25 times over cardboard 5 inches long, put over knot and tie 1/2 inches from top.

For Border going around point at end of scarf, follow instructions as for Border with fringes but instead of having one side with loops make 1 row of 5 s.c., 1 p., 5 s.c. Make Border long enough to go from fringe to fringe on stamped lines around point of linen.

Tassel.

Wind size 1 CORDICHET 75 times around cardboard 6 inches long, tie in center, tie again ¾ of an inch from top and sew to point.

Place crocheted pieces on stamped lines, cut linen away underneath.

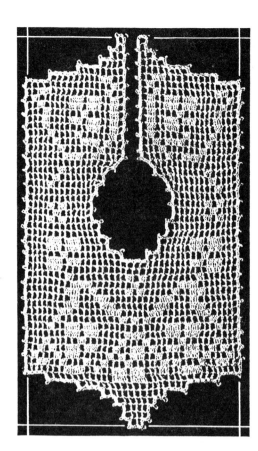

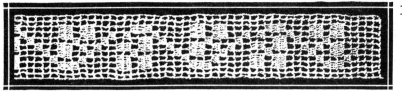

No. 316. INFANTS' YOKE AND BAND

CROCHET COTTON, SIZE 60—1 BALL.

Ch. 11.

1st Row—2 o. m. **2nd and 3rd Rows**—4 o. m. **4th Row**—6 o. m.
5th Row—10 o. m. **6th Row**—18 o. m. Follow design.
EDGE—6 sl. st., 1 p. and repeat all around.
BAND—Ch. 38. **1st, 2nd and 3rd Rows**—11 o. m., then follow design.

CROCHET ART FOR MILADY'S LINGERIE

A BOOK ON YOKES, CAPS, TOWELS. By EMMA FARNES.

Contains 20 Yokes and 60 other illustrations of Kerchiefs, Slippers,
Handbags, Novelties. Ask your dealer for it. **Price 10.**

No. 317. "LONE·STAR," "MULE"

CROCHET COTTON, SIZE 30—2 BALLS.

Star Medallion is worked first.

1st Row—Ch. 7, 5 d. c. with 3 chs. bet. each in first ch. st. Join.
2nd Row—Ch. 3, 7 d. c. in each one of the 6 sps.
3rd Row—1 sl. st. over each d. c.
4th Row—Ch. 7, sk. 1, 1 d. t., ch. 7, sk. 1, 2 sl. st. Repeat 7 times.
5th Row—9 sl. st. over 7 chs., ch. 1 over d. t., 9 sl. st. over next 7 chs. Fasten thread.
6th Row—Start over the first ch. st. in upper point, ch. 4, 1 pt. st. of 2 d. t., ch. 15 to next point. Turn. 5 sl. st. over 5 ch. sts., turn, ch. 3,

1 d. t. in same st., ch. 8, 1 sl. st. all in same st. Turn. 5 sl. st. over 5 ch. sts. leaving 3 ch. sts. untouched, ch. 10 to third point, 1 pt. st. of 3 d. t. in ch. st.

7th Row—13 sl. st. in each large sp., 4 sl. st. in each small sp. Count carefully. This will give 136 sl. st. in all.

8th, 9th, 10th and 11th Rows—Work 4 rows of same sl. st. over this, taking up both threads and always count 136 · sl. st.

12th Row—17 sl. st. over same. Turn, sk. 1 sl. st. on each side, 15 sl. st. for 2 rows, working up from point, 13 sl. st. for next 2 rows. Omit same way until 2 rows of 3 sl. st. are finished, then sl. st. down on left side of point. Work all 8 points same way.

SMALL MEDALLION.

1st Row—Ch. 7, 5 d. c. with 3 chs. bet. each in first ch. st. Join.

2nd Row—Ch. 3, 6 d. c. in each of 6 sps.

3rd Row—8 sl. st. over 8 d. c., 1 p., sk. 1. Repeat 3 times. Connect small medallions bet. every other point of star. Ch. 4, 1 sl. st. in star, ch. 4. Fasten all threads

First upper row of Star Medallion—Start over point on side of star with 2 sl. st., ch. 17, 1 pt. st. of 2 d. t. bet.

first and second point. Turn. 10 sl. st. over 7 sts. of this ch. Turn. Ch. 4, 1 pt. st. of 2 tr. t. over pt. st. bel., ch. 11 to connecting st. of pt. st., 10 sl. st., over 7 sts. of this ch., ch. 10 to next point of star, 2 sl. st., ch. 4, 1 pt. st. of 2 d. c. in first p. of small medallion, ch. 11 to cor. p., ch. 11, 1 pt. st. of 2 d. c. in third p. of small medallion.

2nd Row—12 sl. st. over first sp., 5 sl. st. over second sp., 5 sl. st. over third sp., 12 sl. st. over fourth sp., 4 sl. st. over fifth sp., 12 sl. st. over sixth sp., 12 sl. st. over seventh sp.

Side Parts, upper and lower Edge—Work 48 o. m. over the 2 upper sides of square, then 11 o. m. for 2 rows for side parts, 10 o. m. for next 2 rows, 9 o. m. for 2 rows. Omit same way until there are 7 o. m. left. Then 1 row of 6 o. m., 1 row of 5 o. m., 1 row of 4 o. m. Then 3 sl. st. in each m. on lower side. Work same over other side. Fasten thread.

Row on Lower Side—5 sl. st. over same, 1 p., sk. 1.

First Row on Upper Edge—3 sl. st. in each m.

2nd Row on Upper Edge—4 sl. st. over same, 1 p., sk. 1. If upper edge is desired tight, work 4 sl. st. over 5 sl. st., 1 p., sk. 2.

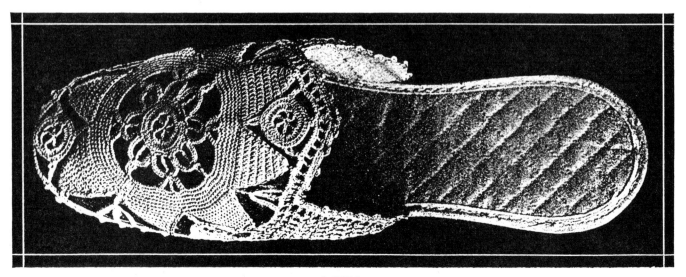

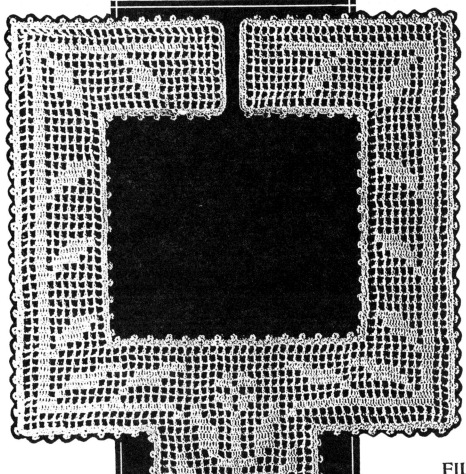

No. 318

CHILD'S YOKE

CROCHET COTTON, SIZE 50.
1 BALL.
Size, 1 Year.

Start at back.

Ch. 83.

1st and 2nd Rows—26 o. m. Next 8 rows follow pattern.

Start shoulder strap with 7 o. m., 1 s. m., 2 o. m.; work next 27 rows following pattern. After both parts are finished, ch. 99, connecting them, then work 2 o. m., 2 s. m., 45 o. m., 2 s. m., 2 o. m. and for next 9 rows follow pattern. Fasten thread. Work 5 o. m., 2 s. m., 2 o. m., 1 s. m., 2 o. m., 2 s. m., 5 o. m., then next 6 rows follow pattern. Work 1 o. m., 2 s. m., 4 o. m., 1 s. m., 4 o. m., 2 s. m., 1 o. m., and next 5 rows follow pattern. Work 4 o. m., 1 s. m., 4 o. m., then next 5 rows follow pattern.

EDGING.

1st Row—3 sl. st. in every o. m.

2nd Row—4 sl. st. over same, 1 p., sk. 1, 4 sl. st.

FILET CROCHET

Book No. 1.   **By Jane Ford**

Contains over 100 designs for cross-stitch or filet crochet. Ask your dealer for it. **Price 10c.**

No. 319.   BABYS' BOOTEES

CROCHET COTTON, SIZE 5—1 BALL PERLE.

1st Row—Ch. 64, join, 1 sl. st. in every st. **2nd Row**—Ch. 4, sk. 2, 1 sl. st. in 3rd st., repeat 5 times; 1 sl. st. in each one bel., taking up back thread only. **3rd Row**—Ch. 2, 1 sl. st. over 1st l., ch. 4 to next, making 5 ls. in this row; ch. 2, 1 sl. st. over 1st one bel.; 1 sl. st. in every one bel. Continue until 11 rows are finished, always 6 ls. over 5 ls. **12th Row**—Count center st. in back, sk. last and first sl. st. in back, 1 sl. st. over center sl. st. Always work 2 rows over each omitting row. Omit 5 times altogether, then 5 rows without omitting. Open part over foot. Work 3 rows same as above, turning work on each side. Then 5 rows—ch. 3 instead of 4 chs. Omit 1 loop on each side. Fasten thread.

FOOT.

1st Row—Start over center st. in back, 1 sl. st. over each one bel. until open part is reached; 4 sl. st. in each l., 1 sl. st. over same. ls.; repeat to end of row. **2nd Row**—1 sl. st. in each one bel. **3rd Row**—Count center st. in front over toe. Increase 1 sl. st. to each side. **4th Row**—Count 3 center sts. in front. Increase 1 sl. st. to each side of these 3 sts. and 2 sl. st. in back of bootee. **5th Row**—Count center st. in front and increase 1 sl. st. to each side. **6th Row**—Same as 4th Row. Then 3 rows without increasing.

SOLE.

1st Row—Ch. 33, 1 sl. st., in each st. to each side all around, 3 sl. st. in first and last ch. st. **2nd Row**—1 sl. st. in each one bel. Increase 4 sl. st. on each end, working 2 sl. st. in each one of 4 sts. **3rd Row**—Same as 2nd Row. **4th Row**—Same, only increase 3 sl. st. on each end. Sole is sewed to upper part.

ORNAMENTS—Made of Silkateen. Medallion.

1st Row—Ch. 5 form ring, ch. 5, 5 d. c. with 2 chs. bet. each over ring. Close. **2nd Row**—1 sl. st., 1 s. c., 3 d. c., 1 s. c., 1 sl. st. over each one of the 6 sps.

STRAPS.

1st Row—Ch. 26, 1 sl. st. in each st. **2nd Row**—1 sl. st. in each one bel., taking up back thread only.

EDGING.

1st Row—1 sl. st. of 2 d. c. in 1 st., ch. 2, sk. 2. **2nd Row**—1 p. over each sp. Cord is made of chs. of double thread.

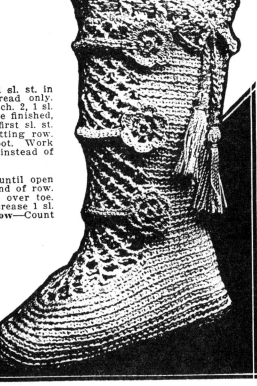

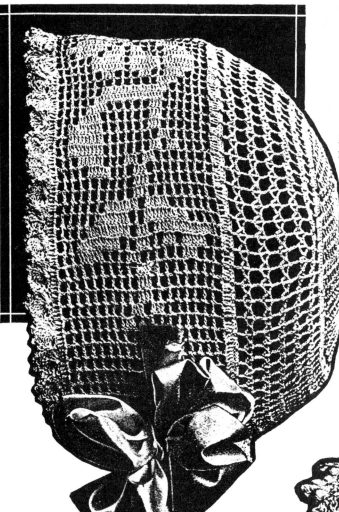

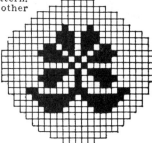

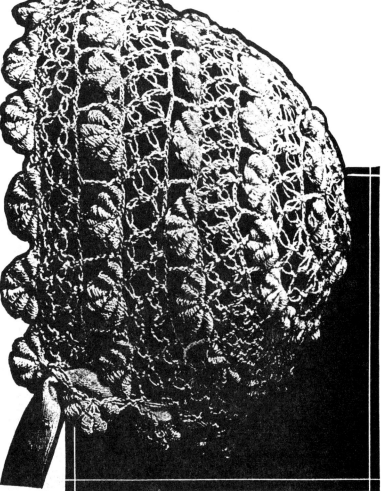

CAP BAND—Work from left to right, which is center of pattern. Work from right to left for other half of pattern.

No. 320
BABY CAP

CROWN OF CAP

CROCHET COTTON, SIZE 60—2 BALLS.

BAND—1st and 2nd Rows—18 o. m. Follow pattern.

BACK—1st Row—5 o. m. Follow pattern.

1st Row around Back—Finish back with 6 chs. fastened around each o. m.

2nd Row—7 d. c. in each ch.

3rd Row—Ch. 1, 1 d. c. and fasten in each 4 d. c. all around.

4th Row—Ch. 3, fasten with s. c. in center of 4th ch., forming the lac. st.; make the next 4 rows with lac. st. and then fasten front and back together. Work around cap with a row of d. c.

Edge—2 d. c. 1 p., 2 d. c., 1 p., 2 d. c., 1 p., 2 d. c., 1 p., in one st., sk. 3 d. c., 1 sl. st. Repeat all around cap.

No. 321
INFANTS' ROLL AND KNOT STITCH CAP

CROCHET COTTON—3 SPOOLS SILKATEEN.

1st Row—Ch. 8, form ring, 11 rl. st. in ring; close.

2nd and 3rd Rows—Work 1 kn. st. over every rl. st.

4th Row—1 sl. st. over 1st kn. st., ch. 7 to next kn. st. This will give 7 chs. 10 times.

5th Row—Ch. 1, 6 rl. st. in 5th ch. st., ch. 1, sk. 5 sts., 1 sl. st., ch. 1, sk. 5, 6 rl. sts. Repeat 7 times. Fasten on chain.

6th Row—Ch. 13, fasten bet. 3rd and 4th rl. st., ch. 7, 1 d. t. bet. groups of rl. sts. in sl. st. bel. This keeps rl. sts. in place. Ch. 7. There are 7 chs. 16 times.

7th and 8th Rows—24 kn. sts., sk. 4 bet. each.

9th Row—1 sl. st. in 1st kn. st., ch. 7 to next kn. st.

10th Row—6 rl. sts. in 1 ch. st., ch. 1, sk. 6, 1 sl. st., ch. 1, sk. 6. There are 14 groups of rl. sts.

11th Row—Same as 6th row.

12 and 13th Rows—42 kn. sts., sk. 4 bet. each.

14th Row—1 sl. st. in 1st kn. st., ch. 4 to next kn. st.

15th Row—15 groups of rl. sts., ch. 1, sk. 6, 1 sl. st., ch. 1, sk. 6 bet. each.

16th Row—Same as 6th row.

17 and 18th Rows—42 kn. sts., sk. 4 bet. each.

19th Row—Ch. 5 over kn. st.

20th Row—19 groups of rl. sts. worked same way as above. 5 of these groups will give the edge in back. Work another set of rows over 14 groups of rl. sts. for front part, connecting front and back edge with group of 6 rl. sts. Draw ribbon through last row of kn. sts.

[122]

13

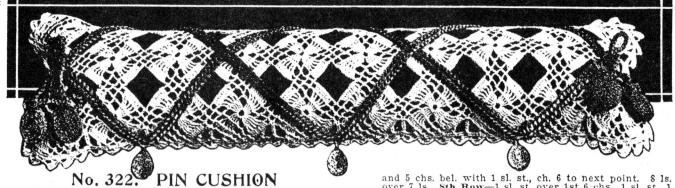

No. 322. PIN CUSHION

CROCHET COTTON, SIZE 30—1 BALL AND 1 SPOOL SILKATEEN FOR ORNAMENTS.

Each square is worked separately. **1st Row—** Ch. 7 form ring, ch. 4, 4 d. t., ch. 5, 5 d. t. in ring. Repeat twice. **2nd Row—**Ch. 5, 4 d. t. with 1 ch. bet. each, ch. 5, 1 sl. st. over 5 chs. bel., ch. 5, 5 d. t. over same with 1 ch. bet. each. Repeat twice. **3rd Row—**Ch. 5, 9 d. c. over 5 d. t. and chs., ch. 4, 1 sl. st. over 1., ch. 5, 1 sl. st., ch. 4. Repeat. Connect squares over corners. Ch. 2, 1 sl. st. in 1st 1. of 1st square, ch. 2 back again and repeat over all 3 ls. **EDGING.—1st Row—**1 sl. st. in 1st 1., ch. 3, repeat twice, ch. 3, 2 d. c. in 4th d. c. of square, ch. 4, 2 tr. t. bet. squares, ch. 4. **2nd Row—**1 sl. st. in each st. **3rd Row—**1 sl. st., ch. 2, sk. 2, 1 d. c., ch. 2, 7 d. c. over d. c. just made, sk. 2. **ORNAMENTS—1st Row—**Ch. 5 form ring, 2 sl. st. in each st. **2nd Row—**2 sl. st. in 1st st., 1 sl. st. in 2nd st. **3rd Row—**2 sl. st. in each st. Repeat until there are 5 rows. **Cord** is made of chs. of three double threads. **Ornaments** are made of 2 of these little disks and sewed together after being filled with cotton.

No. 323. ELECTRIC LIGHT SHADE

WITH COLORED LINING ACTS AS A DIMMER.
CROCHET COTTON, SIZE 20—1 BALL. SIZE 25—1 BALL FOR FRINGE.

Consists of three medallions. **1st Row—**Ch. 7, 4 d. c. with 3 chs. bet. each in 1st ch. st., ch. 3; close. **2nd Row—**Ch. 3, 3 d. c. in each 5 sps. **3rd Row—**Ch. 3, 2 d. c., ch. 3, 3 d. c.; repeat 7 times. This requires 27 sts.; ch. 3, sk. 1, ch. 4, sk. 2, ch. 4, sk. 2, ch. 3, making 4 little ls.; close. **4th Row—**Work thread up to 3 chs. Ch. 2, 2 d. c., ch. 3, 3 d. c. over 3 chs., ch. 2 to next 3 chs., 3 d. c., ch. 3, 3 d. c. Repeat. 5 ls. over 4. **5th Row—**Work thread up. Ch. 2, 1 d. c., ch. 3, 2 d. c. over 3 chs., ch. 5 to next point, 2 d. c., ch. 3, 2 d. c., 6 ls. over 5, ch. 4 for ls. **6th Row—**Work thread up. Same as 5th row only ch. 6 instead of 5. 7 ls. over 6 ls. **7th Row—**Work thread to the 3 chs., 1 sl. st., ch. 6 taking up the 6 chs.

and 5 chs. bel. with 1 sl. st., ch. 6 to next point. 8 ls. over 7 ls. **8th Row—**1 sl. st. over 1st 6 chs., 1 sl. st., 1 s. c., 8 d. c., 1 s. c., 1 sl. st. over every 6 chs., making 14 scallops. 9 ls. over 8 ls. **9th Row—**Work thread to 4th d. c., ch. 2, 1 d. c., 1 p., 2 d. c. over 4 d. c. bel., ch. 5 to next scallop, 2 d. c., 1 p., 2 d. c. over the 4 d. c. in center. 10 ls. over 9 ls. **10th Row—**Work thread with long sl. st. behind p., 1 sl. st. over 5 chs., ch. 2, 2 d. c., ch. 3, 3 d. c. over 5 chs., ch. 5 to next 1., 3 d. c., ch. 3, 3 d. c. Then same figure of 3 d. c., ch. 3, 3 d. c. over 1st and last 1. This will leave 9 ls.; ch. 5 to 1st figure of r. bel. **11th Row—**Work thread up. Then same as r. bel.; ch. 6 instead of 5. There are 15 figures in this r. 10 ls. over 9 ls. **12th Row—**Start at 2nd figure and work thread up. 8 d. c. with 5 ps. over 13 figures, 3 d. c., ch. 3, 3 d. c. over 1st and last figure, ch. 4, 1 sl. st., ch. 4 over 6 chs. taking up chs. of 2 rs. bel., ch. 4, 1 d. c. over 1s., ch. 6 in p. holding fringe. **UPPER EDGE—1st Row—**1 d. c., ch. 3 over every 1., 2 d. c. over figure, ch. 3, 2 tr. t. in center of 5 chs. bel., ch. 2, 2 tr. t. (keep last 2 ls. on hook) in p., 2 d. t. in center, pull thread through all, ch. 2; repeat. **2nd Row—**1 d. c., ch. 2, 1 d. c., ch. 3 over sps. **3rd Row—**1 d. c., ch. 2. **4th Row—**1 d. c. in 1st sp., 2 d. c., ch. 2, 2 d. c. in 2nd sp. **5th Row—**2 d. c., ch. 3, 2 d. c. over 2 chs. **6th Row—**3 ps., ch. 5. Connect the 3 medallions on 3 points with 3 ps.

FRINGE.
Wind thread 8 times over cardboard 4 in. wide, cut off, pull through loop, tie tightly.

For directions on No. 324 Powder Puff Reticule, see page 6.

Materials Required: 3 Balls

Boudoir Cap *Collingbourne's*

Every lady delights in a pretty Boudoir Cap. Here is one that will make you look very "Chic."

Art. C51. No. 50

Start with rose at top of cap. Ch. 10, join into this ring work 6 tr. c. with 5 ch. between. Fill in these 6 loops with 1 s. c., 5 d. c., 1 s. c., this forms the 1st row of petals. Ch. 6 and catch at back of each petal. Fill these with 1 s. c., 7 d. c., 1 s. c. Ch. 7, and catch in back of each petal. Fill with 1 s. c., c. 9 d. c., 1 s. c.

Ch. 8 catch in back of each petal, fill with 1 s. c., 11 d. c., 1 s. c. Ch. 9, and catch in back of petal. Fill with 1 s. c., 13 d. c., 1 s. c. Ch. 10, catch in back of petal, fill with 1 s. c., 15 d. c., 1 s. c., this completes the rose.

First Row.—Make 3 s. c. in 1st 3 stitches of petal. Ch. 8, go back into 3rd stitch, this forms a picot. Ch. 8, go back into 3rd stitch, this forms a 2nd picot. Ch. 3, skip 7, 1 s. c., ch. 8, 1 picot, ch. 8, picot, skip 6, 1 s. c. We will call (ch. 8, go back into 3rd stitch, ch. 8, go back into 3rd stitch, ch. 3). Two picots in order to simplify instructions. Make 2 picots, catch in 3rd stitch of next petal. Two picots, skip 6, 2 picots, skip 6. Repeat all around, and you will have 18 loops of two picots.

Second Row.—Ch. 3, and catch into 1st picot made * thread over needle 4 times, catch into 2nd ch. stitch, skipping two picots. Ch. 3, and work around this loop made by putting thread over needle 4 times, 10 d. c., ch. 3, and catch in same stitch where you made long tr. crochet. Make 2 picots, skip 2 picots, catch in 2 ch., 2 picots, skip 2 picots, catch in 2 ch., 2 picots, skip 2, catch in 2 ch., 2 picots, skip 2 picots, catch in 2 ch. Repeat from * all around. This divides the Cap into 4 sections of 4 two picots between each group of 10 d. c.

Third Row.—2 picots, catch in center of 10 d. c., 2 picots catch in last d. c., 2 picots, skip 1 picot, catch in 2nd st. between 2 picots, skip 2 picots, 2 picots, skip 2, 2 picots, skip 2, 2 picots, skip 1 picot, catch in 2nd d. c. Repeat all around. Now repeat from directions, beginning with thread over needle 4 times (2nd row) and work all around.

You will notice in the 3rd row, you skip only 1 picot, this forms the increase. Work in this manner until you have 8 rows of the 10 d. c. In this last row, you will have 17 groups of 2 picots between the shell of 10 d. c. Now make 1 more row of directions for 3rd row, which finishes top of Cap. Now make 1 d. c. into picot. Ch. 1, 1 d. c. into next picot. Repeat all around.

Fourth Row.—1 d. c., 1 ch., skip 1, 1 d. c., repeat all around.

Fifth Row.—Two picots, skip 1 space, repeat all around. Now make Roses—17 for band.

Directions for Rose for the Band.—Ch. 10, 6 d. c. with 5 ch. between, fill 5 ch. with 1 s. c., 5 d. c., 1 s. c. Ch. 6 and catch in back of each petal, fill with 1 s. c., 7 d. c., 1 s. c. After sewing together the 17 roses, make 1 more row of 2 picots, joining 1st two picots to 1st and last stitch of 2 Petals of Rose.

NUT BOWL

Use *Collingbourne's* Luxura Silk
No. 20

Ch. 5, join with sl. st. ch. 3, 17 d. c. into ring, making 18 d. c. all together. Ch. 4, 1 d. c. in 1st space. 1st space, ch. 1, skip 1 st., 1 d. c. in next space, continue all around, and join with slip st. Ch. 5, 1 d. c. in 1st space. Ch. 2, 1 d. c. in next space, continue all around and join with slip st. Ch. 3, 4 d. c. in each space, and join with slip st. This forms the base. Ch. 3, 1 s. c. in 1st space of next to the last row. Ch. 5, 1 d. c. in next space. Ch. 2, 1 d. c. in next space, continue all around and join with slip st. 1 slip st. in 1st space, ch. 3, 2 more d. c. in the space, ch. 2, 3 d. c. in 2nd space, continue all around, and join with slip st. Ch. 3, 2 d. c. into the other 2 d. c. of previous row. 3 d. c. into the next space, 3 d. c. into the next 3 d. c. of previous row, continue all around, and join with a slip st. Ch. 3, 6 d. c. in the next 6 spaces of previous row, making 7 d. c. Ch. 2, 1 d. c. into the 2nd space, ch. 2, 1 d. c. into the next space, ch. 2, skip 1 st., 1 d. c. into the next space, 6 d. c. into the next 6 spaces. Ch. 2, skip 1 st., 1 d. c. into the next space. Ch. 2, skip 2 sts., 1 d. c. into the next space. Ch. 2, skip 2 sts., 1 d. c. with next space, 6 d. c. into the next 6 sts. Ch. 2, skip 1 st., 1 d. c. into the next space, ch. 2, skip 2 sts., 1 d. c. into the next space, ch. 2, 1 d. c. into the 2nd space, 6 d. c. into the next 6 sts., ch. 2, skip 1 st., 1 d. c. into the next space, ch. 2, skip 2 sts., 1 d. c. into the next space, ch. 2, skip 2 sts., 1 d. c. into the next space, join with slip st. Make about 3 slip sts. back into the middle space, 8 tr. into that space, ch. 2, slip 2 spaces, 3 d. c. into the next 2 spaces, ch. 2, 8 tr. into the middle space, ch. 2, skip 2 spaces, 3 d. c. into the next 3 spaces, continue all around, and join with 2 sl. sts., 2 tr. between each tr. of previous row. 1 d. c. in the middle space 2 trs. between each tr. and continue all around, join with sl. st., ch. 3, 1 s. c. between each tr., continue all around, and join with slip st.

Handle.—Ch. 23, d. c. back on 24th ch. Ch. 2, skip 2, ch. 1 d. c. in next, and repeat to the end. On both sides of the block ch. 3, s. c. in every space, and fasten to the basket.

COIN PURSE Use *Collingbourne's* Artificial Fibre Silk

Chain 66. Into 3rd ch. make 2 d. c. In 6th ch. make 3 d. c., continue around with 3 d. c. in every 3rd ch. Fasten at 1st d. c., 3 ch., 2 d. c. in space. 3 d. c. in next space, continue around. Make 16 rows.

For Flap.—3 ch., 3 d. c. in next space, and continue across for just one-half of purse. 3 ch. to turn each time, and narrow to one space. Fold bag and into each double space at bottom make 2 s. c. Turn. 5 ch., fasten in 6th d. c., 7 c., fasten into 11th d. c., 5 ch., fasten at end. Fill each chain with s. c. Sew a rose at end of flap. Fasten an ivory ring at top with 5 d. c. Under flap, sew two small snap fasteners.

Edge for Curtain Shade, Doily, Collar, Etc. Use *Collingbourne's* Art. C51, No. 20

Square Medallion.—Ch. 7, join, and work in 24 d. c., ch. 6, and make 1 d. c. in the next st. (this forms corner). * Ch. 3, skip 2, 1 d. c., ch. 3, skip 2, 1 d. c., ch. 3, 1 d. c. into same stitch. Repeat from *. Fill in with 3 s. c., 1 p., 3 s. c. in 3 ch. and 3 s. c., 1 p., 3 s. c., 1 p., 3 s. c., 1 p., 3 s. c. in the corner. These directions are for one scallop complete. One can make as many as needed according to article wanted. 4 squares are required for 1 scallop.

Leaf Medallion.—Ch. 24, catch into 13th ch. with s. c., ch. 5, skip 5, catch in next for s. c., make 1 s. c. into each of the next 5 s. c., turn.

Second Row.—Ch. 7, catch in 3rd of 5 ch. with s. c., ch. 5, catch in the middle of next 5 ch., Ch. 5, 1 d. c. in middle of next 5 ch., Ch. 6, 1 d. c. in same st., ch. 5, 1 s. c. in next 5 ch, Ch. 5, 1 s. c. in next 5 ch., Ch. 7, 1 s. c. in end st.

Third Row.—Fill in 7 ch. with 11 s. c., the 5 ch. with 5 s. c.. the 6th ch. (point) with 11 s. c.

Fourth Row.—1 s. c. in each s. c., making 3 s. c. in 6th st. at point. Work in only half (the back half) of st.

Fifth Row.—Same as 4th. This completes leaf with 3 picots at lower end 2 stitches between.

Border Across the Top.—Ch. 24, catch last chain into last of 3 picots into corner of square 1 d. c. in the 4th ch., 1 d. c. into each of the next 7 ch., 11 ch., catch in 1st p. of next corner. Ch. 3, catch in 1 p. of corner of 2nd square, 1 d. c. in the 4th ch., 7 d. c. in next 7 ch., skip 2 ch. and then 9 d. c., catch in last d. c. in 1st p. of 2nd corner of 2nd square. Repeat these instructions until you have the required number of squares joined.

Second Row.—1 d. c., 1 ch., skip 1, 1 d. c. all the way across.

Third Row.—Fasten thread in d. c. * Ch. 5, 2 tr. c. in same st. Skip 2 d. c. into 3rd one, make 2 tr. c., ch. 5, and catch in same stitch with s. c. Ch. 5, skip 2, d. c. and repeat from *.

Fourth Row.—2 tr. c. in the top of 2 tr. c., 5 ch., catch in same stitch, 5 ch., 2 tr. c. in same stitch. Ch. 3. and catch in 5 ch. with s. c.

Fifth Row.—Ch. 5, * catch in top of group of 2 tr. c., 5 ch., ch. 5, catch in top of next group, ch. 5, repeat from *.

Sixth Row.—* 1 d. c., 1 ch., skip 1, 1 d. c., 1 p. and repeat from *. Make 7 leaves for scallop, join squares as in illustration, making a ch. of 11, and catching in the 1st picot of corner. On this work 8 d. c. and ch. 11, catch in 1st p. of 2nd corner, and picot of leaf. 8 d. c. in this ch. Ch. 11, and catch in next picot of leaf, and 1st picot of corner of next square 8 d. c., 11 ch. and catch in corner of square, and work 8 d. c. Join 2 leaves to lower square at corner picot. The center leaf is not joined to square, but only to the outer leaves.

Joining Leaves at Lower End.—Fasten thread in leaf where first loop of 5 chs. come. Ch. 5, skip 2 stitches, 1 s. c. in next stitch. Now make 3 s. c. into this 5 ch., ch. 6, skip 2, 1 s. c., 4 s. c. into this loop, ch. 7, skip 2, 5 s. c. in this loop, ch. 8, skip 2, 6 s. c. in this loop, ch. 8, skip 2, 6 s. c. in this loop, ch. 8, and now go in stitch at point. 6 s. c. in this loop, ch. 8, 1 s. c. in next stitch, 6 s. c. in this loop, ch. 7, skip 2, 5 s. c. in this loop, ch. 6, skip 2, 4 s. c. in this loop, ch. 5, skip 2, 3 s. c. in this loop, join this leaf to the next one, and proceed in the same manner, joining the 5 lower leaves. Now fill in the 1st loop of 3 s. c. with 1 p., 2 s. c. next loop, 1 p., 3 s. c. next loop, 1 p., 4 s. c. and continue up to point with 1 p., 4 s. c. and then decrease again on other side until you reach 2 s. c. Fill in next leaf in same manner. The leaf at either end of scallop is not finished in this way, but is left without the edge.

Jewel or Money Bag Use *Collingbourne's* Luxura Fibre Silk

Chain 75 and join. Then s. S1 around 72 stitches, 35 rows. Then fold as an envelope, for lap over, 7 rows. the same, only in 3rd row, skip one stitch 4 times to make button hole. Finish all around with any scallop. When done begin in middle of 2nd row of flap, crochet 12 c. sts. 4 rows of same, to fasten to corset. Then sew buttons on to fit holes.

20

Kewpie Doll and Hair Pin Holder

Use 5 balls Collingbourne Fibre silk (2 white, and 3 colors) and 1 yard of ribbon to be used for hanging.

UNDER GARMENT:

First Row.—Ch. 35 st. for waist band.

Second Row.—Throw thread over and crochet off twice, or double crochet making 32 sts.

Third Row.—Same as 2nd, only increase over little stomach to 48th st.

Fourth and Fifth Rows.—Plain, no increase, and join skirt.

Sixth Row.—Ch. 23 sts., and join for leg, and make two more rows the same. To finish ch. 5 and fasten in every st. Break thread and return to skirt part, skip 1st. cr. 23 for other leg, same as 1st one.

SECOND GARMENT:

Ch. 40 sts., 2nd row (same as other garment), 8 sts., ch. 4, and skip, for armlets, 12 st., ch. 4 for arms, then 8. Do not join, as it will not go over the head.

Second Row.—The same, only fill in ch. under arms with d. cr. st.

Third Row.—Increase every 6th st.

Fourth Row.—Increase every 3rd st., and join.

Fifth Row.—Increase every 5th st. and join. Make 11 rows until you have about 166 sts. around bottom, then finish with ch. of 5 as in Panties.

DRESS:

Ch. 40, same as skirt, and same for armlets, increasing after 2nd row in 6th and 8th, then 3rd, then 4th, then 6th, then 5th, then 3rd, 4th, 3rd, 4th, and 2nd, last row plain. Finish off bottom same as others. At neck and armlets ch. 3, and fasten. Join clothes with needle and thread, and then put the ribbon on.

KEWPIE CAP:

Ch. 4, join c. 12 double st. Then double in each stitch clear around 3 rows, and in 4th row double every other st., then decrease (skip) every other one for two rows, on until band fits head, and attach to Dress Skirt with needle and thread, tie ribbon on arms up to cap, and sew.

Hot Trivet Mat

Use *Collingbourne's*

Art. 1145.
Crochet Twist. Collienett, 2 Balls.

Chain 35.—Fill chain on both sides with dc., proceed in same manner, taking back sts. only for 5 rows, widening at ends by dc. in same st. twice at each end.

Sixth Row.—* Starting at end make slip st. through both sides of st. chain 6, slip st. in same, ch. 8, slip st. in same, ch. 6 slip st. in same, single crochet in next 7 st., taking back part of sts., repeat from * all around. When last group of ch. is made, slip st. back to top of middle loop just made.

Seventh Row.—Ch. 5, treble crochet in 4th of 7 sts. in row below, ch. 7, slip st. in top of ch. 8 of next group, ch. 7 tr., in 4th of next group below, * ch. 5. Slip st. in next 8 ch., ch. 5, 1 tr. in 4th of next group of d. c. below. Repeat from * 3 times, 7 ch. Slip st. in centre of 8 ch., ch. 7, 1 tr. in 4th, of 7 d. c. below, * ch. 5, slip st. in top of 8 ch., c. 5, 1 tr. in 4th of 7 d. c. below. Repeat from * to end of row.

Eighth Row.—7 s. c. over 7 ch., 1 s. c. on tr., 7 s. c. over ch., 1 s. c. on tr., 5 s. c. over 5 ch. Repeat all around, putting 7 s. c. over each group of 7 ch. at other end.

Ninth Row.—S. c. in each s. c. of last row, always taking back of st. 2 s. c., in st. at each end.

Tenth Row.—S. c., on s. c., 2 s. c. in 5th st. each side of centre at each to widen.

Eleventh, Twelfth, Thirteenth, Fourteenth, Fifteenth Rows.—Same as 10th row.

Sixteenth Row.—Slip st. in center of end, ch. 6, slip st. in same, ch. 8 sl. st. in same, ch. 6, sl. st. in same * 5 s. c., in next 5 s. c. sl. st. in next, ch. 6, sl. st. in same, ch. 8, sl. st. in same, ch. 6, sl. st. in same, repeat from * all around. When last group of ch. is made, sl. st. back to middle of 8 ch.

Seventeenth Row.—Ch. 5, tr. in 3rd of 5 s. c. below, ch. 5, sl. st. in centre of 8 ch., repeat all around.

Eighteenth Row.—5 s. c. over 5 ch. Repeat all around.

Nineteenth Row.—S. c. in each s. c. of last row.

Twentieth Row.—S. c. all around, widen in 8th st. each side of centre s. c.

Twenty-first Row.—S. c. all around, widen in 17th each side of centre and 8th, each side and in centre.

Twenty-second Row.—2 s. c. in centre st. of end, skip 7 s. c., 2 s. c. in next, repeat around.

Twenty-third Row.—Widen in every 7th s. c.

Twenty-fourth Row.—Same as 23rd row.

Twenty-fifth, Twenty-sixth, Twenty-seventh, Twenty-eighth Rows.—S. c. in each s. c.

Twenty-ninth Row.—Sl. st. in centre s. c. at end ch. 6, sl. st. in same, ch. 8, sl. st. in same ch. 6, sl. st. in same, s. c. in next 15 s. c. Repeat all around.

For Back.—On other side ch. 8, tr. in 8th of 15 s. c., ch. 5, tr. in s. c. at left of group of chains. Repeat all around.

Second Row.—1 tr. in center of 5 ch., ch. 4, 1 tr. in center of next 5 ch. Repeat around.

These two rows form the casing to hold mat over asbestos.

Fancy Sewing Apron

Use *Collingbourne's*   Art. 1145. Crochet Twist; Arabian

First Row.—Ch. 7, join in 4th from needle to form picot. 3 p., ch. 7, join in the 4th to form picot. 3 p., ch. 7, join in the 4th to form picot. 6 picot, continue from illustration to the end. Do not turn work. Ch. 11, join in the 4th from the needle to form picot, ch. 2, slip through center picot. Ch. 2, join in last to form picot, ch. 4, picot. Ch. 7, join in 4th to form picot. Ch. 2, slip through center. Finish lace from illustration.

For Insertion.—Take instructions from lace.

Library Rest Cushion

Use *Collingbourne's*   Art. 1145. Crochet Twist, Ecru

First Row.—Ch. 7, join in 4th from needle to form picot. 3 p., ch. 7, join in 4th from needle to form picot, 3 p., repeat 4 times. Ch. 7, join in 4th to form picot, make 6 p., join in ch. with 3 d. c.

Second Row.—3 p., 4 ch. in each p., join in ch. with 3 d. c., continue to end. Do not turn work. Ch. 7, and continue from illustration for 5 points. Finish from illustration.

Center.—Use Hardanger Needle, cast over thread for 4 rows. Then make a web of 7 strands. Mend around to form rose in center.

21

[126]

BAG
Use *Collingbourne's* Art. 1151.   No. 30

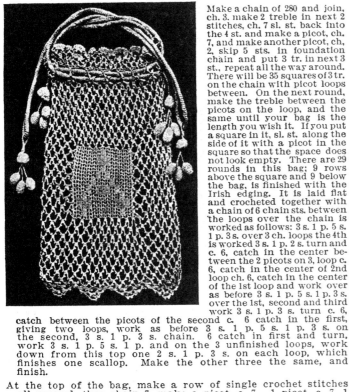

Make a chain of 280 and join, ch. 3. make 2 treble in next 2 stitches, ch. 7 sl. st. back into the 4 st. and make a picot, ch. 7, and make another picot, ch. 2, skip 5 sts. in foundation chain and put 3 tr. in next 3 st., repeat all the way around. There will be 35 squares of 3 tr. on the chain with picot loops between. On the next round, make the treble between the picots on the loop, and the same until your bag is the length you wish it. If you put a square in it, sl. st. along the side of it with a picot in the square so that the space does not look empty. There are 29 rounds in this bag; 9 rows above the square and 9 below the bag, is finished with the Irish edging. It is laid flat and crocheted together with a chain of 6 chain sts. between the loops over the chain is worked as follows: 3 s. 1 p. 5 s. 1 p. 3 s. over 3 ch. loops the 4th is worked 3 s. 1 p. 2 s. turn and c. 6, catch in the center between the 2 picots on 3, loop c. 6, catch in the center of 2nd loop ch. 6, catch in the center of the 1st loop and work over as before 3 s. 1 p. 5 s. 1 p. 3 s. over the 1st, second and third work 3 s. 1 p. 3 s. turn c. 6, catch between the picots of the second c. 6 catch in the first, giving two loops, work as before 3 s. 1 p. 5 s. 1 p. 3 s. on the second, 3 s. 1 p. 3 s. chain. 6 catch in first and turn, work 3 s. 1 p. 5 s. 1 p. and on the 3 unfinished loops, work down from this top one 2 s. 1 p. 3 s. on each loop, which finishes one scallop. Make the other three the same, and finish.

At the top of the bag, make a row of single crochet stitches all around, then chain 7, make a picot, c. 7. 1 picot, c. 7, 1 p., c. 7, 1 p., c. 3, and catch in at one of the squares along the top of the bag. Repeat all the way around, this will make the loops to draw the cord through.

Make a chain for the heading of the bag. Join thread at center of loop between second and third picot, ch. 8 and catch in the next loop at the same place, and so on all the way around, then join.

Second Row.—Chain 5, sk. 2 st. on chain, 1 tr. in next, c. 2, 1 tr. in 3rd all the way around, and join in 3rd of 1 s. c.

Third Row.—Chain 7, 1 p. c. 7. 1 p. c. 2 catch in the 2nd mesh, then make another picot loop, and catch in 4 mesh, skipping one all the way around.

Fourth Row.—On every 6th loop between the picot, make a shell of 1 s. 9 tr. 1 s. turn and over top of them, make a row of single sts., then 6 picot loops, and another shell all the way around.

Fifth Row.—1 picot loop caught in 3 st. of shell and one in 9th st; then one on the center of next loop all the way around.

Sixth Row.—Ch. 2, 1 tr. next loop c. 3, and catch in top of tr. to make a picot, make 6 more trebles with a picot on top for a shell. Ch. 2, catch with a slip stitch on top of next loop, chain 2, and make a shell on the next loop with picots on top that will finish the bag after you get all the way around.

The cord is made by making a ring of five stitches, and work 10 singles in it, and keep on going around on the back thread until you have the desired length; that is about one yard for one cord, then make the other the same and draw through the loops between the bag and the heading. Sew ends together, and make the ornaments.

Ch. 3, 6 tr. in 1st st. join, ch. 3, put 2 tr. in each of last row, making 12 tr. join, ch. 3, and again put 2 tr. in each of the 12 tr. of last row, join. Put 1 tr. in each stitch, but hold the last loop on the needle until the 2nd tr. is made, then crochet together, so that there is only 12 sts. around when you finish, and join. The next round only 6 stitches, then finish.

Stuff it with a little cotton and draw together, putting needle through and catching up the 1st stitch, or the center of the six, and form the Bell Shaped Ornament. The smaller ones are made the same, only the center row is left out, and are stuffed firm with cotton, fastened to the bell by chain stitches.

Young Ladies' Party Slipper Bag
Use *Collingbourne's* ELGIN MAID
Pink or Light Blue

150 ch., join, make a shell of 3 d. c. st. 1 ch. 3 d. c. all in one stitch, skip 3 chs. and repeat all around. Make 30 rows like this with the shell in the center of the double shell of every row. Ch. 5, tr. ch. in every 3rd ch. with 2 chs. between for the ribbon. Ch. 3, 2 d. c. 1 ch. skip every other space, and repeat the 3. d. c. with 1 ch. between around the bag twice.

Finish with a shell of 7 d. c. with a picot between each d. The bottom of the bag is card-board cut to fit the bag, and is covered with satin same as lining.

Lettuce Bag

MATERIALS:

Use 2 Laps *Collingbourne's* Swiss Teidy Cotton No. 4

1 Pair Amber Knitting Needles No. 8. 1 Crochet Hook No. 8. Cast on 30 stitches, knit 52 ribs (104 rows), fold strip and join sides with a single crochet in each stitch. Fasten cotton to top of bag; ch. 5,—skip 1st stitch, 1 dc. in next * ch. 1-skip 1st, 1 dc. in next. Repeat from * around top of bag. Join with slip stitch to 4th of 5 ch. Ch. 1-2 single crochet in 1st chain of 1-2 sc. in next. Repeat around top. Make a twisted cord of the cotton and run through open squares each way so that it draws up at both sides. Knot the cord where it joins for a finish, or tassels may be added.

22

Genuine Parisian Party Bag
Use Collingbourne's Artificial Luxura Silk. No. 20

Ch. 160. In 4th chain make 1 d. c. ch. 1, skip 1, 1 d. c. the (1 d. c. 1 ch. 1 d. c. form a space). Make 10 spaces, then 1 d. c. in the next ch. 1 ch. 2 d. c. this forms the part where strands are drawn through.

FOR THE FLAP: Now make 65 spaces, making 2 d. c. at the end. This is the entire length of bag front and back.

Second Row.— Make 65 spaces, 2 d. c. 1 ch. 2 d. c. 10 spaces.

Third Row.— Make 10 spaces, 2 d. c. 1 ch. 2 d. c. 25 spaces into next space make 7 d. c. drawing together the 1st and last d. c. to form a tuft. This is the border across bottom. Then make 12 spaces, 1 tuft, and work spaces to end 27 spaces.

Fourth Row.— Make 26 spaces, 1 tuft, 1 space, 1 tuft, 9 spaces, 1 tuft, 1 space, 1 tuft, finish spaces to the end of line.

Fifth Row.— Repeat from 3rd row until you have 27 rows with the tufts, and then 1 row of spaces. Crochet 1 row of spaces across flap two sides and bottom with d. c. Fill in spaces with 3 s. c. this joining sides and bottom. Finish bottom with 3 rows of spaces, then make a fringe of 50 chains, catching every 2nd space to join these loops at bottom with 5 ch. and fill in with 4 s. c. 1 p. 4 s. c.

Finish flap: with 5 chains in every 2nd group of 3 s. c. Fill in with 4 s. c. 1 p. 4 s. c. Cover ring with s. c. starting corner of bag under flap, and make 50 chains, draw through spaces of 2 d. c. 1 ch. 2 d. c. and fasten with s. c. on ring. Ch. 50, draw through space, and fasten on under part of bag. Continue across width of bag. In the illustration red beads are drawn into lower edge of flap above and below cluster of tufts at bottom and across center, a row of 3 spaces.

In the fringe loops of beads are entwined between the loops of 50 chains. The use of beads is optional.

Calling Card Case
Use Collingbourne's American Maid, No. 80 White

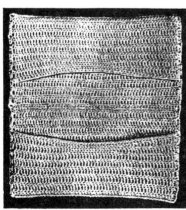

It is worked in alternate rows of single and treble stitches starting at the center or top and working down on one side, then crochet together along the sides. start with a chain of 58 stitches, then work 2 rows of single stitches, and start a 3rd row treble, which is thread over the needle through loop, with 3 loops on needle and crochet 2 stitches at a time.

Fourth row single.

1 loop on needle hook through work bring back 2 loops on needle, crochet both together.

3, 5, 7, 9, 11, 13, 17, 19, 21 are made treble.
4, 6, 8, 10, 12, 14, 16, 18, 20, 22 are made single.

Calling Card Case—Continued

Then comes 7 rows single 2, 23, 24, 25, 26, 27, 28, the 26th row is crocheted on one thread of the stitch of the thread towards you.

29, 31, 33, 35 are made treble.
30, 32, 34, 36 are made single.

Thirty-seventh Row.— 20 tr. 1 h. tr. 16 s. 1 h. tr. 20 tr.

Thirty-eighth Row.— Single all the way.

Thirty-ninth Row.— 15 tr. 2 h. tr. 24 s. 2 h. tr. 15 tr. then 2 more rows of single. Fold it even across the bottom where the 26th row is, so that the loose thread of the stitch is outside. Crochet down the side and across the bottom, up the other side, and you will have one-half of the case; put 1 st. into each across at the beginning, and make the other half the same.

Dainty Little Purse
Use Collingbourne's Luxura Fibre Silk

Ch. 7, join. Fill ring with s. c. and increase until you have a little round piece about as large as a quarter. 28 stitches, now make 1 d. c. 2 ch. skip 1, repeat all around.

Third Row.— Into each loop of 3 ch. work 3 s. c.

Fourth Row.— 1 s. c. on every stitch.

Fifth Row.— 1 s. c. on every stitch.

Sixth Row.— 1 s. c. on every stitch.

Seventh Row.— Now make 3 d. c. on 3 s. c. of row before. Ch. 3, skip 2, repeat all around.

Eighth, Ninth and Tenth Rows.— Repeat 3 rows of s. c. 3 in every ch.

Eleventh Row.— Next row same as 7th row.

Twelfth Row.— Same as 3rd row.

This completes one side. Make another just like it, and join with 1 row s. c. leave opening of about 9 groups of 3 d. c.

FLAP: Work 1 tr. c. 3 ch. between on each one of the groups of 3 d. c. making 9 in all, then fill these 9 loops of 3 chs. with 3 d. c.

Second Row.— 1 row of s. c. skipping 1st and last stitch of row. Turn ch. 3, skip 1, 2 d. c. into next 2 stitches, ch. 2, skip 2, 3 d. c. into next 3 stitches. Make 6 groups of 3 d. c. across row. Turn. Make 5 groups of 3 d. c. in ch. of 2.

Third Row.— 1 s. c. into each stitch, skipping 1st and last.

Fourth Row.— 3 groups of 3 d. c.

Fifth Row.— 1 group of 3 d. c. fasten. Now make a shell of 3 d. c. 1 picot, 3 d. c. ch. 2, skip 2, 1 s. c. ch. 2, and repeat. Make this shell all around bag and flap.

STRANDS: Fasten thread in right hand corner under the flap. Ch. 35, catch with s. cr. in ring. Ch. 35, draw through space between 1st and 2nd tr. c. of flap. Fasten under flap, and continue across opening in same manner.

Very Pretty Bag or Purse
Use Collingbourne's Luxura, No. 20

Ch. 10, into 4th ch. make 1 d. c. in the next 3 ch. make 1 d. c. in each total of 4 d. c. 1 d. c. in last chain.

Second Row.— Ch. 3, 3 d. c. between 4th and 5th d. c. ch. 3, skip 4 d. c. 3 d. c. on 1st d. c. 2 groups of d. c.

Third Row.— Ch. 3, 3 d. c. in 1st d. c. ch. 3, skip 3 d. c. 3 d. c. in next 3 chains, ch. 3, 3 d. c. You will now have 3 groups of 3 d. c. with 3 chs. between. Continue working in this manner, increasing 1 group of 3 d. c. in each row. Work until you reach 25 groups of 3 d. c. This completes one side of bag. Make the second part just like this. If you desire the beads large oval ones are used in this illustration, string them, and join the bag at sides by making 10 ch. 1 bead, 10 ch. and 1 s. c. in each group of 3 d. c. Work down the side, across point, and up the other side, across top make 3 rows of 1 d. c. 2 ch. 1 d. c. in each space between the groups of 3 d. c. The last row at top is made by 1 tr. c. 4 ch. 1 tr. c. in each space, and in each d. c. so made 1 d. c. Make a Fringe the same as at sides (10 ch. 1 bead, 10 ch. across the 1st row of 1 d. c. 2 ch. 1 d. c. catching in every space of 2 ch. Chain desired length for cord, and then 3 beads at each end after cord has been drawn together.

The Young Ladies Week End Bag

Use

Collingbourne's

Elgin Maid White and Shaded Color

With color: Chain six (6) join. **First Row.**—11 d. c. in ring.
Second Row.—1 d. c. between each 11 d. c. of last row, with 1 ch. between.
Third Row.—1 tr. in each of first 9 spaces with 1 ch. between 1 tr.—1 ch.—(tr. in 10th space), 1 tr. in each of next 9 spaces with 1 ch. between.
Fourth Row.—1 tr., 1 ch., all around; widen in every third space.
Fifth Row.—Same as 4th row.
Sixth Row.—Same as 4th row.
Seventh Row.—Same as 4th row.
Eighth Row.—Same as 4th row.
Ninth Row.—Do not widen.
Tenth Row.—Same as 9th.
Eleventh Row.—Same as 9th.
Twelfth Row.—With white—2 tr. in each space.
Thirteenth Row.—1 tr. between each tr. in 12th row.
Fourteenth Row.—Ch. 7, skip 3, 1 s. c. in next, repeat.
Fifteenth Row.—Ch. 7, 1 s. c. in 3rd of 7 ch. below, repeat.
Sixteenth Row.—Sl. St. to center of 7 ch., ch. 7, 1 tr. in center of next 7 ch., ch. 4, 1 tr. in next, repeat.
Seventeenth Row.—With pink, 4 s. c. over 4 ch. all around.
Eighteenth Row.—With white, ch. 7, 1 tr. in center of group below, ch. 3, 1 tr. in center of next, repeat.
Nineteenth Row.—With pink, 3 s. c. over 3 ch., all around.
Twentieth Row.—With white, ch. 7, tr. in center of 3 pink s. c., ch. 3, 1 tr. in center of next—repeat, join to 4th of 7 ch.
Twenty-first Row.—Ch. 7, 1 tr. over last space, ch. 3—repeat, join last 3 ch. to 4th of 7 ch. with sl. st.
Twenty-second Row.—Same as 21st.
Twenty-third Row.—Same as 21st.
Twenty-fourth Row.—Same as 21st.
Twenty-fifth Row.—Ch. 10, skip one space, 1 dbl. tr. over next space, ch. 6, repeat. Join last 6 ch. to 4th of 10 ch.
Twenty-sixth Row.—Slip st. to 3rd of 6 ch. and ch. 3, 2 t. c. over same, 6 ch., ch. 3, 3 t. c. over next 6 ch., repeat. Join last 3 ch. to 3rd of 5 ch.
Twenty-seventh Row.—Ch. 6, 3 ch. 3 tr. in space below, ch. 3, 3 tr. in next space, repeat. Join to 3rd of ch. 6.
Twenty-eighth Row.—1 s. c., 1 d. c. 3 tr., 1 d. c., 1 s. c., in each space.
Twenty-ninth Row.—With pink, ch. 3, 1 s. c. between each of the stitches of shells.
Line with rubber and supply with Wash Cloth, also soap, Dental Paste, Cold Cream, and Toilet Water in sample sizes.

Simple Crochet Ball Holder

Use *Collingbourne's* **Art. 1145 Collienette**

Chain 10, join into this ring. Make 40 d. c. join. On these 40 d. c. make 5 groups of 8 d. c. with 5 ch. between each group of 8.
Third Row.—6 d. c. skipping first and last of 8 d. c. ch. 5, catch in 5 ch. Ch. 5, 6 d. c. Repeat.
Fourth Row.—*4 d. c. skipping first and last of 6 d. c. ch. 5. catch in loop of 5 ch. Ch. 5, catch in 5 ch. Ch. 5 repeat from *.
Fifth Row.—*2 d. c. skipping first and last of 4 d. c. ch. 5. catch in 5 ch. ch. 5, 3 d. c. in loop of 5 ch. ch. 5, catch in loop of 5 ch. ch. 5, repeat from *.
Sixth Row.—*1 d. c. on top of 2 d. c. ch. 5, catch in 5 ch. ch. 5, 3 d. c. in 5 ch. 3 c. skip 3 d. c. make 3 d. c. in first loop of 5 ch. ch. 5, catch in 5 ch. ch. 5. Repeat from *.
Seventh Row.—Ch. 5, and catch in each 5 ch. and in group of 3 ch. make 3 d. c.
Now make 3 rows of 5 ch. catch in ch. 5. This completes the one side. Make another, and join at edges 5 ch. 1 picot, 5 ch.
HANDLE OR STRAP.
Across the top of front make 5 loops of 5 ch. caught in center of 5 ch. Make this until long enough, then join to other side. Same edge as around bag.

Holder for Flat-Iron, Etc.

Use

Swiss Teidy, No. 4 Edge with Classic No. 3

Collingbourne's

1. Chain 33.
2. Sc. back to end of chain, turn sc. back. Repeat until Holder is a perfect square.
DIRECTIONS FOR BORDER.
1. Sc. around Holder once. 2. Five dc. in first st.
3. Skip one and fasten in second.
Repeat until border is complete.

Hair Receiver

Use 1 Ball *Collingbourne's* **Elgin Maid, or Luxura Silk and**

Crochet Hook No. 9, and 1 Yard of ½ inch Ribbon

BASKET: Ch. 3, join 2 rounds s. c. increase on 3rd st.
Fifth Round.—d. c. increase on 4th st.
Sixth Round.—d. c. skip on 5th st.
Seventh and Eighth Rounds.—d. c. taking every st.
Ninth Round.—1 tr. in 1st st. but draw thread through 2 loops only, wrap again, and draw through, 3rd st. in 8th r. pull thread through all loops on hook by 2 loops at a time, ch. 2, wrap and insert hook in centre of treble, and draw through last 2 loops, when you will have a perfect * st. ch. 2, skip 2, repeat * st. all around 9th row.
Tenth and Eleventh Rounds.—d. c. taking every st.
COVER FOR BASKET: Ch. 3, join, 2 rounds s. c. increase on 2nd st. 4 rounds of d. c. increase on 4th st.
Seventh Round.—Same as 9th round of Basket, but make ch. of 2, and skip only 1st between *-cs. 8th and 9th round d. c. increase on 5th st.
Tenth Round.—1 d. c. ch. 4, close picot, skip 2, d. c., and repeat all around.
HANDLE: Make a chain of 20 sts. s. c. 4 over chain, 1 closed picot, 4 s. c. close picot, repeat to end of chain, and fasten to cover in center.
To stiffen use starch or sugar water.

24

[129]

Baby Collar

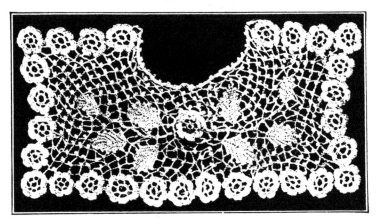

PLATE 67

DIRECTIONS

MATERIALS—J. & P. Coats Mercerized Crochet Cotton, No. 100.

The rose in the center is made by the directions for Irish Crochet Collar, on page 21, using only two rows of petals, and allowing for seven petals in each row.

For small leaf, ch 11, 1 s st into 4th from needle, 1 s st in each of next 7, 3 s st into end chain and 8 st up the other side of chain, ch 3, turn. Repeat for the required number of ribs, having 8 s st each side of the central sts, always putting the needle in the back of the stitch. The large leaves are started with a chain of thirteen and have ten stitches each side of the central three; they have seventeen ribs.

The row of single roses is made as are the other roses, working only one row of petals. For making the yoke, follow the method used in shaping the Irish collar on page 21.

Bag

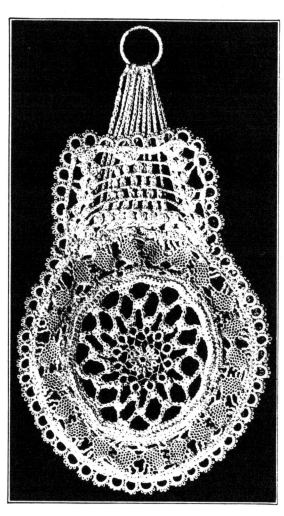

PLATE 68

DIRECTIONS

MATERIALS—J. & P. Coats Mercerized Crochet Cotton, No. 30, for the crocheting and No. 20 for the tatting.

For the medallion, make a ring of 12 double stitches (d st), with picot (p) between sts. Carry the thread up far enough to commence a ring of 3 d st, and fasten into 1st p, 3 more d st. Close ring, leave about ⅜ inch thread and make a ring of 3 d st, p, 3 d st, p, 1 d st, p, 1 d st, p, **3 d st**, p, 3 d st. Close, turn, make another small ring

like the first. Fasten into 2d p of ring; 1 large ring, joining the side p, until you have 12 of each size ring. Fasten thread to No. 20. * make 3 s st, one in each p, at top of tatted ring, 7 ch. Repeat around and join. Sl st to 3d of ch. Ch 3 for 1st tr, 2 more tr, * ch 7, 3 s st into middle of next ch of last row. Repeat around, join. Sl st into 2 sts. * 3 s st into middle of 7 ch, ch 5. Repeat all around, join. Work a row of s st into each st of previous row, ch 1, turn. S st into every s st, taking up back thread, only, ch 1, turn. * 4 s st into 4 s st of last row, 3 s st over the loop between 2 medallions of braid, 4 s st in 4 s st of last row (skipping 1 st between groups of 4 s st), ch 2, catch into 3d p of braid medallion, catch into 3d p from bottom of next braid medallion, ch 2, repeat all around. It will take 22 medallions, which should be joined at the loop between medallions. **Next Row—** * 5 s st over loop between medallions at top, ch 1, s st into 1st p of m, s st into 2d p, tr into 3d p, d tr into 4th p, ch 1, d tr into 4th p of next m, tr into next p, s st into each of next 2 p, ch 1, repeat around. **Last Row—** S st in every st, until there are only 3 loops between medallions. Then make the chains as follows: After the 1st s st over loop, ch 35, s st in ivory ring, ch 35, 3 s st over loop, and continue, making the 35 ch, s st in ring and 35 ch, alternately with 3 s st in the bag until there are 10 chains.

FOR THE BACK OF BAG—Make a tatting medallion like the one for the front. **1st Row around—** (Sc into 3 pcs at top of each tatting ring), 3 ch between. Repeat all around. **2d Row—** * 1 tr into last of 3 s st, 3 tr into the 3 ch following, 1 tr into the first of next s st, ch 3 *. Repeat all around. **3d Row—** * 4 s st into 3 ch between trebles, ch 5 *. Repeat all around. **4th Row—** * 3 tr into 4 s st of preceding row; 5 ch, 3 s st into middle of the 5 ch of last row, ch 5. Repeat around. **5th Row—** * 5 ch over 3 s st of last row; 3 s st into middle of 5 ch *. **6th and 7th Rows—** Same; put front over back and crochet them together until you reach the chains. Then make 4 ch, pull 1 long ch in front of the 4 ch and make 3 sc into 3d of last row. Ch 4, pull another long ch in front of the 4 ch and make 3 sc in back. Repeat until the long chs are through the loops, then turn the work. In the first of these loops, make 3 tr, ch 1, 3 tr; ch 3, 2 tr in next loop; ch 2, repeat until the last one, which is a sh, like the first (you will then have a sh at each end, with 4 ch between sh and next group of 2 tr, and 8 groups. **2d Row—** Turn. Ch 5, sh in sh, ch 4, 7 groups of 2 tr, 4 ch, 1 sh, turn. **3d Row—** Sh in sh, ch 4, 6 groups of 2 tr, ch 4, sh in sh, turn, decrease number of groups until you have 4 groups between shells, finish with sh at each end and one in middle, 4 ch between shs.

Join back and front and make enough tatting to go around the tab and around the bag, except where the chains are. This tatting is made of No. 20 or 30 thread, just as you prefer, and the loops are not drawn up round, but left open at bottom so each ring forms a little more than one-half circle. Each loop consists of 2 double sts, * 1 p, 2 ds, repeat 6 times. First and last p's joined. This tatting can be sewed or crocheted on.

CROCHETED LINGERIE TAPES

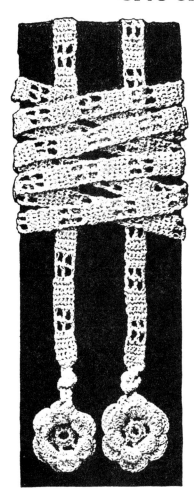

WITH ROSES (left)

No. 70 Crochet Cotton
No. 12 Hook

OVER 6 chain make five rows of doubles, (always make 1 chain to turn), then chain 5, treble in third stitch, chain 2, treble in last stitch, chain 5, turn, treble in treble, chain 2, treble in third stitch of 5 chain; repeat five rows of doubles and two rows of spaces for desired length of tape.

ROSE.—Chain 7, join, 12 doubles in ring, chain 6, treble in second stitch, * chain 3, treble in fourth stitch; repeat from * four times. Make 1 double and 7 trebles in each space of 3 chain. Back of petals make six loops of 5 chain, slip stitch in double; make 1 double and 9 trebles in each loop of 5 chain; repeat loops of 5 chain and petals around rose.

Attach roses to ends of tape by a small cord made of a chain one inch long, slip stitch down one side and up the other.

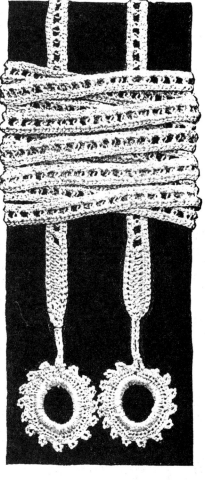

ROSE AND LEAF (centre)

No. 20 Crochet Cotton
No. 10 Hook

ROSE.—Chain 5, join, make 6 spaces of 3 chain, 1 treble in ring. In each space of 3 chain, make 1 double, 5 treble, 1 double. Back of each petal make a loop of 3 chain, slip stitch in double between petals. In these loops make, 1 double, 7 trebles, 1 double. Back of these petals make six loops of 4 chain, slip stitch to double between petals. In these loops make 1 double, 9 trebles, 1 double. After joining last petal of rose make a chain 1½ yards long and along this make 1 double in every stitch; cut thread.

LEAF.—Chain 11, turn, 1 double in every stitch, 3 doubles in end stitch, 1 double in every stitch on other side of chain, chain 1, turn, 1 double in each of 9 stitches (putting hook in the back loop of every stitch to form a rib), 3 doubles in middle stitch of 3 doubles, 1 double in each of 9 doubles. Continue working back and forth around leaf until there are four ribs;

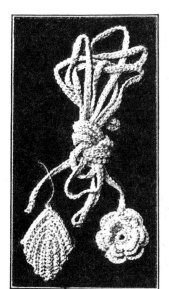

omit one stitch at the beginning and end of each row to form the point, and make 3 stitches in middle stitch of 3 doubles. After running cord through beading of yoke, join leaf to cord securely.

WITH RINGS (right)

No. 70 Crochet Cotton
No. 12 Hook

MAKE a chain of desired length, then 1 double in every stitch, chain 3, 1 treble in each of next 11 doubles, chain 2, treble in every third stitch on chain, ending with 1 treble in each of last twelve doubles; turn, 1 double in every treble, 2 doubles in space to end.

RING.—Wind cotton twenty-five times around little finger, fill ring with doubles, make another row of doubles over this, with picot of 5 chain in every third stitch. Fasten ring to tape with a loop of 8 chain; run tape in underwear and fasten the other ring.

38

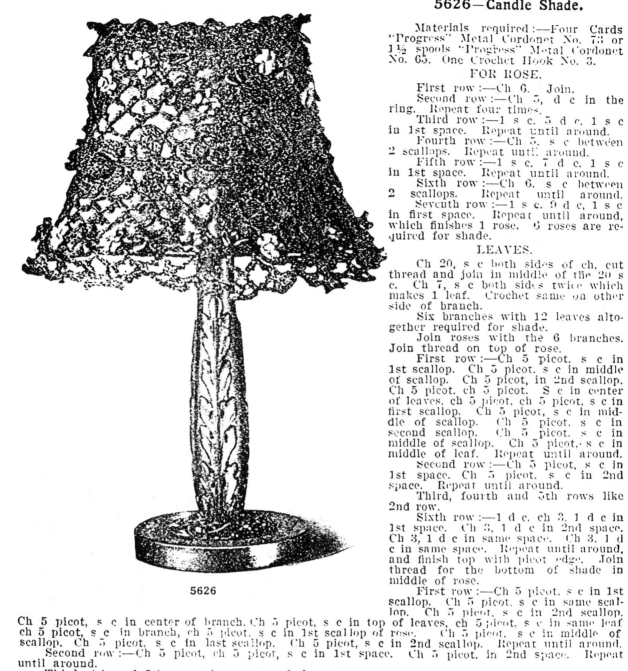

5626

5626—Candle Shade.

Materials required:—Four Cards "Progress" Metal Cordonet No. 73 or 1½ spools "Progress" Metal Cordonet No. 65. One Crochet Hook No. 3.

FOR ROSE.

First row:—Ch 6. Join.

Second row:—Ch 5, d c in the ring. Repeat four times.

Third row:—1 s c, 5 d c, 1 s c in 1st space. Repeat until around.

Fourth row:—Ch 5, s c between 2 scallops. Repeat until around.

Fifth row:—1 s c, 7 d c, 1 s c in 1st space. Repeat until around.

Sixth row:—Ch 6, s c between 2 scallops. Repeat until around.

Seventh row:—1 s c, 9 d c, 1 s c in first space. Repeat until around, which finishes 1 rose. 6 roses are required for shade.

LEAVES.

Ch 20, s c both sides of ch, cut thread and join in middle of the 20 s c. Ch 7, s c both sides twice which makes 1 leaf. Crochet same on other side of branch.

Six branches with 12 leaves altogether required for shade.

Join roses with the 6 branches. Join thread on top of rose.

First row:—Ch 5 picot, s c in 1st scallop. Ch 5 picot, s c in middle of scallop. Ch 5 picot, in 2nd scallop. Ch 5 picot, ch 5 picot. S c in center of leaves, ch 5 picot, ch 5 picot, s c in first scallop. Ch 5 picot, s c in middle of scallop. Ch 5 picot, s c in second scallop. Ch 5 picot, s c in middle of scallop. Ch 5 picot, s c in middle of leaf. Repeat until around.

Second row:—Ch 5 picot, s c in 1st space. Ch 5 picot, s c in 2nd space. Repeat until around.

Third, fourth and 5th rows like 2nd row.

Sixth row:—1 d c, ch 3, 1 d c in 1st space. Ch 3, 1 d c in 2nd space. Ch 3, 1 d c in same space. Ch 3, 1 d c in same space. Repeat until around, and finish top with picot edge. Join thread for the bottom of shade in middle of rose.

First row:—Ch 5 picot, s c in 1st scallop. Ch 5 picot, s c in same scallop. Ch 5 picot, s c in 2nd scallop. Ch 5 picot, s c in center of branch. Ch 5 picot, s c in top of leaves, ch 5 picot, s c in same leaf, ch 5 picot, s c in branch, ch 5 picot, s c in 1st scallop of rose. Ch 5 picot, s c in middle of scallop. Ch 5 picot, s c in last scallop. Ch 5 picot, s c in 2nd scallop. Repeat until around.

Second row:—Ch 5 picot, ch 5 picot, s c in 1st space. Ch 5 picot, in 2nd space. Repeat until around.

Third, 4th and 5th rows the same as 2nd row.

Sixth row:—Ch 4, 1 d c in 1st space. Ch 2, 2 d c in same space. Ch 5, s c in second space. Ch 5, 2 d c in 3rd space. Ch 2, 2 d c in same space. Continue until around.

Seventh row:—Ch 4, 1 d c in 1st shell. Ch 5 picot, 1 d c in same shell. Ch 5 picot, 1 d c in same shell. Ch 5, s c in s c, ch 5, 1 d c in shell and repeat until around.

If desired, finish top and bottom with trimming made of Progress Rococo Ribbon.

USE PERI-LUSTA   USE PERI-LUSTA

2

5691—Bag with Frame & Clasp.

Materials required:—Four Cards "Progress" Metal Cordonet No. 73 or 1½ spools "Progress" Metal Cordonet No. 65. One Crochet Hook No. 3. Twelve Strings Beads No. 8.

String on Metal Thread 1 skein of No. 8 beads.

First row:—Ch 6, leaving 1 bead between every other stitch of ch. Join.

Second row:—Ch 5, two beads. 1 d c with 2 beads. in ring. Repeat 6 times.

Third row:—Ch 3, two beads 5 d c in 1st space with 2 beads between each d c. Ch 2, two beads. 6d c in 2nd space 2 beads between each d c. Repeat until around.

Fourth row:—Ch 3. Two beads 7 d c in the 6 d c with 2 beads between each d c. Repeat around.

Fifth row:—Ch 3. Two beads. 5 d c in the 8 d c with 2 beads between each d c. Draw thread through the 6 d c fasten with s c. Ch 5, s c with 2 beads in 1st space. Ch 5, s c. 6 d c in the 8 d c of last row with 2 beads between each d c. Repeat until around which completes figure. Ch 6 inches for bottom of bag. 2 d c in every other stitch. Repeat 4 rows.

Sixth row:—Ch 5, 1 d c in 1st space. Ch 2. 2 d c in 2nd space. Repeat 4 times. Ch 2. s c in figure. 1 d c in 1st space. turn. 1 d c in 2nd space of figure. Ch 2, 1 d c between 2 d c of last row. Repeat to top of figure. join thread to other side and repeat to the top of figure. 2 d c in every d c. Make 6 rows for top of bag. Crochet back of bag same as front. Join front and back together beginning at point where metal top ends. 4 d c in every space around the bag. Use picot edge for last finish. Sew to metal frame and use a bead to cover stitch.

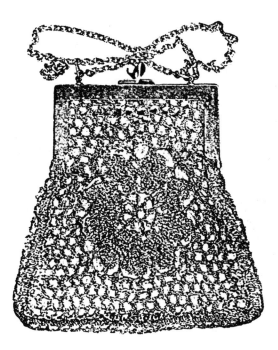

5691

5641—Card Case.

Materials required:—Two Cards "Progress" Metal Cordonet No. 73 or ¾ spools "Progress" Metal Cordonet No. 65. One Crochet Hook No. 3.

First row:—Ch 6 join.

Second row:—12 s c in ch of 6.

Third row:—Ch 20. Join with s c in 3rd stitch from start. Ch 3, s c in 4th stitch of s c in center. Repeat 4 times.

Fourth row:—3 s c in the 3rd stitch. 25 s c in the 17 stitches. 3 s c in the 3rd stitch. Repeat until around.

Fifth row:—Ch 3, d c in 3rd stitch of the 25. Ch 4 make picot. 8 d c with picot between each d c which finishes the figure. Ch 4, 1 d c between scallops. Ch 3, 1 s c in 2nd picot. Ch 3, s c in 3rd picot. Repeat until around. Ch 6, s c in 2nd space. Turn. 6 s c in the ch 6. Turn. Ch 3. 9 d c on top of the 6 s c, ch 3. S c in 1st space. Ch 3, s c in 3rd space. Repeat around. Ch 3. s c in 3rd stitch of the 9 d c. Ch 3, s c again in third stitch. Ch 3, 2 d c in 1st space. Ch 2, 2 d c in 2nd space. Ch 2, 2 d c in 3rd space. Repeat until around. Ch 2, 2 d c in 1st space. Ch 2, 2 d c in 2nd space. Ch 2, 2 d c in same space. Ch 2, 2 d c in 3rd space. Repeat around. Ch 2, 1 d c in 1st space. Ch 2, 2 d c in 2nd space. Ch 2. 2 d c in same space. Ch 2, 2 d c in third space. Repeat around. Ch 2, 2 d c in first space. Ch 2. 2 d c in the second space. Repeat across. Turn. Crochet 16 rows or until case is desired size. Finish with picot edge.

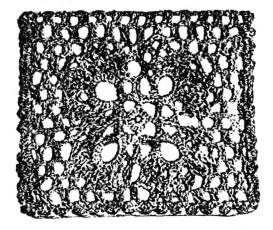

5641

5646—Bag.

Materials required:—Nine Cards "Progress" Metal Cordonet No. 73 on 2¾ spools "Progress" Metal Cordonet No. 65. One Crochet Hook No. 3.

First row:—Ch 4, join.

Second row:—Ch 2, s c in every stitch 3 times around. Widen often to keep flat.

Fifth row:—Ch 4, d c in every stitch with 1 stitch between. Repeat until you can cover completely a 5 inch circle of cardboard for the bottom of the bag.

FOR BODY OF BAG.

Ch 6, 2 d c in 1st opening. Ch 2, 2 d c in same opening. Ch 2, 1 d c in next opening. Ch 2, 2 d c in next opening. Ch 2, 2 d c in same opening, which forms shell. Repeat until around, picking up the chain beginning the row. Crochet 25 rows like the above row. Now make 1 row of tr crochet for draw string or cord, by putting thread around needle twice, and taking up every shell and open space between shells. Make 5 rows like the body of bag, for the top, and finish with heavy scallop. S d c in every shell, 1 s c between shells.

FOR DRAWSTRING:

Crochet cord and balls, as per directions on page 24 or use ribbon.

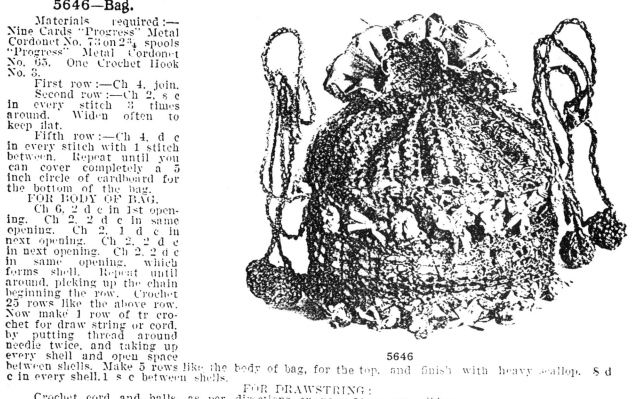

5646

5698

5698—Baby Cap.

Materials required:—One-half Ball "Peri-Lusta" Jewel art. 24. One Crochet Hook No. 3½.

First row:—Ch 6 join.

Second row:—Ch 3, 25 d c in ring.

Third row:—Ch 3, 2 d c in every d c of row below. Repeat 7 rows and widen only when necessary to shape.

Eleventh row:—Ch 3, s c in 3rd stitch. Ch 3, s c in 6th stitch. Repeat until you have 20 stitches left for bottom of cap. Turn. Ch 3, and s c in the middle of the ch 3 below. Go back and forth until you have 22 rows. Turn and go across the bottom of Cap. Make 7 rows the same stitch and finish all around cap with large scallop.

Turn back the front of cap and pull ribbon through and make a bow on bottom of each side leaving enough ribbon for strings.

5695--Purse with Frame and Clasp.

Materials required :—Two Cards "Progress" Metal Cordonet No. 73 or 3/4 spool "Progress" Metal Cordonet No. 65. One Crochet Hook No. 3. One String Beads No. 8.

Ch 4 inches. Turn. S c in every stitch turn, skip first stitch s c across, picking up the back stitch of the 1st row, and skip last stitch. Continue the above solid work until you have 38 rows, and see that the top of purse fits neatly into the metal top, crochet back of purse the same and when finished join front and back together beginning where the stitches in metal top end, and finish with a small scallop.

Sew to metal frame and add a bead to cover stitch.

5695

5653--Coin Purse for Glove, of Metal Thread.
5669—Coin Purse for Glove, of "Peri-Lusta" Crochet Cotton.

Materials required :—No. 5653—15 yards "Progress" Metal Cordonet No. 73 or No. 65. No. 5669—24 yards Peri-Lusta Crochet art. 18, size 20.

First row :—Ch 3. Join.
Second row :—6 s c in ch of 3.
Third row :—12 s c in the 6 s c of 2nd row.
Fourth row :—Ch 4. D c 16 times with 1 stitch between.
Fifth row :—S c in each stitch widen when necessary to keep work flat.
Sixth row :—Ch 4. D c in every stitch with one stitch between until 8 stitches are left.

TO MAKE FLAP :
Ch 4. 12 d c across top. Turn. Ch 4, 6 d c with 1 stitch between. Turn. Ch 4. 3 d c with stitch between. Ch 5, and catch with s c on other side to make loop for button.

TO MAKE FRONT OF PURSE :
Repeat from 1st to 6th rows inclusive. Join front and back with a small scallop all around purse and flap.

TO MAKE BUTTON :
Ch 3. Join. 6 s c in chain of six. Repeat, draw up tight with the metal thread and sew on front of bag :

TO CROCHET ORNAMENT :
First row :—Ch 3. Join.
Second row :—6 s c in ch of 3.
Third row :—12 s c in the 6 s c of 2nd row.
Fourth row :—Ch. 16 d c with 1 stitch between.
Finish edge with s c over a cord to make heavy. Join to purse with a ch of 40 stitches double thread and 40 stitches to join to ornament.

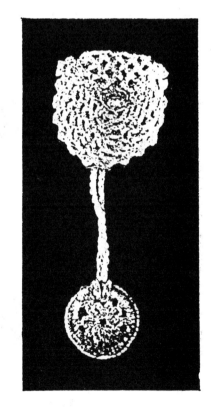

5653—5669

5696—Purse with Frame & Clasp.

Materials required:—Six Cards "Progress" Metal Cordonet No. 73 or 2 spools "Progress" Metal Cordonet No. 65. One Crochet Hook No. 3. One Srting Beads No. 8

First row:—Ch 5 inches, turn.

Second row:—10 d c in 10 stitches of ch. Ch 3, s c in 3rd stitch. Ch 3, d c in the 6th stitch. 9 d c in next 9 stitches. Ch 3, s c in the 3rd stitch. Ch 3, d c in the 6th stitch. 9 d c in next 9 stitches. Ch 3, s c in last stitch of ch. Turn.

Third row:—Ch 5, s c in 1 space. Ch 3, 11 d c in the 10 d c in last row. Repeat twice. Ch 3, s c in last stitch. Turn.

Fourth row:—Ch 5, s c in 1st space. Ch 3, 12 d c in the 11 d c of last row. Repeat across and so on. Adding 1 d c in every other row until you have 24 rows and 24 d c in each point. Make the other side of bag the same. Join sides below clasp with picot edge and across bottom of bag with d c and picot between.

FOR ROSES:

First row:—Ch 6, join. Ch 5, d c in ring. Ch 3, d c in ring. Repeat 4 times. 1 s c, 3 d c 1 s c in 1st space. Repeat around. Ch 5, s c between shells. Repeat around 1 s c, 5 d c, 1 s c in 1st space. Repeat around and sew on the 3 points of the 6th row from bottom of bag. Line with color desired and sew with metal thread to frame using a bead to cover the stitch.

5696

5392—Small Finger Purse.

Materials required:—Two Cards "Progress" Metal Cordonet No. 73 or ¾ spool "Progress" Metal Cordonet No. 65. One Brass Ring ¾ inch. One Crochet Hook No. 3.

First row:—Ch 3, join.

Second row:—Ch 3, 10 d c in ring.

Third row:—20 d c in the 10 d c of last row.

Fourth row:—2 d c in each stitch of last row.

Fifth row:—Ch 3, 5 d c in the 5 d c of last row. 5 d c in same stitch draw thread tight through all 5 stitches to make knot. Repeat around.

Sixth and 7th rows:—D c all around, widen when necessary to keep flat. Crochet two rows of d c across top of circle which completes front of bag. Now make back same as front and for flap, continue across the top 7 rows, dropping 1 stitch each side of flap.

Eighth row:—Ch 5 catch on opposite side of flap for button. Join front and back of bag together and finish all around with picot edge and 7 s c in ch of 5 for button.

FOR BUTTON:

Ch 3 join. 6 s c in ch of 3. Repeat and draw close together with metal thread and sew to front of bag.

FOR HANGER:

Ch 6 inches double thread, cover with s c a ¾ inch brass ring and join to hanger. To crochet the 5 small balls on bottom of bag see directions on page 24.

5692

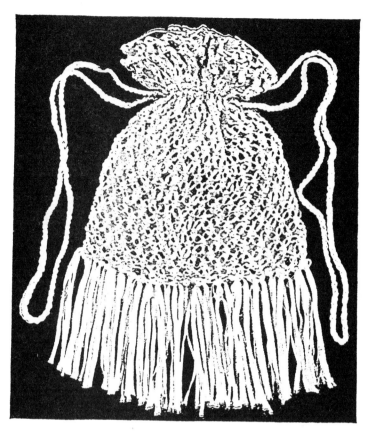

5700

5700—Tape Bag.

Materials required:—One 1½ inch Maltese Pin. One Bone Hook No. 3. One and a half Balls Progress Mercerized Towel Tape No. 1048.

Tie tape around the prongs of the Maltese Pin, slip hook between tape on left side of the knot. Turn the Pin and pick up the tape with a s c, turn pin and s c in center after each turn until you have 58 loops on each side of Pin. Draw work from Pin and tie or crochet together. Be sure work does not twist. Pin to a covered board or cushion firmly, through the heavy part. Cut 58 strands of tape each 1½ yards, fold a strand together in the center and pull through a loop of the hairpin work. Put the 2 loose ends through the loop of tape and draw to a tight knot. Continue until the 58 strands of tape are tied in the 58 loops of hairpin work.

Take 4 strands of the tape for a knot. Now take the 2 outer strands, one in the right hand and one in the left hand, leaving the two strands in center straight. Pass the strand in the left hand over the 2 center strands and the one in the right hand over the left one, and under the 2 center strands and up through the loop on the opposite side and draw up to within ½ inch of top. Repeat using the right strand over, and the left strand under. Draw up close to the other knot, and that completes the single knot. Repeat for a double knot. When around once with double knots take two strands from one knot and two from the next knot for the next row, keeping the knots all an even distance apart. When you have 14 rows, tie front and back together with the single knot.

Crochet cord of double tape for draw strings. Crochet two rows around the top of bag with ch 3, 1 s c picking up two loops together of the 58 loops.

If heavier fringe is desired tie in extra strands.

5672—Spectacle Case.

Materials requires:—Two Cards "Progress" Metal Cordonet No. 73 or ¾ spool "Progress" Metal Cordonet No. 65. One Crochet Hook No. 3.

First row:—Ch 5 inches. Join.

Second row:—S c all around ch, picking up every stitch. Join together at bottom.

Third row:—Ch 4, 1 d c in 5th stitch. 2 d c in every 3rd stitch with ch of 2 between.

Fourth row:—2 d c in every space with ch of 2 between. Join each row as crocheted before starting another. Continue until case is desired length. Finish top with a picot scallop. Crochet ch of double thread 1 yard long. Make 2 hangers 5 inches long and remainder in loops each side of bag with a small crocheted ball as per directions on page 24.

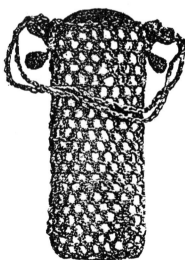

5672

USE PERI-LUSTA   USE PERI-LUSTA

8

5649—Bag.

Materials required:—Seven Cards "Progress" Metal Cordonet No. 73 or spool "Progress" Metal Cordonet No. 65. One Crochet Hook No. 3.

First row:—Ch 14 inches. Join.

Second row:—Ch 2, s c in every stitch of the 14 inch ch.

Third row:—Ch 4, d c in every stitch of the s c taking up both threads until around.

Fourth, 5th, 6th, 7th, 8th rows same as 3rd row.

Ninth row:—Ch 6, s c in every 4th stitch until around. Repeat until you have 18 rows.

Nineteenth row:—Ch 6, tr c in every loop which makes open work for draw string.

Twentieth row:—1 s c in 1st loop, 6 d c in same, 1 s c in same. When around Crochet 7 rows like body of bag with a scallop at top for finish.

For drawstring and balls:—Crochet as directed on page 24.

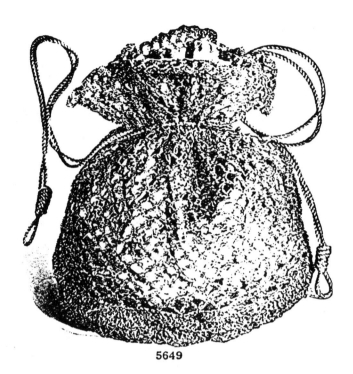

5649

5655—Opera Glass Bag.

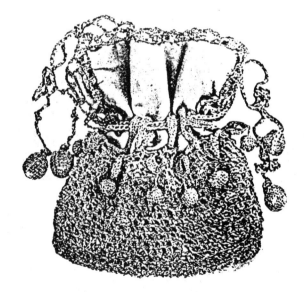

5655

Materials required:—Seven Cards "Progress" Metal Cordonet No. 73 or 2¼ spools "Progress" Metal Cordonet No. 65. One Crochet Hook No. 3.

First row:—Ch 6 inches.

Second row:—Ch 1, s c in every stitch both sides of chain.

Third row:—Ch 4 2 d c in every 3rd stitch around bag. Repeat until you have 18 rows or bag desired depth.

Last row:—7 s c, ch 12, join. Turn, and in ch of 12 1 s c, 15 d c 1 s c. 7 s c, ch 30, s c both sides of ch 30.* Join to bag to make loop for drawstring. 7 s c in top of bag. Ch 30 and repeat from star* until top of bag is finished.

Make a chain the length of sides and top of lining crochet in the chain an edge or scallop for a finish.

For drawstring and balls crochet as directed on page

9

5627—Candle Shade.

Materials required:—Four Cards "Progress" Metal Cordonet No. 73 or 1 spool "Progress" Metal Cordonet No. 65. One Crochet Hook No. 3.

First row:—Ch 12 inches, join.

Second row:—Ch 4, 1 d c, ch 2, 2 d c in same stitch. Ch 5, 2 d c in 5th stitch of ch. Ch 2, 2 d c in same stitch. Repeat until around.

Third row:—Same as 2nd row.

Fourth row:—Ch 4, 1 d c in shell below. Ch 2, 2 d c in same shell. Ch 3, s c picking up the 2 ch's of 5 below. Ch 3, and repeat with shell in shell until around.

Repeat 2nd, 3rd and 4th rows four times.

TO MAKE POINTS ON SHADE:

Ch 4, 1 d c, ch 2, 2 d c in shell, ch 5, 2 d c with ch 2, 2 d c in same shell. Repeat twice. Turn. Ch 4, 2 d c, in ch of 5 below. 2 d c in same space. Repeat twice. Turn. Ch 4, 2 d c in 1st shell, ch 1, 2 d c between shell; repeat. Turn. Ch 4, 2 d c, ch 2, 2 d c between 2 shells. Ch 2, 2 d c in shell. Turn, ch 4, 2 d c, ch 2, 2 d c between shell. Make 6 points on shade. Finish with scallop all around points, and top of shade.

Crochet 12 balls as per directions on page 24 and attach to each point and between points.

5627

5631

5631—Candle Shade.

Materials required:—One-half Ball "Peri-Lusta" Jewel art. 24. One Crochet Hook No. 3½.

BEGIN WITH MOTIF.

First row:—Ch 6 join.

Second row:—5 d c in ch of 6. Ch 3, d c in same stitch. Repeat 5 times.

Third row:—Ch 4, 5 d c in 1st space. Ch 1, 5 d c in 2nd space. Repeat until around.

Fourth row:—Ch 4, 7 d c in 5 d c of 3rd row. Ch 2 and repeat until around.

Fifth row:—Ch 4, 5 d c in 7 d c skipping a stitch on each end. Draw the 5 d c together at top with s c. Ch 7 with s c between shells. Repeat until around, which completes motif.

Make six motifs.

Join motifs together.

For top, first row:—S c in 1st ring at top of motif. Ch 4, 2 d c in next ring repeat until around with ch of 2 stitches between each d c.

Second, 3rd 4th and 5th rows the same as 1st row.

Finish top with picot and 4 s c between each picot.

For bottom 1 st row:—S c in 1st space of figure. Ch 9. S c in 2nd space, repeat until around.

USE PERI-LUSTA   USE PERI-LUSTA

5640—Card Case.

Materials required:— Two Cards "Progress" Metal Cordonet No. 73 or ½ spool "Progress" Metal Cordonet No. 65. One Crochet Hook No. 3.

First row:—Ch 8, join, ch 8, join. Ch 8 join all in same place

Second row:—1 s c, 12 d c, 1 s c in first space. Repeat same in each ch of 8.

Third row:— Ch 10, s c in middle of scallop. Ch 10, s c in last stitch of scallop. Repeat until around.

Fourth row:—24 s c in each ch of 10.

Fifth row:—Ch 5 picot, ch 5 picot, s c in 5th stitch of the 24 s c. Ch 5, picot, ch 5 picot, s c in the next 5th stitch. Repeat twice in the 24 s c and all around.

Sixth row:—Ch 5 picot, ch 5 picot, s c in 1st space. Ch 5 picot, ch 5 picot, s c in 2nd space. Ch 5 picot, ch 5 picot, s c in 3rd space. Repeat until around.

Seventh row:—Ch 5 picot, ch 5 picot, s c in 1st space. Ch 6, s c in 2nd space. Turn. 6 s c in ch of 6. Turn. Ch 3, 9 d c in stitches of 9 s c, ch 3, s c in same place. Ch 5 picot, ch 5 picot, s c in 3rd space. Repeat and s c in the fourth and fifth space. Ch 6, s c in the sixth space. Repeat until around. Ch 5 picot, ch 5 picot, s c in 1st stitch of scallop. Ch 5 picot, ch 5 picot, s c in middle stitch of scallop. Turn. Ch 5 picot, ch 5 picot, s c in the 1st space. Repeat to next scallop. Turn. Ch 5 picot, ch 5 picot, with s c in 1st space. Repeat 10 times. Go around case with 1 d c, and ch of 3 in every space. Finish with picot edge and 3 s c between each picot.

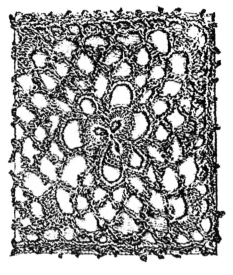

5640

5662—Candle Shade.

Materials required:—Three Cards "Progress" Metal Cordonet No. 73 or 1 spool "Progress" Metal Cordonet No. 65. One Crochet Hook No. 3.

First row:—Ch 12 inches. Join.

Second row:—Ch 4, 1 d c in 2nd stitch. Ch 1, 1 d c in 3rd stitch. Ch 1, 1 d c in next 3rd stitch. Repeat until around.

Third row:—Ch 4, 1 d c in 1st space. Ch 2, 1 d c in 2nd space. Repeat until around.

Fourth row:—Ch 15, s c in 3rd space. Ch 15, s c in 3rd space. Same all around.

Fifth row:—Same as 4th row.

Sixth row:—Ch 15, s c pick up 2 of the ch below with s c, ch 15, repeat until around.

Seventh row:—Same as 6th row.

Eighth, 9th row:—Same as 4th and 5th row.

Tenth row:—Ch 7, s c in the middle of ch 15. Repeat until around.

Eleventh row:—Ch 4, 3 d c in 1st space. Ch 5, 1 s c in 2nd space. Ch 5, 1 s c in same space. Ch 5, 1 s c in same space. Ch 5, 1 s c in 3rd space. Ch 5, 4 d c in 3rd space. Ch 5, 1 s c in 4th space. Repeat until around.

Twelfth row:—Ch 4, 5 d c in the 4th d c. S c in 1st, 2nd, 3rd and 4th spaces, with a ch of 5 between each s c. Ch 5, 1 d c in the 5th space. 4 d c in the 4 d c. 1 d c in 1st space. Ch 5, s c in 1st space. Repeat until around.

5662

16

Thirteenth row:—Ch 4, d c in 1st space. 6 d c in the 5 d c. 1 d c in 1st space. S c in 2nd, 3rd and 4th spaces, with ch of 5 between each s c. Ch 5, d c in 5th space. 6 d c in the 5 d c. 1 d c in 1st space. Ch 5, s c in 2nd space. Ch 5, s c in 3rd space. Repeat until around.

Fourteenth row:—Ch 4, 1 d c in 1st space. 7 d c in the 6 d c. 1 d c in 1st space. S c in 2nd, 3rd and 4th spaces, with ch of 5 between each. Ch 5, 1 d c in 5th space. 7 d c in the 6 d c. 1 d c in 1st space. Ch 5, s c in 2nd space. Repeat until around.

Fifteenth row:—Ch 4, 1 d c in 1st space. 9 d c in the 7 d c. 1 d c in 1st space. S c in the 2nd and 3rd spaces with ch of 5 between. Ch 5, 1 d c in 4th space. 7 d c in the 9 d c. 1 d c in 1st space. Repeat until around.

Sixteenth row:—Ch 4, 1 d c in 1st space. 11 d c in the 9 d c. 1 d c in 1st space. Ch 5, s c in 2nd space. Ch 5, s c in 2nd space. Ch 5, 1 d c in 3 space. 11 d c in the 9 d c. Repeat until around.

Seventeenth row:—Ch 4, 1 d c in the 1st stitch of 11 d c. Ch 5 picot, d c in 2nd stitch Ch 5 picot, d c in 5th stitch. Repeat same in the 11 d c, with picot between. Ch 5, s c in 2nd space. Ch 5, 1 d c in 1st of 11 d c. Ch 5 picot. 1 d c. Repeat until around and finish top with scallop in each space.

5629—Candle Shade.

Materials required:—Two Cards "Progress" Metal Cordonet No. 73 or 1½ spools "Progress" Metal Cordonet No. 65.

First row:—Ch 9 inches Join

Second row:—Ch 4, d c in 3rd stitch of ch. Ch 1, d c in 3rd again and repeat until around.

Third, fourth and fifth rows like second row.

Sixth row:—Ch 4, 2 d c in every space until around.

Seventh row:—Ch 4, 3 d c take up 1st stitch in ch 4 and draw thread through all 4, fasten with s c. Ch 4, 4 d c and repeat until around.

Eighth row:—Ch 2, s c in ch 6. 6 d c in same ch. 1 s c in same which makes a scallop. Repeat same in next ch until around.

Ninth row:—Ch 8. Join with s c in middle of scallop. Repeat until around.

Tenth row:—Ch 4, 4 d c in ch of 8, repeat until around.

Eleventh and twelfth rows are same as tenth row.

Thirteenth row:—Ch 5, 2 d c in middle of 4 d c. Ch 2, 2 d c in same space which forms shell. Ch 5 and repeat all around.

Fourteenth row:—Ch 4, Put shell in shell with ch of 2 between. Ch 3, d c in ch between shells. Ch 3, Shell in shell and continue until around.

Fifteenth row:—Shell in shell with ch of 6 between.

Sixteenth and last row:—9 d c in every shell with picot between each d c. Ch 4, s c in the d c of the fourteenth row, picking up ch of sixteenth row. Finish top with scallop in each space.

If desired finish bottom with six rosettes made of "Progress" Fancy Ribbon.

5629

USE PERI-LUSTA   USE PERI-LUSTA

17

Metal Crochet Bag No. 125.

Materials required:—Four Spools "Progress" Cordonet No. 65 or 11 Cards No. 73. One Crochet Hook No. 3½.

BAG:—Make a chain 8 inches long.

First row:—S c in every stitch of ch, taking up one loop. S c across the other side taking up one loop.

Second row:—Ch fourteen slip-stitch in fourth stitch from the bottom of the ch. Ch three, slip-stitch in the third s c. Ch seven. One d c in third stitch of ch at top. Ch seven, slip-stitch in fourth stitch of ch. Ch three slip-stitch in third s c. Repeat all around.

Third row:—Three s c in spaces below, all around. Repeat alternate rows until the bag is about nine inches long.

FOR THE LARGE ROSE.

Ch 6 and join in ring.

First row:—Ch 5, s c in ring, repeat five times.

Second row:—1 s c then 6 d c then 1 s c in each loop. This forms 6 scallops of first row.

Third row:—Ch 3 turn the work and fasten into first spoke. Ch 6 and fasten into next spoke. Repeat five times.

Fourth row:—One s c, 8 d c, then one s c in each loop. Repeat five times.

Fifth row:—Ch 3 turn the work and fasten into first spoke. Ch 7 and fasten in next spoke. Repeat five times.

Sixth row:—1 s c, 10 d c, 1 s c in each loop. Repeat five times.

FOR THE SMALL ROSE.

Ch 5 join in ring.

First row:—Ch 4, s c into ring. Repeat four times.

Second row:—One s c, 3 d c, 1 s c into loop. Repeat four times.

Third row:—Ch 3, turn the work and fasten into first spoke. Ch 5 and fasten into next spoke. Repeat four times.

Fourth row:—1 s c, 6 d c, one s c into loop. Repeat four times.

FOR THE GRAPES.

Make the grapes separately, working them in s c and with double thread.

Make a chain of three, join in ring.

First, second, third rows:—Widen every other stitch.

Fourth and fifth rows:—Plain.

Make fourteen (14) grapes. Sew together: five in the first row; four in the second row; three in the third row and two in the last row. Make a chain of five and s c all around the grapes.

FOR THE LEAVES.

Make a chain of ten.

First row:—One s c in second, third, fourth, fifth, sixth, seventh, eighth, ninth stitches of the ch taking up one loop of ch; then three s c in tenth stitch, then taking up the other loop of ch 7 s c. Skip one stitch, one s c turn the work.

Second row:—Ch 1. Skip one stitch. Eight s c. Three s c in next stitch. Seven s c. Skip one stitch. One s c. turn the work.

Third, fourth, fifth, sixth rows:—Like second row. This makes one leaf. Make three leaves and join together. For stems make a chain of ten s c in each stitch.

5693—Round Coin Purse with Frame and Clasp.

Materials required:—Two Cards "Progress" Metal Cordonet No. 73 or ¾ spools "Progress" Metal Cordonet No. 65. One Crochet Hook No. 3.

Ch 3 join. 6 s c in ch of 3. S c 14 rows to cover 1½ inch circle. Widen often to keep work flat. D c all around circle taking up only one thread of s c below. Continue until you have 14 rows or bag is desired length. Crochet to band in metal top and fasten in securely with clasps of metal band.

5693

5628—Candle Shade

Materials required:—Four Cards "Progress" Metal Cordonet No. 73 or 1½ spool "Progress" Metal Cordonet No. 65. One Crochet Hook No. 3.

BEGIN WITH MOTIF:

First row:—Ch 6. Join.
Second row:—5 d c in ch 6. Ch 3, d c in same stitch. Repeat 5 times.
Third row:—Ch 4, 5 d c in 1st space. Ch 1. 5d c in 2nd space. Repeat until around.
Fourth row:—Ch 4. 7 d c in 5 d c of 3rd row. Ch 2, and repeat until around.
Fifth row:—Ch 4, 5 d c in 7 d c skipping a stitch on each end. Draw the 5 d c together at top with s c. Ch 7 with s c between shells. Repeat until around which completes motif.
Make 6 motifs for shade and join together.

FOR TOP:

First row:—S c in 1st space at top of motif. Ch 4, 2 d c in next space. Repeat until around with ch of 2 stitches between each d c
Second row, 3rd row, 4th row and 5th row same as 1st row.
Sixth row:—Finish with 4 picot, and 4 s c between each picot until around.

FOR BOTTOM OF SHADE.

First row:—Fasten thread at bottom in first space of motif. Ch 8 in each space of motif until around.
Second row:—5 s c in 1st space. 2 s c in 2nd space. Ch 4. 3 s c in same space. Repeat 3 times in same space and until around the 6 motifs.
Finish bottom and between scallops with balls as per directions on page 24.

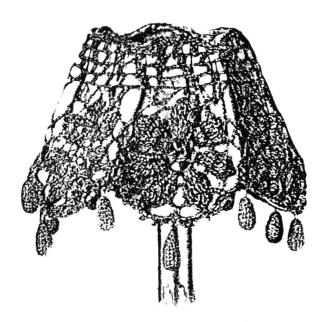

5628

22

[143]

Metal Crochet Bag No. 112.

Materials required: 4½ Spools "Progress" Metal Cordonet No. 65 or Twelve Cards Progress Metal CordonetNo. 73. One Crochet Hook. No. 3½.

112

Bag :—For the squares make one ch of fifteen.

First row :—One d c in the seventh stitch of ch   Ch one d c in second stitch ; repeat till you have five spaces.

Second row :—Ch 5. Turn the work. D c in d c underneath. Ch 2, d c in the next d c.

Third, fourth and fifth rows :—Like second row.

Sixth row :—Seven s c in corner space. Three s c in next space. Ch 1, one d c in next space. Ch 1, d c in same space. Ch 1, three s c in next space. Seven s c in corner space. Repeat all around.

Seventh row :—Ch 5, s c in top of the first d c. Ch 5, s c in next d c. Ch 5, s c in corner. Repeat till around. 7 s c in ch of five . Repeat all around. This forms one square. Make 34 squares for the bag.

FOR THE LEAVES.

Make a chain of ten.

First row :—One s c in second, third, fourth, fifth, sixth, seventh, eighth, ninth stitches of the ch, taking up one loop of ch ; three s c in tenth stitch ; then taking up the other loop of ch 7 s c. Skip one stitch, one s c, turn the work.

Second row :—Ch 1, skip one stitch. Eight s c. Three s c in next stitch. Seven s c. Skip one stitch. One s c, turn the work.

Third, fourth, fifth, sixth rows :—Like second row. This makes one leaf. Make three leaves and join together. For stems make a ch of ten s c in each stitch.

Make two leaves and crochet together with a   ch of five, placing the leaves in opposite corners. (Place so you will have a square of four inches.) Crochet three squares on sides. Crochet two rows of four each across the top, which forms the front of the bag.

The back of the bag :—The back of the bag is made by crocheting together four squares in a row and making five such rows.

FOR THE GRAPES.

Make the grapes separately, working them in s c and with double thread.

Make a ch of three, join in a ring.

First, second and third rows :—Widen every other stitch.

Fourth and fifth rows :—Plain.

Make twenty grapes, placing nine in one bunch, eleven in the other bunch, and sew on bag after the bag is completed.

To Crochet Balls or Pendants.

Ch 3 join. 6 s c in ch of 3. S c around untill you reach the desired size. Widen if a large ball is required ; when the ball is half done, begin to narrow and when nearly finished stuff with cotton and draw together.

To Crochet Draw String.

Crochet chain with double thread desired length and attach balls.

24